Advance Praise for
Jay Pather, Performance, and Spatial Politics in South Africa

"Jay Pather's own artistic as well as curatorial practices are deeply engaged with South Africa's histories and legacies of injustice, segregation, and racialization as well as the country's aspirations for a new dispensation, for a better, more equal, just, and democratic future. He is fully deserving of this full-length study."
— Catherine Cole, University of Washington

"This book offers an important discussion point based on the work of a South African choreographer and teacher who interrogates spaces to offer a political impulse. Land continues to be an issue of political and social context, one that is critical given the South African complex history and the present failures of democracy. The work of Mr. Pather juxtaposes space as a metaphor for social setting and performance."
— Gregory Maqoma, South African dancer, choreographer, and Artistic Director of Vuyani Dance Theatre, Johannesburg

"Jay Pather's choices have never been easy, nor have the routes he has taken been paved with anything but obstacles and mire. Yet, as Ketu H. Katrak shows, Pather's works and achievements are extraordinary records of the challenges faced by those excluded from most places in South Africa by apartheid's drastic laws."
— Sarah Davies Cordova, University of Wisconsin–Milwaukee

JAY PATHER, PERFORMANCE, AND SPATIAL
POLITICS IN SOUTH AFRICA

AFRICAN EXPRESSIVE CULTURES

Series Editors

Patrick McNaughton, editor

Associate editors

Catherine M. Cole

Barbara G. Hoffman

Eileen Julien

Kassim Koné

D. A. Masolo

Elisha Renne

Z. S. Strother

JAY PATHER, PERFORMANCE, AND SPATIAL POLITICS IN SOUTH AFRICA

Ketu H. Katrak

INDIANA UNIVERSITY PRESS

This book is a publication of

Indiana University Press
Office of Scholarly Publishing
Herman B Wells Library 350
1320 East 10th Street
Bloomington, Indiana 47405 USA

iupress.org

© 2021 by Ketu H. Katrak

All rights reserved

No part of this book may be reproduced or utilized in any form or by any means, electronic or mechanical, including photocopying and recording, or by any information storage and retrieval system, without permission in writing from the publisher. The paper used in this publication meets the minimum requirements of the American National Standard for Information Sciences—Permanence of Paper for Printed Library Materials, ANSI Z39.48-1992.

Manufactured in the United States of America
First printing 2021

Cataloging information is available from the Library of Congress.

ISBN 978-0-253-05367-1 (hardback)
ISBN 978-0-253-05368-8 (paperback)
ISBN 978-0-253-05369-5 (ebook)

For the artists of Siwela Sonke Dance Theatre Company in Durban and their founding artistic director since 1997, Jay Pather. May their isiZulu name, siwela sonke, which translates as "crossing over to a new place altogether," continue to resonate in their spirited creative work where the arts foster democratic directions.

For Jay Pather, consummate choreographer, theater director, and curator, whose profound humanity, generosity of spirit, and artistic acumen evoke epiphanies that teach us to see his works with our hearts, and whose political vision participates in art's integral role in transforming society.

CONTENTS

List of Illustrations   ix

Preface: Personal Journey to Discovering Jay Pather   xiii

Acknowledgments   xxvii

Interviews/Conversations   xxxi

Introduction: Pather's Spatial Politics within
  South Africa's Historical and Political Landscape   1

> PART I. *Journeys across Political, Socio-racial, and Geographic Borderlines: Interconnecting the Present, Past, and Future*

1. Crossing (Over): Indian Ocean Migrations   67
2. Race and Space Matter: Outdancing Apartheid's Grip in Pather's Work (1980s and 1990s)   101

> PART II. *The Transitional and the In-between: Theoretical and Creative Engagements with Urban Geography (2000–2015)*

3. Site-Specific Cartographies of Belonging   139
4. Site-Responsive Works of History and Memory   208

> PART III. *Curatorial Choreographies: Challenges of Curating Public Art Festivals (2007–Present)*

5. A New Kind of Performance—Curation of Live Artists   281

Conclusion: Choreographic Reinventions and
  New Directions   339

Appendix. Indians in South Africa: A Chronological Time Line   353

Bibliography   367

Index   387

LIST OF ILLUSTRATIONS

PREFACE

Fig. P.1. Young dancers in training class conducted by Ntombi Gasa at Siwela Sonke Dance Theater (SSDT) studio, Durban. Photographer: Ketu Katrak (hereafter Katrak). *xx*

Fig. P.2. Young dancers in SSDT studio. Photographer: Katrak. *xxi*

Fig. P.3. Ntombi Gasa presenting certificates to youth. Photographer: Katrak. *xxi*

Fig. P.4. Ntombi Gasa and youth. Photographer: Katrak. *xxii*

INTRODUCTION

Fig. I.1. Jay Pather. Photographer: Michael Hammond. https://www.news.uct.ac.za/article/-2016-06-14-jay-pathers-qaphela-caesar-wins-uct-creative-works-award. Courtesy: Jay Pather. *xxxiv*

CHAPTER 1

Fig. 1.1. Family Portrait 1, Chennai/Tongaat, 2017. Digital composite image by Jordache Ellapen. This image is part of Jordach Ellapen's "Queering the Archive: Brown Bodies in Ecstasy," in *Scholar and Feminist Online* 14:3 (2018), which can be accessed at http://sfonline

.barnard.edu/feminist-and-queer-afro-asian-formations/queering-the-archive-brown-bodies-in-ecstasy-visual-assemblages-and-the-pleasures-of-transgressive-erotics/. *69*

Fig. 1.2. Gandhi exhibit at the Old Fort House Museum, Durban. Photographer: Katrak. *70*

Fig. 1.3. *Indian Opinion* newspaper established by Gandhi. Photographer: Katrak. *71*

Fig. 1.4. *Ahimsa-Ubuntu*. Photographer: Val Adamson. *77*

CHAPTER 3

Fig. 3.1. Ancestor with goggles. Courtesy Jay Pather. *182*

Fig. 3.2. *From Before* in New York City. Photographer: Mario Todeschini. Courtesy Jay Pather. *184*

Fig. 3.3. *From Before* in New York City. Photographer: Mario Todeschini. Courtesy Jay Pather. *184*

Fig. 3.4. *rite*. Photographer: Val Adamson. *194*

Fig. 3.5. *rite*. Photographer: Val Adamson. *194*

Fig. 3.6. *rite*. Photographer: Val Adamson. *195*

CHAPTER 4

Fig. 4.1. Robben Island. Photographer: Katrak. *209*

Fig. 4.2. *Body of Evidence*. Projection of foot. Neliswa Rushualang center, Ntombi Gasa in the back, seated. Photographer: Val Adamson. *240*

Fig. 4.3. *Body of Evidence*. Neliswa Rushualang, Ntombi Gasa, and splits in the air leap by Siyanda Duma. Photographer: Val Adamson. *244*

Fig. 4.4. *Body of Evidence*. Rushualang holds Gasa in backbend, Siyanda Duma on the table. Photographer: Val Adamson. *244*

Fig. 4.5. *Qaphela Caesar.* Dancers in flight. Photographer: Val Adamson. Courtesy Jay Pather. 255

Fig. 4.6. *Caesar Interrupted.* Ntombi Gasa crouched under a wooden plank and Nhlakanipho Cele in red high-heeled sandals carrying a fan on his back and a poster. Photographer: Val Adamson. 264

Fig. 4.7. *Qaphela Caesar.* Dancers with string and balloons. Photographer: Val Adamson. Courtesy Jay Pather. 267

Fig. 4.8. Dancer with pig face mask. Photographer: Val Adamson. Courtesy Jay Pather. 269

CHAPTER 5

Fig. 5.1. Cape Town Harbor. Photographer: Katrak. 291

Fig. 5.2. Nelson Mandela's cell on Robben Island. Photographer: Katrak. 295

Fig. 5.3. "Leper Colony Graveyard" on Robben Island. Photographer: Katrak. 296

Fig. 5.4. *Ilulwane.* Athi-Patra Ruga. *Infecting the City* 2012. Photographer: Sydelle Willow Smith. Courtesy Jay Pather. 311

CONCLUSION

Fig. C.1. *The Firebird* at the Hollywood Bowl, Los Angeles. Photographer: Luke Younge. Courtesy Janni Younge and Suzy Bell. 346

Fig. C.2. Backstage at the Hollywood Bowl, August 4, 2016, after performance of *The Firebird* with Ntombi Gasa of SSDT in middle, Katrak to her left, and Katrak's daughter Roshni to Ntombi's right. Photograph taken by a cast member. 349

PREFACE

Personal Journey to Discovering Jay Pather

A HUMAN SKULL. A SILHOUETTE of a bony foot. An S-shaped spinal column with clearly etched vertebrae. Human eyes. A skeletal hand. These startling body parts are projected on the backdrop and the floor, with dancers from Jay Pather's Siwela Sonke Dance Theatre (SSDT) at times dwarfed by the larger-than-life images, at other times stomping, as it were, on a projected rib cage or spine on the stage floor. This was my introduction in 2012 to Jay Pather's innovative work in *Body of Evidence*, clips of which I encountered on the web. I was intrigued, excited, and eager to probe deeper into the work of this artist and his creative inter- and multi-disciplinary choreography.

Body of Evidence, though first performed in 2008, fourteen years after South Africa's independence, touches palpably on the painful continuities of apartheid and the post-apartheid problems of poverty, violence, and physical, mental, and psychological traumas held in the body's bones, muscles, and cells. These wrenching themes are represented in a complex interplay of movement, projections, human sounds, and uncanny juxtapositions such as Pather's dancers interacting with distinctive, symbolic props in order "to elaborate on an existing history to make apparent hidden textures of these lived spaces" (Pather

2003, 434). One harrowing vignette in *Body of Evidence* shows a Black male dancer crouched inside a small chicken coop, as if trapped in a substandard home, loudly shouting out his rage while another female dancer sits inside a clear plastic enclosure, another kind of entrapment, with an impassive face. Such images symbolically evoke vast inequities for Black South African people who face a persisting reality that Pather describes succinctly as "the gap between one's unending labor and the inability to earn a living wage" (Pather 2015b, 320).

The concern with the human body in *Body of Evidence* is deeply poignant, provocative, and politically charged, as in bodies that have to give evidence and testify in courts of law. Pather's probing of bodies and memories is conveyed by startling segments of male and female dancers performing on what feels like the edge of an abyss, with the dark humor of Black male dancers' feet stuck in tins as they try to move or wearing blue flippers that make it equally difficult to walk. In other scenes, male dancers wearing bras jive it up, and a middle-class woman positions her neck stiffly, as if trying to assuage her guilt by walking in with loaves of bread tied to her long gown for distribution to the poor. In another segment, we see male dancers on all fours crawling from one end of the stage to the other, storybook-like model houses with red roofs on their heads, indicating the majority Black population's need for decent housing.

Body of Evidence's medical-legal parameters—body and evidence given in a courtroom—initially inspired Pather to locate this work inside a surgical theater (note the performative resonance of this "theater" where the body undergoes incisions, bleeding, and sewing up, performed by a surgeon) but did not get permission. Hence, he compromised by creating a site-responsive location on the nineteenth floor of the Lister Medical Building in Johannesburg. Pather's choreography meditates on history and memory in particular and probes into what the body remembers. Why does the body store in what Pather describes as "file cabinets" of memories, especially from the wounds of apartheid-era inhumanities suffered by Black South Africans? Can medicine intervene in painful memories held inside individuals as well as in the national body? What legal recourses (beyond the Truth and Reconciliation Commission's efforts from 1996 to 1998) were available in 2008, when *Body of Evidence* was performed, for those who continued to suffer?

My first encounter with Pather's choreography on the web seemed initially to be totally by chance; however, I now regard this as an epiphany from the good spirits. When I discovered Pather, I was at a crossroads in my scholarly work after the publication my book *Contemporary Indian Dance: New Creative Choreography in India and the Diaspora* (2011). I was yearning to discover a project that would bring together my scholarly ardor for African drama with my newly minted role as a scholar of Indian dance. As I let my imagination flow with my breath, without trying to control either, I encountered a segment of *Body of Evidence* online, and the seeds of this monograph were sown. Pather struck me as an innovative artist and thinker who spoke avidly to my scholarly passion in the fields of drama and dance in Africa and in India, and his progressive politics resonated with my own conviction that art is a significant tool in struggles for social change. Along with relating intellectually to Pather's progressive politics, his formidable intellect, and his creative talents, I also connected, as someone who grew up in India, to his biography as a South African of Indian origin—a fourth-generation descendant of Indian migrants (laborers and free traders) who arrived in South Africa from the 1860s onward.

During apartheid's rigid racial system, people were classified as White, Black, "Coloured" (i.e., indigenous peoples [Khoi and San], people of mixed race and people of Malay descent), and Asian. The latter three groups experienced varying restrictions on where they could live and work that did not apply to White people. During the anti-apartheid struggle, especially with the formation of the Black Consciousness Movement in the midsixties "Black" came to include South African Black people, Coloured people, and Asians. In contemporary, postindependent South Africa, Pather who is classified Asian, and specifically South Indian, continues to see himself as Black in academia, ideologically, and consistently throughout his work (interview via phone, May 31, 2020). I will follow this usage for South African Black people in this monograph. He believes that "Coloured" is a problematic reductionist term in which indigenous people "are considered to be peripheral to dominant white culture during apartheid, and considered peripheral in dominant black culture after apartheid" (Pather 2018b, 66).

Before viewing Pather's startling choreography on the web in 2012, I had met Pather very briefly in 2011 in Cape Town. I was standing with colleagues outside the School of Dance at the University of Cape Town (UCT) while attending the Confluences Dance Conference when Gerard Samuel, then head of the School of Dance, introduced me to Pather, who also worked at UCT in the Department of Drama, located on the other side of magnificent Table Mountain, which dominates Cape Town's natural beauty, even as echoes of this "Mother City" where apartheid was born still haunt the lives of South African Black people. My conference presentation was based on my recent book *Contemporary Indian Dance*. Pather was interested in my work, and when we met next in December 2013 in Chennai, where he was invited to present at a conference entitled Purush: The Global Dancing Male, co-convened by contemporary Indian dancer Anita Ratnam, he remembered meeting me briefly. By then, I had begun this project and wanted to interview him. Our first extended conversation took place in Chennai (previously Madras), the city of his ancestral origin; I had grown up in Mumbai (previously Bombay). Since 2013, Pather's profound generosity to me has continued in interviews and conversations in Cape Town,

Grahamstown, Los Angeles, and Irvine, in person and via Skype and phone.

Part of my academic journey since the 1980s has included my scholarship in African literature and drama, which always came with a revulsion for apartheid, that blot on human history. Worldwide political action to release Nelson Mandela from prison and to end apartheid took place as South Africa imposed states of emergency in the 1980s that exacerbated brutal repression of protesters, imprisoning thousands, and forcing many into exile. In the early 1980s, I was at Yale University teaching and working on a bibliography on Wole Soyinka published with coauthors James Gibbs and Henry Louis Gates Jr., the latter of whom had invited me to Yale for this project. The divestment movement pressuring university administrations to remove their monetary assets from South Africa to protest apartheid was at its height. At Yale, students mounted protests day and night in pitched tents. A student in my class on African women writers was very active in this movement; she later spent a few years in Zimbabwe, where she created textbooks with and for local teachers.

The 1980s were also a politically active period among US academics in the field of African studies who condemned apartheid. I belonged to the African Literature Association (ALA, an organization of US- and Africa-based scholars), whose annual meetings included South African writers in exile such as poet Dennis Brutus, an outspoken anti-apartheid spokesman. At ALA's business meetings, members voted on petitions condemning apartheid and making our voices heard across the oceans in racist South Africa. In those days, as a citizen of India, I had to abide by the Indian government, which in opposition to apartheid banned traveling to South Africa. My fervent wish to visit this country, especially after its independence in 1994, was fulfilled in 2011 when I presented my scholarly work on contemporary Indian dance at the University of Cape Town.

In April 2014 I attended the ALA's fortieth conference at the University of Witwatersrand (Wits) in Johannesburg. By that time, my project on Pather had taken shape; while in Johannesburg, I interviewed South African Indian scholars and artists who knew Pather and the apartheid world in which he had grown up. While at Wits, I had a most serendipitous meeting with veteran South African journalist Adrienne Sichel on the recommendation of a South African dance student, Mlondi Zondi, who attended my institution, the University of California, Irvine at that time. Sichel, a speech and drama graduate of the University of Natal in 1970, has worked for over forty years as a renowned arts and dance commentator first for *The Pretoria News* from 1978, then, until her retirement in 2009, aged sixty, in Johannesburg, for *The Star*, a newspaper equivalent in stature to the *New York Times*. She is a repository of knowledge and a most reliable witness of South African contemporary dance. In 2012, Sichel, as a visiting researcher at the University of Witwatersrand's School of Arts (WSOA), cofounded, with filmmaker Jessica Denyschen, the award-winning The Ar(t)chive, hosted by WSOA (at Wits), where I discovered a treasure trove of materials that have been key in writing this book. Sichel's own personal nurturing of my research and her kindness in keeping me informed of events and dance personalities over the years have also been invaluable. I rely on her commentaries of Pather's work throughout this book, as her firsthand accounts of live performances and her astute analyses provide an important foundation for and supplement to my own interpretations of Pather's creative journey. In September 2018, Sichel's book *Body Politics: Fingerprinting South African Contemporary Dance* was launched in Durban at JOMBA! Contemporary Dance Experience. Sichel's valuable text includes her significant journalistic writing over the years, and her research into the evolution of contemporary African dance, in which Pather features as a significant figure (though he is not the focus of Sichel's book).

Another significant stepping-stone along my path to discovering Pather's work was my research trip in July 2015 to the National Arts Festival (NAF) in Grahamstown, South Africa. That year, Pather was chair of the selection committee. I experienced an exciting gathering of artistic works at this festival—drama, dance, installation, performance art, exhibitions, and music—that helped me weave a texture for Pather's work. At that time, I did not know his profound influence on the next generation of artists. I witnessed dancer-choreographer Mamela Nyamza's *19 Born 76 Rebels* at NAF. Nyamza is younger than Pather, and like others of her generation she has been presented at the *Infecting the City* public arts festival and *Live Art* festival that Pather curates in Cape Town.

After attending the NAF, I journeyed to Port Elizabeth airport in the Eastern Cape and flew to Durban, a city where Pather had grown up and that has the largest population of Indians outside of India. Here, I visited the modest office and one-room studio of the Siwela Sonke Dance Theatre (SSDT), which Pather has led as artistic director since 1997. On July 21, 2015, on a narrow and crowded street in central Durban, close to (though in other ways miles away from) the lush Playhouse Theatre, I met Siwela Sonke's founding company members, dancer-choreographers Ntombi Gasa and Neliswa Rushualang, who welcomed me as someone who wished to write a monograph on their mentor. They shared many valuable materials, including multiple scrapbooks Gasa had compiled over the years, which contained newspaper reviews of the company's work glued onto colored pages. I interviewed both Gasa and Rushualang, discussing Pather's choreographic processes and how works such as the harrowing *Body of Evidence*—in which they both participated—came together. Both Gasa and Rushualang come from modest backgrounds that offered no opportunities for dance training; today, they are acclaimed choreographers in their own rights. They acknowledge, with love and humility, Pather's key role in their success.

Fig. P.1. Young dancers in training class conducted by Ntombi Gasa at Siwela Sonke Dance Theater (SSDT) studio, Durban. Photographer: Ketu Katrak (hereafter Katrak).

Pather regards Siwela Sonke artists like them as his "extended family" on a personal level and professionally as his "moral compass" (interview 5, 2015).

I returned a few days later to observe Ntombi Gasa conducting a teaching workshop with Black children and teenagers. Such training is crucial for nurturing the next generation of South African dancers, a labor of love that Siwela Sonke has undertaken from its inception as a "training program" before it became a full-fledged dance theater company.

Since I am visibly Indian, I was often mistaken, during my research time in Durban, for someone belonging to the South African Indian community. Folks would come up to me and speak in Afrikaans, a language that is foreign to me. I was, of course, an outsider in Durban in most ways, though I connected both with the community of Black artists and scholars

Fig. P.2. Young dancers in SSDT studio. Photographer: Katrak.

Fig. P.3. Ntombi Gasa presenting certificates to youth. Photographer: Katrak.

Fig. P.4. Ntombi Gasa and youth. Photographer: Katrak.

connected to Pather's work over the years as well as with South African Indians I met, such as eighty-year-old (in 2015) Harold Samuel, a South African of Christian/Indian origin who had been active in anti-apartheid struggles, eighty-one-year-old playwright Ronnie Govender, and Ashwin Singh of the younger generation. I was an outsider-insider who shared some of my scholarship with the community, such as a talk on contemporary Indian dance, kindly facilitated by Ashwin Singh at the Playhouse Theatre.

These dialogues, which included personal anecdotes of discrimination against Indians during apartheid, illuminated my understanding of the historical and social context for Pather's work. Such interactions also shed light on Pather's unique position as part of and yet apart from the Indian community (discussed in the introduction). Indians were the buffer zone in between White, Black, and Colored people in apartheid's racial hierarchy. Pather's personal/biographical space also ignited my interest in studying spatial politics in his innovative works.

This monograph, the first on Jay Pather, was motivated by my desire to recognize a major artist, an award-winning choreographer, theater director, and curator whose works speak about and to South Africans and to global artists and communities that deploy art to inspire social change. I provide an in-depth analysis and impact of this living, world-class artist's unique, prolific, and multifaceted body of work over four decades. Pather has created several acclaimed original choreographic works as artistic director of SSDT. The words *siwela sonke* translate from isiZulu as "crossing over to a new place altogether," a much desired "new place" in the afterglow of independence. I contend that Jay Pather should be considered of the same creative stature as writers such as Nigerian Nobel laureate Wole Soyinka, who, like Pather, I describe as ethno-global, a phrase I coined in my published essays in 2008 and 2009 to refer to artists rooted in their own ethnicities and locations while being simultaneously global in their creative work.

Throughout his artistic career, Pather has remained profoundly in tune with his nation's changing fortunes and its dark legacies, along with hope for a democratic future. In a 2018 keynote address for the Global Shakespeare Symposium at the University of California, Irvine, Pather probed "contemporary practices of art that face a persistent red herring, namely that art declares reality" and what that means in the South African context: "Art helps us to test it [reality], not just its subject, its very form, authorship, its assumptions. The malleability of art is its striking characteristic allowing for collective and individual consciousnesses to be gnawed at, to be ripped apart, illusions to be whittled away to come face to face with the truth of our desire for something certain. Ultimately, that is all that art can do, to address an unrequited desire for certainty." Pather draws attention to the continuing physical and psychic ache that many Black

South Africans endure even as they search for certainty amid their ongoing struggles for survival.

This book contributes to knowledge about Pather's oeuvre along with analyzing what makes his experience and his art significant today to global scholarly debates on space, on cities, on sexuality, and on art's key role in social amelioration. Pather's emphasis on cities, especially as they demarcate inclusive or exclusive areas, connect his art to urban theories. As a gay artist, he brings to the fore his sexuality in the broader politics of struggle against discrimination based on race, class, and sexuality; his work intersects with sexual/queer politics and queer movement in the arts. Pather's choreography, along with his concept-infused director notes, explore South Africans' continued apartheid trauma and refer to societies dealing with similar psychic and physical devastation caused by war and genocide, as in Rwanda or the former Yugoslavia, or the struggles of foreigners seeking citizenship in new homes. Pather's intersectional choreography and curation make him a relevant and valuable artist today not only in African dance studies but equally in scholarly fields such as space and body politics, theater and visual arts, and postcolonialism inside and outside the African continent. Above all, Pather's highly unique interventions in social justice via original choreography reach beyond their locally situated resonance to serve as models for dance makers and performance curators in South Africa, on the African continent, and beyond.

Scholarship on South Africa has been dominated by the juggernaut of apartheid. Although African theater under visionary directors such as Athol Fugard and Barney Simon, who cowrote plays with Black actors such as Winston Ntshona and John Kani (Johannesburg's iconic Market Theatre's main auditorium was renamed, in 2014, the John Kani Theater) during apartheid, has received scholarly attention, the same is not true for South African contemporary dance and performance, nor for such a prominent South African choreographer and curator as Pather.

To date, Pather's prolific oeuvre, although acclaimed in his country, is underrepresented in South African scholarship on arts and culture; critics have not kept pace with his fecund reinventions as artist and curator and his crossing boundaries of genre and discipline, during apartheid and into "democratic" disillusionments. Pather still remains a well-kept secret in the United States, and I wish to correct this oversight by bringing critical attention to an artist whose work is relevant for scholars and art practitioners in global performance and art festivals. Engagement with Pather's groundbreaking choreography, site work, and curation illuminates the human condition, most immediately for his constituency in South Africa but globally, too, in cities as diverse as Cape Town, Copenhagen, New York, Mumbai, and Durban.

ACKNOWLEDGMENTS

THIS BOOK HAS JOURNEYED WITH me over the past several years from my base at the University of California, Irvine to South Africa and India. I first met Jay Pather in 2011 in Cape Town, his academic home, and next in 2013, in his ancestral home of Chennai, where he was invited to speak at a symposium entitled Purush: The Global Dancing Male. I thank Dr. Anita Ratnam, contemporary Indian dancer and co-convener of the symposium, for inviting Pather and for facilitating my meetings with him while in Chennai.

This monograph owes a huge debt of gratitude to Jay Pather for his generosity and graciousness in putting up with a pesky scholar's interminable questions about his work and for agreeing to several interviews conducted in Chennai, Cape Town, Grahamstown, Los Angeles, and Irvine, including several phone calls during the global pandemic of 2020. I persuaded Jay to travel temporally and spatially down memory lane to discuss his early and recent works. His insights have added invaluable texture to this text. Thanks also to Jay for sharing his unpublished essays and for providing many of the photographs in this book.

This project, from its incipient stages to fruition, owes a great deal to veteran journalist and arts commentator Adrienne Sichel, archivist (with Jessica Denychen) of The Ar(t)chive at the University of Witwatersrand. Adrienne shared invaluable materials with me during my visits to the Ar(t)chive in 2014 and 2015 and over subsequent years with email exchanges. I also thank Tammy Ballantyne Webber, Head of Research at The Ar(t)chive, for her assistance in locating citations during the health crisis lockdown of 2020.

At the University of California (UCI), my academic home, I thank colleagues in the Department of Drama, and Chair Daniel Gary Busby, who has always supported my research. I am profoundly indebted to Distinguished Professor of English and Comparative Literature Ngũgĩ wa Thiong'o, my colleague and friend at UCI whose essay entitled "Enactments of Power: The Politics of Performance Space" first inspired me to undertake a study of space and race in this book. Ngũgĩ and I also team-taught a graduate seminar titled The Politics of Performance Space in the Postcolonial World, which was highly enlightening in shaping many of the ideas in this book. I also thank my UCI friends and colleagues Professor Gabriele Schwab and Professor Julia Lupton for their invaluable insights on drafts of this monograph. I also thank Julia Lupton for inviting Jay Pather to the Global Shakespeare Symposium at UCI in January 2018.

I am deeply grateful to Professor Sarah Davies Cordova at the University of Wisconsin, Milwaukee, whom I first met at a dance conference in 2013 when she came forward to offer me materials from her time in South Africa. With an unwavering belief in this project, Sarah has spent invaluable time on reading drafts and offering assistance on this book's structure. Through the ups and downs of writing, she remained an encouraging and supportive kindred spirit, and we became friends on this journey of understanding Jay Pather's practice.

For enlightening interviews with founding members of the Siwela Sonke Dance Theater Company (SSDT) in Durban—namely, Ntombi Gasa and Neliswa Rushualang, and for Ntombi's friendship over the years, her insights into Jay's works, I am grateful. Ntombi's materials—newspaper reviews and other notices of SSDT performances—were most useful. Thanks also to Elroy Bell, administrator at SSDT in 2015.

I consulted the Archive at the University of KwaZulu Natal, Center for Creative Arts in Durban. Thanks to Ashwin Singh for driving me to this location as well as his assistance with transportation in Durban and for arranging a talk for me at the Playhouse Theatre.

For useful interviews in Durban, I thank Suria Governder, Kribben Pillay, Michael Samuel, Harold Samuel, Ronnie Govender, Manesh Maharaj, and Clare Craighead (also for invaluable brochures and publications of JOMBA! Contemporary Dance Experience).

Many thanks to talented photographer Val Adamson, whose eye captures dancers in flight in memorable images. Adamson had very kindly invited me to her home in Durban and gave me permission to use several of her photographs of Pather's works that are in this book, including the cover image.

My thanks to Gerard Samuel, head of dance at the University of Cape Town (UCT) in 2015, for his time spent in interviews, for sharing dance materials in his office, and for providing contacts of local dancers and scholars. At UCT, Jacki Job kindly shared her work and some of Pather's work with Jazzart Dance Theater.

In Johannesburg, I thank for their time and interviews Gita Pather, Keiron Jina, Dr. Lalloo, and Jeyasperi Moopen, whose Tribhangi Dance Theater Company artists kindly performed in their studio for me.

I thank Lliane Loots, Pravika Nandakishore, and Smeetha Maharaj for phone interviews.

In Malibu, California, I thank South African journalist Suzy Bell for discussing Pather's work with me.

I thank UCI's Academic Senate Council on Research, Computing, and Libraries (CORCL) for research funding to travel to

South Africa in 2014. Carmen Burgess' computer expertise and Leslie Blough's editorial assistance were invaluable.

Among family and friends in Irvine, I thank my daughter Roshni for her patience regarding her mother's projects and for accompanying me to India, where we both met Pather in Chennai. Roshni stands by me as my tech guru; I thank her for helping me to organize the photos in this book. I am grateful to my friend Beheroze Shroff for her emotional support with this project and for her loving care of Charlie, our four-legged family member who has now joined the angels. My thanks to Starbucks baristas on Bison and California—Kevin, Laura, and Alex (the Great!)—for keeping me caffeinated, kindly inquiring about how "the book" was coming along, and often letting me stay past closing time. I miss my Starbucks work-site during the stay-at-home time of the corona virus as I write these words.

I thank my friend Astad Deboo, pioneer of contemporary Indian dance, for discussions on dance and for his understanding while I worked on this monograph and simultaneously coedited with him a special issue on contemporary dance in India for *MARG: A Magazine of the Arts*, published in June 2017.

My thanks to Dee Mortensen, editorial director at Indiana University Press, for her positive response to my idea of writing a book on Jay Pather when I met her in San Diego at the African Studies Association Conference in November 2015. Dee's effective guidance through the prospectus stage and her faith in this project over the years have been key in bringing this monograph to publication. I am also grateful to the anonymous reviewers of this book for their suggestions

I acknowledge with thanks the permission to use materials from my published essays on Jay Pather in *African Theatre* (2016) and in *Dance Research Journal* (2018).

Ketu H. Katrak
Irvine, August 16, 2020

INTERVIEWS/CONVERSATIONS

DATES AND LOCATIONS OF INTERVIEWS/
CONVERSATIONS: JAY PATHER WITH KETU KATRAK

In South Africa: Cape Town, and Grahamstown; in India: Chennai; and in the United States: Los Angeles and Irvine, California.

Interview 1: In Irvine, California, January, 24, 28, 30, 2018.

Interview 2: In Chennai, India. Purush: The Global Dancing Male Symposium with Performances. December 18–22, 2013. Interview on December 20, 2013.

Interview 3: Via phone from Grahamstown to Cape Town, August 20, 2017.

Interview 4: Via Skype, October 29, 2015. Pather in Cape Town and Katrak in Irvine, California.

Interview 5: In Pather's office in Hiddingh Hall at the University of Cape Town, July 29, 2015.

Interview 6: In Los Angeles, August 3, 2016, on the occasion of Pather's choreography for *The Firebird*, which was performed on August 4, 2016 at the Hollywood Bowl.

Phone conversations: Jay Pather (in South Africa) with Ketu Katrak (in Irvine, California): May 20, 25, and 30, 2020, and June 2, 7, and 9, 2020.

JAY PATHER, PERFORMANCE, AND SPATIAL
POLITICS IN SOUTH AFRICA

Fig. I.1. Jay Pather. Photographer: Michael Hammond. https://www.news.uct.ac.za/article/-2016-06-14-jay-pathers-qaphela-caesar-wins-uct-creative-works-award. Courtesy: Jay Pather.

INTRODUCTION

Pather's Spatial Politics within South Africa's Historical and Political Landscape

The politics of space are important to me. I think there is a simple notion that we are a democratic society now ... [that is] something that I'm fascinated with and I keep trying to press against and try to push and see just how democratic we are. I find that actually spaces carry a history against which this kind of questioning ... can really happen.[1]

Jay Pather

JAY PATHER (B. 1959), A South African choreographer, theater director, and curator of Indian descent, is creating some of the most provocative movement and performance pieces in the world today. This innovative, experimental, and avant-garde artist's choreography and curation from the 1980s to the 2010s deploy space—geographical, bodily, mental, psychological—in conjunction with race in order to challenge apartheid (1948–1994) and post-apartheid geographical divisions and persisting psychological trauma via artistic performances that intervene in issues of social justice. As a progressive artist with an aesthetic-political vision, Pather has created inter- and multidisciplinary choreography using movement with video and multimedia. He has also produced site works that challenge apartheid-era divisions of space based on race and has curated large-scale public arts festivals in Cape Town that have transformed art and performance significantly in South Africa, with global impact on artists and scholars.

Pather's evolving spatial politics over the course of his nearly four-decade career are inspired by his creative works, which are infused with his progressive politics, his aesthetic-political vision, and his theoretical essays on space. My ideas on space in postcolonial regions are influenced by prominent Kenyan writer Ngũgĩ wa Thiong'o's essay "Enactments of Power: The Politics of Performance Space." Ngũgĩ remarks that "the struggle between the arts and the state [can] best be seen in performance in general and in the battle over performance space in particular.... The war between art and the state is really a struggle between the power of performance in the arts and the performance of power by the state—in short, enactments of power" (Ngũgĩ 1998, 37). Performance spaces are charged politically, according to Ngũgĩ; they carry memories of colonial dominations in postcolonial societies, and they threaten neocolonial state power. Such ideas resonate in South African society, where spaces that mark racial inclusions and exclusions still exist. In the epigraph, Pather remarks that "the politics of space are important" to him and that spaces "carry a history against which" he questions South Africa's hard-won democracy. The concept of space, I contend, is overdetermined within the context of South Africa's draconian apartheid laws when racial divisions were systemic and into post-apartheid disillusionments today, over a quarter century after the 1994 ushering in of "democracy." Pather's creative choreography probes the colonial and apartheid eras' physical, mental, and psychic wounds which linger in the human body and mind; he critiques the failures of democracy that continue to dehumanize the majority Black and Colored populations in South Africa.[2]

I develop my argument on Pather's spatial vision as challenging apartheid's legacy via his own theorizations of space in essays and his concept-infused director and curator notes as well as in analyzing his spatial politics as they evolve in his creative works in line with his nation's painful history. Pather's innovative uses of space include their political, resistant resonances that aim to democratize space, to provide access to high-quality art, and to ignite communication among diverse South Africans. In site-specific works, he deconstructs certain spaces actively, wrenching them away from their usual functions—for example, having his dancers perform a popular South African dance style that is incongruous inside a swanky mall. Pather deploys the human body as a site that is inscribed with personal, political, and national histories and memories in his site-responsive works; further, as a curator, he selects artists for public arts festivals as well as identifying the appropriate spaces, provocative at times, for performance, installations, and other artistic expressions. Here, Pather is a curator of space itself in enabling the location to showcase, subvert, or question its purpose—such as classical music played on a grand piano wheeled into Cape Town Railway station, where 99 percent of the commuters are Black, during the 2013 *Infecting the City* festival. Pather holds a global stature in performance and curation in contemporary times, when dance and movement collaborate and interface with other disciplines such as visual art and multimedia.

SPACE AS POLITICAL AND HISTORICAL

Pather's uses of space are political and historical in terms of the locations and settings of his works. He locates Black performers in spaces previously forbidden to them. The very occupying of such spaces performs, as it were, resistance to apartheid-era divisions. Indeed, the conjuncture of geography and history during apartheid and into the continuing failures of democracy when it comes to the Black majority guide the innovative forms of Pather's site works. As an artist, Pather's spatial vision draws on diverse performance genres, as in his original site-specific and site-responsive works that challenge controls of space, thereby intervening in social transformation. Such site creations in the spaces that Pather selects confront apartheid's lingering legacy, largely in place today, of the ghettoization of where people could (and can) live, work, and love. Pather connects his immediate constituency of diverse South Africans to local history as well as to global politics, as in his creative adaptations of world classics like Shakespeare's *Julius Caesar*, Stravinsky's *Rite of Spring*, and, most recently, Stravinsky's *Firebird* (a collaboration with Janni Younge) giving them a South African setting and illuminating their wider political resonances of power, justice, and hope.

Spatial locations and the politics attached to them over South Africa's history are part of daily reality for most Black people who live outside cities, in townships, and still search for home and belonging in the land of their birth; they "migrate" daily to and from work. Esha De and Sonita Sarkar, editors of a collection of essays entitled *Trans-Status Subjects*, create the word "placetime" to bring together history and geography and to demonstrate "how individuals and groups re-member, survive in and resist imposed definitions of place" (De and Sarkar 2002, 21). They probe "the radical potential of geography in defin(ing) the production of new histories from these geographies" (21). The significance of location and time, of geography and history, is poignantly and palpably real for most South African Black people. Pather intervenes spatially in his curation of public art festivals such as *Infecting the City* with Sello Pesa and Vaughn Sadie in a work that pokes irony at the reductive nature of memorials such as the Preswich Memorial in Cape Town, a site where buried slave bones were found. The site performance included activities that reveal the humanity of Black people such as barbequing, hair-braiding, and playing music from a car's trunk.

In one of my previous books, *Politics of the Female Body*, I argue that in postcolonial cultures female bodies under patriarchy are exiled internally—that is, they experience alienation from their female bodies—and here I transpose this same argument to South Africa, where Black bodies are exiled geographically, living in the margins of major cities or relegated to "homelands" in arid hinterlands. In colonial and apartheid regimes, and even today, maps still need to be redrawn to enable Black people to afford to live inside cities. Pather's spatial politics critiques such marginalization in his choreographed performances such as *Home* and *Hotel*, which are discussed in chapters 3 and 4.

Pather's (2014a) spatial vision and his attention to history are expressed in his presentation "Legacies of Violence: South Africa, 20 Years after Democracy."[3] He admits that "apartheid sits firmly in each moment that one is. I remember it clearly, not because I want to or am obsessed with the past." He then provides reasons why this painful past persists in the democratic present: "It is because the persistence of poverty and an unabated rage remain as viscous, and as visceral as ever. The denial of this has made the festering wound to turn its colour and shift its form from a space of vulnerability and compromise in the early nineties to a space now increasingly of sudden attack, an unpredictable virulence born of neglect" (this talk was incorporated into "Laws of Recall," Pather 2015b, 334). Although Pather in the same essay, warns that positive emotions are "wearing thin" in the reality of apartheid's continuing, haunting fallout for the majority, he remains hopeful that "the mechanisms inherent in art could possibly fill these spaces and silences in legacy and memory." He meditates lyrically that this is "a legacy inscribed not just in land, in home, in place, not just on kin, in bones, in organs and human tissue but a legacy etched in the shared memory and spirit of a nation" (Pather 2014a). Even as his searing vision probes the debris of apartheid's devastation of physical bodies and minds, he holds on to "the mechanisms inherent in art" that could heal the wounds inside and outside the human body and are carried by "the spirit of a nation."

In an interview with Peter Machen in 2009, Pather reflects on "art-making for his generation" under apartheid's mandated divisions of diverse people:

> In response to the terrible separation, there was a strong need to collaborate, to create strategies to counter the divides. These divides that were not just about race and class, but also divides in cultural forms: what was "classical," what was "good" art and "bad" art, what was so-called "community" art, and what was professional.... We have to be very conscious that we do not continue the legacy of apartheid in subtle forms. Art and culture reflect the unfinished business of redress prevalent in other aspects of our society. Working collaboratively engenders healing, dialogue and a way of developing, more than just a superficial understanding of diverse points of view. (Machen 2009)

Pather's uses of space have historical resonances rooted in the political realities of separations of diverse South African peoples and artists during apartheid, with lingering echoes during post-apartheid.

DEMOCRATIZING, DECONSTRUCTING SPACE: THE POLITICAL IS PERSONAL

Pather aims to democratize space, providing access for diverse bodies; he also deconstructs spaces from their usual meanings. He mediates space and race in serious, provocative, even playful ways. Since challenges of access to performance remain for the majority who cannot afford to attend theaters, Pather offers his work free of charge in public spaces or indoors. He is adept at raising funds that make such goals of access a reality and still pays professional dancers. Pather's careful site selections often involve an emotional response, as he admits: "I have to fall in love with the site that I select" (interview 1, 2018). These include the throbbing city center of Durban, his hometown, which features remarkable buildings: the 1901 Durban City Hall, with bold columns, pillars and figures of warriors, women, and lions etched into the stone surfaces; the Juma Masjid Mosque, with arced gateways and gilt-covered minarets; and the Madressa Arcade, where Pather's grandfather's watch repair shop sat among the small traders in a bazaar-like atmosphere. As noted on a Durban city site, "the intimate contact between traders with the lightweight galleries of the first floor and connecting bridges overhead contribute to an exciting spatial experience with a distinctly eastern atmosphere."[4]

Sites where Pather positions his dancers and dance forms challenge the invisibility imposed on Black bodies. Public spaces that Pather uses for performance foster his deep commitment to inspiring connections among people of different races, sexual orientations, classes, and other affiliations, and to their being in touch with their personal selves. Pather's site works evoke cultural connections among different publics whether on a pavement or inside a coffee shop, which is not separate from cultural practices. His choreography is embedded in South Africa's sociocultural and political fabric of a particular time. It traces ordinary people's hopes, disillusionments, and dreams. These are evoked in the very titles of his dance-theater works *Testimonies* (1997) and *Forked Tongues* (1999), which were presented on state-controlled proscenium stages indoors and dealt with pre- and post-apartheid scenarios of testimonies and the fallouts of the Truth and Reconciliation Commission. Pather remains critical of "reconciliation" in the face of horrific human rights violations and wounds that continue to fester.[5] He was an invited keynote speaker at an international conference entitled Re-moving Apartheid: Postdramatic and Postnarrative Modes of Coping with Trauma at Ghent University, Belgium (September 28–30, 2016).

In South Africa, 2005 marked ten years after independence and also saw Pather's creation of *The Beautiful Ones Must Be Born*, exposing many promises broken by the new government. Pather's work aligns here with Gabriele Schwab's, who "links the cultural function of literature [and performance] to its power to affect and change us and to intervene in other cultural practices" (2010, 10). Further, the way that a story or performance works involves what Schwab calls "the ideology of form," a phrase borrowed from Frederick Jameson. For Schwab, "the aesthetic has always been defined in relation to other cultural spheres" that may emphasize different "priorities" taken from the social, psychological, or political arena.

Pather's spatial politics aim to transform what he describes as "spaces of alienation under apartheid to spaces where different cultures could brush up against one another" (interview 3, 2017). One major change after apartheid is that suddenly Black people came into focus, becoming visible in central spaces in cities such as Cape Town and Durban. Pather capitalizes on this visibility by situating Black dancers in city centers or public parks, trusting that "intercultural communication can happen" for different people who may stop to watch a performance and perhaps talk to the person next to them. Pather's democratic goals are invested in "making place" for all South African citizens, in "unmaking and remaking space" to open them up from previous restrictions (Pather 2013b, 438).

Whether in the public arena or in making private spaces public, Pather remarks (interview 2, 2013) that he "is obsessed with the personal in dance and in how much of the personal, even intimate, is repressed." His spatial politics unfold in what I delineate as "the political is personal," reversing the feminist adage "the personal is political." In another interview (interview 4, 2015), he indicates that "in *Cityscapes*, whether set indoors or outdoors, the idea was always around intimate moments, private moments in public spaces. . . . Even in *From Before* (2004), a version of *Cityscapes* performed on the steps of the Cathedral of St. John the Divine in New York City with twenty-four dancers, and a massive work, the way I use space highlights private dialogue." This indeed is a unique way of using public space, where "the political is personal."

Even when Pather creates public art, he is interested in "personal place-making in public, and intimacy in public spaces" (interview 5, 2015). He considers it "very important to show South Africans to be in touch with their bodies" (interview 5, 2015). He aims to make public spaces personal, even intimate, in his body-based (rather than text-based) work, encouraging diverse citizens to brush up against one another physically with the hope of further communication among groups that were separated by law under apartheid. Pather's intention to foster the "feeling of touch and intimacy in public space" is a deliberate affront to apartheid, which forcibly separated races in housing with little opportunity for social interaction among diverse South Africans, even less for personal or intimate interactions (interview 5, 2015). During apartheid, sexual relations between races was forbidden legally under the 1950 Immorality Act. Open interaction among diverse people was not allowed in public spaces; rather, these were sites for protests and funerals. In all such avenues, the political is personal for Black South Africans. Pather's site selections are distinctive in making indoor, even private spaces public. Pather's award-winning work entitled *Hotel* is set inside a hotel room and viewed by only twelve spectators at a time.

By the 2000s, Pather's spatial explorations journey to site-specific choreographies. The concept of "site-specific" indicates Pather's astute selections of locations in major South African cities where many areas, especially in the central business districts, were forbidden to Black people during apartheid. Such spatial exclusions continue post-apartheid in some cites especially Cape Town. Pather's pioneering 2002 site-specific work entitled *Cityscapes* (performed in various Durban locations and then in Johannesburg and Cape Town) defies such outsiderness for Black South Africans. In it, he places dancers in the city's central business district, where he explores the interface between the human frame and large buildings in urban centers; diverse dancers appear on the previously forbidden beach front, and indoors,

Pather choreographs an interracial couple's struggles inside a hotel room. Pather's deployment and deconstruction of such locations explores cartographies of belonging for diverse citizens.

Other site-specific locations include upscale malls where shoppers are startled by dancers on escalators in Armani business suits, carrying briefcases, who perform the South African popular dance form *pantsula*, usually done in Black townships outside cities. Such site work, in Pather's hands, is creatively mobile. Indeed, in 2003, *Cityscapes* moved to Johannesburg with his core company, who performed with dancers from the new location. In 2004, segments of *Cityscapes* entitled *From Before* traveled to New York City with SSDT dancers along with some local dancers. Other site-specific performances of the 2000s include *Blindspot* in Copenhagen, *rite* in Johannesburg, and *Republic* and a symposium, "LAND," in Cape Town.

Pather's experimental and avant-garde site-responsive performances of the 2000s deconstruct spaces from their usual functions. His spatial evolution continues in four distinctive site-responsive works whose very spaces and settings express his choreographic ingenuity toward increasing interdisciplinarity. The site-responsive concept indicates locations saturated with the nation's history, its seamy past, and its disillusioned present, leaving the majority still hoping for a positive future. A particular site inspires Pather to "respond" to its history artistically, often ironically; such content guides Pather's inventive formal choices such as including Indian classical dance and contemporary Western dance along with video and unusual props juxtaposed in uncanny ways. The site-responsive work *Home* (2003) is particularly close to Ntombi Gasa's heart, as she noted when I interviewed her, because it reassures her and the company of a "home" that Pather was instrumental in securing after Siwela Sonke was retrenched from the Playhouse Theater (their original space) due to the latter's troubling policies. The Brett Kebble Award-winning work *The Kitchen*, part of *Home*, is set (un)cannily inside a public art gallery and witnessed by various publics, whereas a kitchen is usually a private space.

Other site-responsive works subvert official, state-sanctioned histories in unusual sites such as Johannesburg's Constitutional Hill, where Pather locates *The Beautiful Ones Must Be Born* (2005), or a medical building for *Body of Evidence* (2008), whose seeds were sown in *Unclenching the Fist*. Pather selects another history-laden site, the old Cape Town City Hall—where, on February 11 1990, Nelson Mandela first addressed his people and the world after his release from Robben Island prison—for *Qaphela Caesar* (2010), his adaptation of Shakespeare's play that is given "a new habitation and a name" in South Africa's political climate of corrupt leaders and greedy politicians (Theseus's words in Shakespeare's *A Midsummer Night's Dream*, V,1). The political upheavals and fragmentations of 2010 are conveyed in Pather's innovative form that fragments the play, situating fourteen scenes in fourteen different rooms in City Hall. This work had another exceptional site-responsive location: Johannesburg's old Stock Exchange Hall, a site of trading fortunes and lives.

INSCRIBING THE HUMAN BODY AS A SITE OF HISTORY AND MEMORY

Pather's goals of democratizing and deconstructing space to provide access to diverse South Africans who can gather in public to enjoy performances also evoke the dark cloud of memories and historical residues that a particular space may carry "and what longings (it) might generate" (Ngũgĩ 1998, 41). Pather's landmark essay "Shifting Spaces Tilting Time" similarly raises concerns about spaces triggering memories of past traumas. Pather's creativity addresses such deep-rooted physical and psychic realities by inscribing multiple meanings metaphorically on the human body. Pather is as concerned as veteran South African dancer-choreographer Tossie van Tonder, as expressed in her poignant reminder about "what South Africa does to the body."⁶ This is a loaded statement in light of South Africa's painful history of landmark protests, when large numbers of ordinary people's bodies were subjected to beatings, arrests, and political repressions.⁷ "What South Africa does to the body" poses a tactile reality that evokes apartheid's daily outrages of dehumanization caused by harsh legislation such as the Pass Laws, the Immorality Act, the Group Areas Act, and the Terrorism Act, all designed to control where Black bodies could be present and breathe freely at any given time. Pather's site works take on such unjust degradations of the human body, asserting its humanity and visibility in public areas.

Although certain bodies were physically barred and marked during apartheid, Pather's attention to bodies in performance goes further in his fascination with symbolically probing the human body's cells and muscles while "alive," though trapped in abject poverty. He wants to find the oozing wounds of apartheid-era damage that continues in physical and psychological trauma today. Pather's metaphoric looking into the human body for clues echoes the field of forensic science, which dissects dead bodies to discover the causes of their demise. In an interview with Niren Tolsi, Pather remarks that "there are theories that memories of pain can never be obliterated. Part of that memory becomes part of the tissue, of the marrow in our bones. And in our collective history there is so much physical and psychological pain" (Tolsi 2008). Such persistent and painful remembrances throbbing inside sinews and psyches feature most poignantly in Pather's *Body of Evidence* (2008) and also in an earlier work, *Laws of Recall* (2000).

Pather's focus on the body and psyche as sites and repositories of apartheid-era traumas echoes other violent events in human history and their psychic continuation through the generations, as discussed evocatively in Gabriele Schwab's scholarly book entitled *Haunting Legacies: Violent Histories and Transgenerational*

Trauma. These events, Schwab argues, are "hard to recount or even to remember, the results of a violence that holds an unrelenting grip on memory yet is deemed unspeakable. The psychic core of violent histories includes what has been repressed or buried in unreachable psychic recesses. The legacies of violence not only haunt the actual victims but also are passed on through the generations" (2010, 1). Schwab avails herself of a striking image proposed by Nicolas Abraham, namely that of "a *crypt* in which people bury unspeakable events or unbearable, if not disavowed, losses or injuries incurred during violent histories. It is as if in this psychic tomb they harbor an undead ghost" (1). Pather's art is original in his creative excavations of traumatic memories that persist in the bodies and minds of apartheid-inflicted injuries from such "crypts."

Pather engages with the human body, physically and psychically, as he remarks in his "Artist's Statement":

> I am as interested in performance as I am in psychology and the manifestations of the psyche on the human bodily environment. I cut my teeth making work that emerged from the personal made political, and though I have tried working purely with form for the sake of its own vitality, in both a visual sense and within the moving body, I always seem to creep back to locating why things are and not just that they are.
>
> Mixed media, the visual, aural and the kinetic give me a broad canvas to explore the complexity and sophistication of consciousness, and ultimately it is the choices and the playing out of choice in the human consciousness that fascinates me. Live performance and video framed often by existing architecture give me frame and malleable material. Of late, site-specific work has taken me out of traditional spaces to explore new relationships with public spaces and architecture but now extended to an informal, unsuspecting audience who view the work from a range of angles and vantage points. (van Rensburg 2004)

Pather is less invested in having his audience grasp a particular "meaning" of his work; rather, he wants people from different walks of life to respond from their own vantage points. His approach gives huge importance to dialogue, to debate rather than closure in his notion of dialogic open-endedness. Similarly, Pather's bold works encourage discussion on topics such as domestic violence in *Unclenching the Fist*, mental challenges in *Laws of Recall*, and communication lags within a multi-lingual society as in *Forked Tongues*.

Pather's artistic vision remains consistent, rooted in his progressive politics and his recognized role as "a facilitator of Black talent" (Machen 2009) throughout his oeuvre. At times, his choreographic expressions are dark in response to broken government promises a decade or even two after independence. In terms of form, his early dance-theater work evolves into avant-garde performance, a word he favors since it includes his increasing embrace of inter- and multi-disciplines, crisscrossing borders of movement with media and visual art.

Pather's spatial politics are showcased in his award-winning choreography and multidisciplinary performances. As artistic director of Siwela Sonke Dance Theatre (SSDT), he has choreographed several award-winning works commissioned by prominent dance and arts organizations in South Africa such as FNB Dance Umbrella (Johannesburg), JOMBA! Contemporary Dance Experience (Durban), and the National Arts Festival (Grahamstown). Internationally, Pather and his company have been invited to create site-specific works at the Metropolis Biennale in the Netherlands, the World Social Forum in Mumbai, and New York City's African Arts Festival, among others. He has presented work across Africa in Madagascar, Angola, and Zanzibar as well as around the world in India, Germany, London, and Australia. He has received prestigious awards: the Brett Kebble Art Award, a Mayoral Excellence Award, FNB Vita Awards for Choreography, Award for Excellence in the Arts and Humanities from the Convocation of the University of KwaZulu Natal, and a Heritage award, jointly presented by Independent Newspapers, the Heritage Council, the National Arts Council, and

Business Arts South Africa. In 2015, he was honored with the distinguished Living Legend Award by the city of Durban. In 2016, he was conferred with the Chevalier des Artes en Lettres by the French ambassador to South Africa. Currently, in South Africa, he serves as chair of a judging panel for the International Award for Public Art, convened in Hong Kong in March 2017. He has been appointed as "Expert Advisor: Live Art, Africa 2020," commissioned by President Macron of France, and serves as a committee member of Tanzfabrik Berlin—the decolonization of art institutions, Berlin.

Pather continues to work with SSDT. The company specializes in contemporary dance theater and in African intercultural and multimedia performance along with collaborations across disciplines from video art to architecture, as well as site-specific works. Under the directorship of Ntombi Gasa and Neliswa Rushualang, the company runs an extensive community development program in rural and urban communities from KaMashu to KwaMachai townships on the outskirts of Durban.[8] One major and unique aspect of SSDT is their educational "Reachout Training" including "Dance Education, and Youth Development Training" that "develops dance literacy amongst under privileged children (from rural areas, Black townships), the development of choreographic literacy and potential among new choreographers ... and in general to develop an awareness of the power of the arts and dance training in particular through public performances. Above all, along with training the body and mind, Siwela Sonke enables the development of a professional work ethic and discipline."[9]

Pather shared his personal unpublished document (via email, May 20, 2020) outlining SSDT's mission statement that states its goals and scope, including performance and training for those from disadvantaged communities:

- Produce visually compelling contemporary dance theatre performances of high quality

- Develop a dance theatre language that draws from the rich variety of indigenous and contemporary dance styles of South Africa such as the indhlamu (traditional zulu dance) gumboot, isicathamiya, Indian dance, ballet, contemporary European and contemporary African dance
- Recreate our histories, and rediscover the rich myths and legends of marginalized people whose stories have remained untold
- Train and develop dancers from disadvantaged communities who have had no prior access to training opportunities
- Create socially relevant dance theatre that deals with the issues that affect the people we perform to—such as gangsterism in high schools, abuse against women—in places where the people are—community halls, shopping malls, clinics, prisons, clubs and outlying villages
- Be instruments for the ideas of people around us, but also to challenge these ideas

In the same document, Pather states that "Siwela Sonke Dance Theatre defines its identity from partnerships on three levels," as follows:

A. **Professional Theatre**—we produce original dance theatre works that place the company in the forefront of creative production in South Africa and performing in national and international festivals

B. **Education and Community Development**—building a wide and heterogeneous audience base over time and helping to stimulate a culture of theatre and dance

C. **Business and Government**—making strategic and mutually beneficial relationships with the private and public sector, and offering the skills of the company as a vehicle for appropriate social concerns (literacy).[10]

Siwela Sonke's African dance incorporates contemporary and traditional African dance, classical ballet, modern dance, traditional and contemporary Indian dance, hip-hop, and jazz movements. Pather, sensitive to and aware of the fact that traditional Zulu and African dance were denigrated during the colonial and apartheid eras, reclaims them carefully as "classical" with their own idioms. Pather, with SSDT, fosters communication across cultural groups by incorporating a range of dance styles. As Terri Davidoff remarks, "This healthy integration of diverse performance forms can in itself be read as performing the process of transformation from a racially divided to a multiethnic democratic society" (2006, 137).[11]

Pather took Siwela Sonke to perform at the Festival of Dhow Countries in Zanzibar. In 2004, he traveled to Mumbai, India, with twenty-five dancers in a large-scale performance for the official opening ceremony of the World Social Forum. In 2004, he participated in the Personal Affects: Power and Poetics in Contemporary South African Art event in New York City, where he presented parts of 2002's *Cityscapes*, retitled *From Before*. In the latter, Pather involved four South African and twenty-one New York City dancers.

SSDT's work encourages innovation in dance theater, particularly creating space for "people whose stories have not been told." They aim to "create works that develop new South African Dance language, create intercultural performances that break historical barriers, develop indigenous African dances ... [and] create performances in collaboration" with other artists, as well as with art galleries, teachers' unions, and the National Ports Authority.[12] Suzy Bell remarks in *The Independent on Saturday*, "Acclaimed choreographer Jay Pather has taken South Africa's layered landscapes and mindscapes to create the superbly satisfying and insanely lyrical South African interior dance dialogue we've been waiting for. Pather slowly unfolds a distinctly South African narrative with sophistication and an unselfconscious interplay of dance forms from Zulu and Xhosa dance, kathak, bharathanatyam, oddissi, contemporary and classical ballet. It works beautifully. At times it is soft and calm, rational and dignified, comical and camp, balanced and harmonious then petulant and tortured. And yes, of course, even very sexy" (Bell, 2000d). Pather's choreography—attuned to his progressive and aesthetic-political excavations of social problems—draws from a palette of dance languages: South African dance styles such as Zulu and Xhosa; Indian classical dance styles such as Bharatanatyam and Kathak; South African popular dance styles such as *pantsula*, *isicathamiya*, and gumboot dance; and an eclectic layering of modern and contemporary dance.[13] Pather's hybrid style is similar to choreographers in other parts of the world who transform classical styles from within, rendering them relevant for new content in contemporary times, layering them with Western dance vocabularies.[14] Pather is profoundly conscious of South Africa's colonial legacy; hence, even as he deploys Western forms such as modern and contemporary dance or release technique, he transforms them as relevant in the South African context. His use of release technique is especially relevant because it "prepares the body for a greater number of movement possibilities" and appeals to Pather's own anatomical emphasis in his choreography (Roche 2015, 6).[15] Further, in release technique, "images are used to structure the manner in which bones balance or articulate in movement: movement of lines, bridges, bowl shapes in the body, of paths of action-flow, all designed to release the body into easy efficient alignment and action" (6). Release technique serves Pather's aims in representing the human body, its physical movements, and its capabilities as a vessel to contain, evoke, and represent memory and history.

THEORIST OF SPACE WITH GLOBAL RESONANCES: DANCE AND THE BODY

As in the creative work of prominent artists worldwide who deploy their own theorizing to provide useful analytic tools to readers and spectators with which to approach their creative endeavors, so does Pather, who is a prominent theorist of space.

In his landmark essay, "Shifting Spaces Tilting Time," Pather remarks, "I was interested in space, and then public space as animate, as a personal and political phenomenon, a powerful conveyor and custodian of power, emotion and meaning" (Pather 2013b, 433). Along with Pather's other published essays, "Laws of Recall: Body, Memory, and Site-Specific Performance in South Africa," and, cowritten with Mark Fleishman (South African scholar and artistic director of Cape Town's Magnet Theater), "Performing Cape Town: An Epidemiological Study in Three Acts," his director and curator notes and published and unpublished essays enable viewers and scholars of his choreography and curation to recognize his transposition of his theoretical concepts into artistic practice; indeed, he achieves a unique theory and praxis approach to instigate social change.

Pather's theorizations of his site and curatorial works for festivals held in Cape Town belong with other theoretical works on cities and urban spaces. He remarks, "The city has always fascinated me as a living space—where you have your social and living space side by side, and you constantly have to take care of recreating self.... Suburbs determine the kind of people you meet. In the city, there are always accidents, moments of serendipity. Here, in the city [Cape Town], I feel like I'm part of something global, something bigger." His choice to live in urban centers is connected to what he calls his "great idiosyncrasy. I don't drive. I've spent time in places where I simply didn't need to drive" (interview 4, 2015). Pather observes people in their daily activities while walking to many places in Cape Town. In a TedX talk at the University of Cape Town (February 27, 2015) entitled "A Love Affair with Spaces," Pather mentions that he does "a different kind of space travel—by walking a lot, since I do not drive—that keeps my feet firmly on the ground." While walking, as he remarks in his TedX talk, he discovers "mysterious spaces that can become a playground for performance, where [he] connects with [people's] dreams, as individuals, as a nation" (Pather 2015a).

In "Performing Cape Town: An Epidemiological Study in Three Acts," Pather and Fleishman analyze Cape town's current status as a tourist city and its manicured beauty, which is shaken up deliberately by outdoor festival performances and installations in gardens and in warehouses. As in Cape Town, where Black people are relegated to the outskirts, so it is in other global cities like Copenhagen, where Pather was invited to create a site-specific work entitled *Blindspot* as part of the Metropolis Biennale in 2009. *Blindspot* proceeded on Copenhagen's streets from the city's outskirts, where migrants live, into the center. Pather's deep concern for migrants facing prejudice as outsiders extends to "foreigners"—that is, Black people from the continent who confront exclusions as they seek refuge in South African cities. These realities echo beyond South Africa in ubiquitous media images of ordinary people from Africa, Asia, and the Middle East fleeing violence and poverty, risking their lives in overcrowded boats crossing the Mediterranean to arrive on Europe's shores.

Along with movement training, as Pather's cutting-edge choreography demonstrates, and as is increasingly evident worldwide, dance collaborates and interfaces with other disciplines— movement is interwoven with visual art, theater techniques, video, and multimedia. This multidisciplinary vision does not lose focus of the dancer's human body; in fact, as recent critical dance studies illuminate, dance is not simply on the receiving end of other expressive forms such as visual art. Rather, dance as a body of knowledge is recognized as intervening in and transforming other fields rather than the other way around.[16]

Pather's description of life in South Africa as "uniquely and truly post-modern" invokes the kinds of communication and interactions among human beings that were unimaginable during apartheid (van Rensburg 2004) He probes the personal and the intimate in all his work, wherein body politics evoke larger political landscapes that emerge organically from his imaginative juxtapositions, such as "rural Black matriarch meets surfer-boy" (van Rensburg 2004). His postmodernism, a cultural and aesthetic style that is used globally by creative artists, was expressed in a unique layering of his creative choreography—as in dancers in staggered spaces on stage moving in front of visual art, or trapped inside cage-like props, or holding a lightbulb emitting a harsh and naked light.

Pather recognizes astutely the limits of choreography, since he observes that even well-trained Black dancers carry a history of "their own surveillance and self-negation," leading to a self-consciousness in "what the audience would look at" (interview 5, 2015). Hence, contemporary South African dance language, according to Pather, needs to incorporate more than the physical body in performance even as the moving body remains significant. He layers movement with "visual art, text, sound, images, and conceptual material" in provocative multidisciplinary performance (Pather 2015b, 317). The audience picks up the kinetic quality of the "work/dance," he remarks, leading to "a conceptually more complex work than what the dance/body can accomplish on its own" (interview 4, 2015), even in executing arabesques and displaying excellent technique. Pather embraces the word *performance* (as opposed to *dance-theater*, which he used in the 1980s and 1990s) to describe the inter- and multidisciplinary impetus of his work since early 2000.

Much of Pather's creative work is at the forefront of innovative scholarly and conceptual illuminations in the fields of dance and performance across the world. Performance practices such as Pather's are an integral part of global trends in the twenty-first century—inter- and multidisciplinary, collaborative, crossing borders of dance, theater, visual art, multimedia, and technology. He is recognized as a choreographer who "has taken his discipline to the very edge of expression, often blurring the division between dance and fine art in productions—both in traditional performance environments and in public spaces—which are invariably visually stunning, deeply thought-provoking and emotionally honest. . . . Jay Pather is one of South Africa's most eclectic creative talents" (Machen 2009). Pather makes formidable and formative contributions to inter- and multidisciplinary performance in South Africa and beyond.

A significant benefit of working across national and international borders is the richness of collaboration. Pather's aim to engage with "space and place" both locally and globally is influential, as in a noteworthy seven-day collaborative project (from March 21, 2016) between internationally renowned South African dancer-choreographer Boyzie Cekwana and Durban-based Desire Davis's twenty-year-old Floating Outfit Project dance company entitled *Phomoong* train-*Station* (original emphasis). In an interview with Sichel at The Ar(t)chive, Cekwana remarks, "Our interest is to explode the Third Wall. Invent new dialogue with *space and place*. How do we redefine the infrastructure of performance? In Africa, we are fighting on so many fronts. So much re-invention is going on. We have to have strategies and methodologies. Nothing is settled. The generational aspect is important" (Sichel 2016, 3, emphasis added).

Similar to Pather's ethno-global vision, *Phomoong* train-*Station* reached for a broad scope across the African continent and beyond, involving local dancers and networking with international festivals and presenters. They aim to bring together four global projects to converge in South Africa. Collaborations with Studios Kabako of the Democratic Republic of Congo working on *Redefining . . . Home-work* began in 2014 and lasted until 2017, with efforts to extend it extended to 2019 and beyond. Cekwana recognized that such work "incubates the local work we do with artists (in eThekwini) as well as exchanges with and in Congo and Kenya (Opiyo Okach) in Nairobi" (interview, Sichel 2016, 3). Reaching across geographical and artistic borders is at the heart of this collaboration and partnership that "drives this evolving blueprint," comments Sichel, "for dance making and training—not only for the African continent. . . . The *One Space* artists attended choreographic labs in Lisbon, Ramallah, and Kisangani" (Sichel 2016, 4).). Cekwana noted to Sichel that in conversation with Linyekula over fifteen years, they both recognized the need "to find different ways of being in Africa without dealing with the one-dimensional identity of poverty, strife and material needs" (4). Like Cekwana and Linyekula, Pather's style of working with local or international artists is profoundly collaborative, whether creating a work in South Africa with his SSDT company or a site work in Copenhagen or as director of Afrovibes Festival in Amsterdam.

CURATION AND CURATING SPACE

Curation involves a process of selecting and looking after, indeed caring for, the works and artists, usually in a museum exhibit. However, curation today is a skill reserved not only for visual art inside museums; rather, the notion of "choreographer as curator" is highly relevant for an artist like Pather, whose curatorial activity significantly involves his choreographic skills.[17] A "choreographer as curator" brings dance and performance into useful dialogues with curatorial activity and broadens critical dance studies without minimizing the significance of movement and gesture. A discussion of Pather's transformative role in contemporary South African and global performance would not be complete without giving attention to his influential curatorial activities of selecting established artists as well as discovering and mentoring new ones with notable perspicacity; further, he works with them to find innovative locations for their work. His selections are linked integrally to his remarkable and imaginative acumen in curating space in large-scale public arts festivals.

Pather's curation is inspired by and rooted in his spatial politics; he notes that "Public Art now embeds itself in different spaces" (interview 5, 2015). Initially, in 2008, he collaborated with Brett Bailey in conceiving and directing the *Infecting the*

City public art festival, which had "a singular aggressive aim (at its inception)—to infect the city with performances that capture the complexities of our daily lives" (curators' notes, Pather and Bailey 2008). Since 2012 Pather has been sole curator and is involved passionately with selecting a variety of creative artists and aesthetic forms that are set in unique locations for diverse publics. His name is synonymous with the two large-scale public arts festivals in Cape Town—*Infecting the City* and *Live Art*. As curator, he fosters interdisciplinary work and provides platforms for creative, edgy, even risky work.

Pather remarks that since his work has always been concerned with "ideas and concepts, moving into curation was quite natural" (interview 6, 2016). He is interested in "curating an idea," selecting and locating works for a theme, such as "mapping" for *Infecting the City*. Equally, he pays close attention to "curating an audience experience by remaining aware of the kinds of audiences who participate in public art festivals on the street or in historic sites (interview 6, 2016). Pather's curation demonstrates his keen ability to recognize artistic works that overtly and symbolically speak against ongoing systemic violence of all forms against the disenfranchised, as in Mamela Nyamza's ironic recreation of the Soweto uprising in 1976, the year of her birth, in her choreographed *19 Born 76 Rebels*.

Pather's curatorial selections have paved the way for noteworthy South African female dancer-choreographers Dada Masilo (whose solo he curated in Fresh ll in 2007) and Mamela Nyamza, who belong to a generation younger than his. Through his own work, he has forged an aesthetic-political succession/lineage for Masilo's and Nyamza's bold conceptual choreography, through which they take on gender, race, and other sociopolitical issues. Pather is one of the oldest Black choreographer-curators with artists such as Alfred Hinkle (who had hired Pather to lead Siwela Sonke), artistic director of the multiracial Jazzart Dance Theater in Cape Town, and the iconic Robyn Orlin, whose lengthy signature titles include phrases, even full sentences—such as *At the same time we were pointing a finger at you, we realized we were pointing at ourselves*.[18]

Pather's 2013 curation of *Infecting the City* included Dada Masilo's *Death and the Maidens* (with Franz Schubert's music) for the opening event at the Iziko SA Museum Amphitheater. In 2014, he included Mamela Nyamza's autobiographical *Hatch* and her *19 Born 76 Rebels* (with Faniswa Yasa). Such creative choreography that deploys art for social change and forges new directions aesthetically and politically follows in Pather's footsteps. Both dancer-choreographers, trained in ballet, are adept at deconstructing classics such as Masilo's *Swan Lake* into a hybrid of balletic and African traditional hip movements, challenging the beauty of the ballet body.[19] They confront ongoing repressions of the body based on racial, sexual, gendered, and religious dogmas.[20] Violence against lesbians is represented in Nyamza's collaborative work with Modisola Adebayo, strikingly entitled *I Stand Corrected* (2012)—a chilling phrase used by males raping lesbians in order to "correct" them.[21] Similar to Pather, these artists are critical of the broken promises of democracy via their issue-oriented choreography. Nelisiwe Xaba, another dancer-choreographer and a peer of Masilo and Nyamza, describes herself "as belonging to a new generation of post-Apartheid African artists for whom building their art is also a way to challenge enduring forms of voyeurism."[22] Xaba's conceptual works, *They Look at Me and That Is All They Think* and *Plasticization* showcase such voyeurism.[23]

Along with prominent South African female dancer-choreographers, Pather's aesthetic-political goals in interdisciplinary performance and curatorial ventures inspire innovative male performance artist Kieron Jina, who, like Pather, is a South African of Indian descent. Jina boldly explores homosexuality, masculinity, and queer identities in his interdisciplinary choreography, and like Pather goes beyond his Indian ancestry.[24] Similar to Pather, Jina is an inter- and multidisciplinary artist using movement, video, screendance, and multimedia in his work. Pather's aesthetic-political choreography serves as an artist-activist model for Jina's adventurous artistry and his advocacy of gay rights as an out gay male concerned about the erosion of rights for homosexuals across the African continent.[25] Jina makes bold statements via his performance of queer masculinity; in his deeply moving *Werk It!* he "makes the invisible male sex-worker visible."[26] He critiques homophobic attitudes, pointing out the urgency "to research, discuss and understand this criticized and disparaged queer industry." *Werk It* combines materials from African traditions and popular culture as well as from the sex industry. Similar to Pather, Jina aims to be provocative, tearing the veil off middle-class hypocrisy and the status quo to showcase "hate speech and violence towards the queer body that has become a norm." Jina's goals include "celebrat(ing) the body of difference ... in order to challenge our perspectives on what we perceive as 'normal.'"[27] In *Synergy*, Jina is bare chested, wearing a white ballet tutu—almost a signature costume for this artist.

The kinds of creative juxtapositions that Pather uses are seen in Jina's *Emerge-in-see*, set on a construction site with men in hard hats and Jina in a tight-fitting pink dress, carrying a large bunch of pink balloons. The striking combination of images and props, such as the hard hats protecting workers from workplace hazards and the fragile balloons that could be easily popped, is reminiscent of Pather's similar linking of unusual images in performance; balloons often appear symbolically, as in Pather's *Qaphela Caesar*, in which the politicians who carry them embody their short-lived power grabbing. *Emerge-in-see*, "inspired by 'Pink money, religion, protests and liberation,'" "investigates the diversity of masculinity in Africa, sourcing materials from the sex industry, African traditions, religion and popular culture. Spectators are encouraged to participate and join the celebration of difference"[28]

I focus on urban locations for contemporary South African dance since Pather is particularly interested in urban geography and sites that include architectural icons in certain cities, such as Durban's City Hall or Cape Town's Long Street that capture his imagination more than working in rural areas. Nevertheless, one unique 2016 rural project, part of My Body My Space (MBMS) public arts program, is similar to Pather's curating of *Infecting the City* Public Arts Festival in Cape Town.[29] This public arts program, sponsored by the Department of Arts and Culture's Mzansi Golden Economy and curated by PJ Shabbaga, offered bold interventions of Black performers into White rural areas, challenging racial and cultural borders.[30]

PERSONAL AND INTELLECTUAL BIOGRAPHY

Pather was born and raised in Durban, the city where the majority of South African Indians reside even today, making it "the largest Indian city" outside India. He experienced activities of worship, ceremony, even rituals performed particularly by his mother in his parental Hindu household. He remarks that "the smell of the ritual ceremonies" from his youth, such as the incense sticks or oil lamps common in Hindu religious practice, is still with him (interview 2, 2013). Pather brought ritual practices into his work with Jazzart Dance Theater in Cape Town, where he performed *Arati* (a Hindu ritual ceremony for the gods using incense, *diya* [oil lamp], and recitation of religious *slokas*, or verses). Pather's family was politically aware and so he grew up in "a Black consciousness household."

Pather's firsthand life experience of growing up in Durban during apartheid's racialized separations as a South African with fourth-generation Indian ancestry honed his creative choreography by exploring the conjuncture and disjuncture of race and space. The exploration of space in his artistic work is rooted in his own biography, crossing the space between his Indian ancestry and his South African identity. This biographical in-betweenness becomes generative for Pather's inter- and multidisciplinary artistry, which straddles movement and theatre, visual art and multimedia. I discuss in-betweenness further using critical theorists Homi Bhabha's delineation, as well as Gabriele Schwab's notion of "transitional space," in order to show how Pather's works cross the gap (hyphen) between spaces.

Pather's self-positioning is unique: as a South African of Indian origin, he does not deny his ancestral heritage; however, he identifies artistically and politically as South African allied with his nation's Black people. His Indian heritage constitutes his "filiation," to use Edward Said's delineation in *The World, the Text, and the Critic*; but Pather's "affiliation" (also Said's word) resides firmly with diverse South Africans, especially with Black and Colored people. Said describes a writer/artist's "filiation" as an "inherited location" such as one's ancestry and place of birth over which one has no choice, whereas "affiliation" covers a broad parameter that includes, according to Said, "a network of relationships that human beings make consciously [and that] often replace the loss of filiative relations in modern society" (Said 1983, 19–20). Pather's Indian ancestry, family, and birth in South Africa constitute his filiative bonds, whereas his artistic network of connections and his aesthetic-political affiliations remain with South African Black people. Additionally, similar to Said, whose work includes both his filiative and affiliative connections that root his identity within his sociocultural and political reality as a Palestinian who lived in the United States (1935–2003), Pather's allegiance to Black struggle roots him in South Africa, where he continues to reside. Pather, from his youth, connected with South African Steve Biko's Black Consciousness Movement's struggle against apartheid. Pather remains a part yet apart from his Indian background; he describes himself as "Indian in heritage and Black in Ideology."

Pather commented that while growing up, there were "different narratives" about the identity of South African Indians—some insider community members regarded themselves as "progeny of pioneers" while others saw their descent as being from "exploiters" (interview 3, 2017). He notes "a deceptive homogeneity, even a fantasy of homogeneity" among South African Indians. However, there are both reactionary and revolutionary figures in this history, some who sympathized with the African National Congress, who honored Steve Biko's Black Consciousness Movement and Pan-African ideas. "Although his father did not collaborate with the White government" and was an activist who fostered nonracial sports, Pather himself experienced a "claustrophobic atmosphere" in his growing up years, feeling "very conflicted and schizophrenic" (interview 3, 2017). The clashes resided partly in his family's progressive politics versus what Pather perceived as "forced Indianness in ethnicity . . . [being] subconsciously caught" in the middle of these allegiances to family and to a narrowly defined Indian ethnicity. As a youth, he "started shedding the idea of being Indian" since it restricted a sense of freedom and democracy in delineating identity. Yet later he realized as an adult, Indianness itself is not a monolithic concept, but it is "complex and saturated" (interview 3, 2017).

From a young age, Pather was "choreographing dance dramas in his head," and when his family went on picnics, he stayed home, listened to music on vinyl records, and danced (interview 2, 2013). One rather poignant incident that Pather shared in a public talk for the Purush Symposium on "The Global Dancing Male" in Chennai (2013) was his very keen desire to dance for his father's birthday. He borrowed one of his mother's sarees and got dressed up, but when he appeared before the extended family of parents, uncles, and aunts, his father was upset and told his son to return to his room. Pather's intention was simply to dance for his father; draping his mother's saree over his male body was also part of dancing and not intended to make any specific sexual statement. Despite the negative response to this one incident, Pather notes, his father was supportive later, once he understood his son's passion for dancing and drama. Indeed, Pather acknowledges his family's backing of his artistic activities. During his days at the University of Durban-Westville, they would fetch him after late-night rehearsals, and his mother even encouraged Pather's dancing. During apartheid, dance, and in particular, ballet, was for Whites only, but some teachers taught Black people like Pather "in a back room" (interview 2, 2013). Pather's passion for dancing as a young male was not a "coming out" incident, nor did it translate necessarily into a conscious sexual choice of being gay. Pather remarks (interview 1, 2018) that he embraced his sexual identity as a gay man later in life, when he was in New York City on a Fulbright Award in the 1980s. Further, he notes importantly, his own homosexuality has always been part of a larger politics of social justice and equality and not a sole struggle for sexual rights.

During his early twenties, from 1979 to 1981, Pather was director of the Centre for Creative Drama in Durban, demonstrating an early acumen for creative leadership in guiding progressive endeavors in the arts. In 1982, he completed a BA honors in African literature and a BA honors in drama from the University of Durban-Westville, which was for Indians only during apartheid (now University of KwaZulu Natal with unrestricted access). There, students of color were subjected to a colonial practice that enforced drama students to remove "deviant accents," he remembers, that included "all traces of South Asian vernacular and South African English" from their English language speech (interview 2, 2013). In 1981, he researched Russian models and wrote a thesis for his BA honors entitled "Towards an Alternate Theater: Strategies for Political Theatre." That was a "big deal" for him at the time (interview 2, 2013).[31]

Pather received a Fulbright Award to study for an MA in theater (1982–84) at New York University, where he wrote a thesis entitled

"Multi-media Performance Models for South Africa." In this "international, cosmopolitan city," he noted, "possibilities opened up." He was influenced by visual art, by political theater—he saw the San Francisco Mime Troupe, Il Teatro Capistrano—and by performance studies with his teacher Richard Schechner. Having grown up during apartheid with its spatial restrictions that devalued Black people and people of color, Pather commented that he did not feel "fully human" until his time in New York City (interview 2, 2013). He does, however, acknowledge the ongoing fissures caused by race and class politics in New York City at the time. In this US city, as Pather felt less self-conscious about his own race/ethnicity that under apartheid in his home country had created a stifling atmosphere. He also came out to himself as a gay man and has not looked back since. From the inception of his acceptance of his gay identity, Pather has not focused on it exclusively; rather for Pather, art embraces a broad politics that militates against discriminations based not only on gender and sexuality but also on race, class, and nationality. Sexuality is part of an inclusive cavass of struggles for social justice. This breadth about sexuality is similar to Pather's noninsular attitude about his Indian identity.

In 1985, after completing his MA at New York University, Pather returned to South Africa. As he had been before he went to New York in 1982, upon his return he was a lecturer at the University of Durban-Westville. From 1986 to 1989, he was employed at the University of Zululand, a location away from major urban centers, as senior lecturer and acting head of the drama department. In that capacity, he was movement course coordinator and directing course coordinator. He directed plays like Ngũgĩ wa Thiong'o and Micere Githae Mugo's *The Trial of Dedan Kimathi* and Athol Fugard's *The Island*, among others. He recalls that working on ancient Greek dramas such as *Medea*, there were "debates around the human; around how a dancer-actor ceases to be a human being"—concepts with parallels to apartheid-influenced notions of Black and Colored people as being less than human.

When apartheid ended in 1994, Pather recognizes, there was a "sense of a shift connected to what was happening in society, a sense of being lifted" (interview 4, 2015). However, he continues, even until today, "culturally, psychically, the society has not shifted." Colonial and apartheid's negative attitudes, especially those aimed at Black people, still need to be decolonized. Such prejudices continue to cause drastic economic unemployment of the Black majority, which also suffers from a lack of basic living amenities.

Pather has been recognized since the 1990s as a visionary figure on the South African arts scene, playing influential leadership roles in arts organizations and festivals. He was appointed in 1994 by the Ministry of Arts and Culture as coordinator for performing arts on the Arts and Culture Task Group, to develop new arts policies for the new South African Constitution. He contributed to the 1994 government-initiated White Paper on the Arts, a significant document in the history and development of contemporary South African arts. He has served on the National ACTAG, the Arts and Culture Trust of the President, and the Advisory and State Theatre Board. In 2000, Pather coordinated the South African performing arts program for the XIII International AIDS Conference and directed the closing ceremonies for this gathering. He was chair of the National Arts Festival (previously Grahamstown Arts Festival) Selection Committee in 2015.

From 1990 to 1996, Pather was project director for the New Africa Theatre and Community Arts Project in Cape Town. In 1992 and 1993, Pather was resident choreographer of the preeminent multicultural company Jazzart Dance Theatre in Cape Town. Overlapping from 1992 to 1996, he was part-time lecturer at the University of Cape Town and course coordinator for dance. From 2000 to 2003, Pather was a lecturer at the Durban Institute for Technology, where he was also the choreographer and course director of dance.

In 1997, during the afterglow of independence, Pather applied for a position as director of a training company in Durban. The dance trainees were part of a development program under Jazzart Dance Theater's artistic director, Alfred Hinkel, a significant and transformative individual in Pather's career and the careers of others in South African contemporary dance. Pather's application was successful (over others like Robyn Orlin, as he shared with me, interview 3, 2017). He was appointed artistic director of the training program in 1997. The full-fledged Siwela Sonke Dance Theatre Company was launched in 1998 (called Siwela Sonke Contemporary Live Art since 2016).

Although Pather has resided in Cape Town since 2006, when he moved there for a position as associate professor (promoted to professor in 2019) in the drama department at the University of Cape Town (UCT), he notes that "the spirit of eThekwini," which includes Durban, where he grew up, and its surrounding areas, remains "a very strong, intoxicating, intense thing" for him (Machen, 2009). "You grow up with it," he continues, "imbibe it, and it never leaves you, ever. It definitely pervades my work wherever I go" (Machen 2009). Further, in the same interview with Machen, he comments that his company, Siwela Sonke, is based in Durban, and he "seldom works without them, whether in Cape Town or Copenhagen." He was course coordinator for the postgraduate program at UCT from 2006 to 2010, when his leadership skills in envisioning creative avenues for an institution were recognized in his appointment as director of UCT's Gordon Institute for Performing and Creative Arts (GIPCA). A further accolade followed in 2012, when he assumed curatorship of the *Infecting the City* public arts festival, working with GIPCA and other funders. While holding these leadership positions, Pather has continued to teach at UCT in the newly formed (in 2016) Center for Theatre, Dance and Performance Studies, which merged the previously separate drama and dance units. At UCT, Pather is a much sought after MA and PhD supervisor (with several students who have graduated with these degrees) as well as an external examiner for undergraduate and postgraduate students at Universities of Zululand, KwaZulu Natal, Witwatersrand, and Rhodes.

As director of GIPCA from 2010–2015, Pather formulated the center's vision via collaborative programs and projects among UCT's performing arts departments, Fine Arts, Film and New Media, Creative Writing, Drama, and Dance; the School of Music (Classical and Jazz); and faculty in humanities and sciences. With certain GIPCA projects, Pather worked with the city of Cape Town, Baxter Theater [Cape Town], and the National Festival [of South Africa], in addition to international embassies, institutes, and the professional community. In line with Pather's creative engagements with site work and spatial politics in his choreography since the 2000s, the move to curation, selecting artists and sites for performances, was organic. Since 2012, he has curated large-scale public arts festivals across the city of Cape Town. Beyond South Africa, he was co-curator for performance art for Spielart Festival (Munich) in 2016, when he was also appointed curator in 2016 of the Afrovibes Festival (Amsterdam), which Pather considers "an honor."[32]

GIPCA's initial five-year funding ended in 2015, and after a few months in limbo, Pather successfully acquired a three-year (2016–2019) grant of just over nine million rand from the Andrew W. Mellon Foundation (renewed until 2023) to continue GIPCA's mission under a new name: the Institute for Creative Arts (ICA). Pather's spatial sensibilities evolve organically from his site-based work into curation with his distinctive role as curator of festivals. With GIPCA and now ICA as sponsors (along with other funding sources), Pather has continued to curate *Infecting the City* each year since 2012 (moving to a biyearly format after 2019), and *ICA Live Art* festivals every other year. Pather's biographical note for the Global Shakespeare Symposium at the University of California, Irvine (January 19, 2018) states that he "has created structure for interdisciplinary collaboration in the form of Fellowships, a Post Graduate Programme in Live Art, public lecture programmes and interdisciplinary events on a range of subjects, comprising lectures, panel discussion, exhibitions and performance."

In September 2018, I spent a mind-blowing week during the *Live Art* festival in Cape Town, astounded by avant-garde performances and installations in provocative spaces such as installation artist Sue Williamson's *119 Deeds of Sale* on view at the Cape Coast Castle, a holding space for slaves in the eighteenth and nineteenth centuries. Williamson memorialized the slaves transported on Dutch ships from the coast of Malabar in India. Their meager information, such as their age—some only ten years old—was etched on white work shirts dipped in the muddy waters of the castle's moat. In responding to such painful histories, Pather urged spectators like me to reflect on current crises of poverty and unemployment for vast numbers of Black South Africans who endure different forms of enslavement in the twenty-first century.[33]

PATHER AND SOUTH AFRICAN INDIANS: A PART YET APART

While materials on South African Indians' history and sociology abound, there is no scholarly work on expressive artists in this group; such a study would be useful, though this monograph does not undertake that project. Rather, I focus on Pather's creative oeuvre via his spatial politics. He is distinctive and exceptional among South African Indian choreographers and playwrights for many reasons. First, his creative goals have never been insular; rather, his artistic and political vision connects with diverse South Africans, as he considers himself first and foremost South African. Secondly, Pather does not ally solely with Indian arts organizations but with different ones that serve the larger artistic and diverse public in his nation. Thirdly, Pather is more adventurous in terms of form, creatively using space in his avant-garde choreography and theater directing than most South African Indian dramatists and dancers. Pather has played key roles as artistic director of the Siwela Sonke Dance Theatre company since 1997. He has transformed, via his mentoring, the artistic lives of Black dancers, many of whom had no previous movement training. In his curation activities, he presents established and emerging artists in public arts festivals.

One can understand that during apartheid, with its mandated segregation of different races, the South African Indian community in general wanted to "preserve" Indian culture and Indian classical dance and not to critique or intervene in social traditions or artistic forms. Also, as a minority community, they did not embrace internal critiques of their own group. I recognize the value of South African Indian artists training students in classical Indian styles in their traditional idioms and their artistic endeavors, especially during the isolation imposed by the cultural boycott from 1964 to around 1990.[34] However, their work contrasts sharply with Pather's multidisciplinary creations. They continue to validate traditional Indian culture and uncritically endorse the ideals of *simunye*, the "rainbow nation's" slogan, meaning "we are one." Pather finds this idyllic notion problematic since it covers up glaring differences of class, race, language, culture, and sexual choice and hardly functions harmoniously for all South Africans. Pather is also critical of multiculturalism because he believes that it hides power dynamics and the unequal playing field among races in South Africa's artistic and social worlds.

Pather was designated as "Indian" or "Asian" in South Africa and did not grow up with the privileges of White pioneers such as Sylvia Glasser or Alfred Hinkel, who could take personal risks in training Black people during apartheid.[35] "Glasser as dance activist," remarks Sichel, "started the non-racial Moving into Dance (MID) company in the garage of her 'Whites only' suburban Victory Park home in Johannesburg on October 23, 1978" (Sichel 2018, 38). In her book, Sichel describes Glasser, Hinkel, and Germaine Acogny as "Matriarchs and Patriarchs of Contemporary Dance" (37). Glasser is merited with "a pioneering strategy of appropriation," comments Sichel, "in her Afro-fusion dance practice which she charaterises [as] ... guided by principle and achieved by respecting traditional rituals and dances" (38). Pather's choreographic palette favors a different kind of hybrid principle (discussed below) rather than Afro-fusion.

Pather's choreographic and theatrical works have always been edgy, unlike those of South African Indian playwrights such as Ronnie Govender, Kribben Pillay, and Saira Essa, who represented their community's struggles in dramas using traditional dramatic structures and forms. Rather, Pather's intercultural artistry is evident in the themes and forms of all his creative work. Even in his early dance-theater productions that reflect his Indian heritage and South African identity, he includes diverse South African performers and different dance styles.

South African Indian artists who teach and perform classical Indian dance consider the divisions between traditional and contemporary styles as stark and challenging, and as troubling intermedialities. Such differences are neither part of Pather's choreographic vision nor part of his sociopolitical concerns, even as he includes Indian dance styles and their sensibilities in his work via music, *mudras* (codified hand gestures), and costumes along with other contemporary Western and South African dance forms. Pather choreographed two dance-dramas that center on Indian themes, though he uses diverse dance forms and South African dancers of different races—*Ahimsa-Ubuntu* (1996) and *A South African Siddhartha* (1999), both discussed in chapter 1. In *Ahimsa-Ubuntu*, Pather was a pioneer in re-creating artistically the nearly 150-year history of the Indian community's past and its contemporary location. Pather takes a backward glance, historically and geographically, at his ancestors who migrated from India, crossing the Indian Ocean to South Africa starting in the 1860s as indentured and free people, and their struggles for acceptance as South Africans. Mohandas Gandhi evolved his moral-political strategies of *ahimsa* (nonviolence), and *satyagraha* (truth as a weapon in battle) in South Africa before he used them in India's independence struggle against the British. Even in this early work, Pather's vision spans the geographical space between India and South Africa via Gandhi's notion of ahimsa, along with the concept of ubuntu that needs to be acknowledged, as Pather remarks, "as a fundamental Nguni principle: 'I am because you are, I am because of you,' which of course is propounded by Mandela and Tutu, post-1994 as a unifying mechanism in the new democracy" (Pather, personal communication).

In another dance-drama with an Indian theme, *A South African Siddhartha*, Pather recreates and Africanizes the story of the Indian prince Siddhartha searching for enlightenment to a South African discovering his personal and national identity as he wanders in the South African Karoo (an expanse of semi-arid land). Pather's choreography unfolds at the crossroads of India and South Africa, embodied in different dance styles and geographies, evoking synergistic connections among them.

Hence, by 1999, Pather's choreographic universe was immersed in diverse dance forms and dancers, unlike other South African Indian dancer-choreographers who were caught in conflicts between tradition and modernity and whether to "preserve" classical Indian dance styles or to modernize them, along with their own identities as South African Indians. In 2000, Smeetha Maharaj and Vasugi Singh, teachers and performers of classical Indian dance, initiated an international conference on the state of Indian dance in South Africa. Suzy Bell's newspaper article entitled "At Last: A Dialogue on Indian Dance" comments, "Singh and Maharaj are effectively working towards a South African identity in Indian dance.... The conference is essentially about traditionalists sharing ideas with contemporary thinkers.... As a result, they have invited trailblazers of intercultural work like the highly respected Jay Pather to discuss where traditional Indian dance fits in with new contemporary fusion" (Bell 2000c).

Pather's presentation for the conference, entitled, "Searching for the Dance 'between' Dances," tellingly omits words such as *traditional* and *contemporary*. Vasugi Singh, one of the conference organizers, remarks, "There is a major identity crisis with Indian people as there is so much debate about whether to remain traditional or to go forward with change. Mindsets are being challenged and as artists we need to change" (quoted in Bell 2000c). Pather does not relate to notions of "identity crisis" in terms of dance forms since he refuses to be caught between the enervating distinctions between traditional and contemporary dance. Instead, he bridges intermedialities between traditional and contemporary in his imaginative choreography rather than regarding them as binaries, as he notes in South African reviewer Suzy Bell's article "A Dance of National Importance": "I'm interested in the meeting-point of a *mudhra* and a traditional Zulu dance kick, the way the rhythms of say a gumboot dance would flow with *kathak*. It's a reflection of movement seen in Warwick Avenue [in Durban], but it's more complex as I try to debunk this choreography as an advertisement for co-existence.... My work loses immensely if not drawn from classical work, but because I'm deconstructing post-modern consciousness, it's imperative that various frames of dance dialogue with each other where various dancers accentuate various aspects of the body" (Pather quoted in Bell 2000b, 14). In the same piece, Bell describes Pather's process of creating choreography, commenting that he is "adamant that there is a history in this country which reflects a distinct lack of presence of Indian artists." Pather adds, "I think the complexity of the art [Indian dance] just misses people. People think Indian music is just *bhangra* and that Indian dance is exotic and it only happens in some mystical, remote temple. There is an invisibility of the wide range of art created by Indian artists and sadly this also stems from within the communities." Pather challenges the exotic expectations of Indian dance that miss its "complexity." Further, as Bell notes, he "not only smashes the stereotype that Indian dance is a specific dance form but he cleverly creates a new dance that is still 'deeply rooted in classical Indian dance'" (2000b, 14).

In his choreography, India and Indian classical dance create an interethnic dialogue with African and European forms rather than being fused. In the same article, Bell remarks that "Pather does not like the word fusion because he insists that the process of making cross-cultural contemporary work is far more complex than fusion seems to imply. He prefers to describe the process as 'democratic choreography.'" Bell continues, "An intellectual choreographer, Pather makes an astute but unselfconscious attempt to promote either democracy or inter-culturalism, 'but not as a political statement,' he insists" (Bell 2000b, 14).

Afro-fusion, a concept introduced by South African dancer-choreographer Sylvia Glasser in the 1970s, appealed to many South African Indian dancer-choreographers, such as Jayesperi Moopen and Suria Govender, who place Indian classical bharatanatyam next to classical Zulu dance.[36] Pather is distinctive among South African Indian artists in not engaging with Afro-fusion in his choreography, wherein he seeks the space in between dance styles and finds innovative movement to bridge the gaps. Pather remarks, "Fusion is a double-edged sword—keeping the integrity of the original forms while bringing together different disciplines to create something new and layered is always a challenge" (Machen 2009).

Pather intervenes in dance styles with his adventurous and hybrid use of inter- and multidisciplinary forms and media. Deliberate interruptions via irony and symbolism mark his signature choreographic style. It is important to distinguish "hybridity" that aims to transform styles and disciplines from within their traditional parameters and come up with a new creative product from "fusion" that blends different dance styles or places them side by side. Fusion retains distinct movement idioms rather than integrating them in ways where both dance styles come across as refashioned, even "new" in certain respects.

I describe Pather's choreography as hybrid since it creates an imaginative canvas of various dance styles, such as South African traditional Zulu dance, which he among others, during his choreographic activity and after, recuperate with considerable artistry from colonial denigration to classical status. Pather also layers his choreography with South African popular dance forms; Indian classical dance styles such as bharatanatyam and kathak; and Western modern and contemporary dance. These movement styles and their dance idioms are transformed from within in a hybrid mixing where the styles come across as different from their traditional idioms along with interdisciplinary elements from theater, media, and art.

The Oxford English Dictionary defines hybridity as "a thing made by combining two different elements: a mixture." Dictionary definitions of hybridity indicate its origins in biology that explored the mixing of plant species. Later in the nineteenth century, the concept of hybridity was used in linguistic and racial theory. Mikhail Bakhtin "theorized the political effects of hybridity in language" wherein "a single utterance can be double accented"—that is, have multiple meanings as inflected by stylistic, social, and religious influences (Bakhtin, 1981). However, in South Africa, the mixing of cultures travels back to ancient times and is connected also to indentured laborers brought from India to South Africa, whereby the human-cultural contacts create different hybrid realities.

Today, hybridity is a potent concept in postcolonial theory, especially as influenced by scholars Homi Bhabha, Gayatri Chakravorty Spivak, Paul Gilroy, and Stuart Hall. Bhabha's influential text *The Location of Culture* contends that colonial discourse in its very "ambivalence" could be used by colonial subjects to resist colonial authority and cultural imperialism. "Hybridization," as Bhabha notes, "describes the ambivalence at the source of traditional discourses on authority" (1994, 112).

In 2016, as curator of the Afrovibes Festival (Amsterdam and UK), Pather remarked,

> This festival of great lineage and vitality, captures the contemporary and the diverse. *In a vastly changing world with escalating technology and increased migration patterns, the only authentic self is a hybrid self, collapsing space and time.* The Afrovibes Festival demonstrates bringing these illuminating as well as challenging ideas into one Festival. That which is 'Africa' is vast and so complex that in effect the Festival has outgrown its compelling name. It is this that interests me about the Festival. How does it represent what is so vast and yet that which continues to be hidden, causing stereotypes, and misunderstandings. (emphasis added)[37]

In our contemporary globalized world, hybridity is part of many people's identities, as Pather notes above. Migrations lead to peoples' multiple identities (such as origins in a homeland with relocations elsewhere); increased communication is also a reality among artists using various art forms imbibed and shared via the internet. Such a "hybrid self" also "collapses space and time," remarks Pather. The hybrid is part of the mixing of different cultural groups and of linguistic variations among ethnicities; South Africa's Constitution recognizes eleven indigenous ethnic groups and languages that include Zulu and Xhosa.

Pather's choreography avidly creates a hybrid landscape of movement styles, along with other border crossings—musical, geographical, artistic genres and disciplines—resulting in new creative expressions. His vision, which recognizes the various dance vocabularies and theater traditions of his country, actively collaborates with diverse South African dance companies such as Kathak Kendra, Flatfoot Dance Company, and the South African Ballet Theatre, as well as with visual artists. This wholly original choreographer and theatre director's breadth of skills include not only creating works on relevant social and national issues but also developing young choreographers' work through workshops and skills training in lighting or movement, and as curator, presenting emerging artists in festivals.

Pather is regarded with high respect by South African Indian dancer-choreographers such as Pravika Nandakishore of Kathak Kendra, who has worked with Pather and danced with Siwela Sonke. She noted the huge impact that Pather has had on her work, noting that her choreography is influenced by her observation of how Pather "unfolds a piece" (phone interview, July 30, 2014). She acknowledges a debt of gratitude to Pather, describing him as "a brilliant artist and a wonderful person." Nandakishore had also worked for some time as an administrator for Siwela Sonke. When the funding dried up, she had to leave, though she noted how hard Pather has worked to keep Siwela going even with his own personal income. Even when Nandakishore dances with Siwela, she does only kathak along with the *bols* (rhythmic syllables of kathak) "in her head." She asserts, "My kathak is South African. I am South African first, and next Indian. The importance of Africa in me effects my style of thinking, my choice of music and so on. My style does not follow a particular *gharana*" (distinct kathak styles originating in particular regions of India such as Lucknow or Jaipur).

Among Pather's key contributions to contemporary South African dance is his acumen in working with and mentoring artists in interdisciplinary arts that include choreography, video art, sound and lighting design; as in 2005, he was commissioned by the Drama Department at the University of Cape Town to direct eleven interdisciplinary artists in four-week workshops for a work entitled *Paradise*. In this work, Pather's interest in space and location is described as "a quest that informs the purpose of many lives and is yearned for, whether as an actual physical place or a state of mind.... *Paradise* emerges as varying states of mind, all fiercely idiosyncratic. However, these shifts also have enduring points of intersection: moments of beauty and power when the mysteries of longing, ecstasy, comfort, bliss reveal themselves with a vulnerability and humanity that is universal."[38] Geographical place is elided with mental space, as in states of mind that can enjoy moments of joy and longing, asserting a sense of humanity shared by all.

PATHER IN CONTEMPORARY SOUTH AFRICAN DANCE, CONTEMPORARY AFRICAN DANCE, AND GLOBAL PERFORMANCE

Pather's artistic constituency is first with South African and African choreographers on the continent who are on the same creative wavelength as he is—namely, being innovative, provocative, and socially conscious in the themes and forms of their creative work, and also in transcending the continent with choreographers and curators across the world. As choreographer, theater director, curator, and presenter, he holds a highly respected position in contemporary African and South African dance, and in his site work in his country's cities and in Copenhagen, as well as in his position as director of Afrovibes Festival based in Amsterdam.

Pather shares key commonalities with other African and South African contemporary dancer-choreographers, including Gregory Maqoma and Vincent Mantsoe, both from Soweto and trained by Sylvia Glasser at Moving into Dance Mophatong company; Boyzie Cekwana; and Mark Fleishman (artistic director, Magnet Theatre in Cape Town). He also connects with South African scholars of dance Gerard Samuel and Lliane Loots and interlocutors Mike van Graan and Mark Fleishman, along with South African dancer-choreographers Athri Patra-Ruga, Donna Kukuma, Mamela Nyamza, Dada Masilo, and Nelisiwe Xaba, Neliswa Rushualang, and Ntombi Gasa. On the continent, Pather has included in his curations Nigeria's Jelili Atiku, Olaniyi Rasheed Akindiya, Ghana's Bernard Akoi-Jackson, Congo's

Maurice Mbikayi, Kayumba-wa-Yafolo, Angola's Nastio Mosquito, among many others whom he presents in his curations.[39]

Since African literary and expressive traditions were predominantly oral, colonial and racist prejudices denigrated, even decimated them, across the continent. In South Africa, during apartheid, systemic racism fostered hostility to different creative practices— writing, dance, music, drumming—by Black artists. Censorship was so severe that playwrights often worked with actors in a workshop style without a completed script; rather, they evolved a creative work together, still running the risk of arrest by South Africa's security branch. Whether under repressive apartheid-era laws or during colonial times, artistic practices such as drumming, the backbone of oral African cultures, when banned by Christian missionaries, have survived by going underground. Wole Soyinka's essay "Theater in African Traditional Cultures: Survival Patterns" discusses the ingenuity of dominated people in preserving their cultural traditions, at times guarding them in secret spaces where the forms are alive, though they do not appear in public. Such scenarios of creating work in private spaces also pursued South African artists. At other times, artists and writers have transformed the "objectionable" sections and their art forms by adding new hybrid elements. As in Africa, artists in other colonized areas of the world often represent a layering of expressive elements from their own traditional forms that are integrated with palatable Western evocations. Often, once African artists gain recognition in Europe, they move there to avail themselves of artistically nurturing environments and funding possibilities.[40]

A profound difference between the rest of the African continent and South Africa lies in the severe restrictions on Black peoples' movements, their opportunities for training in dance or theater, and the overall fostering of their artistic ambitions during apartheid. Although this unequal playing field has been challenged after apartheid, there is a long way to go before the promises of democracy and equal access are realized for the majority Black population.

My search for the origins of contemporary African dance, to which Pather's choreography belongs and to which he adds significant spatial and interdisciplinary resonances, is part of a history that is discussed effectively in Sichel's book *Body Politics: Finger Printing South African Contemporary Dance* (2018). Sichel shared her archival expertise with me on one of my research visits to the Ar(t)chive at Johannesburg's University of Witwatersrand and showed me a brochure about a pioneering event entitled First Encounters of Contemporary African Choreography held in Luanda, Angola, November 17–20, 1995, under the direction of Alphonse Tiérou (from the Ivory coast, living in France).[41] Sichel attended this event as an invited delegate from South Africa. The brochure outlined the goals of this new style, named contemporary African dance. "Creativity must reflect contemporary Africa in its full richness and specificity—rooted in tradition but just as alive and constantly evolving. An essential dynamic element of African expression, dance must be returned to dancers and choreographers so it becomes live again. These first encounters of African choreography are a major step in the advent of a truly contemporary African dance" (courtesy Sichel, the Ar(t)chive). Pather's thinking resonates with this vision of contemporary African dance in his dedication to train Siwela Sonke dancers and expose them to a variety of dance heritages that include South African classical and popular dance styles, along with those beyond the continent to Western modern and contemporary dance. Pather's choreography innovates from these various movement styles and interfaces at times with other arts, reflecting a South African contemporary reality.

Similar to Tierou's research in his book *Doopié: The Eternal Law of African Dance*, which proposed the first "technical and gestural vocabulary of African dance" (Tierou [1989] 1992, 5) and asserted that Westerners are ignorant of the fact that traditional

African dance "possesses precise rules and codified movements," Pather (and others during and after his choreographic activity in this regard) carefully recuperates South African Zulu and Xhose dance forms from colonial stereotypes. Ballet dance on pointe shoes was regarded as "unnatural by the Elders because it does not respect the body (they claim that the excessive use of points can lead to madness or mental unbalance). However, the use of stilts is not prohibited. The stilt walker does not seek balance but rather explores the limits of balance" (27). This African way of using stilts is a kind of dance en pointe that "respects the body" and is found in rock paintings in Togo, Ivory Coast, and Guinea, among other African countries (26).

As artistic director of the Afrique en Créations dance project, Tierou aims to inspire young artists "to develop vocations for a modern and dynamic African dance together with western contemporary dance."[42] Such a hybrid dance style with traditional African, Indian, and Western forms with other media is characteristic of Pather's choreography from its earliest expressions.

I travel forward from this 1995 gathering in Luanda, Angola, which delineated contemporary African dance on the continent, to August 2004 in Durban, South Africa, when JOMBA! Contemporary Dance Experience (founded in 1998, with Lliane Loots as artistic director from its inception) hosted a significant conference titled Contemporary African Dance: Questioning Issues of a Performance Aesthetic for a Developing and Independent Continent. Pather, along with dancer-choreographers from across Africa, such as Nigerian Adebayo Liadi and Mozambique's Augusto Cuvilas, among others, conducted discussions on defining this genre, on techniques and processes of creating work, on locations, and on funding challenges in different African nations. Among their shared goals, the artists debated definitions of African dance on the continent and how that differs from Euro-American dance. They also aimed to document the discussions, preserving them as a database for African artists.

Pather's talk, entitled "A Response: African Contemporary Dance? Questioning Issues of a Performance Aesthetic for a Developing Continent" points out that "fundamental definitions of contemporary African dance are elusive; inextricably linked... to received notions of contemporary consciousness and dance from the West" (Pather 2006, 10). He proposes an innovative methodology that he terms "'response aesthetics'... (that) would interrogate... a relationship with Western aesthetics and a growing Western audience." He is concerned that a Western inheritance of the arts "has come at a price, in many instances, an alienation of African audiences." Such audience disaffection, Pather believes, is caused by the kind of "contemporary African dance [that] is in danger of remaining uninfluenced by a contemporary Africa." He proposes that by "owning 'response aesthetic', the resulting self-consciousness may cause (South Africans) to unpack received notions and develop contemporary aesthetics that are informed by a life lived in contemporary Africa" (12).

Pather's delineation of an African contemporary dance aesthetic, similar to descriptions by other artists, was "highly contested" (Douglas et al 2006, 107).[43] South African dancer-choreographer Gregory Maqoma usefully remarked that artists have "a responsibility of cultural translation" to make their work accessible. Several participants spoke of researching their own indigenous traditions, creating "new body language," even being open to borrowing or appropriating styles from other places while keeping their own identity and integrity. There is an unspoken expectation, somewhat poignant, that even while doing "contemporary dance" a dancer must show that she or he is influenced by "traditional dance" or else he or she might be accused of trying to be European. Whatever forms, traditional and contemporary, that dancers use, they need to convey an "African" identity. If the latter is lost, an artist may fall into the trap of what Zakhele Mhlongo describes as "conforming to the universal aesthetic of contemporary dance" (112). Augusto

Cuvilas provocatively expressed discomfort with the designation "African dance" since it is not specific about which Africa and which Africans are included in the designation. In talking about contemporary dance, he asked if one "is talking of technique or style or aesthetics." Ultimately, there are myriad ways in which in the postcolonial context, African contemporary dance is delineated as "characterized by hybridity (emphasis on appropriation, assimilation, synthesis and questioning)" (Reddy 2006, 116).[44]

Similar to Pather's goal of creating contemporary choreography that is rooted in South African life, Lliane Loots's remarks on expanding the concept of dance to include dance-theater, performance art, physical theater, and performances that utilize multimedia connect with Pather's approach.[45] In the same interview, Loots spoke of Pather's work as occupying "an unfathomable space between tradition and the contemporary. He creates a new language that can blow one away." Loots regards herself "as excavator, as architect working with dancers and recognizing their own embodied languages and stories" that are expressed through intercultural methods that guide her choreography. Loots's connection to Eastern spiritual practices is embedded in her location in KwaZulu Natal, with its vast Indian population. Like Pather, she explores movement and rhythmic connections with Kathak and modern dance, and among percussion instruments such as *tabla* (drums used in North Indian music that accompanies kathak) and African sounds of *maskanda* (Zulu folk songs accompanied by guitar and drums). Loots spearheads initiatives that refuse to get mired in colonial legacies that have had negative impacts on much of the continent and that embrace, as Pather does, the role of artist-activist who is "fighting to continue to be the conscience of our nation," remarks Loots, "no matter what.... It is up to us to refuse silence."[46]

Another significant aspect of contemporary African dance is evaluated by Sichel as "the Laban component" that was brought into South Africa by the University of Natal's Speech and Drama Department's pioneering founder, Professor Elizabeth Sneddon, in 1949. The Laban method "laid one of the foundations," remarks Sichel, "for our formal contemporary dance development" (Sichel 2010b, 43).[47] Pather also studied at the then University of Durban, Westville (for Indians during apartheid) from 1977 and was offered a curriculum that was founded on Laban principles, inherited from the University of Natal (for Whites). However, earlier, prominent South African dancer-choreographer Gary Gordon studied Laban at the Speech and Drama Department at the University of Natal in his home city of Durban. Gordon, who pioneered contemporary South African physical theater in 1993 from his base at Rhodes University in Grahamstown, is considered the father of the current training and performance of this style in South Africa.

Gordon's First Physical Theater Company (FPTC), established in 1993, is renowned for its training, which includes "choreographic research, and conceptual performance."[48] At FNB Dance Umbrella in 1994, Gordon's *Shattered Windows* showcased "First Physical's bruising theatricality . . . explosive physicality and vocal force." The performance, just weeks before the first democratic elections, "was an outpouring of white angst and desperation to survive against the looming catastrophic odds" (Sichel 2010b, 45). Earlier in 1989, Gordon reflected on his choreography in *The Anatomical Journey of a Settler Man*, an interracial and multimedia collaboration:

> "The work spoke of where we lived; this was my world represented in contemporary dance; there was improvisation as well as silliness and pain; there were animals but also roller skates and a bicycle; the score had ordinary noise as well as sounds from inside your head. . . . This anatomical journey contemplated struggle, humour, power, emptiness, aspiration and loss. The breath of this settler man inspired shapes, sounds and movements of this work of his in the Eastern Cape." He started the work in silence and he continued

in it dancing his part in a land that was still waiting to be reimagined. It was after all 1989. (Quoted in Sichel 2010b, 45)

Gordon's choreographic talent with its unusual juxtapositions such as "animals, roller skates and a bicycle" provides possibilities for Pather's adventurous choreography, which also places paradoxical objects and people together. Gordon focuses on the "anatomical" and includes uncannily original physical jumps and drops in his movement vocabulary; Pather, too, is focused on the physical body and its capacity for unusual movement (though not to the extent that Gordon takes it). Along with the physical, Pather's choreographic universe delves into the inner truths held inside the body's cells and organs.

During the 1970s, '80s, and '90s in South Africa, arts commentator Sichel gave credit to "a living legacy left in the form of methodologies and techniques such as Sylvia Glasser's 'Afrofusion,' and 'Edudance', educational institutions (and) dance companies" (Sichel 2016, 5). Although Pather does not favor Afro-fusion (discussed earlier), which places different dance styles side by side, Glasser is an important figure in mentoring now influential and world-renowned dancer-choreographers such as Gregory Maqoma and Vincent Mantsoe via her Moving into Dance Mophatong company. Glasser's essay "Is Dance Political Movement?" discusses "indigenous black South African forms of cultural expression in which dance and music are referred to synonymously" (1991, 112). She traces the changes in indigenous forms during colonization with class- and race-based judgments followed by cross-fertilizations between colonists and indigenous populations in the eighteenth century. However, European settlers of the nineteenth and twentieth centuries preserved their social and performance styles in isolation from indigenous Black dance forms that they treated with "disdain." Glasser connects personally with one avenue of traditional dance—namely, the integral role of music with dance in religious practices that were "the means through which trance-like states were reached whereby mediums could communicate with ancestors" (114).

Overall, Glasser argues that dance's "non-verbal" nature makes it a powerful political tool for oppressed people to express resistance as well as the desires they cannot express in literary avenues for lack of education or due to state censorship. Glasser provides the striking example of the *toyi-toyi*, a warrior's dance used in political protests and demonstrations, which Pather has interwoven in his choreography. "In South Africa, where you dance, whom you dance with, what kind of dances you do, and your attitude toward dance," comments Glasser, "will say something about you as a political being, as well as a performer or 'artist'" (1991, 120). Glasser continues, looking forward to a time when traditional dance forms will be understood and there will be increased "cooperation and collaboration in the dance community. Dance not only reflects the society, but it can also mould society." Such aspirations have been realized by artists like Pather, who, like Glasser, has mentored Black artists' talents in his Siwela Sonke company.

Sichel's essay "Enigmatic Bodyscapes: Sampling South African Dance" explores "the rich ambiguities, dazzling eccentricities, entangled histories and complexities of South African contemporary dance" (2016, 2), wherein she argues that this style "has disrupted, displaced, connected and survived. Other trademark qualities are invention and re-invention of artistic and cultural forms and functions" (2–3). Such characteristics are visible in Pather's choreography, which draws on a variety of South African movement languages and sociopolitical histories—English, Black, Dutch, Indian—prior to, during, and after apartheid. According to Sichel, different ethnicities provide "very rich pickings for dance-makers who have been sourcing, de-constructing, and re-imagining strands of centuries-old experiences, histories, facts, myths and the Western classics" (5).

In concluding this introduction to *Jay Pather, Performance, and Spatial Politics in South Africa*, I move ahead to the next five chapters in which I analyze Pather's evolving spatial politics, always guided by his keen connection to his nation's "political unconscious," to use Fredric Jameson's resonant phrase. Pather's creative deployments of space are choreographed in site works and in curations that inspire, even instigate a just society. Apartheid's legacy hovers over his oeuvre, during its worst repressions in the 1980s and in its haunting shadows today.

Part I, entitled "Journeys across Political, Socio-racial and Geographic Borderlines: Interconnecting the Present, Past, and Future," includes a preface, an introduction, and chapters 1 and 2. The preface includes my personal discovery of Pather and why I wrote this book. The introduction presents my argument on Pather's uses of space within his aesthetic-political and progressive vision, which has been consistent since the 1980s and his own journey in relation to his peers' work in contemporary dance. Chapter 1 discusses the historical and geographical realities faced by Pather's Indian ancestors who arrived in South Africa beginning in the 1860s and offers my interpretation of two of Pather's early dance-drama choreographies with an Indian theme along with a brief outline of South African and Indian dance forms and dancers. Chapter 2 analyzes Pather's spatial politics and its evolution specifically in response to apartheid during the 1980s. After independence in 1994 and the establishment of the Truth and Reconciliation Commission (TRC), Pather's early dance-dramas are critical of the TRC and of slogans such as *simunye* (all South Africans are united) which remains an ideal. This chapter analyzes Pather's early work as actor and dancer during the 1980s, moving into his decision to be a choreographer that informs the body-based topics such as the burdens on the physical human body, including the gay body, and Pather's indictment of the social disease of domestic violence that haunt his dance-dramas of the 1990s during and post-apartheid.

Part II, entitled "The Transitional and the In-between: Theoretical and Creative Engagements with Urban Geography (2000–2015)," starts out with chapter 3 that discusses Pather's spatial politics in racially divided South Africa relying on his published essays, conceptual program, and director notes in dialogue with scholars of geography and space whose relevance undergirds and illuminates several of Pather's site-specific choreographies. Chapter 4 focuses on site-responsive performances that are increasingly inter- and multidisciplinary. Pather's spatial sensibilities evolve organically from his site works into curation with his distinctive role as curator since 2012 of large-scale public art festivals such as *Infecting the City* (over thirty productions each year) and *Live Art* (over forty each year) across Cape Town, as discussed in part III, entitled, "Curatorial Choreographies: Challenges of Curating Public Art Festivals (2007–Present)" (chap. 5). Pather has conducted a dizzying number of curatorial activities each year since 2010, organizing symposia with performers, scholars, filmmakers, and interlocutors as director of GIPCA, now ICA. His increasing international profile is evident in his prestigious appointments: curator for *Body Image Movement*, Madrid (2019–2020); curator and area expert for *Live Art* and Theater in English for Africa 2020; President Macron's commissioned season, Paris, Lyons, Marseilles (2019–2020); curator of visual art, dance, theater, and performance art for *Fragile Democracies* at Afrovibes in Amsterdam, Rotterdam, Utrecht, and Den Haag.

The conclusion sums up Pather's site-based creations, his inspirational curatorial contributions, and his mentoring and inspiring the next generation of artists to make meaningful work that speaks to many audiences. My discussion of Pather's evolving spatial engagements in various works with bodies and psyches as repositories of history and memory, with curating ideas and audiences, concludes with underlining his choreographic talents that crisscross racial/spatial and social/gender divides in his 2016 choreography for Stravinsky's *Firebird*. In this collaborative venture with Cape Town's Handspring Puppet Company, Pather reinvents himself by mixing genres and bodies—human and nonhuman puppets, returning to an early fascination with Stravinsky's music (he had choreographed *Rite* in 1991). *Firebird* premiered in Cape Town, then toured major US cities in summer 2016. This work augments Pather's international renown, with previous work in European cities such as Copenhagen and Madrid, and in Asian cities such as Chennai, Mumbai, and Hong Kong.

Pather's commitment—namely, that the performing arts are vehicles of change—remains consistent throughout his own passionate creative journey. They are processes of shared learning and methods for seeking social justice in public spaces that carry their exclusionary past and present hope of inclusion for all. This book is an intellectually rewarding journey as I travel this artistic road with Pather, his company, and his many collaborators including visual artists, scholars, scientists, filmmakers, videographers, and musicians. Pather's award-winning choreography and curation influence and shape the direction of contemporary artistic expressions in South Africa and beyond. Pather's aesthetic-political vision, aligned with his spatial politics, explores multiple artistic avenues to encourage continued hope and to insist that "the beautiful ones must be born" in independent South Africa, despite continuing struggles for social justice.

NOTES

1. Jay Pather, interview by Terri Davidoff and Ameera Patel, University of Cape Town, 2005.
2. The word "Coloured" in South Africa, which has included different people in particular eras, has a complicated history. The earliest designation of Colored describes South Africa's indigenous Khoi-khoi and San populations, who were generally light-skinned (yellowish brown) and of small build. After the post-eighteenth century European arrivals—English, Dutch, German, and French Huguenots—the term Colored has referred to mixed-race people, some descendants of slaves, and, after the abolition of

slavery, those born of Dutch and Malay heritage (Malaysia was a Dutch colony in the eighteenth and nineteenth centuries) as well as Black and European and other racial combinations including Irish, German, Zulu, Xhosa, and Indian. The Colored population lives primarily in the area around Cape Town called the Western Cape. The latest Census records, from 2011, report 79.2 percent of South Africans (41 million) as Black Africans, 8.9 percent as Colored (4.62 million), 8.9 percent as White (4.59 million), and 2.5 percent as Indian or Asian (1.29 million). The next Census will be conducted in 2021. "Colored People (South Africa)," encyclopedia.com, https://www.encyclopedia.com/people/history/historians-miscellaneous-biographies/colored-people-south-africa, accessed January 30, 2017.

3. My thanks to Pather for sharing an unpublished copy of this essay with me.

4. "Madressa Arcade: Linking Dr. Yusuf Dadoo St and Cathedral Rd," Kwazulu Natal Institute for Architecture, City Architecture Department, Durban 4001. Details and map: https://www.kznia.org.za/durban-city-guide/islamic-architecture/madressa-arcade, accessed May 4, 2019.

5. In such critiques, Pather is in line with world-renowned artists such as Wole Soyinka (Nobel Laureate 1986) in his volume of essays *The Burden of Memory, the Muse of Forgiveness*.

6. Quoted in Adrienne Sichel, "Tossie van Tonder, Dance Umbrella [Festival, Johannesburg]," *Face to Face*, March 13, 2015—a postperformance interview on the John Kani Theater stage after the second performance of van Tonder's commissioned *Chthonia*.

7. March 21, 1960 marked the Sharpeville Massacre, when over five thousand protestors against the Pass Laws faced police brutality and many were shot in the back. June 16, 1976 marked the Soweto student uprising. Innumerable political detainees included Nelson Mandela (released after twenty-seven years) and Steve Biko, founder of the South African Student Organization (SASO) and leader of the Black Consciousness movement, who was murdered by the regime.

8. Siwela Sonke's Educational Training and Reachout Program described here was accessed at www/siwelasonke.com.za on November 1, 2012 (the site does not exist at this time).

9. Ibid.

10. Jay Pather, 1996–1997, "Mission Statement," Siwela Sonke Dance Theatre Company, unpublished.

11. Davidoff's comments and Siwela Sonke's training program echo a similar venture, Dance for All (DFA), that offers movement training to

underprivileged children in the Cape Town area. Information on DFA (accessed in the office of Dr. Gerard Samuel, head of dance at the University of Cape Town, who kindly invited me to see the DFA program in July 2015 when I was in Cape Town) is useful:

> Since 1991, DFA gives students a chance to reach beyond their circumstances through being taught skills that could open doors to a career in the performing arts. Their training includes a firm foundation in the disciplines of ballet, African, contemporary and Spanish dance which gives them the versatility needed to succeed in the profession. However, the life skills that underpin the training such as discipline, focus, and self-confidence will be an advantage whatever they choose to do. Most of DFA's students live in very challenging circumstances where poverty and unemployment are rife and social ills such as gangsterism, and substance abuse are common. By providing an enjoyable and constructive extra-mural activity open to all, DFA gives children the opportunity to spend their afternoon off the street, in a safe and stimulating environment.

12. Sonke, "Educational Training and Reachout Program."
13. Pantsula, isicathimaya, and gumboot are popular South African dance styles with their own origins. Pantsula, which evolved in Black townships, is marked by quick steps and is performed in signature Converse sneakers. There are competitions among pantsula groups. Isicathimaya, from neighboring Namibia, is marked by slow, gentle movements. Gumboot dance, originated by Black miners who wore gumboots inside mines, evolved into a popular style with signature foot stamping. Popularizing this style also brings dignity to miners' labor.
14. I analyze this hybrid style in the Indian context in my book *Contemporary Indian Dance: New Creative Choreography in India and the Diaspora*.
15. Release technique was introduced in the UK by Mary Fulkerson, who "referred to her work as Anatomical Release Technique" (quoted in Lepkoff 1999).
16. This is argued usefully by Erin Brannigan in *Dance Research Journal* (2015).
17. This is discussed in a 2014 special issue of *Theater* entitled "Performance Curators"; further analysis in chapter 5.
18. Robyn Orlin's Daddy, *I have seen this piece six times before and I still don't know why they are hurting each other* premiered at the 1999 FNB Dance Umbrella, toured internationally for twelve years, and won a British Olivier Award. Originally, the audience was required "to stand to

view the performers who were wreaking havoc with SA dance history and politics" (Sichel 2016, 12).

19. Dada Masilo's *Swan Lake* (2010), presented at the Lyon Biennale in 2012 and in Ottawa and Montreal in 2016, showcases an impeccable ballerina who startles with her signature blending of this European form with African dance in her original choreography, in which the tutu bounces up and down with strong hip movements. At other moments, Masilo gracefully executes pirouettes and arabesques interrupted by grounded, African-style stamps.

20. In Nyamza's *De-Apart-Hate* (2016), she dances courageously with the Bible open at her crotch, with her legs spread out wide.

21. The word "corrected" is used negatively by people hostile to lesbians. In an unpublished essay, Sichel evaluates this work as "a passionate response to an epidemic of rape and murder in South Africa." A real event—the gruesome murder of a lesbian woman whose body was dumped into a garbage bin—provided urgency and inspiration for *I Stand Corrected*. Nyamza plays the murdered woman, who returns to her female lover after her death to "correct herself." According to Sichel, "*I Stand Corrected* weaves a theatrical spell through a fractured, dramatic narrative which succinctly choreographs an epitaph for ordinary people textured with love, pain, loss, brutality and dignity . . . a landmark dance theatre work which marries the skills, experience, sensitivity, sensuality and artistry of two African artists—a theatre director, actor and playwright and an uncompromising dancer and choreographer. The final message is love is stronger than death."

22. JOMBA! 2006, contemporary Dance Experience, program notes.

23. *They Look at Me and That Is All They Think* is a performed critique of the story of Sarah Baartman, the "Hottentot Venus," who was taken from her homeland in South Africa and displayed in exhibitions in Europe. Baartman symbolized the oppressive ways in which colonizers looked at female African bodies as more akin to animals than to humans. "For Xaba," the brochure states, "this story is an allegory for her own artistic journey, from Soweto to the Eurocentric world of art today." Exoticization of the Black female body is also undercut in Xaba's work, *Plasticization*, which presents a fascinating critique of materialistic, even "plastic," lives that have lost their connection with "human touch." The piece also connects the church's objection to "plastic condoms" needed for protection from HIV/AIDS. Xaba has performed across Africa and Europe and has collaborated with one of South Africa's iconic and subversive

dancer-choreographers, Robyn Orlin, well as with visual artist William Kentridge.

24. When I met Jina in Johannesburg on a research trip in April 2014, I was struck by how uncannily similar he looks to Pather. When I mentioned this, he agreed, noting that he was familiar with this comparison.

25. Jina was born in Durban and completed his MA in performance studies at the University of Witwatersrand, studying physical theater, filmmaking, and theater as used in education and for activism. In 2010, he started, with other artists, a performance art company called Stash the Suitcase Collective. He wishes to create a screendance organization in South Africa. He has a particular interest in fashion that combines Afro-chic and a contemporary modern look and plans to start his own label of fashion clothing called Afrohomo to draw attention to the stigmatization of homosexuality on the African continent and the larger social terrain of accepting differences in sexuality, race, nationality, and other categories. See "Kieron Jina: Performance Artist," October 11, 2015, https://www.youtube.com/watch?v=dF4UcskbZJo.

26. Kieronjina.com has clips and descriptions of Jina's works. Werk It! can be seen at link https://www.youtube.com/watch?v=O4QP6b7QboY.

27. The clip on Jina's site shows a bare-chested Black dancer in a white gown down to his feet, held by steel bands (echoes of the Hottentot Venus held stiffly in beautiful poses to be gazed upon). Jina, in his signature tutu, wears high heels and carries a leather whip that he cracks often as the dominatrix who moves around the Black dancer in threatening attitudes. Then, he goes under the wide skirt, his head supposedly touching the Black dancer, who moves as if responding to sexual touching. Other dancers join in as the "werk" of sex unfolds via costume, props, and movement. Like Pather, Jina provides conceptual notes: "*Werk It!* is a form of rebellious celebration that embraces diversity, creativity, decentralization, horizontality and direct action. Human connection flourishes and flows when individuals embrace their own diversity. Living and Performing the queer within the 21st century South Africa has become vital. . . . This performance work is an activist approach that pays homage to queer expression and masculinity, weaving a visual kaleidoscope that challenges what it means to be a man in South Africa and the continent of Africa . . . a reflection of queer expression as well as the diversity of masculinity."

28. Kieron Jina, *Emerge-in-see*, http://kieronjina.com/projects/emerge-in-see/, accessed March 2, 2017.

29. According to Sichel, MBMS involved "a series of flash mobs in the Emakhazeni district comprising the towns of Belfast, Dullstroom, Machadodorp and Waterval Boven. These free, public interactions were themed around social issues including gender violence, HIV and AIDS" (2016, 7).

30. Sichel (2016) describes the 2016 performances, giving significant credit to PJ Sabbagha's Forgotten Angle Theater Collaborative (FATC) for organizing this public arts festival with thoughtful curating and partnerships that fulfilled FATC's aim of breaking cultural and aesthetic barriers. MBMS's achievement in penetrating racially White towns like Machadodorp enabled "humanis(ing) and un-demonis(ing) the black South African performing body," remarks Sichel. "FATC has met the challenges of its new rural relocation by producing thoughtful dance work." Some well-established urban dance companies joined the rural Mzansi Project—such as Glasser's Moving into Dance Mophatong (MIDM), Gregory Maqoma's Vuyani Dance Theatre, Wits University's Drama for Life, Cape Town's Unmute Dance Company (integrating both physically able and differently able bodies) under the direction of MIDM graduate Themba Mbuli, and Cape Town's dancer-choreographer Mamela Nyamza.

31. Pather's bio-note also mentions that he has an ATCL (Associate of Trinity College, London), a prestigious musical degree earned by advanced students in arts, drama and music, for playing different instruments such as piano. These tests were usually administered in the ex-British colonies, as I recall from my youth in Bombay, with British piano examiners who flew in from London's Trinity College to the former colonies. As a youngster of twelve or fourteen, I was struck by how reddish these White examiners looked, undoubtedly suffering from the heat of a blazing Indian sun.

32. Pather made this comment on his appointment as director of the Afrovibes Festival in 2016 (accessed July 25, 2017, under Afrovibes and Jay Pather: https://www.afrovibes.nl/2016/en/news/214-jay-pather-new-artistic-director-of-afrovibes-in-2016).

33. For further discussion of the *Live Art* festival 2018, see Ketu H. Katrak, "Defying Boundaries, Excavating Histories, Revising Trauma," October 8, 2018, http://www.ica.uct.ac.za/ica/news/LAFreport2018. A different version entitled, "Legacies of Loss and Trauma, Healing and Redemption" is published in *The Drama Review* 63:4 (Winter 2019) 172–80.

34. There are several classical Indian dance schools for training students mainly in bharatanatyam and kathak. Several South African Indian teachers have been trained in India, such as Kantharuby Moodley, who

established Natyakalalayam School of Music and Dance in 1978 in Greytown, Pietermaritzburg, after she trained in India, first in bharatanatyam and later in kathak. In 2010, she presented a performance entitled *Chaturanga*, which means "four limbs or parts, a word taken from the *Mahabharata* that refers to four divisions of the army" (commemorative brochure that Katrak saw during her research time in South Africa in 2015). The four parts include the showcasing of four classical Indian dance styles: bharatanatyam (performed by Yshrene Moodley), kathak (performed by Manesh Maharaj), kuchipudi (performed by Sandhya Raju, visiting from India), and odissi (performed by Supriya Nayak, a prominent performer of odissi from India). The year 2010 marked the one hundred fiftieth anniversary of Indians entering South Africa in 1860. Vasugi Singh, arts and culture convener of the 1860 Legacy Foundation, dedicates the program to the "indentured laborers whose sacrifice and suffering gave rise to this rich cultural tapestry which you and I proudly embrace." *Chaturanga* was performed in Durban, Port Elizabeth, Pietermaritzburg, Pretoria, and Lenasia. The word *Lenasia*, in use since 1958, is based in apartheid-era policies of the Group Areas Act, which segregated people by race. Johannesburg's Indian population was moved to an area called the Lenz Military Base, owned by Captain Lenz. Lenasia is a combination of the words "Lenz" and "Asia."

In Cape Town, the Vadhini Indian Arts Academy, with Savitri Naidoo as artistic director, produced several graduates and was connected to individuals such as Jay Pather and associations such as Artscape, Cape Town Festival, Jazzart, and UCT School of Dance. Vadhini created an initiative called Adopt a Dancer that invited donors to support promising dancers from underprivileged backgrounds to nurture their talents in the performing arts (commemorative brochure for Natyakalalayam).

Kala Darshan Institute of classical music and dance, headed by Manesh Maharaj in Durban, follows the curriculum of studying Indian dance and music as set by Bharatiya Vidhya Bhavan in Mumbai, where Maharaj himself trained in Hindustani *sangeet* (music) and earned a bachelor's degree in music. He also trained in kathak with late Guru Sushri Madhurita Sarang and is dedicated to fostering kathak in its "purest form" to his students. He has collaborated with South African choreographer Lliane Loots in a work called *Bhakti* (Devotion), which features creative, hybrid choreography.

Smeetha Maharaj, based in Durban, is artistic director of Nateshwar Dance Academy, founded by her mother, Draupadi Singh, in 1980.

Nateshwar was the first school in South Africa established to teach kathak and Indian folk dance. Smeetha Maharaj, trained in these styles and in bharatanatyam, has presented dance programs in these styles, along with African, Western, and Bollywood styles, for over thirty years.

Jhankaar School of Dance, established in 1986 in Lenasia (on the outskirts of Johannesburg), celebrated its twenty-fifth anniversary in 2011. This school was founded and run under the dynamic Dr. Ranjit Lalloo, a medical doctor whose lifelong passion for Indian dance led him to evolve a style that draws freely from Hindi film dance and various Indian classical traditions to create thematic works such as *Shraddha (Faith)* in 2009 and *Tere Naina (Your Eyes)*, among others.

35. "Asian" included Indian, Chinese, and Vietnamese South Africans. Indians, at different historical times of their struggle to belong to South Africa, self-identified as Indian South African, South African Indian, or simply South African.

36. Both Jayesperi Moopen and Suria Govendar were most generous in giving me interviews during my research time in Johannesburg, where Moopen's Tribhangi Dance Theatre company is based, and in Durban, where Govendar's Surialanga Dance Company are based. Moopen's company members also very kindly presented some works from their repertory for me at their studio. Both dancer-choreographers have a body of work, such as Moopen's *Talas in Conversation*, the winner of the FNB Vita Award, and Govendar's *African Dream*, which was presented at Nelson Mandela's inauguration on May 10, 1994.

37. Accessed July 25, 2017, under Afrovibes and Jay Pather: https://www.afrovibes.nl/en/news/214-jay-pather-new-artistic-director-of-afrovibes-in-2016.

38. Brochure, 2005, accessed by Katrak during research trip to South Africa, 2015.

39. To cite only one example, when I attended the ICA *Live Art* in September 2018, the two-week program included over forty creative works. Hence, Pather's curation of the two large-scale public arts festivals, *Infecting the City* and *Live Art* since 2012, has presented many hundreds of creative artists.

40. It is a sad reality that African artists get resources to travel to Europe more often than to other African nations. As scholar Dr. Gerard Samuel remarked (at Confluences 8 Dance Conference in Cape Town, July 2015), how can we change the trajectory of artists taking "the road to Paris"?

41. First Encounters of Contemporary African Choreography, Luanda, Angola, November 17–20, 1995. Among the fifteen participant countries, which included Angola, Burkina Faso, South Africa, Cameroon, Cote-d'Ivoire, Gabon, Madagascar, and Zimbabwe, there were similar approaches: the company from Angola aimed to create a common language of African dance using traditional movement with modern African body language; the Burkina Faso company wished to deal with "the problems of the moment; and the dancers from Gabon expressed interest in depicting philosophical issues.

42. Brochure, 1995.

43. Gilbert Douglas, Adrienne Sichel, Adebayo Liadi, et al, "Under Fire: Defining a Contemporary African Dance Aesthetic—Can It Be Done?" Conference catalogue 2006, 107–12. Further quotations are from this same source.

44. For further discussion, see Vasu Reddy's review of Lliane Loots and Miranda Young-Jehangeer's edited volume *African Contemporary Dance? Questioning Issues of a Performance Aesthetic for a Developing and Independent Continent* (2006).

45. Phone interview with Loots, July 21, 2015.

46. Opening speech, JOMBA!, 2013.

47. Among Sneddon's prominent graduates were Gary Gordon, who founded First Physical Theatre Company in 1993 at Rhodes University in Grahamstown with founder members PJ Sabbagha, Athena Mazarakis, and Craig Morris.

48. A doctoral dissertation completed in March 2020 by Dr. Juanita Praeg at Rhodes University makes a major contribution analyzing First Physical Theater's training and its various works at Rhodes University, in which Praeg participated as dancer-choreographer. Praeg also discusses contemporary dance in South Africa by graduates of First Physical's training of prominent South African dancer-choreographers such as PJ Sabbagha and Athena Mazakaris, among others. Gary Gordon and I served as supervisor and co-supervisor of Praeg's dissertation, entitled "The Political Promise of Choreography in Performance and/as Research: First Physical Theatre Company's Manifesto and Repertory, 1993–2015."

PART I

JOURNEYS ACROSS POLITICAL, SOCIO-RACIAL, AND GEOGRAPHIC BORDERLINES

Interconnecting the Present, Past, and Future

ONE

CROSSING (OVER)
Indian Ocean Migrations

SPATIAL POLITICS UNFOLD WITH A backward glance at Pather's ancestors who crossed the Indian Ocean, migrating from India to South Africa, beginning in the 1860s, as indentured and free people, subsequently seeking acceptance as South Africans. This struggle is marked by historical milestones such as the role of Mohandas Gandhi during his years in the country. Gandhi was a household name during Pather's upbringing in Durban; later, in 1996, on the invitation of Fatima Meer, Pather choreographed a dance-drama entitled *Ahimsa-Ubuntu* (discussed below) that revolves around Mohandas Gandhi's life in South Africa while also tracing the over 150-year history of the Indian community in South Africa. Pather was a pioneer in artistically re-creating this history. Even in this early work, his vision includes both India—the land of his ancestors—via Gandhi's notion of *ahimsa* (nonviolence) and Pather's home in South Africa via Nelson Mandela and Desmond Tutu's potent idea of *ubuntu*, that translates as recognizing the humanity in each person. In 1999, another choreographic work with an Indian theme, *A South African Siddhartha* (discussed below), Pather's choreography unfolds at the crossroads of Indian and South African dance styles and identities, evoking synergistic connections among them; an example of this is Pather's *Siddhartha*, based on the Indian Prince, who searches for enlightenment as he wanders in the South African Karoo, an expanse of semi-arid land.

While excavating the history of Indian migration, the Indian Ocean itself plays a major role in many people's crossing from one part of the world to another. As one of India's preeminent writers, Amitav Ghosh delineates it lyrically: "The Indian Ocean is not merely a theoretical or geographical construct but a human reality, constituted of a dense (and unexplored) network of human connections. . . . Exploring transoceanic migration . . . [it] reiterate(s) the centrality of human relationships in bridging this vast expanse of water" (2010, ix). Contemporary Indian Ocean studies excavate "the human reality," as Ghosh notes, of sojourners who left India and embarked on a path to create new homes in their adopted lands. Studies of the Indian Ocean world bring significant insights into human stories of migrants, their cultures, and their possessions. Pamila Gupta argues that there is

> a growing trend to look at the Indian Ocean as a space of transformation, immersion and mobility. . . . Fluidity, the defining property of water [is regarded] as a metaphor to ask how the Indian Ocean transported, kept afloat, and drowned ideas and concepts, and how it became a pathway dividing as well as connecting people. In the act of crossing the Indian ocean, people transformed places and formed new identities. Ideas and objects also travelled the water in the luggage of imperialists, pirates, merchants, pilgrims and traders. Diverse languages and faiths reached the shores on both sides of the water. Thus, it was the melding of ideas, peoples and material objects that became the basis for conceptualizing the Indian Ocean as one of flows and fluidity. (Gupta, Hofmeyr, and Pearson 2010, 3)

Although it is more common in human history to discuss land-based societies than to regard "the world's seas and oceans as real places" (Rediker, quoted in Pearson 2010, 9), Michael Pearson and historian Karen Wigen claim in "The Idea of the Ocean"

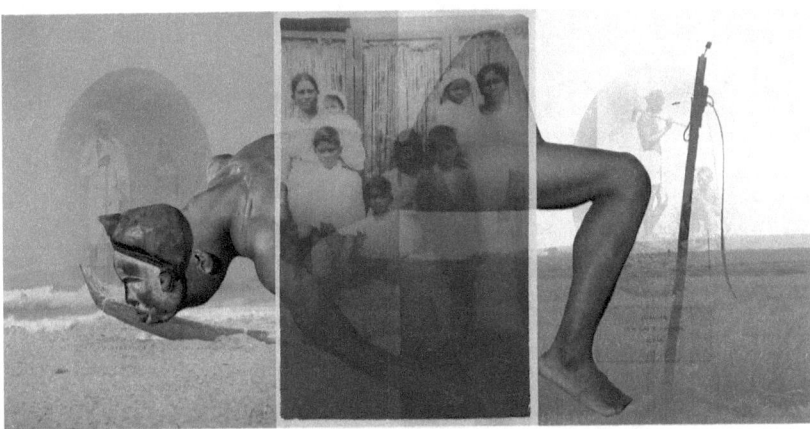

Fig. 1.1. Family Portrait 1, Chennai/Tongaat, 2017. Digital composite image by Jordache Ellapen. This image is part of Jordach Ellapen's "Queering the Archive: Brown Bodies in Ecstasy," in *Scholar and Feminist Online* 14:3 (2018), which can be accessed at http://sfonline.barnard.edu/feminist-and-queer-afro-asian-formations/queering-the-archive-brown-bodies-in-ecstasy-visual-assemblages-and-the-pleasures-of-transgressive-erotics/.

that oceans have their own histories that can "enrich traditional histories" (2010, 8). As geographer Steinberg posits, the coastlines touching oceans can be "claimed, controlled, regulated, and managed" by individuals (quoted in Gupta, Hofmeyr, and Pearson 2010, 10). The Indian Ocean world, with its parallels and differences to the Black Atlantic, brings to the fore "previously unwritten histories of transnationalisms" notes Gupta in the introduction, "migration and diasporic imaginings. The spectre of race ... as a category of personhood [is significant] ... just as [is the case with] the biography of the Indian Ocean as a history of different faiths, languages, colonialisms, commodities and capitals" (Gupta, Hofmeyr, and Pearson 2010, 4).

British imperialists responded to labor shortages in their various colonies, components of the British Empire, by actively encouraging migrations of colonial subjects from one geographical region to another—such as Indians sent to Mauritius since 1842, to the British Caribbean since 1844, and to Natal province

Fig. 1.2. Gandhi exhibit at the Old Fort House Museum, Durban. Photographer: Katrak.

in South Africa since 1860 for labor on sugarcane plantations.[1] The India Office in London "authorized the Government of India to pass the necessary enabling legislation, and India Act XXIII of 1860 extend[ing] the system of indentured Indian emigration to include Natal" (Huttenback 1971, 7). Although the Indian government initially resisted the proposal since it did not offer opportunities for free Indian laborers, it relented, reassured by false claims that the indentured laborers would be well provided for in terms of food, lodging, medical care, and wages. Historian Robert Huttenback recounts that recruiters deployed several devious means to secure Indian laborers.

Racial hierarchies, buttressed by British divide-and-rule policies and by colonial notions of civilization, lie underneath what historian Isabel Hofmeyr posits as "one major fault line of Indian Ocean studies (and indeed schemas of south-south solidarity)

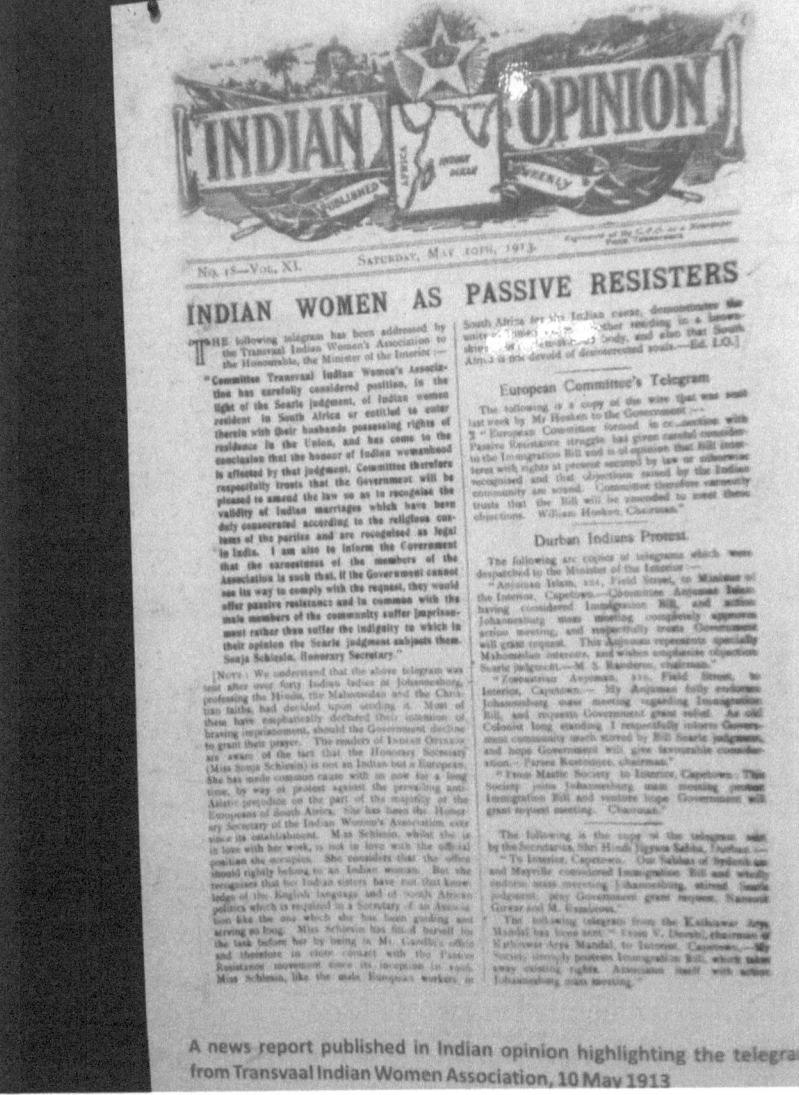

Fig. 1.3. *Indian Opinion* newspaper established by Gandhi. Photographer: Katrak.

[namely] the prominence of India as opposed to the invisibility of Africa," indeed, an "occlusion of Africa" (2010, 101). Hence, "sites of Indian indenture were used for creating and demonstrating African-Indian conflict. On Natal plantations, it was not uncommon for White overseers to instruct Africans to carry out punishments of flogging on Indian workers. Notions of civilisationism with 'India' ranked above 'Africa' fed into and exacerbated these structures of colonial dominance" (101). Hofmeyr proposes a revised historiography that examines the complexity of Indian-African relations, an idea that resonates in Pather's work and that invites scholars to remain open to "paradox and contradiction" when referring to eras of conflict and others of solidarity.

The many challenges the Indian community in South Africa faced from White colonists and settlers prior to, during, and after apartheid provide a significant historical backdrop for Pather's personal and political development as a choreographer and curator. The Indian community's struggle for equality and social justice overlaps at points with the dire situation of South Africa's majority Black population in the late nineteenth century and throughout the twentieth century until independence in 1994. Jay Pather and his family are fourth-generation descendants of Indians of Tamil origin (from Tamil Nadu State in South India) who arrived in South Africa in the 1860s. *Ahimsa-Ubuntu* spans the crossing of geographical space—from India to South Africa—and the passage of time from the 1860s into the next fifty years, when the community grew to nearly 150,000 people. Pather choreographs an embodied retelling of key historical milestones of Indian migration from the 1860s onward, during colonial domination, and later explores alliances with Black people during apartheid in movements such as the Defiance Campaign (1952), among others.

Pather's use of dance to convey history resonates with dance scholar Susan Leigh Foster's seminal concept of the "body as an analytical category" in her introduction to Foster's edited volume entitled *Choreographing History*. She connects a "focus on body as an analytical category ... in the writing of history" (Foster 1995, 3). Her evocative concept of "bodily writing [that] ... emerge[s] out of cultural practices, verbal or not, that construct corporeal meaning" connects to Pather's rendering of historical events via bodily movement in *Ahimsa-Ubuntu* (3). As Foster animates the figure of the historian as one seeking knowledge of the past by "consort[ing] with dead bodies," so does Pather represent historical figures such as Mahatma Gandhi and Nelson Mandela. Foster provides insight into what motivates historians as they re-create past lives through documents, evaluating and interpreting bodily movements, the spaces they occupy, and their engagement with political and social environments.

Rather than regarding the past as "fixed," Foster conceives of the past as "embodied," which would then "move in dialogues with historians, who likewise transit to an identity that makes such dialogue possible" (Foster 1995, 10). In language evocative for Pather as a choreographer, Foster suggests a creative notion of bringing historians and their past subjects together "in a kind of improvised choreographic process.... To choreograph history, then, is first to grant that history is made by bodies" (11). She continues, "Neither a historian's body nor historical bodies nor the body of history become fixed during their choreographic process. Their edges do not harden; their feet do not stick. Their motions form a byway between their potential to act upon and be acted upon. In this middle ground they gesture toward one another, accumulating a corpus of guidelines for choreographic signification as they go, making the next moves out of their fantasies of the past and their memory of the present" (11).

Apart from choreographing history à la Foster, the past is also studied, translated, and interpreted by "anthropologists, literary critics, novelists and others," as Amitav Ghosh remarks in his foreword to *Eyes across the Water: Navigating the Indian Ocean*. These different experts, literary or sociological, are adept, in

Ghosh's tactile description, at "stirring handfuls of [their] own spices and condiments into the pot of [their] common interest" in order to trace human links across the Indian Ocean.

INDIGENOUS POPULATION AND LAND DISPOSSESSION

Since Pather's artistic concerns encompass diverse South Africans though it is important to recognize the severe discriminations that Black people endured from colonists and settlers—most crucially, the dispossession of their land from the seventeenth century onward. The earliest history of Black populations on the southern tip of Africa (before it became the Union of South Africa in 1911) can be traced back nearly two thousand years and predates the Indian migration beginning in the 1860s. This indigenous population, composed of the San and the Khoikhoi, were identified by their occupations—the San as hunter-gatherers and the Khoikhoi as pastoral herders. They lived and cultivated the land in what is now the Western Cape and Namaqualand. In modern history, their earliest encounter with Europeans was with the Portuguese at the Cape around the late fifteenth and early sixteenth centuries.

By the end of the sixteenth and into the seventeenth century, English and Dutch seafarers entered the Cape; Europeans traded metal for the Khoikhoi's cattle. When the Dutch established the Dutch East India Company in 1652 and became settlers, battles ensued over land ownership, which remains an ongoing issue for many South African Black people even today. Although there were three Khoikhoi-Dutch wars—in 1659, in 1673, and from 1674 to 1677—the Khoikhoi population was defeated, expelled, forcibly removed from their land, and forced into servitude and indentured labor. They suffered an enormous loss of life due to a smallpox epidemic, "against which the Khoikhoi had no natural resistance or indigenous medicines. The disease had been brought to the Cape by Dutch sailors."[2] Black population groups in South Africa today include the Bantu-speaking people—the AmaZulu and AmaXhosa—who migrated to South Africa from areas around the Congo in the sixteenth and seventeenth centuries. Other groups such as the Sotho, Tswana, Venda, Swazi, and Ndebele peoples settled in the interior.

Traumatic encounters between the indigenous people and the colonists are re-created by contemporary South African dancer-choreographer Gregory Maqoma in his solo *Exit/Exist*. Maqoma conveys the nineteenth-century history of his ancestor, a renowned chief of the AmaXhosa nation who was at odds with the English over the possession of cattle in the Eastern Cape. *Exit/Exist* "blends storytelling with a powerful dance vocabulary and dynamic live music in an examination of race, political power, and the melding of past and present. Maqoma reveals the history and fate of his ancestor, a 19th century Xhosa warrior, who fought to maintain cultural traditions in the face of colonial rule. Through his signature integration of traditional and contemporary dance, Maqoma invites audiences to reflect on who we are, where we come from, and how all of these facets, past and present, inform our personal and collective identities today."[3] The title, *Exit/Exist*, refers to how indigenous Black people were forced to "exit" their land, surrender their cattle, and simply "exist" while the White settlers took over.

Maqoma embodies his ancestor's forgotten history in a transformational and poignant performance with spirited live music. Along with singers, world-fusion guitarist Giuliano Modarelli performs a lush score by Simphiwe Dana, the acclaimed singer and composer from Maqoma's native province of the Eastern Cape. In a TedX talk, Maqoma notes that when he witnessed Black dancers who lived in hostels in Soweto, their "euphoria" went beyond "movement." Rather, it captured the stories of where they came from and "how the landscape was reflected in their faces, using their dance as a form of connecting to themselves, their lives" (Maqoma 2016). Similar to Maqoma's re-creation of his AmaXhosa ancestor, Pather as choreographer-historian animates the sojourn of his Indian ancestors in *Ahimsa-Ubuntu*. Pather remarks, looking back to the 1990s, that now "his approach to his ancestry is critical given the ebbs and flows of political loyalty by South African Indians to the African continent and to India" (phone conversation, May 20, 2020).

It is with full recognition of this history of indigenous Black peoples' lands and livelihoods being stolen by European colonists and settlers that I excavate Indian migration into South Africa, since I focus on one of their descendants, Pather. His ancestors from Madras (renamed Chennai) in South India were among the earliest Indian migrants who came to Natal Province in 1860. Although Indians usually preserved strong group affiliations along religious, cultural, caste, and subcaste lines, with elders among the early migrants valuing a protective insularity, this was not the case for members of the younger generations like Pather, who grew up in the 1970s and 1980s. They instead forged allegiances with South African Black people involved in progressive anti-apartheid struggles. In the 1980s, when Pather was studying at the University of Durban-Westville, students there were forging political alliances between Black people and South African Indians. Although Pather does not deny his Indian ancestry, he was never invested in ethnic insularity or in struggling for social justice for the Indian community alone. This was not necessarily the position taken by many South African Indians, many of whom tended to be protectionist of their own culture; some demonstrated a disturbing sense of superiority to Black people.

Unlike them, Pather's dance-theater choreography for *Ahimsa-Ubuntu* includes diverse dancers and dance styles even as he represents the Indian community's struggle initially as outsiders and their sociocultural and political realities over the late nineteenth and twentieth centuries.

Fig. 1.4. *Ahimsa-Ubuntu*. Photographer: Val Adamson.

Pather choreographed and directed *Ahimsa-Ubuntu* at the invitation of Professor Fatima Meer, who envisioned a play about Gandhi's life in South Africa. High Commissioner to India Jerry Matsiela commissioned *Ahimsa-Ubuntu* in association with the Indian Council for Cultural Relations (ICCR), New Delhi. The program notes (October 1996) describe it as "a special programme of cultural exchange between India and South Africa." Sichel notes that "the production was conceptualized and scripted by IBR [Institute of Black Research at the University of Natal] director, sociologist and writer Fatima Meer and was originally performed (and televised live by SABC last year) at Durban's Springfield College of Education to launch Meer's book *The South African Gandhi 1893–1914*." The IBR "specializes in recording oral history and the history of this country's disenfranchised peoples" (Sichel 1996, 19). Sonia Gandhi, the widow of India's assassinated prime minister Rajiv Gandhi, saw the work at Durban's Springfield College; later, *Ahimsa-Ubuntu* was performed at the Playhouse Theatre in Durban. On the invitation of Mrs. Gandhi and the South African High Commission, it toured India and Sri Lanka in 1997.

When asked about his early memories of Gandhi and what his family thought of this historic figure (interview 3, 2017), Pather responded that initially his personal connection to Gandhi was that of "a father and teacher, predominantly good." That "lens" through which he regarded Gandhi then "gets blurred" around the time he created *Ahimsa-Ubuntu* and subsequently. Pather recalled that in 1981 he acted as Gandhi in a play entitled *Satyagraha* by Saira Essa; to prepare for this role he read many articles and discovered that "Gandhi's approach to black Africans [was] negative, as opposed to positive for Indians." Gandhi's own "racism," as complicated and problematic as it is, "can more productively be read," according to Hofmeyr, "as part of Gandhi's early understanding of Indian nationalism." In line with moderate Congress thinking, he envisaged India as being contained within Empire: India would attain dominion status within Empire, a dispensation which gave India and Empire a shared boundary. Just as the "native"/"African" marked the boundary of Empire, so too did this figure signal the limits of Indian nationalism (Hofmeyr 2010, 101). Hofmeyr also argues that the uneasiness in Indian-African relations "has been the way in which Africa functions as a disavowed boundary for Indian nationalism" (101).

Pather was troubled by the fact that Gandhi fought for Indians only, excluding Black people. Pather himself identified as Black, was inspired by ideas of Black consciousness, and became "self-conscious about calling [himself] Indian. This had nothing to do with India," he adds, "but with the attitudes of Indians," especially ones who did not connect with the Black struggle. For Pather, a certain kind of "Indianness equated racism," and he "wanted nothing to do with that." These attitudes "caused divisiveness in his immediate society." Gandhi himself "became a flashpoint" for ideas of racism and ethnic affiliation (interview 3, 2017). Among the contradictions of "shedding the idea of being Indian" as racist and connecting with the Black struggle, Pather was also caught between being respectful of Fatima Meer, who had requested he create a work on Indian history in South Africa and Gandhi's role in it, and having to represent a revered historical figure, Gandhi whose views on Black people were profoundly flawed. This revealing personal history furthers an understanding of Pather taking on the challenge of choreographing this historical dance-drama, *Ahimsa-Ubuntu*. The word *ahimsa* comes directly from Gandhi's philosophical-political ideology, developed while he was in South Africa, along with the principles of *satyagraha* (*satya* is truth and *graha* is a weapon—hence truth is the weapon with which to battle social, political, and moral inequities). Later, Gandhi used these political tactics against the British during India's independence movement.[4]

Despite Gandhi's objectionable thinking about Black people as inferior to Indians, Pather is in line with Gandhi's strong advocacy against injustice, which is similar to Pather's own devotion to training and mentoring young dancers—some of whom he has cultivated from modest township origins to becoming choreographers in their own right (such as Ntombi Gasa and Neliswa Rushualang of Siwela Sonke Dance Theatre). Gandhi's work in the 1890s was galvanized by resisting the same key components of "racial superiority, arrogance emanating from colonial plunders, and misplaced notions of divine sanction for segregation" that also inspire Pather's aesthetic-political creative works (Mathur 1986, 19). It is noteworthy that even in pre-apartheid days, as Mathur attests, "apartheid had already taken firm roots in South Africa, long before Gandhi landed there in May, 1893" (29).

Pather's original 1996 choreography of the Indian migrant history came just two years after the official end of apartheid. Later, South African Indian dancer-choreographers dealt with this ancestral narrative—Smeetha Maharaj, artistic director of

Durban's Nateshwar Dance Academy's 2001 dance-drama *Sunghursh* (revolution), and Jayesperi Moopen, artistic director of Johannesburg's Tribhangi Dance Theater's 2010 docudrama *From Canefields to Freedom*.[5] Both Maharaj and Moopen's choreography take the audience on a journey similar to the one represented in Pather's *Ahimsa-Ubuntu*.[6] *From Canefields to Freedom* uses drumming, recorded music, multimedia, and sound effects to retell the history, similar to Pather's use of such theatrical elements in *Ahimsa-Ubuntu*.[7] Rajesh Gopie's depiction of this history in a 2003 play entitled *The Coolie Odyssey* has similar goals to Moopen and Maharaj's dance-theater works—namely, to educate the audience about prejudicial laws, such as the unfair taxes imposed on Indians called "coolies," who were known via their identity numbers rather than as human beings.[8] An educated indentured laborer was considered a hindrance, as a line in *The Coolie Odyssey* states: "Kaffirs and Coolies don't need to read and write."

Ahimsa-Ubuntu opens with Mandela's inauguration on May 10, 1994, a world-stirring event.[9] In 1996, Mandela was a guest of honor in the audience at Springfield College in Durban (Interview 1, 2018). At the end of the show, Pather recalled, Mandela "looked very moved," and—ignoring the concerns of his bodyguards—he walked up onto the stage in an open environment and shook hands with all the cast members. Pather captured the feeling of all present: "how did we get from there [apartheid] to this amazing moment [democracy]?" (interview 1, 2018).

The title, *Ahimsa-Ubuntu*, contains the synergistic connection between India and South Africa. As the program notes state, "Gandhi lays the basis for the anti-racist struggle underpinned by Ahimsa which strikes a kindred chord in the African Ubuntu." Gandhi's influential concepts of ahimsa and satyagraha, which were developed in South Africa, initially reflect the essence of ubuntu, as explained evocatively by Michael Onyebuchi Eze in his *Intellectual History in Contemporary South Africa*:

"A person is a person through other people" strikes an affirmation of one's humanity through recognition of an "other" in his or her uniqueness and difference. It is a demand for a creative intersubjective formation in which the "other" becomes a mirror (but only a mirror) for my subjectivity. This idealism suggests to us that humanity is not embedded in my person solely as an individual; my humanity is co-substantively bestowed upon the other and me. Humanity is a quality we owe to each other. We create each other and need to sustain this otherness creation. And if we belong to each other, we participate in our creations: we are because you are, and since you are, definitely I am. The "I am" is not a rigid subject, but a dynamic self-constitution dependent on this otherness creation of relation and distance. (Eze 2010, 190–91)

Pather's dance-drama focuses on Gandhi's time in South Africa, while also tracing the history of Indians in South Africa, beginning in 1860 when the Indian government agreed to the British "request" to send indentured laborers to Natal Province, and going through many milestones of South African history. These include the 1911 Revolt of the Zulus, led by Chief Bambatha, against unjust taxation; the 1952 Defiance of Unjust Laws Campaign, which brought Indians and Black people together in a common struggle; the rise of Black consciousness; the women's resistance against carrying the Pass; the youth revolts of the 1970s and 1980s; and finally the nonracial democracy established in 1994 that celebrated ubuntu. This work is so much about ordinary people and the context of the time when Gandhi was in South Africa that Gandhi (played by Black actor Thabani Sibisi) is not a major presence except for a significant meeting that he had with Black lawyer Dube.

Although the Indian government agreed to supply indentured laborers to Natal, there were also free traders called "passenger Indians" on the same ships. Historian P. Pratap Kumar notes that the early classification between "indentured and passenger Indians" was "aimed at safeguarding the economic concerns of the European community. It is simply part of the larger colonial distinctions based on race and color" (Kumar 2004, 376). Kumar comments that even when they were indentured, the Indians' "enterprising spirit could not be curbed"; hence many became small traders, carpenters, and the like (378). Related to (though different from) the Indians facing the harsh conditions of indenture and racial prejudice is the historical reality of indigenous groups being robbed of their lands and displaced despite resistance and wars against British and Dutch colonizers.

Today's South African Indians, descendants of Indian migrants, are diverse and pluralistic, comprising "four culturally and linguistically homogenous groups" demarcated by different languages (Hindi, Gujarati, Tami, and Telugu); different social customs, food habits, and practice of the arts; and "sub-identities based on their caste, and region" in India (Kumar 2004, 57). Further, "colonial discourse often conflated a certain region with the religion of the group that originated from there" (58).

Pather's choreography is punctuated by a voice-over tracing key moments of the history. In this dance-drama, Pather uses only one narrator to trace the history of Indians interwoven with colonists and settlers—the British 1820 settlers and the conflicts between the English and Zulus when the latter refused to plant and cut sugarcane, causing the need for Indian laborers. Pather then represents Gandhi (played by Vaibhav Joshi) along with a Black lawyer, Mr. Dube, "as figureheads," remarks Pather, "bringing together the ANC and the NIC."

Beginning in 1824, British settlers were keen to develop Natal's sugarcane belt, which stretched for nearly a hundred miles from Durban to Eshowe, the capital of Zululand, but they faced labor shortages after slavery was abolished in the British Empire in 1834; indigenous Black people, understandably, did not wish to labor on their own land for the profit of European settlers. As explained by the Cape of Good Hope's colonial secretary, Rawson W. Rawson, "The male Kaffirs are, in their independent state, exempt from toil. They are the warriors and hunters of their tribes, but agricultural and domestic labour devolves upon the women. . . . Hence in the manufacture of sugar . . . that requires constant and certain labour . . . the introduction of coolies is expected to produce results as advantageous as it has done in some other settlements" (quoted in Chattopadhyaya 1970, 21). Hence, the British were forced to search beyond this region into other areas of the empire, such as India, for field laborers. In *Satyagraha in South Africa*, Gandhi recounts that Natal, including Port Natal, was not only the first British colony but also the site where the majority of Indians landed.[10]

From the beginning of their arrival in South Africa, Indians were neither the indigenous inhabitants of the land nor the White colonizers and settlers. They were outsiders, like the Whites, though the latter's racial domination was exerted on Indians and Black people in like manner. The Indians' in-between status marks and mars their struggle to integrate as South Africans over many years. Pather, as fourth generation Indian, could make his ethnic in-between status productive rather than disempowering. Politically, he aligned with the Black struggle; however, he remains exceptional in his ability to "cross over"—as the name of his dance company, Siwela Sonke, translates—and further, to cross over "to a new place altogether." However, during the nineteenth century, Indians' struggle to belong to South Africa was challenging in a different way than it was for Pather nearly a century later.[11]

INNOVATIVE CHOREOGRAPHY IN THE
HISTORICAL DANCE-DRAMA *AHIMSA-UBUNTU*

Pather's choreographic choices in *Ahimsa-Ubuntu* reflect different historical periods since the arrival of Indians in the 1860s— during colonial, apartheid, and post-apartheid times. Zulu classical dance demonstrates colonial times, when the English tried to extract work from Zulus and faced resistance. It was the first time, Pather remarked, that he brought together the Indian classical dance style of kathak and the popular South African gumboot dance in his choreography, with rhythmic commonalities that he has used again in future work. In the middle section, with the rise of apartheid and the 1950 Groups Areas Act, then the June 16 riots (the student revolt), he choreographed a large dance section blending African and Indian styles. He noted that he wanted "to introduce the idea of networks, of people coming together—students, workers, exiles" (interview 1, 2018) culminating in Mandela's election as the new president.

Pather's skill at working with large groups was showcased in *Ahimsa-Ubuntu* with twenty-three dancers—including six classical Indian dancers, thirteen Black dancers, and four ballet dancers (interview 1, 2018). Pather made a fascinating comment about his use of space that conveys significant spatial politics in *Ahimsa-Ubuntu*, namely that since different dance forms need different amounts of space on stage, he used that concept symbolically to evoke the political reality of White colonists and settlers taking over land and territory belonging to Black people in South Africa (interview 1, 2018). Pather conveyed this via classical ballet dancers *en pointe* (on points) executing jetés and extensions that occupy a huge amount of space, similar to and representative of the conqueror-invaders. As the dancers propelled across the space, they symbolized the eating up and taking over of large areas of land. The stage space in Pather's choreography created "dance maps" indicating how geographical territory was stolen from Black people. He deliberately used only four ballet dancers to demonstrate the notion of conquest, whereas there were nineteen other dancers who performed African and Indian dance styles. "One can't beat ballet," Pather added, "as symbolic of colonization" (interview 1, 2018).

In contrast to ballet's movements needing a lot of space, gumboot and kathak can almost be done in place. Pather's interest in space and geography, and his evocative phrase "dance maps," echoes Gilles Deleuze and Felix Guattari's influential analyses of spatiality and borders (*A Thousand Plateaus: Capitalism and Schizophrenia*, 1987, and *What Is Philosophy*, 1991); aspects that resonate in Pather's work include both materialist realities and conceptual dimensions. As Keith Woodward and John Paul Jones III remark, "Deleuze and Guattari's conceptual spaces—and their political leverage—are anchored in a resolutely materialist understanding of spatiality" (2005). The material reality for Black people is land, whereas the space taken over by Whites is about both material and conceptual power.

Along with Pather's insightful and symbolic use of different dance forms that have certain values ingrained in them, he added that for ballet dancers "the chest is the center of levity that mimics the notion of a spirituality that reaches for the heavens above as opposed to the pelvis as the center of gravity, a feature of much African [and Indian] dance that indicates a spirituality directed at ancestors and the earth" (phone conversation, May 20, 2020). Further, a close connection to the earth indicates for Pather "a grounded spirituality that is not divorced from materiality" (interview 1, 2018).

In placing kathak beside gumboot dance, Pather was not interested in fusion but in "pure forms" that have a context, whereas fusion ignores the context of different styles (interview 3, 2017). Pather recognizes that the forms are different, hence forcing them together by "fusing" them results, ironically, in "pull[ing] them apart." He believes that "only in special places as in *Ahimsa-Ubuntu*, can different forms come together" rooted in their historical time and space—in particular, the scenario of the Natal Indian Council (NIC) and the African National Congress (ANC) working together during the 1952 Defiance Campaign.[12] Such synergy provides him with a rationale to place two distinct forms, gumboot dance and kathak, together. For Pather, "this was a big deal. It was purely historical" and more significant to explore "the place of tension between forms rather than [claiming] fusion."

He asks, "How much room" is there for two forms to perform on stage "rhythmically and aesthetically"?[13] Pather continues, "The confluence of classical Indian dance and traditional African dance, the rhythmic quality of both forms is very complex.... The semiotics are so rich in all the traditional performance from *indlamu* to the reed dance to *isicathimiya*.... My concern is that dance is not just foot stomping. I was anxious to keep the forms with their centres. The African dancers worked hard at finding the original steps. The same with the classical Indian dancers. The deeper you drill, you deepen those natural forms and things start happening at an intrinsic level" (Sichel 1996, 19).

Pather's creative and critical eye recognizes each dance form, kathak and gumboot, "with their centres"—with their own distinct movement idioms and identities. If they were fused, each style would lose its core, which for Pather would be reductive of the particular style. He would rather explore "the place of tension between forms" than fuse them. His choreographic process here is also different from simply juxtaposing two styles, as is done commonly in Afro-fusion dance. He keeps the styles separate as he probes the "tension" between them.

In a positive review, Adrienne Sichel describes *Ahimsa-Ubuntu* as "a new form of oral history" that endorses "the new breed of South African story-teller/history teacher [who] takes dance class and connects with the past and the present through a rainbow of rhythms" (Sichel, 1996, 19). *Ahimsa-Ubuntu* opens in precolonial times, represented by relatively harmonious traditional dance styles. Next, the European arrival is conveyed by classical ballet. The arrival of indentured Indians in Natal is expressed through Indian folk dance. Resistance to injustice deploys the Gandhian tools of satyagraha, performed using Indian classical dance *mudras* (hand gestures). The program notes state that "in the Defiance Campaign, the coming together of African and Indian finds expression through the shared rhythms of the African gumboot dance and the Indian kathak."

In performance, the kathak and gumboot dances showcase two movement styles and cultures whose differences begin with something as basic as bare feet (in kathak) versus gumboots. Sichel notes that the amount of time that it takes for kathak dancers to put on their ankle bells—fifteen minutes—is very different from the ease of wearing gumboots. Sichel adds, "There's also the constant trauma of opening old wounds," including cultural and emotional wounds of the recently "ended" apartheid system (Sichel 1996, 19).

The danced history in *Ahimsa-Ubuntu* evokes significant events in India's colonial history that parallel those in South Africa—for instance, the 1857 Indian Mutiny protesting the British, resulting in the Jallianwala Bagh massacre when the British shot fleeing protestors; or the courageous resistance of women fighters such as Rani Lakshmibai of Jhansi. Colonial violence was common in both South Africa and India during the late nineteenth and early twentieth centuries. *Ahimsa-Ubuntu* conveys, as stated on the show's program notes, "the spirit in which disenfranchised peoples of South Africa struggled against and overcame apartheid. . . . Racism was a creature of colonialism, nurtured in violence and that violence was as ubiquitous in India as it was in South Africa."

The Group Areas Act of 1950 was one of the most detested apartheid-era laws; it was a calculated spatial strategy to separate the races that had a major impact on the Indian community, and it features prominently in *Ahimsa-Ubuntu*. This law enforced illegal "confiscation of properties, and forced relocation" and was "a calculated attack on Indians who had prospered through hard work, had purchased their own homes, and were running their own businesses" (Bhana 1997b, 102). Areas of residence and business were separated.[14]

The issue of land and where Indian and Black people were allowed to live, even to own houses, can be traced back to 1885, when the colonists passed Law 3, which placed Indians into separate areas (Bhana and Pachai 1984). In response, the British government protested on behalf of Indians, and the law was amended. However, Bhana and Pachai contend that "the efforts to segregate Indians into 'locations' and 'bazaars' continued" even after 1901. In Natal, the main business area of Grey Street— still a thriving location for Indian businesses and one that Pather uses for his site-specific work *Cityscapes*, discussed in chap. 3— allowed only a few Indian traders to set up shop since "the colonial legislation used the trade license laws effectively to regulate the location of Indian traders" (99).[15]

Pather successfully re-creates South African Indian history via different dance styles "against a backdrop of iconic historical photographic or filmic images. Similarly, the musical score, arranged and composed by Jurgen Brauninger, synthesizes national anthems and melodies as diverse as Rossini's *Thieving Magpie* and Raghupati Raghav Raja Ram" (Sichel 1996, 19). Pather noted to me that there are "difference phases" in his working with music composers; with Brauninger, he would discuss the concept of the work and the sound that would work best.[16] "The Finale," as the program notes convey, "brings together traditional and modern, classical and folk, African, Indian, and European, to express the dancers' final plea: 'To realize Ahimsa, to live in Ubuntu.'"

Ahimsa-Ubuntu was performed in 1996, a landmark year for Pather. He was appointed director of a training program that became "the fledgling Siwela Sonke" dance company, notes Sichel, "which has a unique intercultural training and performance policy drawing on its regional cultural identity" (1996, 19). Pather's own artistic trajectory before 1996, adds Sichel, includes his travel to Angola "to direct Amandla Awethu, the ANC's cultural group in exile . . . while working with Cape Town's Jazzart Dance Theatre." These experiences, Sichel contends, "empowered Pather to take historical material and events and re-find them in the dance through a choreographic character" (19).

In 1999, a mere two years after it was launched as a training program that was part of the Playhouse Theater, and despite the resounding success of *A South African Siddhartha* in the same year, Siwela Sonke Dance Theatre's very survival was in danger in the face of retrenchment. As Sichel remarks, "Tragically, this prototype democratic dance company created in the spirit of socio-political redress by the Playhouse Company to celebrate the cultural diversity and identity of KwaZulu Natal, has become a casualty of the very history it was meant to serve" (Sichel 1999). The company performed *Miracle* (a fitting title that reflected its struggle to survive) to find studio space for their work and to continue to be funded for their deeply committed and significant work training dancers from disadvantaged communities. Sichel describes *Miracle* as "a collaboration between Pather's continuing choreographic concern with lives within landscape, [as it] transposes the life of Christ to present-day South Africa" (Sichel 1999). Christ returns to Durban beach, interacts with the dancers, and Sichel remarks, the "series of sequences and encounters lead to a dramatic crucifixion."

Siwela Sonke Dance Theatre (SSDT) did rise from its near death with Pather's help in securing another studio space on a small street, Albany Grove, very different in social status although close to the Playhouse Theater. SSDT continues to conduct training for the next generation of dancers and to be a thriving company with national and international renown, performing Pather's choreographies and sharing his vision of art as a powerful tool in inspiring social change.

A SOUTH AFRICAN SIDDHARTHA (1999)

A South African Siddhartha, featuring collaboration among dancers from South Africa and India, was commissioned for the Main Program at the 1999 Standard Bank National Arts Festival for their twenty-fifth anniversary in Grahamstown and cosponsored by the Indian embassy in South Africa. It was performed from March 10 through March 19, 2000 at the Playhouse Theatre in Durban. Jurgen Brauninger, composer of *Ahimsa-Ubuntu*, provided original composition and sound design with additional classical sitar music by Ravi Shankar, flute by Deepak Ram, and soundscapes by Philip Glass and Bernd Konrad. Reviewer Suzy Bell comments glowingly that "If J.M Coetzee's *Disgrace*, which just won the Booker Prize [in 1999], is currently the great South African novel, then Jay Pather's seminal dance piece *A South African Siddhartha* is the great South African dance. The dance is so entirely South African and contemporary in tone that we have a Siddhartha in the Karoo, travelling by minibus where he meets a taxi driver and then he lands up at a cyber café in the Transkei!" (Bell 2000a). In the same review, Bell also admires the "exquisite sonic art—bells, rattles, Warwick Avenue's lively street clamour, the gentle swish of *isangoma*'s *ishoba* [whisk] the soft pat of bare feet on the stage." Set designer Sarah Roberts' white cloth strips created vertical lines on stage. Bell describes the costumes as "fabulous and highly original with cheeky reference to Issey Miyake pleats in *isangoma*'s skirt and very street camo-homo-boy and homo-girl grunge." Thulebona Mzizi, who played the lead role of Siddhartha with appealing vulnerability, won the prestigious FNB Dance Umbrella Award in 1998–99 for best male dancer in a contemporary style. Along with Siwela Sonke, Pather got an FNB Vita Award for choreography for his Africanization of the Siddhartha story. Hermann Hesse's *Siddhartha* had won the Nobel Prize in Literature in 1946.

Siddhartha's story in Hesse's novel portrays the journey of a wanderer from youth to adulthood; his quest for spiritual enlightenment—he eventually transforms into the Buddha—leads him through many temptations, including a life of excess that almost destroys him. In Hesse's account, Siddhartha Gautama, the Prince of Kapilavastu, leaves home and becomes an ascetic, though after he crosses a river with a ferryman who turns out to be saint Vasudeva, he falls in love with the courtesan Kamala, who urges him to acquire wealth so that he can enjoy her. In Pather's version, Siddhartha, rather than crossing a river, traverses the arid South African Karoo, not easy for human habitation. The courtesan, with whom Siddhartha falls in love, is played by acclaimed *odissi* dancer Jayati Bhatia, who flew from India to Durban for the role and is described by Suzy Bell as "devastatingly alluring" (Bell, 2000a).

Pather's choreography conveys the powerful story of Siddhartha's life interwoven with mythology. It describes the search of one voyager who chooses to be an outsider, alienated from family, wealth, and his princely heritage, as he seeks truth and enlightenment. Siddhartha's son, conceived during the wanderer's wild days, rejects his father. Siddhartha finally understands what it is to give up everything he loves. Nonetheless, the fact that he does attain enlightenment makes the work highly positive.

A South African Siddhartha's program notes quote an extract from Hermann Hesse's *The Glass Bead Game* (1943, also published under the title *Magister Ludi*) that analyses the parameters of passion, ambition, and spiritual goals:

> What you call passion is not spiritual force, but friction between the soul and the outside world. Where passion dominates, that does not signify the presence of greater desire and ambition, but rather the misdirection of these qualities, towards an isolated and false goal, with a consequent tension and sultriness in the atmosphere. Those who direct the maximum force of their desires toward the centre, towards true being, toward perfection, seem quieter than the passionate souls because the flame of their fervor cannot always be seen. In argument, for example, they will not shout and wave their arms. But I assure you, they are nevertheless burning with subdued fires.... Truth is lived, not taught.

Pather weaves Indian and South African dance and ritual forms in *A South African Siddhartha* that include Zulu and Xhosa dance, kathak, bharatanatyam, contemporary dance, and ballet.

Vaibhav Joshi plays Siddhartha's father and is described by Bell as "the moneyed Daddy Bollywood with his manic Danny Osmond smile. He miraculously transformed from his serious, decidedly solemn role of Siddhartha's father" (Bell, 2000a). Joshi also plays the role of a businessman, crucial in the show as offering the temptations of capital and money, even moving towards corruption. Ntombi Gasa, a practitioner of *sangoma*, a traditional Zulu healing ritual, plays Siddhartha's mother, and Jayati Bhatia, the odissi dancer, is the temptress. These different styles "work beautifully" in Bell's judgment. "At times, it is soft and calm, rational and dignified, comical and camp, balanced and harmonious then petulant and tortured. And yes, of course, even very sexy" (Bell 2000a). Pather commented to the staff reviewer of *Berea Mail* (2000) that he wanted "to get across all the stereotypes of what these people should be and to look at how all these different dance forms come together to tell the same story. Siddhartha is a contemporary African dancer. His father is a kathak dancer, his mother is a sangoma dancer, and the woman he falls in love with is an odissi dancer."

In my July 2014 interview (in Durban) with Siwela Sonke's founding company members, choreographers Ntombi Gasa and Neliswa Rushualong, about Pather's choreography for *Siddhartha*, I learned that Indian dance mudras were used for segments in the story—such as when Siddhartha leaves home, when he is told to kiss his mother and tell her where he is going, and when he is told to come back to his family and teach them his spiritual discoveries. "A magnificent production" comments Bell, "so potent in storytelling as essentially it's about the power of myth" (2000a). For Bell, "*A SA Siddhartha* is sensual, evocative and elegiac. It's epic South African dance theatre."

The video recording of a live performance (with audible clapping) of *A South African Siddhartha* demonstrates clearly Pather's uniquely hybrid signature style; this piece synthesizes different dance genres and their cultures while giving each one its distinct identity and re-creating each into novel effects.[17] This is seen and heard in Indian dancers wearing traditional ankle bells in the show's opening and in a Black female *sangoma* dancer wielding a traditional whisk used for healing. The kathak dancer in the middle playing the young Siddhartha's father, covers the stage in kathak's characteristic *chakars* (pirouette-like circles). The *sangoma* dancer moves across the stage also making circles while a chorus of dancers moves in a bigger circle around the kathak and *sangoma* dancers. Their movement styles, rooted in their own cultural contexts, begin to mirror one another uncannily in the circular movements. The music is distinctly Indian but incorporates Western sounds. As this movement goes on, a voice-over informs the audience that Siddhartha "had begun to feel the love for his mother and friend. His soul was not at peace, his heart not still." In a respectful gesture, he bows and asks his father for permission to leave. "If you go," notes the voice-over, "you will leave what is yours. Would you rather die than obey your father?" Siddhartha is at his father's feet. Finally, his father relents, as we hear, "Go to the forest, find freedom, or a solution, come back, and we will make sacrifices to the ancestors together." Soulful, even mournful Indian music fills the stage as Siddhartha bids farewell to his *sangoma* mother, conveyed beautifully by contemporary dance style lifts. Elegiac sounds accompany this emotional farewell as Siddhartha bows in front of his father for his blessing, then leaves.

In the following scene, vertical lights in parallels indicating large trees take viewers into a forest, and circles of light on the floor mirror circles of movements. Six choral dancers undertake floor work and lifts, moving across the stage as Siddhartha enters and dances balletic pirouettes to Western music. The voice-over draws a parallel between Siddhartha's personal search for enlightenment and the South African nation, "just as when a country is ravished, heal the afflicted." The female odissi dancer enters, playing a temptress enticing Siddhartha away from his spiritual path. Siddhartha tries to leave "to hear the teachings," but his friend is distrustful of all teachers. "You mock me," complains the friend, but Siddhartha asserts, "I've taken a path; you'll always be my friend." The costumes in this forest scene are camouflage tops and loose pants, as if blending with the natural world, indicating Siddhartha's renunciation of everything including friendship. "Tomorrow, I will leave" says Siddhartha as he exits the stage.

The odissi dancer reenters, taking the iconic *tribhangi* pose with one hip displaced, creating a sensually curved bodyline, her hip movements accompanied by flute music. Her body casts large shadows as Siddhartha passes in the back, his own figure dwarfed. There is a video of a truck. Siddhartha holds the dancer at her waist. She goes into a low crouch with hands folded as if in prayer as Siddhartha dances around her. Then, she dances with seductive hip movements, enticing Siddhartha, who stands from a very low backbend, and the two kiss.

Three dancers enter and break up the sensual couple. They dance in an effeminate manner, as if parodying the beautiful odissi dancer. Other dancers enter; Siddhartha watches from the side behind a scrim before emerging with a garland around his neck. In a duet, the odissi dancer and Siddhartha take the statuesque poses of odissi; though untraditional to odissi, the female dancer's leg is lifted in the front while Siddhartha's is raised in the back. He holds her foot as the two bodies come together in romantic movements. He carries her in a move very different from traditional odissi, which is usually a solo female form. She supports him, also untraditionally, and then takes this further by lying on the floor and opening her legs. He does the same, suggesting subtle lovemaking, accompanied by flute sounds. Siddhartha puts a necklace around the odissi dancer, indicating, as in certain Indian customs, that they are married. He lies down, and she joins him, saying, "Best lover I've had, stronger, more supple than others. Yet my dear, you love nobody."

Many pieces of fabric in parallel strips roll down, and music with repeated rhythms sounds insistently as Siddhartha and the odissi dancer move in a synergy of Indian dance and contemporary dance movements. The flowing fabrics on stage convey the tumultuous emotions of the male and female dancers—one battling to seek enlightenment, the other content with the pleasures of the flesh.

In "Siddhartha: An Uncontested Triumph," reviewer Bell recognizes that "Pather's talent in his original selections from the multicultural creativity of South Africa, and unlike many of his contemporaries, [he] is able to skillfully draw on the resource without lapsing into superficial or naïve connections. Instead, his work is at points able to render a profound sense of the interconnectedness of all South Africans in our great wisdom and stupidity, ugliness and beauty, humanity and brutality. It is a seamless production that parallels one man's search for truth with a nation's" (2000d). Echoing this sentiment, *Natal Witness*'s staff writer in "Modern Parable of One Man's Search for Enlightenment" describes Siddhartha's personal quest as "emblematic for the transformation of a nation" (*Natal Witness* 2000). The same review draws symbolic parallels between Siddhartha's temptations and arduous journey and the excesses "that come with a newly liberated third world country."

In Pather's hands, spatial journeys—geographical and of the body-soul—are represented in the themes of both *Ahimsa-Ubuntu* and *A South African Siddhartha*. Indian and South African history are related dialectically to different dance forms that convey significant historical times—as ballet embodies the coming of the Europeans in the re-creation of Indian history in South Africa, so does the Indian classical dance style of odissi, along with contemporary dance, embody Siddhartha in the Karoo. The Indian themes of both works, with Gandhian *ahimsa* and Siddhartha as a seeker for enlightenment, are rooted firmly in the fabric of South African society. Pather's choreography showcases the synergy of his Indian heritage and South African identity; at times they mirror one another, as in the South African ideal of *ubuntu* embodied also in Siddhartha, whose quest to attain a higher self is ultimately for the benefit of all humankind. Pather's creativity, and his breadth and generosity of vision in these 1996 and 1999 works, encompasses such humanist ideals while keeping his feet planted on the ground of his native South Africa.

The next chapter explores spatial politics in Pather's involvement as a dancer and actor in the 1980s and 1990s, during apartheid and after. His choreography confronts Black people's exclusions from many sites as exerted brutally by apartheid laws. Pather is deeply aware of this geography of ravage for the majority of Black people who carry their wounds, often invisible, under the skin and in the bones. He continues to work in dance-drama, though his movement into multidisciplinary performance is fully in view by 2000. In *Unclenching the Fist, Laws of Recall, Shifting Spaces,* and *Tilting Time,* Pather counters apartheid's repressive measures that seeped harmfully into the private and intimate lives of Black South Africans, often causing unpredictable and sudden violent responses. Post-apartheid, Pather creatively challenges the goals and shortcomings of the Truth and Reconciliation Commission (TRC), and *simunye* slogans of "the rainbow nation" in works such as *Testimonies* and *Forked Tongues*.[18] In response to the TRC, I argue in the next chapter that Pather effectively reverses the feminist adage of "the personal is political" to "the political is personal" in the South African context.

NOTES

1. Since South Africa's independence, Natal is now known as Kwa-Zulu (land of the Zulus) Natal. Similar changes in names of universities is noteworthy: during apartheid, the University of Natal was for Whites only with some exceptions; University of Durban-Westville where Pather studied was for Indians only and a few Black people. During democracy, the two have merged to be called University of KwaZulu Natal with access for all South Africans.

2. South African History Online, "Smallpox Epidemic Strikes at the Cape," accessed December 12, 2016, http://www.sahistory.org.za/dated-event/smallpox-epidemic-strikes-cape.

3. A clip of *Exit/Exist* can be viewed at: https://www.youtube.com/watch?v=SPOwuUvXugI, accessed December 28, 2016.

4. Gandhi had completed his education as a barrister in London in 1891 and returned to India, though he was not very successful in the Bombay courts. He realized that the practice of law required moral compromises with which he was uncomfortable. An opportunity came up when a family friend offered Gandhi a position as "consultant lawyer to the trading firm of Dada Abdulla" in Durban. His "welcome" into South Africa in 1893 was a rude shock when he was thrown off the train for sitting in the White section, which he felt was justified since he had a first-class ticket. But to no avail; he had to spend a cold night in a third-class waiting room and was outraged at the injustices Indians faced. Gandhi later described this incident as "the most creative experience" of his life (Mathur 1986, 21). Another early experience with racism occurred when he was required to remove his turban in court and was called "a coolie barrister." He mobilized the Indian community in South Africa to fight unjust laws, forming the South African Indian Congress, which worked with the African National Congress in key historical struggles. Although Gandhi intended to stay in South Africa for a year and "try his luck," he stayed until 1914 (from 1893) and later led public struggles from India to abolish indentured labor in South Africa.

5. Maharaj, along with forty dancers, traces "the story of South Africa's Indian community, their origin, growth, culture and history" in *Sunghursh*, discussed at Artslink.co.za: https://www.artlink.co.za/news_article.htm?contentID=25180. Maharaj remarks on the same site that "as South Africans belonging to the fifth generation of indentured Indians, our pride in our forebears lead us to reflect on the early Indian settlers—their labour, their political, educational and cultural struggle." Maharaj uses dance, music, and narration along with slides of historic materials that aim to educate the audience and correct misinformation and stereotypes about the Indian community.

6. On July 30, 2015, I interviewed Smeetha Maharaj of Nateshwar Dance Company. Maharaj teaches the Indian classical style of kathak that she studied with guru Gopi Krishna in the 1980s in India. She noted that artists like herself, dedicated to classical Indian dance, faced severe isolation for nearly forty years during the cultural boycott. Only after apartheid

ended could South African Indian dancer-teachers like herself enhance their skills in classical dance forms by inviting artists from India to hold workshops and dance camps.

7. Moopen's docudrama is a collaborative project with Devan Moonsamy, who based the script on Uma Dhupelia-Mesthrie's book *From Canefields to Freedom: A Chronicle of Indian South African Life* (published in 2000) and Ashwin Desai's *Inside Indenture* (2007). Moopen, who considered it her responsibility to tackle this history, remarks, "Creating this work [*From Canefields to Freedom*] has not only filled in the historic gaps but dispelled the misconception that all Indian South Africans are rich and own businesses. Tribhangi's Indian dancers also did not know all the details. It has given all of us a lot of insight" (quoted in Sichel 2010a). Part of this painful history concerns the British colonizers' betrayals—they had promised the Indians "a safe passage and a new life" in South Africa that they did not deliver. In fact, hundreds died on this difficult ocean crossing. Nonetheless, "out of these hardships and slave conditions was born a spirit of political resistance" remarks Sichel, "which became part of South Africa's liberation struggle."

8. *The Coolie Odyssey*, a two-act, twenty-six-scene play within a play, begins in present-day Durban with the male protagonist, Neelan Naidoo, in despair about his future in South Africa. Since Neelan did not get into medical school, he wonders if "maybe, just maybe, we *charous* are not getting the message—we not wanted here." Neelan believes that Indians have no future in South Africa; he wants to immigrate to Australia. The action then moves to the past as Neelan encounters the ghost of an indentured laborer, Ramlall, who dramatizes his story of leaving India and the racism and prejudice he faced in South Africa. In September 2010, as noted by Lee-Anne Naicker in an unpublished "Master Techonologiae" thesis, "On the eve of the 150th Commemorative anniversary of Indians arriving in South Africa, Gopie extensively reworked and directed the play, which was then performed in theatres in and around Durban, Pietermaritzburg and Cape Town and also in India," in cities like Bombay, Delhi, and Calcutta (Naicker 2014, 112).

9. I am grateful to Pather for providing a video copy of *Ahimsa-Ubuntu*. Since its quality was damaged, Pather kindly spent time with me discussing the show and its dance styles, along with his invaluable insights (interview 1, 2018).

10. Gandhi was a prolific writer throughout his life, having published over twenty-four books, including his autobiography, *My Experiments with Truth*. In his foreword to *Satyagraha in South Africa*, Gandhi notes,

"The original chapters were all written by me from memory... partly in Yeravda jail [in India] and partly outside" ([1928] 1954, front matter). This text is a compilation of his political views in *Indian Opinion* written during his stay of more than twenty years in South Africa. Gandhi founded *Indian Opinion*, a popular publication, in June 1903 "to assist Indians in fighting for their civil liberties."

11. There is an extensive history tracing the changing fate of Indians in South Africa from the 1860s onward, through unfair laws that ostracized them from full citizenship rights in their adopted home. Although this historical record is significant, it does not relate directly to Pather's life and work, hence I include it in Appendix, "Indians in South Africa: A Chronological Time Line." In order to keep my focus on Pather in this monograph, I analyze only the historical landmarks that he includes for his choreographic purposes in *Ahimsa-Ubuntu*. For further historical details with a time line and archival materials culled from historians of this field, please refer to Appendix.

12. Alliances between Indian and Black organizations guided the struggles of the 1950s. In the Defiance Campaign of 1952, the ANC (African National Congress) and the SAIC (South African Indian Congress) joined forces for the first time to fight together against the fierce succession of laws passed to promote apartheid—the Population Registration Act, the Group Areas Act, the Mixed Marriages Act, the Immorality Act, and the Suppression of Communism Act. Many Indians such as Fatima Meer, Navi Pillay, Jay Naidoo, Ebrahim Patel, Yusuf Cassim, and Anand Naidoo were active in resisting apartheid's racist laws. Resistance rose against these laws—some of which had more impact on Indians, others on Black and Colored peoples—and although the struggle to repeal them was unsuccessful, the link between the Indian and African Congress was solidified.

13. In his 1998 dance-theater work *Shifting Spaces, Tilting Time*, Pather expressed his "irritation with fusion" by portraying *pantsula* (a popular South African dance form that originated in the Black townships) with kathak (interview 3, 2017), though conveying a dramatic effect with Pravika Nandakishore dancing kathak with bandaged hands. This made it impossible to perform this classical dance's signature *mudras*, taking away the decorativeness of hand gestures that is characteristic of Indian dance.

14. The 1950 Group Areas Act was imposed on communities of color who had lived harmoniously side by side; under the act, they were suddenly forced to relocate to racially segregated enclaves, no doubt to

prevent their ability to organize against the apartheid state. This was experienced most bitterly by Indian families, some of whom had to give up their treasured homes bought after a lifetime of work. In his book *At the Edge and Other Cato Manor Stories* (which won the 1997 Commonwealth Writer's Prize for best first book), South African Indian writer Ronnie Govender, now in his eighties, remembers his trauma as an eleven-year-old boy when his family was forced to move from their home in Cato Manor. United opposition to the Group Areas Act of 1950 rallied the people under the slogan "Defend Our Homes."

15. Bhana records that at a Group Areas Conference on May 5 and 6, 1956, Monty Naicker's paper provided a breakdown of the groups displaced: "81,886 Africans, 6,292 Coloreds, 64,745 Indians, and 3,462 whites" (Bhana 1997b, 103). Indian-owned land was appropriated, and families were forcibly moved from the city to areas outside central Durban such as Chatsworth. "There was severe housing shortage for the growing Indian population—from 107,000 in 1946 to 144,000 in 1951" (106). Further, the Indian-designated areas had poor civic facilities, and in allocated low-lying areas, flooding was common during heavy rains.

16. Pather worked with the same music composer James Webb for *Body of Evidence* (chap. 4). Pather discussed this work conceptually; he mentioned the use of Gray's *Anatomy*, and then Webb created his uniquely disturbing soundscape. Pather noted to me (interview 1, 2018) that Webb actually managed to record the sounds within his body and "created little tracks of body sounds" that Pather then used in *Body of Evidence*.

17. I am grateful to Pather for providing me with a video of *A South African Siddhartha*.

18. *Simunye* translates as "we are one," as if imposing a unity that does not exist in reality among all South Africans. Pather adds that "*simunye* comes from an advertising jingle for South African Broadcasting Corporation (SABC) Channel 1, capitalizing on the national unity project and the number of the Channel" (phone conversation, May 20, 2020).

TWO

RACE AND SPACE MATTER
Outdancing Apartheid's Grip in Pather's Work (1980s and 1990s)

SPATIAL POLITICS OF THE 1980S and 1990s, during apartheid, controlled nearly all aspects of life for Black South Africans and imposed severe restrictions on artists and their works; such controls dictated which spaces were available for creative work and what works could be performed or even spoken about, as well as which artists were allowed to showcase their work in public. Pather's creative work as a dancer and actor from this time openly embraces sociopolitical issues that concern the majority of Black people. Indeed, Pather's aesthetic challenges to political injustices come across as a reversal of the feminist adage "the personal is political" to "the political is personal"—a painful truth under apartheid's systemic racism with mandated geographical segregations as well as after apartheid's demise in 1994.

DURING APARTHEID: 1980–94

Pather deployed his considerable imagination and artistry as an actor, director, dancer, and choreographer to counter apartheid's draconian measures. However, as a college student during the early 1980s, between student protests and stayaways, he experienced bring pushed in different directions—while studying authors like Ngũgĩ wa Thiong'o, Virginia Woolf, and Chinua Achebe and performing in Santha Rama Rau's *Passage to India* (an adaptation of the E. M. Forster novel), to dancing in *Curriculum Capers* that connected movement with various subjects, directed by Irene Oakley, at the Asoka Theatre. Devi Bughwan, who directed *Passage to India* was the first Black woman Head of Drama in South Africa and was a formative influence in Pather's artistic life. He remarks that developing his skills as a student in a range of shows reflected the turbulence and tensions of the 1980s, also the period of the state-imposed emergency. His professional performance credits in Durban in 1982 include *Fortune and Men's Eyes*, a play by John Herbert about queer lives in a prison, directed by Dawie Malan, and playing Gandhi in the provocative *Mahatma Gandhi*, directed by Saira Essa. Pather recalled that during a workshop when Essa was interested in digging into Gandhi's personal life, there was a moment when Gandhi's rage comes momentarily to the surface when he is faced with his wife Kasturba's dismay at giving away her jewels—for Gandhi, this was simply to benefit other people. Pather also connected Gandhi's behavior to that of his own activist-father, Manickum Nadarajan Pather, who would do the same as Gandhi, to take from the family for the greater good (phone conversation, May 25, 2020).

Later in 1982, in New York City for his MA, he was involved in plays such as *Rhubarb and Roses*, directed by Ralph Gordon, and *House of Cards*, directed by Ritha Baidaroy. From 1982 through 1984 in New York City, he was a dancer for Kaleidoscope Dance Theater, in their repertory and in new works directed by Jan Abrahamovitz and Mary Sichel. In 1983, at New York University, Pather devised a production of *Hector Peterson*, based on the life of the twelve-year-old of that name killed by South African police during the 1976 Soweto uprising; the youth's dying image, carried lovingly by another Soweto resident, is captured in a famous photograph by Sam Nzima that was published worldwide, galvanizing many to speak out against apartheid. Pather directed

Twice Fallen, Black Women in Apartheid South Africa (dedicated to his mother, Bakiavathee Pather) in 1983 with Amandla Awethu Dance Theatre. In 1984, while still in New York City, Pather performed in *Chaturanga*, directed by Nancy Smithner, in the Afro-American Storytellers Festival in Harlem, and with the Ito Japanese Dance Company under the direction of Sachiyo Ito.

Pather remarks that during the 1980s, debates regarding the South African struggle revolved around the concept of the "human" under apartheid. While in NYC, he personally felt like more of a human being than he had during his time growing up under apartheid in South Africa. Often, the inhumanity Black males experienced resulted in hypermasculinity that Pather regards as "a response to apartheid policies that emasculated males" (interview 3, 2017). His creative work from the 1980s to the present has been concerned with physical male and female bodies and their struggle for acceptance as humans of whatever race, class, gender, and sexuality.

Pather returned to South Africa in 1984, despite the fact that this meant losing the daily freedoms that he cherished in New York City during his two years there. At home, he became involved as a dancer and actor in various projects. In 1985, he danced in *Duel in Black and White* presented by Jazzart Dance Theatre at Cape Town Cultural Festival, and in *The Homosexuals (Out in Africa)* with actor, playwright, director, and advocate for gay rights Peter Hayes at the National Arts Festival in Grahamstown, at the Arena Theatre in Cape Town, and at Wits Theatre in Johannesburg. He acted in 1985 in *The Island*, directed by Saira Essa, commissioned by International Political Theatre Festival, Prithvi Theatre, Bombay, India, and in *Shades of Brown*, directed by Junaid Ahmed, commissioned by Cultural Festival, Durban and Zululand. Since 1985, Pather has been entranced by Stravinsky's *Rite of Spring*, which he choreographed initially with students at the University of Durban-Westville. Then, in 1991, his imaginative choreography re-presented *Rite* in Cape Town; in

1993, *Rite*, seventy-five minutes long, was developed further at the Durban Institute of Technology. In 2014, *rite* was commissioned as a site-specific work for Dance Umbrella in Johannesburg at the Museum of African Design (MOAD); a proscenium stage version followed in 2015 (discussed in chap. 3).

From 1986 to 1989, Pather, who had grown up in urban Durban, worked as senior lecturer in the Drama Department at the University of Zululand (first established in 1960 as University College of Zululand, then renamed in 1982), located in rural KwaZulu Natal; this post allowed him to enhance his own exposure to rural areas of his country, to work with students in this environment, and to take on the challenges of this location. At the University of Zululand, with predominantly Zulu and Swazi students, he directed dramas such as Ngũgĩ wa Thiong'o and Micere Githae Mugo's *The Trial of Dedan Kimathi* (1986); John Kani, Winston Ntshona, and Athol Fugard's *The Island* (1988); and *The Tempest in Africa* (1988).[1] Pather's version had several indigenous inhabitants of the island emerge at the end, leading a revolutionary struggle to take back their land from the likes of Prospero. This was a reflection on the struggle against apartheid, during which the minority Whites held power over the majority Blacks.[2] From 1990 to 1993, Pather was a dancer with Jazzart Dance Theatre in Cape Town, where he featured in various performances directed by Alfred Hinkel—*Arathi*, *Knoc-Turn-Blue*, and the award-winning *Bolero* (restaged in 1998) at Cape Town's Nico Malan Theatre (now called the Artscape Theatre).

Even these few titles clearly indicate Pather's political opposition to injustice and his boldness in confronting racial and sexual discrimination. These were difficult times for artists, when restrictions of state censorship and banning were rampant, making it extremely difficult to engage in creative activity like live political theater in public. Apartheid enforcers could invade a theater at any time; hence, dramatists did not print written copies of their work ahead of scheduled performances. When I interviewed artist Benjy Francis (April 2014, Johannesburg) about this dark time, he remarked that to avoid state censorship of completed scripts critiquing apartheid, playwrights would distribute written sheets to actors just before shows. Hence, the productions were performed workshop-style, with actors reading the scripts for the first time even as they were ready to face arrest or imprisonment.

Apartheid laws banned creative works as well as the use of certain people's names, such as the ban on mentioning Nelson Mandela by name. Nonetheless, creative artists found unique ways to evoke their heroes via indirect, symbolic expressions instead of speaking or writing their names overtly, as in poems by Dennis Brutus entitled "It Is the Constant Image of Your Face" and "A Troubador I Traverse."[3]

In 1992, Pather served as a board member of the Hearts and Eyes Theatre Collective under founder-director Peter Hayes providing early evidence of his ability to envision and guide such an arts collective.[4] In several of Pather's works from 1992 and later, he engages with the human body in asserting its literal humanity, withstanding literal and symbolic violence and racial and sexual discrimination, and as a site on which history and memory are written. He also deconstructs the body to reflect scarred memories of apartheid-era brutalities. The Black physical body was rendered invisible under apartheid; recognition of full humanity includes sexuality and necessary challenges to discrimination against gays and lesbians. The Hearts and Eyes Theatre Collective "was launched at the National Arts Festival with *The Homosexuals (Out in Africa)*, the first play in South Africa to be directed, written and performed by out gay men."[5] This work showcases Pather's personal identity as an out gay man and his lifelong commitment to gay rights. He respects and advocates for the gay human body, challenging exclusion, prejudice, and violence. The very name of Hayes's Hearts and Eyes Theatre Collective resonates with the body, as stated on their site: "The company name comes from *Jesus of Montreal*, a movie about actors making a play, and the lead actor getting killed for his art. Having no family, the doctors ask his friends and fellow performers if they could use this brain-dead actor's organs in transplants. Permission is given and without delay, his heart and his eyes are given to people who need them. For the founders, this symbolises what a director gives her actors, and an actor his audience: their heart and eyes."[6] The sources of Hearts and Eyes Theatre Collective's name and goals echo Pather's future work as a choreographer and theater director in landmark performances. Pather goes further than "heart and eyes" in his concern with the human body's metaphoric dissection of external skin to probe the muscles, bones, and cells that hold memories of violence, as evoked in his choreography in *Body of Evidence*.

The Hearts and Eyes Theatre Collective's methods of conducting workshops with dancer-actors, enabling them to share "personal and true stories, and work that focuses on gender and sexuality," are also processes that Pather later used for his own works. For Pather, thematic choices are never separate from formal choices in the dialectic connection between form and content; hence, I posit that he was inspired by the adventurous spirit of Hearts and Eyes's "body of work that is diverse and spans genres from cabaret to circus.... Visual theatre and puppetry are emerging as a signature style."[7]

Hearts and Eyes's mission statement (on their website) mirrors Pather's evolving aesthetic-political and local-global vision that uses "the stage to reflect and interpret contemporary inspirations and issues that affect the lives of South Africans. Classic or contemporary, our view is local, while our ethos is global." Pather's later work echoes this collective's "cutting edge and brave" work, pushing "the boundaries of theatre," as well as its multidisciplinary impetus "that gives full voice and expression to a range of artistic visions, styles and subject matter." The collective aims to inspire, delight, and even transform their audiences' ability "to examine and explore the world with a clear eye & an open heart."[8]

POST-APARTHEID: 1994 ONWARD

The year 1994 was a watershed in South Africa's history; the entire population voted, ushering in a new democracy with Nelson Mandela as the first Black president. One key vehicle used in the South African transition to democracy, the brainchild of Archbishop Desmond Tutu and Mandela, was the 1995 Truth and Reconciliation Commission (TRC), which states that perpetrators of horrific crimes, mainly state police and security forces, could come forward to confess their violent acts to surviving victims or to their families in the process of healing and moving forward.[9]

Post-independence, in 1995, Pather was active in various projects. He choreographed *Six Solos in Search of a Story* with Jazzart Dance Theatre, Cape Town. He cowrote and performed in *Stories I Could Tell*, directed by Peter Hayes. It was commissioned by Artrage Festival, Australia, and performed also for Jazzart Dance Theatre. Pather notes that in these works he "was obsessed with the personal, with how much is repressed." For their work *Journey*, with Peter Hayes, Pather remarked that they "traveled throughout South Africa in a car, researching prototypes of characters in small towns and cities" (interview 4, 2015). Pather explained further that he played the prototype of an "outsider" character, one who lived on the margins of society. In this role, he once played an Indian shopkeeper in a small town with his family, building their lives in amazing ways. "The fact that the Indian shop was on the periphery" (interview 4, 2015) connects this portrayal in *Journey* with issues of displacement and dislocation that apply to South African Indians coming from outside South Africa and living in between racial groups. In recent years, Pather has been engaged through his curation of *Live Art* festivals in Cape Town with the figure of "outsiders," that is, migrants called "foreigners" from across the continent to South Africa and treated in hostile ways.

Pather's creative journey as actor and dancer evolved into his finally settling on choreography as his modus operandi. Pather embraces what he describes as "the onus of choreography," which for him is to express "the underbelly of oppression, the sheer physicality of it, the separation, the very meaning of apartheid that resonates spatially through exploration of rhythms of silence and defiance, discord, interruption, discord and utility" (Pather 2018a). Pather's choreographic purposes go "beyond fulfilling a pressing need to give shape to a sense of annihilation." His dance-theater work discussed below "has always been a response to the socio-political environment," he remarks, and "as a South African choreographer, it was not difficult to draw connection to sociopolitical issues with choreographic principles such as proxemis, kinesis, cellular memory during and after apartheid" (Pather 2015b, 317).

Pather expertly choreographs such nonverbal (though bodily) means of communication as indicated by "proxemis," which determines the space between and among people, and the expression of touch or distance as accepted within different cultures. During apartheid, the physical Black body was not free to touch non-Black bodies in friendly or intimate ways. Another useful bodily and nonverbal means of communication that serves Pather's choreography is from the field of "kinesis" that includes gestures, facial expressions, eye contact, and body language that convey emotions without physical touch. In the Indian classical dance vocabulary, *abhinaya* includes an extensive codification of the use of hand gestures, facial and eye expressions, and body stances to convey narratives and emotions (called *rasas*) ranging from love to fear, valor, and disgust.[10] And finally, in Pather's inclusion of "cellular memory" as part of his choreographic vocabulary, he conveys the universal physicality of human bodies (irrespective of race) that contain cells, and further that memories are caught inside these microscopic containers, of which humans have 30 to 40 trillion. Many die each day and are replaced. Even if the "offending" cells that hold memories of trauma die, that does not eliminate the human being's trauma, which lingers inside the body, mind, and psyche.

Pather gives expression to pain and trauma through his art; he has made "trauma accessible," to use Gabriele Schwab's phrase. Schwab's argument that "a form needs to be found that translates into language or symbolic expression an experience that is only unconsciously registered and left as a mere trace on the affective and corporeal levels" is realized in Pather's innovative performance forms. Schwab's assertion that "literature and the arts can become transformational objects in the sense that they endow this knowledge with a symbolic form of expression and thereby not only change its status but also make it indirectly accessible to others" is portrayed in Pather's choreographed works (2010, 8).

Schwab asks probing questions that evoke the haunting of violent pasts continuing into the present: "What happens when we build a grave within ourselves? While we can foreclose mourning by burying the dead in our psyche, those dead will return as ghosts. Violent histories have a haunting quality even before their legacy is passed on to the next generation. . . . How do we deal with a haunting past while simultaneously acting in the present, with its own ongoing violence?" (2010, 2).

Pather underlines his interest in the body itself, "its flesh, skin and muscle on which to write meanings beyond the linguistic," in his post-2000 works that he describes not as dance-theater but as "performance." This is rooted in his artistic trajectory; he remarks, "Over time, dance itself ceased to interest me on its own, and it became more important and interesting to work with texts, visual arts, and music" (interview 5, 2015). Such multidisciplinary forms used in unique spaces engage Pather's representation of sociopolitical issues.

THE TRUTH AND RECONCILIATION COMMISSION (TRC): MEMORY, VIOLENCE, AND THE LINGERING HURT OF APARTHEID

Pather's choreography, guided by his spatial and aesthetic-political vision, has been concerned with persisting violence after the hard-won independence in 1994. Although proposed as a hopeful "truth commission," South Africa's TRC left many oozing apartheid-era wounds. The TRC did accomplish some goals of hearing confessions aimed at peacemaking with families of those killed or tortured; however, it remains controversial for victims of violence who need to undergo a more complex process of healing that would take longer than a single hearing. Further, and problematically, forcing closure on still festering injuries represses violence and leads to dark consequences when delayed and suppressed violent energy, which continues to throb just under the surface, reemerges.

Here, it is worth recalling Frantz Fanon's prophetic vision in *The Wretched of the Earth*, in which his foundational analysis of colonization, similar to apartheid-style controls, posits that since these are violent phenomena, dominated peoples' responses must involve violence to come to terms with unjust realities. Fanon explains, "The violence which governed the ordering of the colonial world which tirelessly punctuated the distinction of the indigenous social fabric and demolished unchecked the systems of reference of the country's economy, lifestyles, and modes of dress, this same violence will be vindicated and appropriated when, taking history into their own hands, the colonized swarm into the forbidden cities" (1963, 2004, 6). If violent responses by the colonized are repressed or closures are forced, often by charismatic leaders such as Mandela and Tutu (architects of the TRC) or Gandhi, who upheld nonviolence, the colonized people continue to be haunted by memories of violence, and their lingering wounds can erupt without warning long after political independence.[11]

Pather agrees with Nigerian Nobel laureate Wole Soyinka's skepticism of the long-term impact of the TRC, in particular its lack of adequate monetary compensation for victims, as discussed in Soyinka's text *The Burden of Memory, The Muse of Forgiveness*. While Soyinka recognizes the ethical value of the TRC, he questions if truth alone can set one free: "Truth as prelude to reconciliation, that seems logical enough; but Truth as the justification, as the sole exaction or condition for Reconciliation? That is what constitutes a stumbling block in the South African proceedings" (1999, 77). Soyinka recognizes that memory, as preserved by the ancestral griots (who remember a community's history) and by modern-day poets and expressive and visual artists, can imaginatively assist healing for those seeking reparations for past wrongs, though closure may not always be possible. Soyinka continues, "Memory obviously rejects amnesia, but it remains amenable to closure that is, apparently, the ultimate goal of social strategies such as Truth and Reconciliation . . . seek[ing] the cathartic bliss, the healing that comes with closure" (80).

Pather, like Soyinka, is not seeking what Soyinka describes as "the cathartic bliss, the healing that comes with closure." Rather, Pather is keenly aware of the lingering hurt of apartheid post-1994, which continues in the face of devastating poverty that was hardly addressed by a truth commission focused on moral healing. Hence, in 2008, over a decade after the TRC, Pather's work *Body of Evidence* "appears to question the unfinished business of the Truth and Reconciliation Commission," comments Niren Tolsi, "highlighting the 'lines of continuity' that exist between violent action in 1976 and in 2008. He [Pather] seeks to understand how brutalised psyches, ignored in the post-1994 drive towards rainbow nationalism, carry the scars of violence" (2008). Pather's open-ended dance-theater works, rather than seeking closure for past wrongs, aim a critical lens at the reasons, often economic, for continuing violence.

In a path-breaking book, *Performing South Africa's Truth Commission: Stages of Transition*, theater scholar Catherine M. Cole explores how theater and performance have been used "within the nascent field of transitional justice. . . . [The latter] is an 'invented tradition' of the late twentieth century. Devised as a way to cope with the aftermath of systematic and large-scale violations of human rights, transitional justice has achieved its most notable impact via truth commissions" (Cole 2010, x). Prior to the TRC there had been sixteen truth commissions in the world, including what Cole describes as Slobodan Milosevic's "theatrics before the International Criminal Tribunal for the former Yugoslavia in 2002" (Cole 2010, x), a commission regarding atrocities in Argentina, and later the same in Rwanda. The South African TRC was different because the voices of ordinary victims and perpetrators entered "the public record. An extraordinary feat both in South African history and in African history in general" (Cole 2010, xii). Spectators from the general public gathered in the modest spaces of community halls and churches to hear the proceedings, which were broadcast on radio and TV for nearly two years, from 1996 to 1998. Cole is attentive to both the "time-based public enactments and the archives, repertoires, and memories they leave behind" (xiii). Such "embodied enactments before an audience," comments Cole, "embrace performance" (xii). However, Cole acknowledges that her textual "representation lacks the kinetic, sonic, and visual registers of embodied communication that made the TRC so distinctive" (xxi). Nonetheless, Cole is an excellent scholarly "interlocutor" in debates on the TRC.

The violence that continued after the "end" of apartheid—a system that lasted in its most brutal form for thirty-four years—belies the initial rhetoric about "the rainbow nation" and the unity of a diverse population with vast differences. Cole recognizes both the benefits of giving ordinary people a voice along with the drawbacks of the TRC, especially in persistent violence.

Cole does not glorify what the TRC attempted to accomplish in terms of its cathartic goals but asserts "that the commission was a performance ... a public enactment. The TRC's public hearings constitute what Diana Taylor might call its 'repertoire'—the performed, embodied expressions of the endeavor that stand in contrast to the many traces the TRC left behind in transcripts, photographs, videotapes, and audio recordings in the archive" (Cole 2010, xvi). It is ironic, as Cole points out, that the TRC archive is largely inaccessible to scholars. The Department of Justice owns the materials while the National Archives and Records Service in Pretoria is the "custodian of the collection" (xviii).

A remarkable aesthetic work by South African composer and sound artist Philip Miller, *REwind: A Cantata for Voice, Tape and Testimony* (2007), is a poignant representation of personal testimony that also raises questions at the heart of the TRC— namely, whether recounting personal memories of violations and human rights abuses is indeed cathartic. *REwind* plays and replays the tape of a TRC session, since a mother begs to have the tape repeated over and over again, as if to confirm the awful finality of her son being brutally killed by security personnel. The mother's plight is illuminated in Schwab's profound analysis of such trauma that is "experienced after catastrophic losses, such as the violent death of a loved one [that] annihilates a shared sense of time and forecloses proper mourning ... one remains forever tied to a loss that never comes real.... Where there is no grave, one cannot mourn properly" (2010, 3). Pather, like other artists, made dance theater works (discussed below) that reflected and critiqued the TRC, when horrendous acts were spoken about with expectations of healing and reconciliation. The negative fallouts of such goals have provoked different artistic responses to this type of truth inquiry, such as a play entitled *Truth in Translation* (especially relevant for Pather's *Forked Tongues*) that was staged in Kigali, Rwanda, in 2006, on the tenth anniversary of the TRC, and the *Truth in Translation Project*.[12] Apartheid's dark history is replete with state authorities allowed to intervene with weapons against protesters without arms.[13]

"RE-MOVING APARTHEID" TRAUMA: SEEKING NEW STRATEGIES

Since the massive physical and psychic damage apartheid caused continues for the majority of South Africans, there is a need for new ideas and social action that is different from the street protests common in the 1980s. Worldwide rallies against apartheid and for Mandela's release came with demands that Western governments, corporations, and universities divest from the apartheid regime. Indeed, new ideas include a new spatial imagining as reflected in the evocative conference title Re-moving Apartheid. Over twenty years after apartheid officially ended, what innovative strategies can creative artists discover to continue their struggle for justice and equality in South Africa? In that vein, the conference was held at the University of Ghent in Belgium, September 28–30, 2016, with Pather as one of the keynote speakers. The conference examined both "the 'eventfulness' of trauma" as well as its lingering aftereffects of "quotidian violence inflicted on humans."[14] Such trauma includes the nearly half century of apartheid-inflicted pain that endures for many in post-apartheid society. This timely conference described "non-eventful forms of trauma such as apartheid and racism, sexism, political oppression, colonialism and the daily fear of persecution." In 2016, the hard-won twenty-two-year South African democracy faced enormous challenges: high unemployment for Black people; their inability to earn a living wage even when employed; and the lack of affordable, decent housing and education. Such social problems are violent realities in themselves, often eliciting rage and harmful actions. In "Shifting Spaces, Tilting Time," Pather quotes Ranjit Hoskote's analysis of international economies and cultural productions that succeed by imposing oppressive local structures that "sharpen economic asymmetries that already exist and produce new cultural discontinuities; it generates social conflicts and political uncertainties, all of which factors develop into a general crisis of stability" (Pather 2013b, 434).

By 2016, Nelson Mandela, the father of the nation and an inspiring leader in the struggle for independence, had died (December 5, 2013).[15] Even in 2016, race remained a major factor in an individual's success in South Africa, along with vastly unequal social opportunities. The numbers are sobering: 39 percent unemployment among Black people compared to 8.3 percent among Whites, along with a lower quality of education and life expectancy for a Black child born in an urban township or rural area versus in a White suburb.[16] Although Black people comprise nearly 80 percent of the population, Whites 8.4 percent, Coloreds 8.4 percent, and Indians/Asians 2.6 percent, the majority Blacks endure the harshest poverty. Land is disproportionately owned by Whites. Income inequality is rife.

"Re-moving apartheid" indicates the need, once again, to deal with "cultural trauma [that is] not easily removed . . . and that keeps on moving a person in a way that outwits common sense." The concept of "re-moving" evokes both spatial and temporal dimensions—which physical location and what span of time does a cultural trauma survivor face, and how can these be overcome? The politics of emotion help to break through the paralysis of trauma by "moving" memories of pain from the deepest recesses of the psyche into the open, where the sores may heal. As historian Berber Bevernage puts it, the notion of a "persisting 'past' . . . blurs the strict delineation between past and present and thereby even questions the existence of these temporal dimensions as separate entities" (2012, 5). The act of re-moving apartheid encourages traumatized individuals to face their demons head-on without averting the resultant suffering on rational and emotional levels. In such endeavors, art plays "a transformative role . . . in creating non-verbal and embodied transformative encounters in violated and traumatized communities and it can provide a critical perspective on the restrictive Western memory regime at work in several practices of healing and reconciliation."[17]

This is reminiscent of Wole Soyinka's theory of Yoruba tragedy. He posits that in the course of a tragic drama, a protagonist is caught in a conflict that draws the individual into what he calls "the transitional gulf" or "the metaphysical abyss." In this space, the protagonist moves beyond recognizable realms of time—past, present, future—and enters "the fourth stage," wherein the protagonist is at the edge of human consciousness; this is a sort of near-death experience from which he may return to the world of the living with new knowledge, or he may succumb to his suffering and die. The challenge in Soyinka's theory is for the protagonist to stay alive in order to bring transformational insights to the community (Katrak 1986, 19–20; Soyinka [1976] 2006, 140–60).[18] In today's South Africa, many Black people face the kind of suffering seen in "the transitional gulf," experienced in daily denials of humanity that defy description, and do indeed border on the tragic.

The organizers of the Re-moving Apartheid conference critiqued TRC hearings in which "telling one's story" was regarded, in itself, as healing and liberating. Rather, the narrative simply contained and controlled the affective realms. The wounds were not healed, and, as Thompson notes, "the realities of suffering 'are often prevented from being given their embodied character'" (2009, 128–29). Temporality and the passing of time involves further common misconceptions about dealing with trauma. There is faith in the human ability to conquer the painful past in order to move on with life in the present. This belief is "grounded in a modernist historical regime . . . and modernity's linear conceptualization of time and its belief that the past lies behind us."[19] Rather, the conference aimed "to adopt Jacques Derrida's spectral notion of time in the work of mourning. With his notion of the 'spectral past,' Derrida deconstructed the archeo-teleological concept of history and the linear and chronological alignment of narration with time and space. He pointed at 'the persistence of a present past or the return of the dead which the worldwide work of mourning cannot get rid of'" (Derrida 1994, 101). When past traumas are not healed, they persist harmfully in individual psyches as well as in social and national memories in the present.

The concept of time in traditional African societies' belief systems that the past, present, and future proceed in not a linear but a cyclical manner indicates that present time contains past events via human memory, particularly in recalling traumatic events that were recounted in TRC hearings. Deaths of youth via state violence is tragic. However, the hopeful aspect of a cyclical worldview does not consider death, mainly the passing of an elder of natural causes, as tragic; instead it is celebrated, since the elder has joined the ancestors. In sacred death rituals such as the *egungun* among the Yoruba, ancestors are brought back to the living family via elaborate dramatic enactments of how a dead father or grandmother walked or talked. The dead are embodied by the living performers trained in the sacred practice of the masked *egungun* figure, whose body is covered completely in colored cloth.[20] The cohesiveness of a ritual world order is difficult to realize in the face of the continuing violence of hunger and poverty for the majority in South Africa. Nonetheless, Pather collaborates and consults with his dancers in using the Zulu tradition of *sangoma* healing in his performances, such as in *A South African Siddhartha* (chap. 1) and in *Qaphela Caesar* (chap. 4).

Pather's response to and critique of the TRC is expressed in several dance-theater works such as *Testimonies* (1997); this critique deepens in *Laws of Recall* (2000), which delves into the difficulties of remembering and the extreme unreliability of memory. Six years after democracy, *Laws of Recall* is a powerful indictment of the government conveniently "forgetting" its pledges and failing in its responsibility to improve the Black majority's basic necessities. Who remembers and who is heard in this post-apartheid era?

Pather was as concerned with deconstructing *simunye* (a slogan asserting unity among all South Africans) and fusion as he was with domestic violence that reached epidemic proportions, as he represented in *Unclenching the Fist* (1992 and later productions). Further, for progressive artists like Pather, it was deeply important to engage critically with valorized nationalist, *simunye* slogans as though independence had wiped clean the deep divisions of race, class, gender, and sexuality that persist in society, as portrayed in Pather's *Forked Tongues* (1999). Pather's skepticism about *simunye* is similar to his playful yet serious take on the much-touted "fusion" in dance forms in South African dance-theater that he represents in *Shifting Spaces, Tilting Time* (1998).

TESTIMONIES (1997): CRITIQUING THE TRC

Pather's *Testimonies*, evoking the dark fallout of the TRC, is significant as his first work as artistic director, performed at the launch of Siwela Sonke Dance Theatre Company. A twenty-minute work with two actors (Thulani Ndlovu and Shanitha Jugmohan), and two dancers (Simphiwe Magazi and Claire Beruidenbout) performed in Durban at the Loft Theater, *Testimonies* raised the specter of "forgiveness" and "truth," questioning if there are other alternatives to dealing with apartheid-era hurts.[21]

The voice-over, by Indian performer Shanitha Jugmohan, intones as if giving testimony at one of the TRC hearings: "At two o'clock, they came to take my son and arrested him. I could see him only after two weeks." Although this work presented Black, White, and Indian performers, Pather remarked (Interview 1, 2018) that the spirit of the work was misunderstood, as though it were spotlighting a Black and White issue, whereas he focused on the force of justice rather than only on race. The men of Siwela Sonke danced "in a cold way," remarked Pather in the same interview, evoking "an atmosphere of hate, mutual suspicion, and a vicious cycle" of trying to get "understanding and forgiveness." The voice-over repeats incessantly and tragically, "How did my son die? Who were his torturers?" The speaker notes that she "has suffered for nineteen years." The ideal of justice through forgiveness via the TRC remains "idyllic" rather than a reality for those who have lost loved ones.

Pather's critique of the TRC goes deeper in *Laws of Recall* (2000), winner of the FNB Vita Grant, performed at JOMBA! Contemporary Dance Festival in Durban and at the Dans en Creations/Sanga 2 Festival in Madagascar, where Pather was selected as one of ten African choreographers to present work. This dance-theater work delves into the difficulties of remembering and the unreliability of memory. This twenty-minute work with five dancers does not directly portray the TRC, as Pather noted; however, he wanted to convey his anger "at the lack of responsibility of the government to black people" in 1994 (interview 1, 2018). By 2000, whatever had happened in the aftermath of independence appeared to be "forgotten" and swept under the rug. Pather's characteristically subtle and evocative style ironically depicts the female protagonist, played by Ntombi Gasa, as one of the few who actually remembers very well, but she is in a mental institution suffering from schizophrenia and psychological disturbances. Pather explains that "Eric Shabalala, ostensibly her 'husband' but doubling as benefactor" to please her temporarily with cheap material goods, visits her, carrying two white plastic bags, adding texture to the choreographic presentation. "He [Shabalala] presents a swanky figure, tap dancing in his white shoes, wearing a white suit, hat, and sunglasses" (phone conversation, May 25, 2020).

Pather's essay "Negotiating the Postcolonial Black Body as a Site of Paradox," analyzes the body that deals with "a constant ebb and flow of recovery and catastrophe" (2017a). In *Laws of Recall*, Gasa is placed spatially inside a mental institution because of her unstable state. It is unlikely that this antiseptic space could offer healing and repair her strained mind. Despite this, Pather was not making a direct connection between psychic breakdowns and the ways in which the TRC "was putting people in a terrible position, [forcing them] to be nice about horrific things" (interview 3, 2017). However, "things in her [Gasa's] head" about people being sacrificed and having to line up for basic food items reflect her trauma.

Trauma theories that originate in psychoanalytic studies of repressed memories and amnesia caused by horrific events such as genocide, post-traumatic stress emanating from wars, sexual violence against women, and rape as a weapon during political conflict illuminate Pather's choreographic translation of mental trauma suffered by ordinary people in the post-apartheid era in *Laws of Recall*. Gabriele Schwab's influential book *Haunting Legacies: Violent Histories and Transgenerational Trauma* covers a wide scope of traumatic events from slavery to genocide to apartheid violence that Schwab argues "have lives far beyond the horrific moment. They engender trauma that echoes for generations, in the experiences of those on both sides of the act" (2010, 3). The spectators of *Laws of Recall* recognize that Gasa suffers from troubling memories that continue to haunt her. In *Critical Trauma Studies: Understanding Violence, Conflict and Memory in Everyday Life*, editors Monica Casper and Eric Wertheimer (2016) recognize that academics who study trauma, and those who experience it, as well as choreographers like Pather who portray trauma as embodied in their performer-dancers "inform one another." Trauma such as Gasa's in *Laws of Recall* is both neurological and expressive, related to "things in her head."

Factors of race, gender, and sexuality inform the intensity of responses to traumatic events. "The fact that trauma has been a highly racialized and sexualized concept," argues Maurice Stevens, is "dependent on visual metaphors for its description and models of spectacular for its rendering." The "dilemma" in understanding trauma is that it is "both specific and enigmatic, both discursive and material" (2009, 3).

Pather is highly adept at finding the most appropriate musical scores for his choreographies. In *Laws of Recall*, he depicts the disassociation of traumatic memories by opening the piece with the grand, overblown music of Mozart's *Requiem*, which effectively undercuts the pedestrian lives of the Black performers. Three young men—"messianic figures," notes Pather—enter and dance to Mozart, which reflects "the heightened, epic thing in Gasa's head" (interview 1, 2018). Pather described to me that the male lead, Eric Shabalala dances with tinned fish cans, in the two gleaming white plastic bags, with movement choreographed in contemporary and tap dance styles, and set to Mozart's powerful orchestration.

Pather's vision here is dark in his portrayal of a Satan figure as "the holy spirit," whose "godliness" could not fathom the "truth" of apartheid violence. Only Satan's original form as "a fallen angel" can grasp the "truth." He is a very charming character, not sanctimonious, notes Pather, but a rather seductive street person. Along with his two sidekicks, he dances and connects with the female protagonist. They seem fascinated with who she is, and they recognize that she is "not insane," as she is branded by the mental hospital. They help Gasa to probe levels of continuity in her own memories. They strap the male protagonist upside down, as if in a duel with his wife, who escapes with the "errant character," conveying that there is no possibility of getting to the "truth" (much desired by the TRC). The best route is to escape, even as her dance indicates her vacillation within her strained psychic condition, which remembers the hurt, and her "over-reactions," comments Pather, "are very affecting" for the audience. Gasa, with her traumatic memories, feels lost about the best course of action: will she be able to come to terms with what lies behind her trauma, or will she continue to find escape routes and somehow survive with the painful memories? (interview 1, 2018).

UNCLENCHING THE FIST (1992, 1993, 1997): THE DISEASE OF DOMESTIC VIOLENCE

Pather choreographed and directed a hard-hitting dance-theater work entitled *Unclenching the Fist* in 1992, a severe dissection of the social disease of domestic violence, primarily perpetrated against women. The initial production was commissioned as part of CAPAB (Cape Town Performing Arts Board, now Artscape), a space offered to Jazzart Dance Theatre in Cape Town, where Pather was the resident choreographer. The piece was also performed at the National Festival of the Arts in Grahamstown and at Nico Malan Theatre, Cape Town. In 1993, this same work was restaged by Jazzart Dance Theatre as *Unclenching the Fist II* and in 1997 at the Women's Arts Festival at the Playhouse Theatre, Durban.

Pather remarked that while at Jazzart in 1992, he was caught up in working with jazz and rock musicians that gave "a different kind of edge" to *Unclenching the Fist* than in later versions (Interview 1, 2018). In the first version, Pather was struck, as he notes in his essay "Laws of Recall," by forensic scientist Leonard Lehrer's research in investigating dead bodies. Pather conceived *Unclenching the Fist* "in collaboration" with Dr. Lehrer, whose "findings of a culture of violence that turns in on itself... formed the basis of the production include[ing] the conclusion that, for every one killing motivated by political violence in the early nineties in the Eastern Cape, there were seven deaths of women who were killed by someone they knew. The forensic research traced uses of blunt instrument injury to ascertain proximity and familiarity in the execution of this growing kind of violence in South Africa" (Pather 2015b, 334).

These startling statistics spurred Pather to choreograph *Unclenching the Fist* with the goal of drawing attention to domestic violence against women, especially because society was caught up only in matters of political violence. As in most struggles for social change, women's issues—including violence against them—are considered secondary. Pather recalled Frantz Fanon's analysis of the native male coveting the master's position, and when he is unable to achieve that, his frustration is exerted on the females closest to him. Pather confirmed my interpretation that *Unclenching the Fist* is a precursor to *Body of Evidence*, which continues an exploration of violence and memories of physical and mental traumas that are held in the interstices of the human body (interview 6, 2016).

The first version of *Unclenching the Fist* with Jazzart, noted Pather, involved a very long process with particular kinds of ritual and performance practices, which enabled the dancers to get close to this difficult reality. Pather noted that this "first version was closer to the issue" of domestic violence whereas the second version, which he created after he left Jazzart and became artistic director of SSDT in Durban, was "closer to the audience" (interview 6, 2016). He changed the choreography, translating it to a production during which the audience can get close to the narrative. He included different women's voices, talking, shrieking, and, "intentionally," he added in the same interview, "bordering on the didactic," with the presence of an advice desk for abused women handing out pamphlets about where to get help. He recalled that the production had an impact in Durban on the number of calls received by the advice desk when it toured around the city.

The piece, although dealing with a serious subject, balances light and dark. For Pather, it was not simply encapsulated in going from humor to a dark topic but rather to get the audience "to feel relaxed so that they could accept the more serious issues" (interview 1, 2018). This same impulse guided Pather to include *pantsula* in a club setting where people were enjoying themselves, and the audience was entertained even as he was "creating a space to really understand the devastation" of violence against women. As the lighthearted scene was winding down and the women were leaving the club, Neliswa Rushualang (a veteran Siwela Sonke dancer), by then feeling quite "upbeat," "tries to get home [when] she is raped by four men" (interview 1, 2018).

In *Unclenching the Fist* (1997) at the Playhouse Theatre in Durban, Pather included some of TRC's public hearings based on personal, real-life stories to "paint a dire and daunting picture of ... pain endured," as noted by reviewer David Coleman, who found "more trauma than drama" in this production (1997). The women undergo a range of violence, continues Coleman, from sexual harassment to rape, that is "defined as invariably being a predetermined assertion of male power." Pather, according to Coleman, was "testing his eight dancers to their physical and emotional limits (1997). The dancers included Ntombi Gasa, Neliswa Rushualang, Angela Lardant, Claire Beruidenbout, and Pravika Nandakishore. The audience was reminded that even as it watched this forty-minute work "16 women were being raped country-wide." It was possible to engage with the seriousness of this subject even as, provocatively, the women harassed the male dancers.

The dance styles included Indian classical style kathak (by Pravika Nandakishore) "to a mix of tap, traditional tribal [*sic*] and, of course gumboot ... performed on a bare stage to recorded music, live drumming, and vocals" (Coleman 1997). Reviewer Suzy Bell notes that Pather is "in tune" with various dance styles such as "the blistering street rhythms of *pantsula*, *kwaito cool*, and gumboot, the liquidity of poetic dance with its snake-like rattle of ankle bells, or the classical lines of ballet" (Bell 1998). He layers indigenous dance forms—*indlamu*, gumboot, and *isicathamiya* as well as bharatanatyam and kathak—with contemporary dance, gangsta rap, and street poetry. On opening night, Professor Anshu Padayachee, along with Playhouse Theatre's director of dance Lynn Maree, invited the audience to stay for a discussion with the dancers. Pather's aim was to take the production from the Playhouse Theatre (August 20–24, 1997) to factories, prisons, and centers for abused women with a counselor who would be available to answer any questions.

Reviewer Suzy Bell writes passionately about violence against women in her article "Taking a Stand" (August 14–20, 1998). Bell recognizes that abused women are "emotionally, physically and psychologically abused by their husbands, lovers, bosses, friends, or neighbours. They're the victims of rape—that meditated physically violent act of power and control. With stats that record the horror of 2160 women being raped a day in this blighted yet beautiful country of ours, it's high time that someone as street-sussed as Jay Pather, the widely acclaimed and visionary artistic director of Siwela Sonke Dance Theatre, offered us the highly emotive, compelling dance theatre piece that is *Unclenching the Fist*" (1998).

Pather does not stop with simply retelling real-life stories via dance, song, and personal memories; this piece raises significant questions as well as options for social change. As reviewer Siza Ngqwebo comments in "Placing Women's Abuse Centre Stage" (*Sowetan*, July 31, 1997, 35), "This dance theatre is an exceptional work" that is also, as Pather notes to Ngqwebo "about empowering women firstly, by doing away with a social disease that has been, for a long time kept behind closed doors and hampered a healthy family life." Bell also appreciates that Pather not only takes on this troubling domestic violence issue but also inspires hope in empowering women against this evil. "Pather knows exactly how to weave the light with the dark in dance theatre" remarks Bell. "It's not all heart-sinking dance. There is cheek and char, and even laughter within this serious social sub-text" (1998).

Bell also recognizes the key work of Gitanjali Pather, director of the Women's Arts Festival, who secured the necessary sponsorship to make the festival a reality. "At this festival," remarks Bell, "*Unclenching the Fist* was received by a damn fine, ululating audience. Among them were 30 Sisekelo High School pupils all the way from Swaziland."[22]

At this stage of the evolution of his spatial politics, expressed via his aesthetic-political vision, Pather chooses in *Unclenching the Fist* to be overtly didactic in revealing the horror of domestic abuse along with an agenda to empower women and provide help via counselors available to speak to victims. By 2008, nearly a decade later, when he creates the performance (beyond dance-theater) *Body of Evidence*, which also deals with violence held inside the body's bones and muscles, he does so through symbols, interrupted narratives, and video projections (chap. 4).

FORKED TONGUES (1999): PATHER'S PLAYFUL YET SERIOUS TAKE ON SIMUNYE

Forked Tongues, commissioned for the second JOMBA! Contemporary Dance Festival, featuring Thulaboni Mzizi and Claire Bezuidenhourt, "questions notions of 'authentic' South African identity" (Loots 1999). Pather used "intercultural elements in a parodic way. It was a satiric take, and it was challenging *simunye*" (interview 3, 2017). Pather also indicated that the word *forked* in the title, in addition to evoking the notion of colonial lies, evokes a fork in the road and the choices before the newly independent country. The word *tongues* in the title evoked the challenges faced by people divided across different languages, along with their dual or multiple ethnic identities and other allegiances. Pather also mixed in popular songs like "Speaking in Tongues" by Sheila Chandra, the kind of music that was "breaking new ground in the mid-1990s," along with Indian classical dance syllables (interview 3, 2017). Such interventions, he continues in the same interview, "indicated the levels" at which he was "approaching Indianness," that included his use of Indian dance syllables, and rhythms, turning them into music. "Both sound and music were important," he adds. He observes that even contemporary artists like

Alfred Hinkel "were dismissive" of this work. Nevertheless, for Pather, *Forked Tongues* was "an emotional piece, breaking new ground" in his lighthearted yet critical approach to slogans of *simunye* in the rainbow nation.

Forked Tongues, with eight dancers, begins with the title music "Chariots of Fire." Claire Bezuidenhourt, the female lead, dressed as an Afrikaaner commander, drags in, in slow motion, a traditional rickshaw, often seen drawn by Black men in Zulu regalia transporting tourists on the Durban beachfront; she stops. The tables are turned in terms of who holds power in this scenario when a Black male in a pinstriped suit steps out of the rickshaw and pulls out a ringing cell phone that is heard by the audience through the sound system. The offending cell phone is in his fly! He takes it out and dances to Indian music on top of a table with the spoken syllables (such as *ta dhin dhin na*) of the *taal* (rhythm) section. Four other men in Black pinstriped suits also have cell phones hanging out of their trouser flies.

In the next section, two female dancers, Neliswa Rushualang and Pravika Nandakishore, enter and listen to the popular song "Speaking in Tongues." Each section of *Forked Tongues*, notes Pather, "is about languages coming together [and people] trying to understand each other" (interview 3, 2017). The duet conveys people trying to communicate despite differences. It is clear that there is no single or simple way to unite and dance together. At the very end, Louis Armstrong's song "What a Wonderful World" comes across as a satiric pastiche with different layers and languages, an ironic soundtrack to a space in which people can hardly fathom one another, all conveyed in the atmosphere of an overblown Hollywood sound blast.

Along with a light tone, Pather showcases the hollowness of unity slogans in the new five-year-old nation. His perspicacity in seeing through such glib words as *simunye* is remarkable. He also asks serious questions such as, what would such an idealized unity really mean? How could the racial divisions, so entrenched in the very sinews of apartheid, be dismantled? Would that kind of enterprise, of undoing racial exclusions, need much more serious interventions into diverse communities than can be accomplished by *simunye* slogans? Would White people still in power, as played by an Afrikaaner commander in *Forked Tongues*, be willing to embrace a Black male and help undo the scars of racial hatred? Although he is dressed in a suit, his nervous state is conveyed by the incongruity of a cell phone ringing from inside his fly as though displaying his sexuality for both entertainment and censure, since cell phones have to be turned off inside a theater. Ultimately, "we are one" only pays lip service to a future that is deeply desired but that remains unreachable. Pather concretizes these disillusioning realities by choreographing different dance styles working at cross purposes; he deliberately does not let the dance styles unfold harmoniously. Similarly, the reality of eleven South African languages recognized by the Constitution poses huge challenges in communication. Language and power are integrally linked, especially in postcolonial nations that still labor under the hegemony of English as the language providing access to employment and other opportunities in life.[23]

SHIFTING SPACES, TILTING TIME (1998): INTERDISCIPLINARITY IN PATHER'S PLAY ON "FUSION"

Winner of the First National Bank Vita Award for Best Choreography, *Shifting Spaces, Tilting Time* is the first of Pather's choreographies in which he places the human body spatially in relationship to architecture, via photographs of Durban buildings projected as a backdrop with the dancers' shadows visible on the structures. Pather's interest in exploring connections between bodies and buildings moves further in what I interpret as an organic development only two years after *Shifting Spaces, Tilting Time*, when, in his 2000 site-specific work *Cityscapes*, he places dancers in front of actual Durban buildings, inside a coffee shop, and on the beachfront. In *Shifting Spaces, Tilting Time,* only the dancers' shadows appear on the building photographs, as if they are about to step outside.

Pather critiques fusion in *Shifting Spaces, Tilting Time,* as also in *Forked Tongues,* by juxtaposing different dance styles in superficial shows of the new rainbow nation. Although Pather brings together *pantsula* and a unique form of kathak by having Pravika Nandakishore dance with bandaged hands, taking away the beauty of the hand gestures, he is more interested in the "place of tension between forms rather than in fusion" (interview 3, 2017).

This twenty-minute work with nine dancers and one drummer, performed at the Playhouse Theatre in Durban and then for Dance Umbrella in Johannesburg, opens with a male dancer representing a bird or a spirit flying through different architectural buildings projected via black-and-white photographs on the backdrop, connecting the physical and spiritual worlds.[24] As the dancer is spotlit, creating a large shadow of his body on the buildings in the background, specks of light forming five circles appear on the stage floor. Blue and red lights animate the dancer's contemporary dance style. Movements and shadows are visible as he picks up a cape and runs with it around the stage, throwing it forward and back as the visual image of a building appears in the background.

The backdrop changes to five interlocked rings, the symbol of the Olympic Games, indicating five linked continents. The five rings in five colors—blue, yellow, black, green, and red—encompass the colors of the world's national flags. Pather plays subtly with the idea of "an Olympics of cultures," though even in these games, the goal of unifying disparate cultures remains an ideal (interview 1, 2018).

In *Shifting Spaces, Tilting Time,* eight rings (disrupting the Olympic five-ring symbol) descend from the top of the performance space to circle the faces of the dancers, who stand in a straight row, their bodies, except their faces and feet, covered by a long horizontal fabric. Their foot patterns mark different dance styles such as tap, kathak, and other stamping rhythms, and the genres seem to be conversing. The ballet dancer looks upset at all the competing styles, and with an aggressive arabesque dislodges the cloth. Pather, subtly and humorously, critiques *simunye* style unity. As the male dancer embodying a bird spirit returns, the women—impressed with him—giggle. He disrupts the straight line of the cloth around the dancers, who want to stay in their separate spaces with their own dance styles. As the cloth falls to the ground, the dancers feel exposed. The rings, now "headless," float up and down over the dancers' heads.

Live drumming begins as the dancers are huddled in a diagonal line. The male dances a contemporary solo as photographs of run-down homes in townships appear in the background. Four dancers enter as a photograph of a barbed wire fence is projected. Couples dance to jazz music and live drumming while background images include a skyscraper reaching for the sky, whereas a contrasting movement is executed by kathak dancer Nandakishore's fast *chakars,* which are very grounded to the earth.

The projected photographs transport spectators through Durban. A church spire is etched into the skyline in front of a sign that has long fascinated Pather: "Welcome to Durban, Where the Fun Never Sets." Some dancers perform *isicathimaya*; others dance ballet. Then the projected image shows a rural part of KwaZulu Natal along with an anachronistic Coca-Cola sign on a long pole. One ballet dancer's tutu, multicolored like a flag, evokes the "rainbow nation." But in this new South Africa, a classical ballerina *en pointe* becomes a metaphor for a democracy teetering precariously.

In the next segment, a male dancer wearing a hard hat and goggles enters on crutches. He has one boot missing and stamps his foot in synergy with the ballet dancer. A Black female dancer enters with his missing boot. She throws the ballerina to the floor while making traditional gestures invoking ancestors. She appears to lecture the man, telling him that he is a worker, but he is happy with any compromise. She trips him on his crutches, and as he falls, she waves the crutches around, trying to remind him of traditional dance. He is on the floor as she throws the crutches into the wings. The backdrop photograph shows the Madressa Arcade buildings where Pather noted that his grandfather had a watch repair shop (interview 1, 2018). The man, without his crutches, which were only a ploy to get sympathy, is able to dance as he remembers the traditional movements. The bird-spirit dancer reenters and dances a duet with the Black woman. The jaunty music of a popular song of the time, the "Mango Tango," plays, and the dancers move to its rhythm.

The background image shifts to a rural scene, with a McDonald's sign and a blind person with a stick. An Indian-styled Mughal-era architectural building with typical oval arches appears in the background, and as Nandakishore executes the chakars, her shadow falls over a dome on the building indicating a mosque. Ntombi Gasa takes the bandages off Pravika Nandakishore's hands that had prevented her from doing the mudras. The ballet dancer's pointe shoes are off, indicating, as Pather notes, "that we are getting closer to the truth" even as the struggle to communicate and to be together continues (interview 1, 2018).

Pather's remarks illuminate "what happened in this final moment [namely] that the image of the spirit dancer observes as he sits on a bridge overlooking trains coming in and out of Durban where many workers congregate as they get ready to go home. Looking into the camera, his face appears strong, with eyes reflecting the scene around him. The image is then done twice, four times and then the same image is repeated multiple times on the screen" (Pather email to Katrak, May 25, 2020). The image of several eyes projected on the backdrop indicate an effort to communicate visually rather than through verbal languages of which eleven, spoken by Black people, are recognized by the South African constitution. As the dancers take their final bows, there are colored circles in the background, indicating the tendency of people to retreat into their own "colors"—i.e., their race—and remain in their segregated enclaves, as during apartheid, and to not risk the challenge of stepping out of their circles and reaching across races and spaces, shifting old paradigms and "tilting time" to usher in a different era during post-apartheid.

Shifting Spaces, Tilting Time's highly effective structure is "fragmentary, even alliterative," remarks Pather, who, I contend, continues in future works to create choreographic vignettes that are nonlinear and elliptical. Space and time unfold "in a continuum in an emerging nation," he remarks, adding poignantly that "we never imagined that we would be as 'normal'" in terms of several races trying to communicate across barriers of language, class, and other differences so deeply entrenched by apartheid, which thrived on forced separations. However, nothing is predictable, remarks Pather, since "each moment is tilting and history comes flooding in" (interview 1, 2018).

Pather reflects (in conversation with Katrak) that the race situation in the United States, despite violent police killings of unarmed Black men, is different from the reality of White people's power pervading South Africa even in 2018. Hence, people still construct someone like Pather as "locked in a particular time" no matter how professional and successful he is as a professor at a university and even though his circumstances have shifted dramatically from his early youth during apartheid. At present, he is a renowned artist and academic who has presented work across the world; however, a recent incident that he narrated was deeply sobering. In Cape Town, after a show at the Baxter Theatre, while Pather was deep in conversation with a student, two middle-aged White women—as if doing him a favor, "bequeathing visibility" on him, as he remarked—stuck a cell phone in his face, telling him to "fix it." They saw Pather as locked in that past space and time when he could only be seen "as an Indian, as functional."

Such demeaning treatment wrenches into him almost viscerally. The notion of "the Indian boy" goes way back for Pather, as when that moment at the Baxter "tilted time" back to the memory of seeing his father, who, although an activist, behaved in a servile manner with White people.[25]

Pather also recalls from his childhood days that White people would cross the road when they noticed Indians on the street. The recent incident at the Baxter Theatre was "a tilting time moment" for Pather, who was asked to behave in a particular way, although an epoch had passed both in his own life and in South African society. The present time tilted to confront Pather with a past time when social hierarchies among races was legal in South Africa. He reflected further that the daily subjection of Black people to such treatment—expecting them to be subservient, obliterating them from visibility and decent treatment as full human beings—leads to psychotic and violent behavior that can erupt without warning. Pather thought back to his early days in New York City, when it was most refreshing for him to be treated as a New Yorker, even an "upstart New Yorker," as one of his artist colleagues who admired Pather noted. For Pather, that was a compliment, the kind he would not get in South Africa's fractured society even today.

This chapter has analyzed Pather's creative journey from actor and dancer in the 1980s to his award-winning work as a choreographer in the 1990s, and his artistic responses to the evolving history of his nation, both during apartheid and after. Pather's choreography, rooted in his politically progressive vision, critiques the TRC and fusion dance and openly rejects hollow *simunye* slogans that cannot erase the real racial and economic differences among South Africans.

From *Shifting Spaces, Tilting Time*, where photographs provide the setting of streets or rural environments, I follow Pather's spatial imagination in his site works of the 2000s, when he places his dancers on the streets themselves in *Cityscapes*, on the beachfront in Durban (off-limits for Black people during apartheid), or inside swanky shopping malls. His remarkable site-specific and site-responsive choreography germinates organically from his goals of access and social justice for all South Africans.

NOTES

1. See chapter 4 for a discussion of *Qaphela Caesar* and for details on Pather's reworked *Tempest in Africa*, shared at his keynote for the Global Shakespeare Symposium at the University of California, Irvine, January 18, 2018.
2. Shakespeare's play *The Tempest* has been adapted widely—for instance, Aime Cesaire's *Une Tempete* (1969). For details on other adaptations, see "The Tempest," Adaptations, November 15, 2013, https://davidgreetham.wordpress.com/2013/11/15/the-tempest/.
3. Dennis Brutus (1924–2009), an anti-apartheid activist, was imprisoned on Robben Island in a cell next to Mandela; both worked in the quarry cracking stones even as they kept resistance against injustice alive in their hearts.
4. Peter Hayes, born in 1966, died in 2013.
5. More information on the Hearts and Eyes Theatre Collective can be found at http://theatrecollectives.weebly.com/hearts--eyes.html, accessed July 13, 2016.
6. Hearts and Eyes Theatre Collective[0], http://theatrecollectives.weebly.com/hearts--eyes.html, accessed July 13, 2016.
7. Puppets appear in Pather's choreography for *The Firebird* (2016) when his dancers carried giant puppets made by Cape Town's Handspring Puppet Theater Company. This work is discussed in the conclusion.
8. The Hearts and Eyes Theater Collective's complete mission statement is at https://theatrecollectives.weebly.com/uploads/1/9/0/9/19098411/heartseyes_company_background.pdf.
9. The TRC operated for seven years, from 1995 to 2002. Its original mandate was for three years, 1995 to 1998, but was extended. See https://www.usip.org/publications/1995/12/truth-commission-south-africa accessed July 12, 2018.
10. The ancient Indian text of drama, dance, and dramaturgy, *The Natyasastra*, includes a chapter on the nine primary rasas (emotions), and other chapters on single- and two-hand gestures.

11. Gandhi is revered as the leader in India of the nonviolent struggle for independence from the British. Ironically however, the tragic reality that Fanon warned against, namely, repressed violence that erupts, was unleashed in the bloodbath at India's Partition from Pakistan at independence.

12. *Truth in Translation* includes stories of interpreters who undertook simultaneous translation of the stories of victims and perpetrators: "Everything flowed through them—lies and truths, forgiveness and rage, pain and celebration. They absorbed everything... without getting involved" (http://globalartscorps.org/home/truth-in-translation/, accessed July 15, 2018). It is significant to note that the men and women who translated testimonies also suffered trauma by listening to and transcribing stories of brutal human rights abuses. This theater piece evolved into the *Truth in Translation* project, which continued the work of the TRC in different nations and contexts including South Africa and Palestine, among others (http://www.truthintranslation.org, accessed July 15, 2018). See also South African playwright Yael Farber's (2008a) *Theatre as Witness: Three Testimonial Plays from South Africa*. In *Molora*, Farber (2008b) adapts Aeschylus's ancient Greek plays *The Oresteia Trilogy* in the South African TRC context.

13. Protesters against Pass Books that stated where an individual was allowed to live and work were shot in the back during the Sharpeville massacre on March 21, 1960. The Soweto student uprising on June 16, 1976, against Bantu education enforcing Afrikaans (a regional language) rather than English (with currency as a world language) as the medium of instruction, injured thousands, including killing young Hector Peterson.

14. "Re-moving Apartheid: Postdramatic and Postnarrative Modes of Coping with Trauma/Theme," https://www.re-movingapartheid.ugent.be/themes/, accessed September 29, 2016.

15. Winnie Mandela, Nelson Mandela's wife of thirty-eight years from 1958 to 1996, his partner in anti-apartheid struggles, the one who kept his name and memory alive during his twenty-seven-year prison sentence, died on Easter Sunday, April 2, 2018, a sad milestone in South African history. Winnie was revered by many as a stalwart freedom fighter and mother of the nation.

16. Statistics from *Businesstech South Africa*, https://businesstech.co.za/news/general/96887/white-vs-black-unemployment-in-south-africa, accessed December 2, 2016.

17. Re-moving Apartheid conference materials, "Re-moving Apartheid: Themes," https://www.re-movingapartheid.ugent.be/themes/, accessed January 12, 2017.

18. See my book *Wole Soyinka and Modern Tragedy: A Study of Dramatic Theory and Practice* for an analysis of Soyinka's theory of Yorba tragedy, in "The Fourth Stage." The latter is included in Soyinka, *Myth, Literature and the African World*.

19. "Re-moving Apartheid: Themes," https://www.re-movingapartheid.ugent.be/themes/.

20. In Wole Soyinka's play *Death and the King's Horseman*, the colonial officer and his wife desecrate the sacred *egungun* vestments by wearing them for a fancy-dress ball.

21. Pather made the 1997 original VHS copy of *Testimonies* available for my viewing, and since the video was damaged, he spent time with me (interview 1, 2018) explaining details of *Testimonies* as discussed here.

22. South African dancer-choreographer Mamela Nyamza's choreographed works that speak against domestic violence also educate the community where she grew up, in the township of Gugulethu on the outskirts of Cape Town.

23. See Ngũgĩ wa Thiong'o's influential books *Decolonizing the Mind: The Politics of Language in Africa* and *Globalectics: The Politics of Knowing*.

24. The image of a bird returns nearly eighteen years later, in 2016, when Pather choreographs *The Firebird* (discussed in the conclusion) to Stravinsky's music, with a giant firebird puppet on stage. This work was in collaboration with Janni Younge, director of *The Firebird*.

25. On reading this passage, Gabriele Schwab, my friend and colleague at the University of California, Irvine, noted Freud's interpretations of his dreams with his own dead father. Although different from Pather's memory of his father (who had passed away by 1999), it is instructive to find connections with Freud's dreams of his dead father that "constitute a set of related wishes and ambivalent unconscious thoughts," remarks Doug Davies, "in this case having to do with filial relations, paternal death, and railway travel." Freud notes that these "absurd" dreams deal "'by chance, as it may seem at first sight' with deceased fathers of the dreamer" such as "Freud's 1899 dream of being billed for hospital expenses someone has incurred in 1851 in his birthplace" (http://ww3.haverford.edu/psychology/ddavis/psych212h/fdream.1851.html, accessed July 25, 2018).

PART II

THE TRANSITIONAL AND THE IN-BETWEEN
*Theoretical and Creative Engagements with
Urban Geography (2000-2015)*

THREE

SITE-SPECIFIC CARTOGRAPHIES OF BELONGING

> My site-specific performances [also] stemmed from an interest in the essential connectedness of the moving body to the space within which it moved: the body as it is framed variously by the architecture of a building, the pavement or concrete concourse, a narrow, stony road of desolate recently bulldozed waste land rendering the human frame vulnerable under an open sky.
>
> Jay Pather, "Shifting Spaces, Tilting Time"

PATHER'S KEEN ATTENTIVENESS TO SITE and location emanates organically from racial divisions that he experienced growing up during apartheid, whose rigid color lines he challenged in his own biography and in his creative engagements and responses to South African politics. In owning his identity as Black, Pather recognizes the tensions inherent in contemporary South Africa's race-conscious society when he perceives certain people wondering about this and particularly during recent anti-Indian sentiments. However, for Pather, his identification as Black has remained consistent, indeed "as a through line" in his life and work (phone conversation, May 31, 2020). Pather's significant theorizing of space in several published essays illuminates the choreographic and conceptual processes underlying his site work that challenges racial and class exclusions and that discusses the reasons behind his selections of locations. As he notes in the epigraph, he places the human body in dialogue, literally and symbolically, with site and architecture. In public spaces, Pather is interested in cultivating new audiences who may simply "glance" at a performance and decide to stay or move on. Edward Casey's work on the primacy of a "glance" is useful here, as is his discussion of feeling "out of place" that I relate to Black people residing in "exilic" homes on city margins or in so-called homelands in hinterland areas.

In this chapter, I discuss Pather's urban site-specific works that are inventive, vibrant, even risky at times, and all geared to fulfilling the democratic goals of inclusiveness and interconnectedness of diverse South Africans. Before analyzing *Cityscapes* and *Blindspot*, I discuss Pather's theorizing of space that resonates with critical thinkers on geography and postcolonialism— Achille Mbembe and Sarah Nuttall (both based at the University of Witwatersrand) and with seminal theorists Henri Lefebvre, Edward Soja, Edward Casey, and Michel Foucault.

I demonstrate Pather's unique contributions to theories of space as in (1) his spatial concerns that include not only external locations but also the human body as a "site" in its physical, emotional, and psychological realities (as rooted in South Africa's sociopolitical environment), and also the "space of social practice" as articulated by Lefebvre. (2) Pather's major approaches to space include locations of daily life such as the marketplace, shopping malls, and parks, whose usual functions he delights in subverting. (3) He is skilled at playing with artistic/performative forms that relate to the function of a location and that connect, sometimes uncannily, to ritual roots of performance. This takes place in his site-specific work *Hotel*, in which an interracial couple inside a hotel room play out their anxiety and secrecy via contemporary dance, words, and human sounds; they are interrupted and perhaps alleviated by the sudden appearance of a nonspecific ancestral figure carrying a CD who "comes in like the wind, like an apparition on the winds of history and heritage" comments Pather (phone conversation, May 20, 2020). Pather also imagined this figure twirling a CD around his finger like the Hindu god Vishnu holding his discus. (4) Pather's various uses of space include an aesthetic engagement with, for example, a beautiful building or a seashore, or a deconstruction and undercutting of a site such as a city hall, with its security operations (especially during apartheid). (5) Pather's spatial politics evolve in response to shifting political times; here, his thinking is in sync with geographer Edward Soja's persuasive argument about the primacy of geography with history, of space with time, rather than the usual preference accorded in critical theory to history and time.

Spatial theories are part of contemporary times. Michel Foucault posits that the twentieth century (and we can add the twenty-first) is "an epoch of space." Such "an epoch of space" that is palpable via "simultaneity ... juxtaposition, the epoch of the near and far, of the side-by-side, of the dispersed" features as choreographed elements in Pather's site works (Foucault 1984, 1) Foucault contends further that "our experience of the world is less that of a long life developing through time than that of a network that connects points and intersects with its own skein" (1984, 1). The concept of "networks" that connect and even intersect places is more liberating than apartheid's tight space controls; the openendedness of networks also guides Pather's spatial politics.

Pather's contributions to the theorizing of space is unique, both abstract and grounded in his South African context, where the very definition of space as "a continuous area or expanse, which is free, available, or unoccupied," according to the Oxford English Dictionary, needs to be deconstructed. Historically, colonizers in South Africa, as elsewhere on the African continent and in other parts of the world, illegally occupied geographical areas that were regarded falsely as "empty." Often, colonizers appropriated the best land, dispossessing and displacing indigenous populations. In South Africa, lands belonging to the Khoi and the San peoples were taken away forcibly; land reclamation claims continue to haunt South African Black people even a century later.[1] Next, apartheid imposed another regime of colonial-style appropriation during Pather's upbringing in Durban, legislating that certain spaces, though "free and available," such as urban centers, were reserved for White people only, thus forbidding access to the Black population.

The condition of many South African Black people is illuminated in Edward Casey's recognition in his book *Getting Back into Place*, as he states that place is "at issue in the alienation and violence from which human beings have suffered so devastatingly in modern times." Further, Casey delineates that "the alienation is *from* [a given] place and the violence has been done *to* [some] place, and not only to people in places" (xiv, original emphasis).

The very notion of "empty space" that colonizers used to justify stealing land belonging to local peoples is connected significantly by Ngũgĩ wa Thiong'o, to a "performance site" that can never be "empty as in the title of Peter Brooks' book" (Ngũgĩ 1998, 435). Rather, Ngũgĩ analyzes different ways "of looking at performance space. One is to see it as a self-contained field of internal relations: the interplay between actors and props and light and shadows—the mise-en-scene—and between the mise-en-scene as a whole and the audience.... The entire space becomes a magnetic field of tensions and conflicts ... potentially explosive, or rather, poised to explode. That is why the repressive state has its nervous eyes on performance space" (Ngũgĩ 1998, 436). Ngũgĩ's personal experiences of cocreating a play, and building a modest theater in Kamiriithu with workers' and peasants' ingenuity and personal labor, were judged as "criminal." He was imprisoned by Kenya's neocolonial government. Pather's own site interventions, bold and risky, have not resulted in his personal voice being silenced. After all, during post-apartheid, the South African state is tolerant of creative ventures, even those critical of the government's failures. Pather's challenging of restricted access to

Black people in public arenas echoes Ngũgĩ wa Thiong'o's defiant argument that despite the state's brutal efforts to silence political prisoners like himself, their power did not extend into his imagination. From behind bars, Ngũgĩ wrote an entire novel on the only paper available to him: prison toilet paper, luckily thick and rough.[2]

THE TRANSITIONAL, THE IN BETWEEN, AND THE CROSSING OVER

Concepts of the transitional, the in between, and crossing over that have temporal and spatial dimensions are dynamic and productive in interpreting Pather's ideas on space. His deployment of built structures and architectural facades for site creations evokes transitional space, defined in architecture studies as bringing together a physical, concrete space and the human interactions in front of or inside it. Further, Pather's choreography deliberately "invades" iconic buildings that were forbidden to Black people during apartheid and creates performances inside and around concrete structures, archways, and plazas connecting an urban landscape. Often, clear-cut distinctions between indoor and outdoor areas blur in transitional spaces, such as in passageways and walkways via bridges linking buildings to parking structures or to open-air environments.

In contemporary times, urban spaces often are not welcoming for communities to spend time in; an office worker may transition from a work desk to a park, but this is not as common as attending to increasingly functional urban spaces, such as going to a city hall for permission to use a street for a performance. In the South African environment, with its legacy of controlled spaces, Black people may find themselves more in transitional, even liminal spaces such as railway stations that are in between one station and the next. Pather has immense faith in the human body's ability to "control meanings within what can potentially be alienating urban spaces" (Pather 2013b, 433). He argues that there is a productive synergy in his dance works between "spaces [that] shape the movement and gestural languages of people who in turn shape those spaces, how they are used or even whether they are used at all" (433).

Pather's critical theorizing on space contributes to debates on the transitional. The notion of transition is used commonly in postcolonial studies to mark the period of transitioning, or moving from colonial rule to independence. The changeover to a government of the local people (at least on the surface, despite colonizers' deep-rooted economic strangleholds long past independence) involves time during which local institutions are formed, and a new state order with its own police force and military is formulated for power even in democratic societies. South Africa underwent a huge transition from apartheid rulers to a new government under President Nelson Mandela. Local peoples' hopes and aspirations await a reasonable amount of transition time, though when societies still claim to be transitioning after over two decades, then the word *transition* is not accurate, and disillusionment sets in.

Apart from this political valence of understanding transition in postcolonial nations, I evoke a different, psychologically rooted notion of "transitional space" as articulated very usefully by critical theorist Gabriele Schwab in her book entitled *The Mirror and the Killer-Queen: Otherness in Literary Language*. From the base of her theory that "reading [and, I add here, performance] is a form of cultural contact," Schwab argues that within such contact among cultures, literature (and performance) also involves "an experience of otherness" (Schwab 1996, 24). Schwab relies on psychologist Winnicott's analysis of children's identification with fictional/fantastical characters who take them into "transitional reading," where they recognize their own selves and their transformation into a princess or a frog that may captivate their imagination. The literary or performative experience brings together the self and the other (characters in fiction). "Such 'transitional reading' may never completely disappear," comments Schwab, citing George Poulet's "phenomenological theory of reading.... Poulet's metaphors describe paradoxical aesthetic experiences similar to those Winnicott considers typical for the transitional space" (25). In such an experience, "barriers" between book and reader, or between dancer and spectator, "fall away." The reader or spectator is "inside" the book or performance. "There is no longer outside or inside" (25).

Schwab's analysis brings together the conscious and unconscious in the psychological makeup, especially relying on Winnicott's early childhood developmental theories. Winnicott "emphasizes the ways in which we transpose early patterns of relating to otherness onto later cultural encounters" (Schwab 1996, 26). I relate this to Pather's probing of the psychological hurt of apartheid, during childhood and youth, that is imprinted on grown-up Black people whose unresolved rage often spills over in unexpected violence. They have to relearn new ways of trusting and responding to diverse people in democracy. Pather is fascinated with how memories of pain are retained inside the body and inside what Schwab might describe as the "coming together of the psychological and the cultural," how the two are "inextricably interwoven," crediting Winnicott's "perform[ing] a systematic transcoding between psychological and cultural aspects of maturational processes" (26).

The power of "transitional space," according to Schwab, is that "it allows a certain license from the constraints of the social, the requirements of censorship, and other normative operations of consciousness. Therefore, we may, in the transitional space, act out fantasies and fears, enact relations that would otherwise be restricted if not taboo or temporarily dissolve boundaries that are necessary to maintain in actual cultural encounters" (1996, 26).

The concept of the in between, somewhat different from the transitional though related to it, is theorized as "the third space," the location "where the cutting-edge of translation and negotiation occurs" in critical theorist Homi Bhabha's formative text *The Location of Culture* (1994, 6). Bhabha argues that the realm of the "interstices" can enable a bridging of the divide between "theory and political practice" (22) since

> it is the trope of our times to locate the question of culture in the realm of the beyond ... the "beyond" is neither a new horizon, nor a leaving behind of the past.... We find ourselves in the moment of transit where space and time cross to produce completed figures of difference and identity, past and present, inside and outside, inclusion and exclusion.... What is theoretically innovative, and politically crucial, is the need to think [of] ... "in-between" spaces [that] provide the terrain for elaborating strategies of selfhood—singular and communal—that initiate new signs of identity, and innovative sites of collaboration, and contestation, in the act of defining the idea of society itself. (1994, 1)

Bhabha relies partly on Stuart Hall's injunction of "'intervening ideologically' as a practice of politics [that] ... occupies a discursive space ... exist[ing] in-between these [right or left] political polarities" (1994, 22). The very locations of Pather's creative works radically challenge the in-between existence of Black South Africans by making them inhabit the very cracks that keep communities apart. Pather's use of in-between spaces carries forward his commitment to create performance that challenges divisions and includes diverse South Africans.

Along with the in between, the notion of "crossing over" politically "to a new place altogether" (translated from isizulu for "siwela sonke") is resonant in post-independence South Africa. "Crossing over" includes temporal, spatial, and artistic dimensions as well as the interstitial spaces in between, like Black people who reside spatially in between rural and urban areas or in townships such as Soweto on the outskirts of Johannesburg, KwaMashu and Umlazi outside Durban, and Langa, Gugulethu, and Khayelitsha on the outskirts of Cape Town. Temporally, "crossing over" indicates time lags between the recent past of apartheid and the present of post-apartheid, with hope for a future time of a functioning democracy and freedom for all South Africans. Spatially crossing over from areas with substandard housing to the cities remains distant for most of the majority Black people.

Pather's company members work in between and cross over and across the disciplines of dance, theater, multimedia, and visual art. There is risk involved both in Pather's adventurous choreography and in the performers' embodiment of abstract notions of the in between or of crossing over. The specific challenge in dance, to quote dance theorist Randy Martin, is "*to embody the theoretical as a kind of practice*" (1998, 5, emphasis added). For instance, Pather's concept-driven choreography deals with memory and violence embodied by his performers in *Body of Evidence*, in which the process of accessing personal stories was harrowing (discussed in chap. 4). In other situations, performers could be in physically dangerous positions—such as when Pather has a female performer "rap-jumping" down the wall of a mall (*Cityscapes*) to convey the dangers of conspicuous consumption. He adds significantly that "this was a long time in building up through ethical considerations, safety, and talking through with the artist" (email to Katrak, May 29, 2020). His purpose for this bold act is reminiscent of, though different from, Friedrich Nietzsche's tightrope walker, who struggles to keep his balance but falls to his death when distracted by a jester (*Thus Spake Zarathustra*). Nietzsche's tightrope walker mirrors a contemporary dancer negotiating his or her position in between one safe area and another, though Pather's hopeful vision embodied by Siwela Sonke dancers enables his performers to "cross over to a new place altogether," brimming with possibilities after independence.

In betweenness connects people across social and racial divides, in line with Pather's commitment to inclusiveness for all South Africans. The very locations of his creative ventures, whether situated in historical, medical, or financial sites, radically challenge the in-between existence of Black people by inhabiting the very barriers embodied in cracks and gaps that keep communities apart. Pather enables bodies to interact in various sites: domestic, public, legal, and governmental. His politically progressive goals recognize that space itself is animate and plays a role in transforming society. Pather is a risk taker. He does not dictate specific meanings to performances he creates or curates; instead, he allows audiences to respond from their own experiences.

One of Pather's primary goals in his site-specific work is providing unmitigated access and belonging to public spaces that previously excluded Black people. His site-specific work is "available to people who might not have stepped inside a theatre" (Pather quoted in Davidoff 2006, 139). He involves the general public by providing them access to enjoyable and provocative art, such as live classical music performed on a grand piano inside a train station in South Africa's prime apartheid city, Cape Town, which has no apparent interest in Black people experiencing excellent art.

Pather selects locations, he remarks, based on "the space's unique 'personality'" (quoted in Davidoff 2006, 138). It is "'something about [the sites] that is iconic, the *genus loci* or spirit of the place rather than for the brilliant architecture. It has to do with underlying raison d'etre of the spaces themselves that are sometimes aesthetically loaded and at other times proffer other possibilities, not least of which is to comment on the space itself" (quoted in Davidoff 2006, 141). Pather interrogates discriminatory attitudes that regulate who belongs in certain public spaces, who is left out, and how public art can foster "the development of belonging." He is self-critical in admitting that his early work, while well received, "did not reach the kind of audience [he] was interested in, an audience whose roots [he] shares" (Pather 2013b, 435). Pather notes that the "remedy for not reaching audiences was specifically about changing site not necessarily dance styles that emerged as early as 1979–80" (email to Katrak, May 29, 2020). Hence In *Cityscapes*, Pather situates performers on the Durban beachfront, a Whites-only space during apartheid and places his Black artists inside an expensive mall dancing *pantsula*, a popular style in townships.[3]

Pather's aesthetic-political vision, intercultural and progressive, speaks to various South Africans in a variety of spaces that may contain personal stories and that may evoke national history. Pather works with local communities and creates from multiple movement vocabularies, along with visual art and multimedia, in hybrid works. He emphasizes the languages of gesture, physical theater, and the body that can transcend linguistic divisions, as in aspects of *Cityscapes*.

Pather's uses of city spaces echo what Sarah Nuttall and Achille Mbembe assert in their coedited book entitled *Johannesburg: The Elusive Metropolis*. Their analysis of Johannesburg as "the premier African metropolis, the symbol par excellence of the 'African modern'" applies with differences to Durban and Cape Town, where Pather locates his site works (Nuttal and Mbembe 2008, 17). Pather would agree with Nuttall and Mbembe that "the African modern is a specific way of being in the world. As elsewhere in the global south, it has been shaped in the crucible of colonialism and by the labor of race.... Modernity and worldliness, here, have been so intrinsically connected to various forms of circulation—of people, capital, finance, and images—and to overlapping spaces and times" (Nuttall and Mbembe 2008, 1).

Pather's deployment of different kinds of spaces—physical, mental, sociopolitical—echoes Henri Lefebvre's exploration, in his seminal book *The Production of Space*, of "'real' space, namely, 'the space of social practice'" (Lefebvre [1974] 1999, 114). Pather's creative works portray space as "a social reality" and "a set of relations and forms," to use Lefebvre's words (116).

Spatial designations of everyday life—a marketplace, a shopping center, a park—were regulated and heavily coded and still need to be decoded in post-apartheid society. As Lefebvre asks, "What paradigms give them [spatial codes] their meaning, what syntax governs their organization? . . . If indeed spatial codes have existed, each characterizing a particular spatial/social practice, and if these codifications have been *produced* along with the space corresponding to them, then the job of theory is to elucidate their rise, their role, and their demise" (original emphasis, 16–17). Pather's site-specific work challenges old racial codes that determined spatial rules of exclusion targeted against specific people. As Lefebvre comments, "The job of theory is to elucidate their [spatial codes'] rise, their role, and their demise" (18). Pather's conceptual essays and his choreography explore the changing role of "spatial codes" in South Africa's democracy, with possibilities for human interaction across race and other barriers.

Pather remarks usefully that that he does not work "theoretically," that is, with an external theory in mind when he choreographs, but rather via "a combination of political consciousness, and then an instinct to disrupt, to re-make, re-inscribe [that] pervades, but that the theoretical emanates from and after, and does not lead to the event [performance]" (email to Katrak, May 29, 2020). He adds that in his creative process, theoretical ideas are embedded in the production, rather than working from a preconceived theory, an approach that he finds "stultifying" (phone conversation May 31, 2020). He does begin with concepts, even objects, or a site, or the human body, and such conceptualizing is germane to his choreographic process. Further, it is significant to recognize Pather's complex conceptual essays as theory, similar to such intellectual contributions by African writers like Ngũgĩ wa Thiong'o and Wole Soyinka. I caution against a narrow-minded approach that confines "theory" to Euro-American thinkers, with postcolonial creative writers who theorize being viewed as "simply" discussing issues of culture and identity.

During apartheid, "social spaces," partitioned by racialized divisions, relegated Black people to the margins via draconian laws such as the Group Areas Act that forced them into government-designated ethnic enclaves and into townships with poor amenities. They could enter White neighborhoods only to provide labor, then return to their homes outside the cities. Black people who had no jobs in the cities were forced to return to the so-called "homelands" (a misnomer of "home") located in remote, arid areas where food and employment were scarce. When men traveled out of the "homelands" for work, their wives and children usually remained behind since, during apartheid they rarely found employment in cities.

A feeling of being out of place in a situation or in a dislocated, exilic "home," or not feeling "at home" even in one's own home, is poignantly applicable to Black South Africans dispossessed of their land or displaced internally in "homelands," similar to increasing numbers of migrants worldwide. Pather's choreography for *Blind Spot*, discussed below, creates a site work in Copenhagen that evokes the realities of life for migrants living on the outskirts of this "cosmopolitan" city. "Separation from place," remarks Casey, "is perhaps most poignantly felt in the forced homelessness of the reluctant emigrant, the displaced person, the involuntary exile" (1993, x). Black South Africans feel homeless living in townships on city margins in order to work as domestics for White families, or as miners living in male hostels that resemble prisons, as represented in Pather's choreography in *Hostel*, part of the *Home* series (discussed in chap. 4). A miner inhabiting a prison-like hostel cell "feels dislocated, even lost," suffering from what Casey terms "place-panic," which elicits "the emotional symptoms of placelessnes [as] homesickness, disorientation, depression, desolation" (1993, ix, x).

Performances in unique sites with evocations in between the historical and performative, and crossing disciplinary boundaries such as movement and visual art, play a crucial role in social transformation. Pather's politically progressive goals in recognizing how space can transform society echo Henri Lefebvre's passionate words in *The Production of Space*:

> A revolution that does not produce a new space has not realized its full potential.... A social transformation to be truly revolutionary in character, must manifest a creative capacity in its effects on daily life, on language and on space—though its impact need not occur at the same rate, or with equal force, in each of these areas [Lefebvre, 54].... "Change life! Change society!" These precepts mean nothing without the production of an appropriate space ... a critical analysis of all spatial politics [Lefebvre, 59–60]....
> *State-imposed normality makes permanent transgression inevitable.*
> (emphasis added, Lefebvre [1974] 1999, 73)[4]

The very forms of Pather's creative works related to their spatial locations, whether set indoors or outdoors, are "intimately bound up with function and structure" since "space is a social morphology: it is to lived experience what form itself is to the living organism, and just as intimately bound up with function and structure" (Lefebvre [1974] 1999, 4). For instance, in Pather's site-responsive work entitled *Kitchen*, set uniquely inside an art gallery (chap. 4), Pather plays with and subverts Lefebvre's description of space as "bound up with function." Contrary to what a kitchen usually means—a nurturing, safe, and comfortable area to eat and fraternize with family and friends—Pather portrays it as a space of painful drama between a Black couple with nothing to eat and empty kitchen cabinets. Similarly, Pather deconstructs the accepted uses of an art gallery for public viewing of artworks when he makes the private space of a kitchen public, showing spectators the private emotions of rage and frustration; Pather makes the site speak, as it were. Further, he renders the politics of hunger and anger as personal, reversing the feminist adage of "the personal as political" to "the political as personal." *Kitchen* evokes a sense of despair in the situation facing the couple, who seem stuck in this space, with no choice of moving to a different location with a better future.

As a contemporary artist, Pather is "strategically aware" of what geographer Edward Soja describes as our "collectively created spatiality and its social consequences [that] has become a vital part of making both theoretical and practical sense of our contemporary life-worlds at all scales, from the most intimate to the most global" ([1996] 2000, 1). Soja delineates what he terms "the *spatiality* of life" within his provocative "transdisciplinary scope"—namely, "a growing awareness of the simultaneity and interwoven complexity of the social, the historical, and the spatial, their inseparability and interdependence" (3). In *Kitchen*, the social, historical, and spatial coalesce—video footage, Zulu ritual, and contemporary dance with symbolic props create a palimpsest of affects. Pather's inclusion of Zulu ritual in contemporary work in city settings, emanating from the dictates of the work and his collaborators connects his audience to their memories of indigenous ritual. Here it is significant to underline that although Pather conceives and directs projects, his method of collaborative choreography in all his work, and especially the inclusion of ritual, is done carefully "through collaboration, negotiation, and unanimous agreement" with Siwela Sonke dancers such as Ntombi Gasa and Neliswa Rushualang (email to Katrak, May 29, 2020). Pather is deeply cognizant of not appropriating Zulu ritual without consultation and shared knowledge with his dancers who connect personally to certain ritual practices.[5]

Pather's spatial politics enable us "to keep our contemporary consciousness of spatiality—our critical geographical imagination," to use Soja's words, "creatively open to redefinition and expansion in new directions" ([1996] 2000, 2). Pather connects South Africa's modern urban sites that have opened up in the new democracy to ordinary people's desire for freedom of movement and speech, as well as to what Soja describes as "postmodern epistemological critique," which is not simply a rejection of modernism. Rather, both postmodernist and modernist perspectives enable an opening up of a space "where issues of race, class, and gender can be addressed simultaneously without privileging one over the other; where one can be Marxist and post-Marxist, materialist and idealist, structuralist and humanist, disciplined and transdisciplinary at the same time" (Soja [1996] 2000, 5). Soja's own geographical imagination is broad and profound enough to accommodate various critical theoretical approaches and different disciplines in his text. Pather, too, is as cognizant of "post-modernity," which haunts cities with hidden spaces for shantytowns and others for upscale business areas.

Pather is as interested in geographical spaces as he is in the history behind them in his society. In philosophical and theoretical studies, history and time usually take precedence over space; indeed, the spatial is regarded as controlled by the temporal. Soja makes a persuasive case for the equal significance of geography and history in his book *Postmodern Geographies*. Geographers like Soja and Gillian Rose, and choreographers like Pather, recuperate the significance of space/place along with time in their theoretical work.

Soja brings time and space together in his evocation of time lapses in between spaces or between notes and harmonies, much like Pather's uses of different musical traditions—African, Indian, Western—and is mindful of the gaps and fissures among them, along with their dissonant or melodious sounds. Soja uses a musical analogy evoking lags in between notes when he imagines Lefebvre's rich text, *The Production of Space* "as a musical composition . . . a polyphonic fugue that assertively introduced its keynote themes early on and then changed them intentionally in contrapuntal variations that took radically different forms and harmonies. Composing the text as a fugue . . . was a way of spatializing the text" (Soja [1996] 2000, 9). Pather's choreographic orchestration of his dancers' movements and his musical choices conversing with one another on stage function as a fugue, wherein a musical phrase is introduced and taken up by others as different segments are interwoven.

Pather's *Cityscapes* unfolds across Durban in the post-apartheid era, though memories of exclusions and lack of access haunt performers and spectators as Pather invents ways of recuperating the rights of all South African citizens to inhabit all parts of a city. "To be in the world, to be situated at all," comments Casey, "is to be in place. Place is the phenomenological particularization of 'being-in-the-world' ... we are in place primarily by means of our own bodies.... Embodied emplacement" (2007, xv, xvi). Pather recognizes his dancers' bodies in literal and symbolic ways and places them in different locations—on the street, in the park, inside a coffee shop—to convey particular meanings. The body's role in a particular place is significant in performance. Pather's concern, like Casey's, is "to refind place, a place we have always already been losing—we may need to return, if not to actual fact then in memory or imagination, to the very earliest places we have known.... Place ushers us into what already is.... If imagination projects us out *beyond* ourselves while memory takes us back *behind* ourselves, place subtends and enfolds us, lying perpetually *under* and *around* us" (original emphasis, 2007, x, xvi–xvii). Pather takes his spectators via memory and imagination to familiar places in their lives via popular dance forms; he also takes them beyond the recognizable to reinhabit forbidden sites during apartheid whose distasteful repercussions linger in the bodies, minds, and psyches of Black people.

Pather's method of situating site-specific outdoor performances in public spaces where diverse South Africans of varying economic statuses rub shoulders and even glance at one another while congregating draws attention to the primacy of sight. The experience of performers and spectators in Pather's *Cityscapes* or

Blindspot relies on what the human eye sees and perceives, even in a glance. Casey analyzes the "glance" as "a scopic scout" that is

> stationed at the outposts of human perceptual experience. It discovers whole colonies of the to-be-seen world, places where sight has never before been—or if it has, it now sees differently. The glance guides the eye as it comes to know the perceived world, leading it out of more staid and settled ways of looking.... The glance is incompatible with most Western paradigms of knowledge. It lacks the motive of mastery; it has no pretense to be encyclopedic or systemic... glancing [occurs] in a virtual feel... glancing alleviates my visual life. (2007, xi, xiii)

The importance of the glance is particularly palpable for Pather's site-specific work, which occurs, for instance, inside shopping malls or art galleries, triggering surprise among passers-by viewing unexpected movement and sound and encouraging them to glance cursorily or to watch intently and respond, or to move on, as they please. Pedestrians glancing at a site-specific work may look at "surfaces," may take in unique "places," or may even notice unusual juxtapositions, as in one segment of *Cityscapes* during which dancers in business suits performed *pantsula* on an escalator in a shopping mall. Such activity interrupts the usual business of shoppers who may glance at the work in its unusual locale, and in that glance they are "taken out of [themselves]" as Casey argues persuasively, "out of [their] formally defined, defensive egoic identities." Sichel recounts that "the *pantsulas* from Umlazi, in pinstriped suits, jiv[ed] up escalators to a remix of Carl Orff's *Carmina Burana*, stopped traffic in West Street" in Durban; the same scenario occurred when part of *Cityscape* called *From Before* was performed on Amsterdam Avenue in NYC, and traffic was brought to a standstill (Sichel 2002).

As spectators encounter unexpected sights and sounds in Pather's site work, even their glancing as "the most poignant point of access" takes them to new places in their imagination (Casey 2007, xiv). When spectators are caught off-guard with the familiar rhythms of *pantsula* inside an expensive mall, instead of its usual practice among competing groups in townships, their imaginations can coinhabit two different spaces, economically modest or posh, without restrictions.

ANCHORS FOR PATHER'S SITE PERFORMANCES

Pather describes the trajectory of his site work as moving from using a site "aesthetically" to "deconstructing" it, to "having a conversation with the site," "to undercutting the space" (interview 5, 2015). In *Cityscapes* (2002), he was interested in placing the bodies of dancers "in relation to architecture, i.e. using the space aesthetically" as he remarks in the same interview, "even working around a particular aesthetic" such as challenging the elitism of certain dance forms such as ballet and instead showcasing South African popular dance forms. Later, in *The Beautiful Ones Must Be Born* (2005), his purpose in using Constitution Hill was all about deconstructing the site, to evoke the 'tension, an uneasy meditation not of the state of the nation but of *a* state, a state of ... dissatisfaction ... of dreams deferred, a state of limbo inside spaces of concrete, brick and mortar of a remembered past [a site that held political prisoners] and a new one, the Constitutional Court itself, of hope" (Pather 2015b, 327, original emphasis).

One commonality for site selections resides in artists' connection to particular urban places. Pather has noted his fascination with the architecture of his home city, Durban. The impetus to engage with local sites as Pather does is described evocatively by Lucy Lippart as "the lure of the local [that] is the pull of place that operates on each of us, exposing our politics and our spiritual legacies. It is the geographical component of the psychological need to belong somewhere, one antidote to a prevailing alienation" (quoted in Kloetzel and Pavlik 2009, 1). The goals of creating a sense of belonging and providing access inspire Pather's site-specific choreography in *Cityscapes* and other works. He aims to connect such work to the sensory feel of a place and to communities' emotional connection to a site. As noted in *Site Dance*, and as Pather demonstrates, engaging with space in "novel ways" encourages unexpected "physical exchanges between audience and place" and between audience and performers. Such interactions, note Kloetzel and Pavlik, "are not merely symbolic; they are physicalized with the indelible stamp of experience to amplify their import" (3).

Pather articulates several key goals in his selection of sites:

> My singular pleasure in site-specific performance beyond its interplay of architecture, urban spaces and dance is that the moment of interaction is largely uncontrolled and uncontrollable in so many respects.... This performed moment is so alive and unyielding on risk, vulnerabilities, truth and openness. This for me encapsulates what living in South Africa requires us to face and build; the coalface of what we as individuals can do in those rich moments of interaction. There is this need and opportunity in an emerging democracy to find something new and miraculous... in each other, in those private moments in those public spaces that continue to shift and tilt. (Pather 2013, 442–43)

Pather believes that the human body can "control meanings within what can potentially be alienating urban spaces." He claims that his dance pieces "derive their core concept and momentum from the notion that spaces shape the movement and gestural languages of people who in turn shape those spaces, how they are used or even whether they are used at all" (Pather 2013b, 434). Interactions between people and sites animate both as the combined synergy provokes unforeseen connections and outcomes.

Pather's outdoor, site-specific creations aim to provide opportunities for interconnection among diverse South Africans—Black, Brown, "Colored," White, mixed, able-bodied, differently able, gays and lesbians—gathering on a street or in a public park to witness a high-quality performance. In urban city squares, train stations, or prominent streets, different kinds of bodies—large Black women who defiantly challenge the stereotypical skinny, female ballet body, and "men who are not the Princes of the ballet" share public space, perhaps even experience physical touch that was denied among the races during apartheid (Davidoff 2006, 137). In outdoor work, Pather reclaims the *public* in *public space*, playing with and challenging the overt and covert "rules" limiting spaces to Black people during apartheid, when it was legally mandated, and after apartheid, with the psychological and emotional remnants of such disenfranchisement.

In Pather's site-specific work, interrelationships between the dancers' bodies and the outdoor architecture or physical indoor objects suggest alternative epistemologies in the power dynamic of racial divisions in South African urban landscapes. He strives for new ways of thoughtfully, even joyously reclaiming and inhabiting formerly denied spaces. Pather believes that a playful approach can inspire "symbolism, deeper meanings, recognition and connectivity, and coherence" (Pather 2013b, 434) rather than being heavy-handed about the significance of a work. Instead, he is interested in "inconclusive, incoherent and tentative" affects, very different from fixed meanings. He aims for spectators to tune in to "the lack of resolution, this flux, this inchoate matrix and so shift space and tilt time and strike balances that are not always apparent" (438).

Pather aims to bring both popular and high art that is affective, open-ended, and at times disturbing into the everyday lives of ordinary South Africans, thereby fulfilling their desire for joy, beauty, and community. Pather does not claim to be doing something brand new, since outdoor performances, including ritual performances, have existed globally in both ancient and modern times. In ritual, there is transformative potential whether in connection with a temple or on a street. Outdoor spaces differ uniquely from the confined, walled spaces of indoor theaters, where the audience's responses are conditioned in part by the space itself. Not to romanticize the freedom (and rigors) of the street, but there is an open-endedness to the affect produced by dancers/actors in a public setting; there is a similar ease of movement for the spectators who can move around, engage with the performance, or simply enter or leave the space whenever they like. The flexibility of outdoor space allows dancers/actors to interact with spectators, some of whom may have stopped simply out of curiosity. This can lead to unplanned or unexpected responses, ones that may echo ritualistic practices of storytelling or communal sharing. Indeed, contemporary site-specific and site-responsive performances have their roots in such traditions.

In his book *Places of Performance: The Semiotics of Theatre Architecture*, theatre historian Marvin Carlson discusses how places of performance embody social and cultural meanings "which in turn help to structure the meaning of the entire theatre experience" (1989, 25). Site-specific performance as a phenomenon has ancient roots. As Carlson remarks, "City street and market places continued to serve for the ancient forms of civic entertainment—the parades and processions . . . the acrobats, farceurs, and mimes whose descendants may still be seen today in the clowns, mime, fire-eaters, and jugglers found in such popular urban gathering places" (26–27). Even as cities around these performances change, and even as traditional city squares may disappear, their "modern equivalents [are] found in pedestrian malls" (27) where walking and shopping both occur. In Pather's *Cityscapes*, shoppers' consumer activities are interrupted by performers inside a mall. Pedestrians walking can be, in Michel de Certeau's words, "a sort of articulation" (1984, 103).

In Pather's choreographed outdoor performances where dancer-actors interact with architecture and social spaces, there is a concern with "theater as a place and institution within society" (Wihstutz 2013b, 1). The very etymology of the word *theater* is illuminating, as Wihstutz points out: "*Theatron* in Greek initially described nothing more than a place for viewing"; hence, apart from theater as an art, it equally meant "a place and a space" (2). The "spatial turn" in theater studies was influenced by cultural anthropology, by ideas of "framing and site-specificness, as well as the relationship between performance, urban politics, and geography. The now much broader term 'performance' allowed for the traditional link between theatricality and politics to be highlighted in all forms of 'cultural performance'" (2). Pather is adept at recognizing the very semiotics of the street as he mines, skillfully and artistically, the political effects of certain locations and their overdetermined resonances in racially divided South Africa.

In ancient theaters, space was initially demarcated by the sections that spectators occupied. Later, "the emergence of theater as a public space is just as intimately tied to politics. The theater as a place of assembly for the polis is directly linked to the idea of democracy" (Wihstutz 2013b, 3). This connection made theater dangerous for the masses, according to ancient Greek philosopher Plato. For Pather, a politics of space is influenced by the locations that performances occupy and how they challenge state regulations. This has been a serious reality in spaces occupied by diverse South Africans both during and after apartheid.

When accosted by an unexpected performance on a busy city street, such an encounter, remarks scholar Andrew Houston in *Environmental and Site-Specific Theatre*, is "an act of social geography: a way of being-in-the-world and bringing to bear a social, political and historical consciousness upon our navigations through and experiences of lived space" (2007, vii). Pather's site-specific performances in city spaces echo Houston's description of "environmental theatre" as "the placement of a particular text in a given environment, wherein the environment [*sic*] then begins to operate as an active agent in the process of developing the text in this particular place" (xiv).

The phrase "environmental theatre [was] coined by Richard Schechner [who] first theorized it in the late 1960s and early

1970s" (Knowles 2007, 67). Schechner was Pather's influential teacher at New York University, where Pather completed an MA in theater (1982–84). Schechner "traces its [environmental theater's] contemporary roots in the West to modernist developments in music and the visual arts," comments Knowles, "notably composer John Cage, Dada, and a number of avant-garde visual artists, mostly American" (68).[6] Schechner exposed his South African student to innovative performance, visual art, and music.

Taking "environmental theater" in a different direction, Ric Knowles seeks "an explicitly political way," resonant with Pather's goals, "that has more to do with Linda Hutcheon's articulation of 'the politics of postmodernism' than with the depoliticized excesses of post-modernism" (Knowles 2007, 69). Knowles values environmental theater's "politicization of space and democratization of focus, its insistence on the engagement or implication of audiences . . . and its deployment of socially transformative modes such as ritual, shamanism, or magic" (69). Victor Turner's (via Arnold van Gennep) paradigm-shifting notion of liminality itself "functions as a site of transition" remarks Knowles, "between realms" (77).

Houston further distinguishes site-specific and environmental theatre: "Site-specific theatre may be meaningfully transferred from its site of origin to another site," as was true for Pather's *Cityscapes*, performed in four different cities—Durban, Johannesburg, Cape Town, and New York City. Site-specific works "are conceived for, and conditioned by, the particulars of such spaces [that] recontextualises them" (Pearson, cited in Houston 2007, xv). The particular mobility of this kind of performance is different from "environmental theatre [that] *will become specific to the given site in which it is developed*, and in that sense it will not be mobile" (emphasis added). In some decrepit sites such as inner-city areas, the performance itself can activate the site through technology, which enlivens seemingly "dead" spaces, validating locations belonging to underprivileged populations.

In chapter 5, I discuss a multiplicity of performances "specific to a given site" during the *Infecting the City* festival and *Live Art* curated by Pather.

Underpinning political history with mixed media performance raises overt and symbolic meanings for the general public inhabiting Lefebvre's "l'espace vecu" (lived space) (quoted in Soja [1996] 2000, 6). Soja proposes an alternate direction "of spatial inquiry that extends the scope of the geographical imagination beyond the confining dualism of what he describes as 'first-space' and 'second-space epistemologies'" ([1996] 2000, 7). "'First space' is grounded" notes Soja, "whereas 'second space' is subjective; and fluctuating"; both spaces influence human beings' connection to place, both real and imagined (9). Soja proposes a "third space" that combines both the material and subjective to reach for alternate modes of spatial thinking. Pather's site choreography draws upon all three of Soja's valences of space, giving them new habitations in South Africa.

SITE SELECTION INSPIRED BY PATHER'S AVANT-GARDE SPATIAL POLITICS

Pather imaginatively selects sites for his choreography and analyzes his choices in concept-infused director and program notes. As an artist and scholar, he creates what Anne Carlson describes as "a critical language" needed to explain, even justify site work and to link artistic processes of serious art making with sociopolitical critique (Carlson in Kloetzel and Pavlik 2009, 18).[7] Pather's spatial politics are concerned as much with inclusion and access as with freedom of movement for performers and spectators in urban centers and inside government buildings. Wihstutz links "aesthetic theory and geography, art and sociology, architecture and political theory, geometry and history that shed a new light on performance, politics, and space, thereby transforming this historically intertwined triad into a transdisciplinary subject"

(Wihstutz 2013a, 3). Such links function in Pather's aesthetic-political world, wherein he evokes new meanings for iconic architecture that intrinsically identifies a space and its history.

Even with links between "geography and history," among other dyads noted above, Wihstutz believes that in any performance, a distinction is needed between theatrical space and everyday social arenas, however much an artist may intervene in and even try to conflate these different spaces. Avant-garde artists often succeed in breaking boundaries by forcing theater out of indoor auditoriums and onto the street, as Pather does, and performance art out of museums and art galleries into pedestrian areas. It is useful to bring in Michel Foucault's contention that theater space is "outside all places, although they are actually localizable" (quoted in Wihstutz 2013a, 8). In other words, theater can simultaneously occupy a utopian space outside of recognizable places and an identifiable place such as an auditorium or a beachfront.

Pather discusses the challenges of getting permissions for performances in certain locations (interview 1, 2018). The politics of space are interwoven into the locations of theatrical performances—outdoor, indoor, or in what Richard Schechner describes as theater epitomized in nontheatrical structures, in "found spaces" such as "civil rights marches and confrontations" with state authorities (1988, 2004, 3). During apartheid, protest marches were common on the streets and even funeral processions turned into political rallies. Post-apartheid, occupations of spaces once forbidden and that carry uneasy memories for performance are in themselves resistant political acts. The state's representatives, mainly the police, secret service, and intelligence-gathering personnel, can be at loggerheads with artists and performers, especially when it comes to managing outdoor spaces.[8]

The challenge for artists like Pather is to select from among a variety of sites for their creative work. Mike Pearson, in

Site-Specific Performance, similar to Pather, does not define a "type" of site since there are overlaps among "site-determined, site-oriented, site-referenced, site-conscious, site-responsive, [and] site-related" (Pearson 2010b, 1). We find such links between Pather's site-specific and site-responsive works. Nonetheless, in theater studies, site work is often defined, continues Pearson "with a negative," remarks Pearson, because it uses "non-theatre locations" (2).

Pather embraces the word *performance* to delineate his multifaceted work, which uses movement, theatrical action, visual art, and symbolic use of props and video in both outdoor and indoor sites (interview 5, July 2015). This is similar to Pearson's delineation of "performance [as] embrac[ing] the fullest range of practices originating in theatre and visual art, and to demonstrate affiliations with the academic field of performance studies" (2010b, 7).

When inside a theater, the audience is focused on observing the stage and responding to what takes place there. Even if actors sometimes use the aisles, the action remains mostly on the proscenium stage. Outdoors, there are different, even "unruly elements," notes Pearson, "always liable to leak, spill, and diffuse" (2010b, 3). This is why performers must be prepared for unexpected encounters with spectators or police. Pearson works toward "a theory of practice rather than adopting a position of critical spectatorship" by following particular companies that create work for "special events" or that are "devised for special locations" (2010b, 2). Pather's work draws upon both kinds of artistic goals: creating work for "special events" and for "special locations," such as *The Beautiful Ones Must Be Born* (2005); this piece was located on the "special location" of Constitution Hill to remind spectators of that site's unjust past along with the present and future represented architecturally in post-apartheid's Constitutional Court. Additionally, Pather subtly critiques the disappointing realities of "a special event"—namely, South

African democracy's tenth anniversary in 2005, when there was not much to celebrate for the majority. He aims to make spectators respond to the performance unfolding in this site of justice, succeeding, to use Pearson's phrase, in "performance as placemaking" while Pather remains open to varying interpretations of both the site and the show (Pearson 2010b, 7). Pather's selection of Constitution Hill as a performance site may be read as literally instrumental, but by bringing significant attention to "the memorialization of place" he empowers underprivileged communities as South African citizens to continue fighting for their rights, even legally at the Constitutional Court.

THE BODY AS SITE

Throughout Pather's work, the human body is a central icon, a site on which history, memory, and politics write their scripts, especially given South Africa's violent racial history, which operated as successfully as it did precisely because of the forced segregation of physical bodies of different races. The human body is a symbol that contains the nation's collective history. However, even with physical, mental, and psychic scars, the body, mind, and spirit endure in Pather's vision, which asserts hope in the human spirit's resilience, even as that hope is "wearing thin," as he has warned.

Pather's 2017 essay "Negotiating the Postcolonial Black Body as Site of Paradox" articulates the sociopolitical reality imbued with "the combination of a poorly performing government, unchecked racist attitudes and widespread access to social media [that] has seen this attack on the black body grow" (Pather 2017a, 140). In the same essay, Pather cites Penny Sparrow, who compared "the presence of thousands of Black people on Durban's beaches [out of limits for them during apartheid] on New Year's Day to an invasion by monkeys. The backlash was passionate and severe" (140). Regarding another incident at the University of

Cape Town, where Cecil Rhodes's statue was covered in excrement, Pather remarks that

> the continued centrality of colonial symbology at South African institutions remains unaddressed.... For those who claimed that the statue was just part of a dormant history, the efficacy of the response that followed... challenged these assumptions and claims to long-gone memory and dormant oppression. The symbol of "people's shame" associated with the poor state of sanitation in South Africa's townships superimposed on one of the persisting bastions of colonial oppression occupying central space at the University seemed to expose the suppression of the pain of black people in the wake of the "rainbow nation" ushered in by Nelson Mandela. (139)

Pather makes a strong case against "colonial symbology," represented publicly at educational institutions, while those same places of learning allegedly work to counter such racist history.

In the same essay, Pather probes the continued reality of "the perpetuated image of the black body as *less than* against this backdrop of a 'free' South Africa" (original emphasis). He aims "to illuminate the abnegation of the black bodies and explore how this abnegation may be instructive in how we think about the curation of live performance—especially with black bodies. In light of the recent and ongoing demonstrations [of the #fees must fall protests at several South African Universities and discussions on decolonizing the curriculum], the need for such a study is more urgent still" (141).

Pather is acutely conscious of racialized human bodies that carry not very distant historical memories of Black bodies displayed in European capitals as "curiosities." He is just as cognizant of Blackness not as an "absolute" but as a multifarious category, citing Stuart Hall's analysis of race as a "'floating signifier' that can never be 'finally fixed', but which is 'subject to the constant process of redefinition and appropriation'—a multiple, contextual, complex variable" (141).

For Pather, "the delineated black body implies a special project, a particular brand that turns race into a category and a frame" (141). Given that the Black body is rendered invisible in much of South African history, it is important to "show up this invisibility, exclusion and failure of nuanced representation" (141). Pather does not embrace what he calls "the myth of the postracial" that he describes as "a wonderful fantasy" (142). Racial identity, he contends, continues to remain significant, complex, and shifting. He agrees with Homi Bhabha's idea in *The Third Space* interview, which articulates the dangers of a multiculturalist perspective that attempts to understand—but instead ends up containing—cultural differences within "a particular universal concept" (142).

Pather's discourse on race engages centrally with notions "of power, economics, access and agency" (142). Whiteness as normative and largely privileged maintains "a dominant, racially inscribed cultural narrative." For Black people, moving in and out of these deeply entrenched power structures favoring Whites, "the performance of race and identity, started over four hundred years ago. Realities, languages and cultural forms imposed on complex belief systems and traditions set up a denigration of self to varying and often violent degrees. For people of color, the presence of metanarratives appears long before the twentieth century; indeed, meta-consciousness was present at the onset of the colonial experience (141–42). Pather situates the psychological realities of racial discrimination that are significant from the very start of colonial conquest.

In "Negotiating the Black Body as Site of Paradox," Pather analyzes the public fallout over a 2012 painting called *The Spear* by White South African artist Brett Murray, displayed at the prestigious Goodman Gallery in Johannesburg, which displays President Jacob Zuma's genitals. (This incident was prior to the 2015 incident of Cecil Rhodes's statue being pelted with excrement at UCT). A court case was filed to remove the painting, but while that was being debated, the painting was vandalized and destroyed by two men—Barend la Grange and Lowie Mabokela; this was unexpectedly televised nationwide, as a national broadcasting agency was in the gallery that night interviewing the manager.

Public responses both condemned and supported the artwork as an expression of free speech. However, the dehumanization of a Black body by a White artist carries brutal racial memories, as expressed poignantly by "composer and singer, Simphiwe Dana," remarks Pather, "in a letter to City Press" (144). Pather quotes, "The image of a black man with his penis hanging out on display in galleries, plastered all over the internet, in your newspaper for our children to see, for the whole world to see, shifted something in me. An animalistic howl died in my throat, perhaps a gene memory flashback coupled with the reality of my existence today. It felt like giving birth to death. Like this new SA is stillborn. This hurt is deep" (144). For philosopher and political theorist Achille Mbembe, the same hurt—"like sticking a needle in the heart of a figurine"—has brought to the surface "that once again, the black body is the repository of all the anxieties and neuroses of White South Africa. What has irked many is that, after twenty years of freedom, the black body is still a profane body. It still does not enjoy the immunity accorded to properly human bodies" (Mbembe quoted in Pather 2017a, 144).[9] This incident brings into present consciousness the racial inhumanities perpetrated on Black bodies over nearly four hundred years.

Similar to Pather's analysis of how the excrement on Rhodes's statue raised important facts such as lack of basic sanitation in townships, so too did he see the desecration of *The Spear* as "a performative gesture—a quintessentially South African moment when the surface of reconciliation and the sheen of normality are forced to give way to probing questions about art, ownership, the body, culture and race" (145). Further, Pather regards the incident as a "a microcosm of the forms of subjugation inscribed on the black body" that needs to be placed in "a wider context" in South Africa and beyond in tracing the contemporary, continuing fate of the abuse of black bodies (145). He cites the August 16, 2012, Marikana massacre, a dark blot on South Africa's history when nearly twenty years after democracy thirty-four Black miners were killed while protesting for a living wage. He connects such brutality to the killings in recent years of Black men by White policemen in the United States, which also incarcerates disproportionately large numbers of Black people within the general population. "Each of these 'moments,'" comments Pather, "has re-opened the association of blackness with crisis" (145).

Even as the nostalgia for reconciliation has faded, the promise of equality "is vigorously alive," remarks Pather, "in our consideration of blackness" (146). The realities of equality remain distant since, as Pather reminds his readers, "the holders of South Africa's wealth and land remain largely unchanged since apartheid" nor have disparities shifted between rich and poor. *Daily Maverick's* Greg Nicholson notes that "53.8% of people ... fall under the widest definition of poverty in South Africa, surviving on under R779 ($47) per month" (146).

Pather's creative forays into exposing such inequities via performance include his challenges to sacrosanct Whites-only spaces where he places Black performers. His artistry occupies the potent gaps and fissures in between lingering apartheid policies of separating the races, crossing over to a new place even if that location can only be imagined, as he states forthrightly in the title of his site-responsive work *The Beautiful Ones **Must** Be Born* (emphasis added).

CITYSCAPES (2002)

In the 2000s, Pather reimagines cartographies of belonging for diverse South Africans through his site-specific choreography in *Cityscapes*. Here, spectators view the performances of the human body as a site of historical and political resistance, in dialogue with architecture in urban landscapes, city squares, and shopping malls. Sichel vividly describes this stunning site work, new to Durban: "*Cityscapes* plays with various clichés, textures, histories, architectural contexts and iconographies to create fresh aesthetics, which contain familiar touchstones but are wide open to interpretation" (email to Katrak, March 31, 2014).

Cityscapes (2002) was originally set in Durban; it was performed next in 2003 across Johannesburg, with his company members and local artists. A further iteration in 2004, entitled *From Before*, reimagined parts of *Cityscapes* on the steps of the Cathedral of St. John the Divine in New York City as part of *Personal Affects: Power and Poetics in South African Arts*, sponsored by the Museum of African Art in Queens, New York City. *Cityscapes* was part of the *Infecting the City* festival in Cape Town in 2012, where it was described as "bringing the smells, sights and sounds of KwaZulu Natal [where Durban is located] and reinvok[ing] these on Cape Town streets. Often happening in between other performances, the CityScapes provide pathways, links and bridges, and points of intersection, meeting and departure" (Pather 2012a). In 2015 (June 16 to July 11), *Cityscapes Re-Routed* was performed again in Durban, though in different sites from the original 2002 iteration that demonstrated an inspired synergy between Pather, Siwela Sonke dancers, and Durban.

Sichel credits Pather's 2002 *Cityscapes* in Durban for "lovingly hijack[ing] architecture and landscape that he impregnated with dance and music forms which tap into the city's glorious cultural contradictions and dazzling incongruities. It also plugs straight into Pather's yeasty social transformation and displaced identities. Race, religion, tradition and art are catapulted into fresh aesthetics and expressions" (2002). Durban carries enormous history for Pather's own Indian community as well as for the region's Zulu people. This city is, as Lliane Loots delineates, the province of both geographical and political crossing over points ... as a former British colony, the place where Indian indentured labour arrived in South Africa in 1860 to work on the sugar farms, it is home to one of the largest Diaspora Indian communities outside India, it is the historical home of Shaka Zulu and the Zulu nation. It is also a province that has been torn apart by apartheid wars and faction fighting but it is also a province that continues to mediate peace and reconciliation in the wake of our first democratic elections in April 1994. It is a space of fusion and interculturalism.[10]

Cityscapes unfolds in carefully selected Durban sites that are archetypal of a city Pather has seen evolving as people of color inhabit spaces previously reserved for Whites. His own artistic venture in placing work in Durban's Central Business District (CBD) would not have been possible for him as a South African Indian man during apartheid. Pather's vivid memory from his inner-city childhood in Durban underlies *Cityscapes*:

> "My sister, three brothers and I lived in a small flat opposite the Shah Jehan cinema and the Himalaya Hotel on the corner of Beatrice and Grey streets. [From this location] the skyline [included] a tower of a church, a turret of a mosque and the spiraling apex of a modernist building." He recalls peering through a small window of the flat on a Saturday night, watching the dressed-to-the-nines patrons of the Mountains club at the Himalaya transform after 11pm when all hell broke loose, with fists and bottles flying. It's this kind of ambiguity and incongruity that Pather sews as a thematic thread through Cityscapes. (Pather quoted in Robertson 2002)

Pather's tactile description of his early memories resurface in his selection of sites and performances in his home city of Durban.

Cityscapes was Pather's "first consciously created site-specific body of work," notes Clare Craighead, scholar and assistant director of Durban's Flatfoot Dance Company. She continues that it marks "a pivotal moment in Pather's career.... The sheer scale and scope of *CityScapes*, with its relocation into non-theatre, public spaces and its engagement not only with a variety of local dance forms/styles and companies, but also with local video artists, renders it an historical moment within the local South African performance-scape" (2010, 260).

Craighead argues persuasively that Pather's site-specific work challenges the post-apartheid slogan of *simunye*; this "ideal, premised on the equal value of cultures, which should in turn offer equal access," remarks Craighead, "is not a reality in social and cultural practices" (262). The paradox of an enforced unity is that separation of local cultures is still encouraged—for instance, by state funding policies for rural and urban artists. "This is not dissimilar," notes Craighead, "to apartheid policies around 'separate but equal' development of racial groups living in South Africa" (262). Along with *simunye*, multicultural performance that places different cultural forms side by side is also problematic, as Lliane Loots comments: "Multiculturalism in South African performance practice has lulled us into another type of stereotyping (dare one say racism)" (2001, 12). Loots also raises related concepts of "cultural ownership" that, in South Africa, remain embedded in racial hierarchy to promote the idea that "cultural togetherness often overshadows cultural difference" (12).

Rather than an uncritical celebration of a multicultural place "where cultures meet, dialogue and often clash" as Craighead delineates, Pather works with interculturalism that can also be challenging, since encounters between or among cultures hardly take place on a level playing field; overt and covert power dynamics play out between dominant and subordinate cultures. Craighead argues that Pather's interculturalism is effective in his "consciously [though often implicitly]engaging cultural layering and clashes within spheres of cultural practice and production" (2010, 262). Such an approach "presents his performance works as critical, especially in relation to cultural access to, and ownership of, performance forms that are racially identified, determined or 'owned'" (262).

Cityscapes, funded by South Africa's National Arts Council, the National Arts and Culture Trust, and Durban Arts, is remarkable most especially for "its collaborative impetus," remarks Sichel (2002). The work includes forty-two dancers from different companies: Eric Shabalala's Shwibeka Dance Company, One Hour Pantsula Company, the Celtic Dance Company, Nandakishore's Kathak Kendra, Lliane Loots's Flatfoot Dance Company, and video artists Junaid Ahmed, Thando Mamma, Virginia MacKenny, Storm Janse van Rensburg, and Greg Streak, who shared their work in the Durban Art Gallery for a paying audience. The gallery location adds "a further dimension," remarks Craighead, "to this location-inspired artist who can move fluidly from exterior spaces where his performers interact with built structures or the natural world (as in the sea waves), into an interior art gallery space" (265). Pather challenges the ways in which "gallery spaces have been defined," remarks Craighead, "through use as inanimate spaces, inactive and voyeuristic."

The month-long production of *Cityscapes* in Durban unfolds in five urban sites—320 West Street, the North Beach Pier, the Out of Africa Coffee Shop, a room on the fifth floor of the Albany Hotel, and an installation at the Durban Art Gallery that showcased five video/visual artists' documentation of *Cityscapes*' site performances from their own perspectives.

Each site is transformed innovatively as Pather links classical and popular dance movement forms that enable him, comments Craighead, "to subvert a multicultural façade" (2010, 264). The segments created in specific sites seemed to speak to the spaces in which they were set "and for the most part," adds Craighead, "were made in." Sichel describes the artistic process as "consisting of two phases—rehearsed and performed outside on location and then relocated inside—this merger of theatre aesthetics with street smarts culminated . . . in a four-day innovative performance cycle at Durban Art Gallery for a paying audience. . . . Irony, cultural context and conceptual wizardry deliciously fused in one marvelously entertaining fell swoop. This formula was echoed in each of the five innovative segments accompanied by their own video installation filmed on location" (2002).

In visualizing the five segments of *Cityscapes* unfolding across Durban, I rely on commentators such as Sichel, journalist Heather Robertson, and scholar Clare Craighead. Sichel describes the outdoor performance at North Beach, where Pather used "Shembe reed rattles, Celtic steel taps and Kathak bells [that] echo, and transmogrify Indian Ocean waves." Craighead vividly describes "these three culturally distinct dance forms [as] mov[ing] to the natural ocean rhythm.... Each form interprets and accesses differently, while sharing a vast space where no form in particular dominates—spatially, there is no 'centre stage' as it were. Rather than merely sharing rhythms, each form listens to the others to create a percussive soundtrack" (2010, 266).[11] Craighead envisions Pather as creating the space for the "three cultural forms to meet, converse, and at times clash in a cacophony of sound and un-matched rhythms in their responses to the ebb and flow of Durban's Indian Ocean" (266).

In a review of *Cityscapes* entitled "Space Explorer," Heather Robertson notes the shifts "in mood from spiritual spectacle, to carnival, to intimacy." She continues, "On Durban's North Beach, I was hypnotized by a whirl of White and peppermint green as Shembe-inspired dancers shuffled in a serpentine movement, merging with the angular movements of Celtic and kathak dancers.... At the Albany Hotel, 10 of us were crammed up against a wall of a tiny room watching a relationship fall apart in tumbles, rolls and helicopter kicks. Each of the pieces offers an explosive commentary on urban life" (2002).

Pather's "Director's notes," comments Robertson, "speak of the interface between public spaces and the people whose imprints shape them, but the primary impetus he offers for his work is less prosaic: 'I'm fascinated by Durban's architecture and the reason is quite pedestrian. I'm a pedestrian—I don't drive.'" He describes his goals for the performance set inside the Out of Africa Coffee Shop: "Seven dancers draw from the carnival atmosphere that surrounds an intimate, sunken coffee shop in this space of variety and kitsch. The dancers combine intimate gestures with burlesque, working with dance forms such as tap and jazz. The work is wacky and energetic, using athletic tumbling, jumps, lifts and falls to produce slapstick comedy with zany characters" (quoted in Craighead 2010, 255).

Pather remarks in Robertson's piece entitled "Space Explorer" that he is parodying consumerism and the risks involved when people move up in economic class and gain the privilege of using credit cards instead of cash. Pather is fascinated by shopping malls that showcase especially the growing Black middle class with purchasing power. The Musgrave Shopping Centre incorporated the rap-jumping wall into the parking lot at ground level: "The image of a black woman in a big dress rap-jumping down the wall of Musgrave Centre is a very contemporary symbol... at once powerful and vulnerable, it's parodic of consumerism but it's also very risky" remarks Pather. He continues: "I wanted to capture the combination of dread and admiration that come with a rise in class. That leap of faith is best epitomized by rap-jumping. The shifts in consciousness from rural to urban, from cash to credit cards can be very giddy" (quoted in Craighead 2010, 266). Craighead describes this Musgrave Shopping Centre site performance as "probably the most overt in its mixture of contemporary and traditional cultural identities, explor[ing] contemporary contradictions within post-apartheid [urban] Black African identity. A black kugel abseiled down the side of the shopping centre serenaded by an is'Chatimiya group and eventually whisked away with her shopping bags in a rather battered and rusty 1985 Toyota Corolla with gaffer tape holding the passenger door in place and Perspex sheeting in place of a back window" (2010, 266).

One section of *Cityscapes* unfolds in a "fading Durban shopping center" with a woman wearing tap shoes and dark glasses that hide a black eye, carrying shopping bags and dancing to Frank Sinatra's "Strangers in the Night" (played by the center's resident pianist). Pather notes that this seemingly "spontaneous event in a public space can be miraculous, exciting, and invigorating [even though] there are sometimes reservations by managements and irritation from die-hard shoppers, most times in my experience the risk has been worth it" (Pather 2005, 2).

Shoppers also saw gumboot dancers placed in an expensive shopping mall that typically would be frequented used by White people. Pather's masterful juxtapositions, such as gumboot dance inside a posh, glittery mall, can "not only erode decades of prejudice," remarks Davidoff, "but ultimately develop understanding" (2006, 148). Hence, well-off shoppers who may never have encountered gumboot dance, done usually by Black miners, are suddenly pulled into the rhythm and movement of the dance. Pather describes such encounters evocatively as "public spats of concrete and humanity" that can generate enjoyment along with respect and dignity for the actual labor of miners requiring gumboots in mucky surroundings.

The site performances at 320 West Street, a prominent spot in Durban's Central Business District, "a space of transit... of violence, where muggings are common," reflect "cultural juxtapositions and clashes," notes Craighead, "through Pather's use of contemporary and classical iconography" (2010, 157). Craighead describes unusual linkages:

> Merging of a popular township form of youth dance, is'Pantsula, within the contemporary corporate environment of 320 West Street and its iconic escalators that disappear from ground-level view. Cell phones, Armani Suits and briefcases were all part and parcel of this performance spectacle (*CityScapes* programme notes 2002). Through his strong visual sense, Pather created an image of corporate contradiction—rather than merely engage is'Pantsula in

and of itself as a popular dance form, Pather costumed the dancers as businessmen. They danced to remixed versions of classical music most noticeably Carl Orff's 'O Fortuna' from *Carmina Burana*. Pather's bringing together of popular, classical and corporate cultures created a kind of visual chaos that really embodied the space that is 320 West Street. (2010, 260)

Spectators who recognized the popular *pantsula* style were stunned by its contemporary representation and location. Further, Craighead relates how one of the "businessmen" performers suddenly acted as though he was having a heart attack. This "event" was followed by a single helium-filled balloon being released to float up alongside the front of the West Street building—perhaps the businessman's soul? One audience member inferred the balloon to be a representation of the rising HIV pandemic in KZN's city spaces.[12]

Lliane Loots's review entitled "Reinvention of Dance" describes "Pather's brainchild *Cityscapes* [as] a moment of performance anarchy that celebrates the beauty and danger of our city" (2002). In the same review, Loots evaluates "Pather once again reinventing himself (and his company) and pushing pure dance out of the confines of theatrical spaces into the popular spaces through which we walk every day." Loots recognizes that such site work is not new, though Pather's twenty-first-century version "is offering . . . a celebration of our chaos as Durbanites, often living in spaces that are not the privilege of the first world." Pather himself noted that his choreography of *Cityscapes* required "'negotiating the spaces between architecture and people in a way that celebrates our uniqueness as Durban; a place that has more cross-over points than any other city in South Africa'" (quoted in Loots 2002).

Sichel judges this collaborative enterprise as setting "new parameters for public art . . . and rais[ing] the bar on cultural tourism. *Cityscapes* is about exposing heritage and cross-pollinating peopled spaces" (2002). Sichel quotes Pather: "The public is fully interested in aesthetics that shift consciousness. When the *pantsula* dancers started you'd swear you were at an Idols concert. But when the music changed, when we dealt with death, the people went dead quiet. They stayed with it" (2002).

In 2003, the prestigious FNB Dance Umbrella invited *Cityscapes* to Johannesburg. Animate sites that Pather selected in this city included the Oriental Plaza, the Carlton Centre escalators, Sandton, an upscale shopping center, and a room inside Devonshire Hotel in Braamfontein. As in Durban, the performances culminated in a performance by fifty dancers from Johannesburg and Durban in the Johannesburg Art Gallery, with video artists all "insinuating" themselves, in Sichel's vivid words, "into the crevices of public life and individual imagination with creative stealth and artistic guile" (2003). Different dance styles unfolded like a palimpsest, such as sylph-like ballet dancers from the South African Ballet Theatre who appeared alongside classical Indian dancers of the Tribhangi Dance Theater company, Shembe worshippers from Moving into Dance Mophatong, and Siwela Sonke dancers carrying silver umbrellas. An amazing juxtaposition unfolded when, amid the sounds of ankle bells and Shembe rattles, someone on a skateboard zoomed by in the shopping center. While he appeared to be a neighborhood kid, he was, in fact, Siwela Sonke's Denton Douglas.

Since Pather critiques *simunye* in the "rainbow nation," he uses what Sichel describes as "an ingenious ploy" by having all his performers' "bodies and faces painted white with Umako powder used for rituals," including ballet dancers, classical Indian dancers, and others. "Skin-tone becomes irrelevant in this most color-conscious of societies," remarks Sichel. "What counts are the rhythmic bodies, dancing to recorded ocean waves and Baaba Maal" (2003).

A segment of *Cityscapes*, Pather's eighteen-minute site-specific *Hotel*, takes place inside a hotel room, evoking the poignancy of a Black woman, Ntombi Gasa and a White man, Denton

Douglas torn apart under apartheid-era laws that controlled not only the public but also the private lives of Black people under the "Immorality Laws" that criminalized sexual relations across the races. Pather's choreography creates a kind of danced activism that resists state-mandated controls of the human body. He re-creates a racialized world inside an "inner-city hotel room" that "resonates for [him] with what is typical of an acutely South African space in the emerging democracy" (Pather 2013b, 433). Pather created *Hotel* in 2002—eight years after apartheid "ended," though its legacy lingers, as he remarks in "Shifting Spaces, Tilting Time": "These fading hotels such as the Devonshire in Braamfontein, Johannesburg, and the Albany in Durban crumble and are resurrected in turn like the once abandoned city frantically being brought new blood, organs and entrails. They still stand in limbo ... powerful sites for paradoxes" (433). *Hotel* symbolically portrays the "paradoxes" of "crumbling" architecture and two human beings trying to connect across barriers of race, class, and language.

The small hotel room with the two performers and two twin beds and side tables was viewed by some twelve spectators standing close together. Their proximity made them witnesses, even voyeurs, in this private space. The spectators were part of a general public watching the troubled relationship unravel in front of their eyes. Pather made the private public, to evoke the politics of race and space as they impact the lives of so many, and here, this interracial couple.

The movements vary between tenderness and violence, as if an element of secrecy haunts the relationship. Pather uses "language as a point of communicative clash (where performers Gasa and Douglas speak across each other in isiZulu and English respectively) and at other times engaging a more subtle communicative clash through the notion of secrecy and how the two performers (physically and emotionally) hold secrets from each other" (Craighead 2010, 265).

Viewing a video of this site-specific work, I noticed the camera following a hotel corridor and entering room 78 at the Albany Hotel in central Durban. What the audience witnesses in this cramped space as they enter the room is a woman's hair on a pillow (Gasa) facedown on a single bed, wearing pink bunny bedroom slippers that she keeps on throughout the dance movements. The White male dancer, Denton Douglas, enters. Gasa's disjointed narration conveys that she is trying to heal Douglas who is suffering from hallucinations. The tension mounts in the interracial sexual encounter and is "amplified," notes Sichel, by a figure "clad in traditional white clay [who] dons a pair of dark sunglasses and is wrapped in brown/gold tulle. Perhaps this figure represents ghosts of the past or the emergence of secrets— visually he is a mixture of both traditional and contemporary cultures within South Africa" (2003). Craighead points out that this ancestral Zulu male emerging from the closet is "a visual icon common to many of Pather's works." Pather himself favors an interpretation of a nonspecific ancestral figure who blows in as if with the wind, and with the changing flows of history and heritage. This figure emerges with a CD in his hand, which he twirls around his finger. Pather noted an imaginative connection to the Hindu deity Vishnu who carries a discus in his hand (phone conversation, May 20, 2020).

As this figure carrying a CD invades the room, a fascinating clip of a film from India (in Tamil, the language of Pather's ancestors from Southern India) is playing. An Indian dancer in a red sari and a male figure, dressed like a king portray a heterosexual couple of the same Indian race playing out a courtship as the interracial couple, Denton and Gasa, struggle in their relationship. They move in front of the video, creating a layering effect between the video with a harmonious romantic scene in contrast to the interracial couple's emotional struggles.

The piece ends with Douglas climbing on top of the ancestral male's shoulders, and as he is carried, he touches the ceiling as if

Fig. 3.1. Ancestor with goggles. Courtesy Jay Pather.

climbing the walls, until he is taken out of the room and dropped gently to the floor. The phone rings; Gasa answers it, says nothing, and leaves the receiver off the hook on the table.

Pather notes in an unpublished interview with Clare Craighead that "the seeds" for his choice to place an interracial couple inside a fifth-floor room at the Albany Hotel were planted in 1996 when he stayed at that hotel for four weeks while working on *Ahimsa-Ubuntu*. Pather neither drives nor owns a car, and thus he notes that "walking a lot, but also walking on late afternoons, early morning, I would see the city in a very different way and almost, it was like seeing in black and white. I began to be aware of a city, that without the people, speaks . . . is resonant . . . there are these ghosts . . . these voices . . . but when you put people in . . . the dialogue is so rich."[13]

In his 2018 keynote at the University of California, Irvine, Pather reflects that *Hotel* "was about the possibility and impossibility of two people from two different race groups coming together at that time [in 2002]." He adds that in staging this work "in hotels on the periphery of various cities [he was exploring] as if it was outside the center that there was this possibility. In exploring ideas, I became more aware how truth was available in this non-narrative way" (2018a).

In 2004, Pather's work *From Before* was performed on the steps of and inside the Cathedral of Saint John the Divine in New York City in 2004. As in Durban and Johannesburg, Pather's choreography in the Big Apple showcased diverse dancers performing traditional South African dance, ballet, and Indian dance. Pather traced the genesis of *From Before* to his "sumptuous" work *A State of Grace*, performed outdoors at the KZNA (KwaZulu Natal Society of Ars) Gallery in Durban, with ballet, Shembe, Indian dancers, and Gasa and Douglas in a duet. This was the beginning of *From Before*, so technically it is a different work from *Cityscapes* (phone conversation May 31, 2020).

Fig. 3.2. *From Before* in New York City. Photographer: Mario Todeschini. Courtesy Jay Pather.

Fig. 3.3. *From Before* in New York City. Photographer: Mario Todeschini. Courtesy Jay Pather.

Over a decade after *Cityscapes* was performed, Pather notes his continuing fascination with urban sites for performance in his 2015 TedX talk entitled "A Love Affair with Space": "The city as sensorium, as a space of wonder, as a space of rest, a city of wonder, inside shopping centers, inside shop windows, making parts of the city come alive with sound, through body paint, through smells, music, and touch.... Ultimately it is about you and us as a group owning the city [with] a sense of wonder, of occupying a land and a country, a city that actually feeds us not in a utilitarian way, but in a spiritual and in a centered, in a communal, a social way" (2015).

Pather gives new meaning to working "on the edge," startling spectators with creative interventions that challenge the history of Whites-only spaces and embodying what Henri Lefebvre describes as "the long *history of space*" (Lefebvre [1974] 1994). Pather ignites the "long history" of apartheid and post-apartheid era spaces with evocative juxtapositions that could inspire conversations among communities who usually inhabit segregated neighborhoods.

In his curator note for the 2012 *Infecting the City* festival, Pather reflects back on the production of *Cityscapes* ten years before, which had provided "space for sharing subjectivities, for recognition, contact, improbable conversation, even a knowing or bemused glance or smile cannot be underestimated. It is on this premise that my early works, a series called 'CityScapes'... emerged.... Infecting the City [2008 onward] is about public engagement" (2012a).

Pather cites two main elements that have attracted him to site-specific work. Firstly, to take contemporary art onto the street, "not to patronize this so-called informal audience but create performances as [one] might inside a theatre with all due regard to detail of timings, music, costume, lighting and the like and make such work available to a people who might not have stepped inside a theatre" (Davidoff 2006, 139). The second impulse lies in Pather's interest in dialogues between the moving body in space and spatial tension. The performer interacts with space that is regarded "as animate, as a powerful conveyor of meaning and emotion. The performer engages with the space in both a physical and an emotional manner" (139–40).

Pather's commitment to and indeed passion for creating and curating site work in public began with *Cityscapes* and continues to evolve in his artistic journey. His provocative work, in which ordinary people become involved as spectators, contains a forceful message about accessibility: performances can reach those who cannot afford formal indoor theaters in Durban or Johannesburg and indeed across Africa and even beyond, to India, Southeast Asia, and Latin America. Pather's bold uses of space call out to passersby to witness high-quality artistic work in public.

REPUBLIC: SITE-SPECIFIC INSTALLATION PERFORMANCES

For JOMBA! 2004, Pather conceived of and directed *Republic*, a cutting-edge contribution to contemporary African dance, performed in Durban at ArtSpace and the Albany Grove. *Republic* included twenty visual and performance artists—Sifiso Majola, Mlu Zondi, and Vusi Makahanya, among others—who created "a series of site-specific installation performances" using a combination of indoor and outdoor spaces. One segment was located inside a room with a laundromat under the Siwela Sonke office on Albany Grove Street in central Durban. Pather enabled various communities to participate in making public art in *Republic*, a collaboration between a community of professional Durban artists that included "emerging choreographers, architects, urban planners, musicians, and video artists—20 participants in all" (Davidoff 2006, 134).

Pather describes this ambitious project as "more about curating from a concept"—namely, the idea of the "republic" that is dealt with ironically (interview 3, 2017). As he notes in the program brochure, "A series of site-specific installation performances . . .

about REPUBLIC: the body politic and the concentric circles of space that form and dissolve around the moving body, personal space, street, alley, show window, parking lot, inner city, suburbia, province and country, other countries, small countries subsumed by big ones, land dispute, ownership, monopolizing, edging in, circumnavigating, dissecting, enveloping, unveiling, burning, celebrating and pissing on the REPUBLIC, jiving all the way" (Pather 2005, 6).

Adrienne Sichel's article "Happy to Be Back at Home," while noting Pather's return after the performance of *From Before* in NYC, comments on how *Republic* takes Pather's site work further by incorporating visual art and international musicians: "Also lined up for South African viewers is an international edition of *Republic*—performances of the body politic. This landscaped interaction between dancer-choreographers and video artists made a huge impact at the 2004 Jomba Contemporary Dance Experience, in downtown Durban. This time, Pather's site-specific mediations, targeting the personal and the sociopolitical, aim to incorporate visual artists, musicians and performers from Palestine, Iraq, and Israel. Nothing is too tall an order for the barrier-bashing Jay Pather" (Sichel 2004). In 2002, *Cityscapes* did not feature visual art or international musicians, as did *Republic* in 2004; this is a testament to Pather's ever-evolving artistry, which consistently showcases how a variety of artistic forms can function in the processes of social justice for all South Africans.

STRAVINSKY'S *RITE OF SPRING* INNOVATED IN PATHER'S SITE-SPECIFIC *RITE* AND OTHER INCARNATIONS

Rite has haunted Pather ever since he choreographed his first imagining of the classical Stravinsky music in 1985, and then in Cape Town in 1991 and 1993. In another version, commissioned by Johannesburg's FNB Dance Umbrella (February 2014), Pather presented *rite* as a site-specific work at Johannesburg's Museum of African Design (MOAD). *Rite* was also presented on the proscenium stage at the seventeenth JOMBA! Contemporary Dance Experience, in October 2015 in Durban. *Rite* is Pather's first foray into deconstructing a classic, inspired by Stravinsky's music for *Le Sacre du Printemps* (*Rite of Spring*); Nijinsky's bold choreography in 1913 France, set to *Le Sacre du* Printemps, represented the ritual of a young maiden sacrificed to appease the gods of rain and has been a controversial work ever since its earliest presentation. "The thing about Stravinsky," remarks Pather, "is the connection with Russian folklore; the combination of music sometimes both atonal and driving, plus pulling back with the folkloric. I'm constantly going back to ancient societies and looking at dramas. We catapult into modern times. But we're so locked inside Grand narratives that we forget to find similarities" between ancient and modern (interview 6, 2016).

Pather's program notes for his site-specific *rite* inside the museum in Johannesburg provide his "re-imagining [of Stravinsky's] original work written in several demarcated movements: these formal rituals of adoration, grief, sensuality, choosing the maiden, ancestral dances and finally of sacrifice become vehicles in this production to probe roots of the abnegation of the feminine through a traditional archival-re-staging of the classic work interrupted by the contemporary fragment. Both narratives first punctuate each other, then, merge" (Pather, quoted in Sichel 2014b). *Rite* presented sixteen Siwela Sonke-trained dancers, including founding members Ntombi Gasa and Neliswa Rushualang, along with Cape Town's Chuma Sopotela. The soundscape—which was challenging to some audience members, as discussed below—included Stravinsky's discordant composition along with contributions by musicians James Webb and Colin Peddie. Characteristic of Pather's layering technique, *rite* includes what he describes as "a conversation amongst forms: classical and contemporary African dances, image, ritual performance and video. Closed forms and open-ended porous edges allow Stravinsky's work to bleed in and out of a contemporary South African moment, played out as it is in downtown Johannesburg."[14]

Pather's continuing passion for *rite* since 1985 is driven by Stravinsky's music and this story, replete with archetypes of communal sacrifice, scapegoats (the horror of selecting one maiden as a sacrifice), survival, and death. These notions that seem to belong to humanity's collective unconscious have captured the imagination of other artists such as Pina Bausch, whose memorable *Rite of Spring* portrays her dancers enacting rituals of celebration, along with the palpable tension of who the sacrificial female will be. Vanessa Manko comments in *The Paris Review* that she was haunted by "the ritualistic circles, the bodies contracting and convulsing to Stravinsky's driving score, the lighter moments of frolic. . . . And I saw the terror on the chosen woman's face, her desperation as she grabbed at the air and pulled her clenched fist to her gut, again, and again, and again."[15] Bausch's characteristic choreography embodies the raw emotions of anger, fear, and despair, evoking primal responses.

In "Riotously Creative Rite Debuts on Home Ground," Sichel describes Pather's innovative uses of the various architectural levels of the MOAD, including "metal stairs, dramatic arched windows and basement . . . transform[ing] [it] into a compelling playground" (2014b). Sichel continues, "This is not empty spectacle. As we travelled from site to site we journeyed through dance, South African dance, as well as post-colonial and post-apartheid history. This processional quality reminded me of a medieval miracle play—albeit a heavily deconstructed one. The opening erotic, exotic images of male dancers in stilettos parading their sexual wares high up on window sills immediately connected with the hustling and human trafficking happening below in these very streets" (2014b).

The challenge of site work can make spectators uncomfortable in particular spaces, especially if the space feels too cramped, and also if the work requires them to move from one location to another. Despite Pather's specific request to the organizers to limit the audience for *rite* inside MOAD to a specific number of people, more tickets were sold, which led to a difficult experience for some audience members such as Robyn Sassen. This South African arts commentator judged the tight space as "disregard for one's personal space in a dark unfamiliar context" (2015). She was angry about the jarring "strobe lights" and "audience abuse" that forced them to move around in a small space. Sassen, who has been writing about contemporary South African dance for the past sixteen years, has noticed that "some contemporary dance insinuates itself into the audience in a way that not only speaks of lazy choreography and sensationalism, but downright disrespect towards the abuse of Joe Public through either the effects of excessively loud noise; intolerably bright lights, particularly strobes; smoke, either real or artificial" (2015).

Sassen was also offended by the extremely loud soundtrack that distorted the original Stravinsky music in order "to support a silly tale about rape and drugs." Clearly, she was uncomfortable with the issues that Pather raised; however, she obfuscates them by feeling "physically and psychologically assaulted." As a privileged White audience member, she demands disclaimers in the program. She also questions who the audience for this type of work is—should it just be the arty types under age forty who can withstand these loud sounds and strobe lights? She admits that Dance Umbrella needs audiences, but she wants choreographers to be more responsible in recognizing that there is always a fourth wall, whether the show is on a proscenium stage or right in your face. The fourth wall "exists and a paying audience has the right to be respected for who they are and the role they play in the industry." Sassen's response takes me back to the deeply rooted inequities, the racial and spatial divides, within which Pather grew up and the continuing privilege of some White spectators who declare their right to demand disclaimers, since facing "a silly tale about rape and drugs," as Sassen notes dismissively, feels like an "assault." Ironically, the violence in *rite* is exerted on Black bodies.

Although Sichel acknowledges some of Sassen's "genuine concerns," Sichel asserts that there have been "radical shifts in choreographic and performance approaches, hard core strategies [and] performance art tactics [that] are now firmly entrenched in South African theater dance which is attracting eager, adventurous audiences" (2015, 118). Dance writer and freelance critic Nondumiso Msimanga reviews Dance Umbrella 2015 in "State of the Nation in Dance" for *Creative Feel Magazine* as "an unorthodox self-referential questioning of history, performance and nation" and comments that "the lack of dance in the main Programme of the Dance Umbrella stood as a testament to a new movement in dance performance in this country and the African continent. The theatre is of excess as indicative of emptiness, the style is non-performative absurdity, the form is a collage of fragmentation and the kitsch aesthetic tells of a need for redefinition. . . . And it is a new world for South Africa's Contemporary dance. It is resistance" (quoted in Sichel 2015, 118).

Pather's avant-garde work is a vital part of what Sichel describes as the current situation of contemporary south African dance—namely, as "flagrantly conceptual 'non-dance' driven by the moving, thinking, sentient, critical body and choreographic intelligence [that] is very much a reality on our theatre dance stages. Yet again the choreographed South African body resists being pigeon holed in a society, a country, and on a continent, in which it is performing and insists on not only being seen but being heard. Writers, critics and academics ignore this *fait accompli* at their peril" (2015, 119). Pather's "conceptual" creations unfold at the intersections of movement, theater, and visual art, challenging the boundaries of racial and spatial experiences for Black South Africans. Bold artistic interventions such as *rite* are crucial in South Africa's still developing democracy.

The violence in *rite* is stark, as the audience watches a group of male elders decide on a sacrificial maiden. However, Pather argues that it is not enough to blame individual men for violence; rather, we must work to uncover "the layers of institutional violence" (interview 6, 2016). The idea of an innocent woman being killed is hideous, though violence is widely prevalent in South African society, especially against women, as echoed by Sichel in "Riotously Creative *Rite*," where she remarks, "Violence was happening everywhere—in an urban kitchen, in a rural KwaZulu Natal village. Sacrifices were physical, spiritual, cultural and intellectual as traditions, techniques and form, including performance art, are cross-pollinated and transfused choreographically. Cultural practices and African touchstones such as chicken and cabbage are used ingeniously to create startlingly original iconography" (2014b).

Pather does not wish to simply "bash black men" as abusers; "there are men engaging in gender conversations (interview 1, 2018). In the same interview, he remarks that it is important to work with "subtleties of oppression, with gradations," he remarks. He shares with me a "nice moment" in rehearsal when the men were sitting and the women were doing a circle dance wherein one of them is "chosen" for the sacrifice. Pather notes that he stopped the rehearsal and let Ntombi Gasa turn to the audience and tell a story of a friend of hers who was threatened by the community that she would lose her house because of a virginity test, which the male members subject a young woman to after her mother has hidden the fact that her daughter is not a virgin.

After this incredibly gruesome and violent story, the males took off their robes, and a young female dancer asked Gasa how she could share this private, indeed intimate story, one that is part of their culture, with the audience at Dance Umbrella. Gasa defended her story, asserting that it was relevant; this was followed, remarks Pather, by a "big argument among the cast." The issue of land forcibly taken away came up, and then Gasa was accused of "giving away the little that is ours." The issue of keeping what's ours was linked to economic issues, to land, agency, and possessions. Pather does not wish to criticize individual males who censor Gasa as a simple and flip response; rather, he perceives their patriarchal authority as part of a system of oppressing women. For Pather, it is not a matter of "just attacking patriarchy" when men are from different economic classes; one cannot argue for agency when Black men are disempowered in so many ways in South African society (interview 1, 2018).

In these last sections of the choreography, not the ending itself, Pather comments that Gasa and Rushualang play a huge role in ritualistically getting the woman ready to be sacrificed. The horror of that impending disaster conveys, noted Pather, "a Greek tragedy like sense of catharsis" accompanied by a "wailing sound" that surrounds the actors and audience (phone conversation, May 31, 2020).

Pather's reincarnation of *rite* for the proscenium stage (JOMBA!, October 2015) in Durban included three generations of his Siwela Sonke dancers, marking the company's twentieth anniversary. In an interview on South African TV news on SABC, Pather commented that "Jomba inspires contemporary dancers to move audiences to think about their contemporary life." Stravinsky's thirty-five-minute score inspired Pather's choreography for an hour and fifteen minutes, moving between traditional and contemporary movements and narratives. Male dancers in white shorts with blond wigs and red stiletto shoes were striking on stage. After each of Stravinsky's musical movements, they performed in contemporary movement style and in some instances storytelling. In one scene, a tight circle of women dressed in white danced as if protecting a young girl caught in the middle.

Pather's essay, "Caught up in Multiply-Layered Skirts or What's a Stripper Doing in Julius Caesar?" explores "forms of

Fig. 3.4. *rite*. Photographer: Val Adamson.

Fig. 3.5. *rite*. Photographer: Val Adamson.

Fig. 3.6. *rite*. Photographer: Val Adamson.

choreography and theatre making that are akin to writing an article, a book or research paper" (Pather, forthcoming). He probes what "'literary' dance might look like" in his works such as *Body of Evidence, Qaphela Caesar,* and *rite*. He locates his own multilayered and at times "obscure" works in "the intersection of media, the various sites of the works, the perpetual interplay between tradition and a modernity imposed on us by the West, or the collaborative processes of research and creation." He argues convincingly that integral connections between form and content of his works are "an exercise in disruption, fragmentation, impressionistic collage and unresolved conclusions."

Under a subtitle, "Interrupting Structure, Suspending Narrative," Pather discusses *rite* based on the Stravinsky score and story of sacrificing a young maiden to bring rain (Pather, forthcoming). Pather is profoundly aware of gender-based violence in his society, and the disrespect endured by traditional African traditions. He "interrupts the flow of the [Stravinsky] music after each section with video projection, text, conversation with the audience etc." The show opens with an argument between a man (Mxolisi Nkomonde) and a woman (Chuma Sopotela) about a film they had just seen. Nkomonde's "verbal assault catapults him into a kind of psychic darkness," remarks Pather. In the end, as the sacrificial maiden dances herself to death, and rain does come, the dancers "remove their traditional cloth and put on plastic raincoats and hold open white umbrellas onto which television static is projected." This is followed by an encounter again as at the beginning between Nkomonde and Sopotela when she puts her hand on his mouth, forcing him to be silent during the last two minutes of Stravinsky's score.

Relocating a site-specific work to a proscenium stage involves significant choices since the two have different goals and agendas and provide alternative meanings. Pather noted that these site choices are

> ultimately not just the spaces themselves, but the movement of the audiences is extremely important. They can be led by how the space narrates [meaning] and how they negotiate that. I'm very aware of rhythm and time and how these intersect [with space]. The audience can see something that challenges the sequence. Still, a sequence determines how and when the audience moves [from one area to another]. This is very exciting for me, to see how the audience is getting a really good feeling of how to make sense of time and space in a work. Except that the large-ish audience for *Rite* in Johannesburg made it very difficult to maneuver [relocate] the audience. Since there were twice as many people [than I wanted], the time of the performance really bothered me because people were not seeing the work in its rhythm; they had to wait for spectators to move from one space to another. This starts to tear at the elasticity, the tension of the work. (interview 4, 2015)

Pather's creative use of sites, moving his own work from a site-specific location to an indoor theater or vice versa, brings new illuminations to the same work. Pather undertook a similar move from site-specific to proscenium stage for his *Qaphela Caesar* (chap. 4).

BLIND SPOT AT THE METROPOLIS BIENNNALE IN COPENHAGEN (2009)

Pather's essay "The Making of *Blind Spot*: From Lab to Biennale" discusses his participation with some twenty-five other invited artists that began in 2008 with "an audacious tour through the city of Copenhagen ... trawling through buildings, roof-tops, concrete and over water to come to grips with this lush city, its people, its architecture, politics, its splendor, charm and oddities" (2012b, 89). Pather recognized feelings of "confusion and chaos" in terms of what the participants were looking at, and then he realized that "apparent chaos in a city belies the intricate pattern that remains invisible." The recognition of which people were visible and which others remained invisible inspired Pather and "became the genesis of the project *Blind Spot*, a term borrowed from Physiology, meaning 'a small oval-spared area of the retina in which vision is not experienced' (Farlex's Free dictionary)" (89). The term *blind spot* is used commonly to instruct and warn vehicle drivers that they must look over their shoulders before changing lanes since another moving vehicle may be in their blind spot and may cause an accident. Pather returned to this city three times between 2008 and 2009 to select sites and prepare the performance of *Blind Spot* at Copenhagen's Metropolis Biennale (August 3–9, 2009). Performers included "dancers from South Africa, Malaysia, UK, Norway and Denmark [who] danced their way from Nørrebro to central Copenhagen" (89).[16]

In this site-specific work, Pather uses several locations on Copenhagen streets, where performers attract passers-by who gather to watch, even as their view may be interrupted by passing cars and buses.[17] It is as important to lead spectators to the performance site as it is to inspire them to stay and view the show. Striking columned city buildings, sculptures, large courtyards, and ordinary streets provide a background for dancers.

One segment of this multisited work evokes the title *Blind Spot* when on a cobblestone street in front of a building with a religious stone figure, a woman puts weights like stones on her eyes and walks as if blind to symbolize blind faith. Pather's essay "The Making of Blind Spot" notes that "a title emerged on the street" when his eye was first caught by a sign in the city center, visible suddenly as if from nowhere, advertising a restaurant, before he noticed the man holding the sign, who did not draw attention to himself. "To be invisible," remarks Pather, "he devolved into the perfect blind spot on the street. Who was this man? Where did he live?" (2012b, 91). Since he was a man of color in the midst of the majority White crowd, these questions, Pather states, had "a searching political" valence. Pather grew uncomfortable and put away his camera, leaving with the crowd and "submerging [himself] further into the streets and sites of Copenhagen. And accorded him his space as a blind spot" (91).

Another unexpected experience occurred late at night when Pather was walking down a dark street in Copenhagen and suddenly saw "dancing shadows" in one of the tenements and heard a Hindi song from a popular movie called *Pakeezah*, which he remembered from his own childhood in a working-class area of Durban. The song is "about an ostracized prostitute," Pather comments, and adds that it is "a beautiful film about another blind spot" (2012b, 91). At the Copenhagen jazz festival, which is held in various areas, Pather was bothered by the invisibility of Black people. "Not even the jazz could bring people of colour out of the peripheries into the centre. This blind spot thing was running deep" (91).

These personal experiences during the 2008 Laboratory phase of *Blind Spot* enabled Pather to zero in on the issue of migrants who lived in marginal areas of Copenhagen. No doubt, this resonates with the township locations for most Black people in South Africa, who come into cities for work and then return home to the city fringes. Pather sensitively describes the search for home, for comfort and security, that migrants anywhere share as well as their links to traditions from homes left behind and conflicts with their children growing up in the host country, "a site of great deliberations and tension." Pather includes among their desires and "existential longings" a need "for space, land, home, a better life, and above all, to know oneself... acceptance and above all visibility a cornerstone and perennial theme of the metropolis" (2012b, 91). Pather quotes Georgio Agamben's characterization of the metropolis as "having a strong connotation of maximum dislocation and spatial and political dishomogeneity" that is palpable in Blind Spot. Pather also finds Foucault's concept of "contemporary urban space" inspiring, namely that it is "a convergence of two paradigms: leprosy and the plague" one that demands exclusions (lepers) from civic society and the other (plague) that demands confinement, surveillance, and control (91). Notions of inclusion and exclusion of particular peoples from cities, and their realities of visibility and invisibility, are part of Pather's site work.

Armed with these conceptual tools, Pather proceeded to interview migrants in the Norrebrogade locality, gathering testimony and responses to their notions of home, where they see themselves in a decade, and their expectations of their current locations. Many answers evoked how migrants felt "othered" within dominant populations, leading to efforts to adapt or isolate themselves. "They desire paradoxes," remarks Pather; they are "yearn[ing] for rest and are restless, anxious and angry, grateful and sad, eager and resistant, thankful and restful" (2012b, 92). Even as migrants want freedom from some of their confining traditions, they hold on to them in an alien culture.

Ideas from Pather's process of gathering testimony and then creating an analytic frame for the core concepts of *Blind Spot* are worth quoting, since these inspirational notes are part of his site work as a whole:

> Showing the spatial tension between the insular and the global
> Mapping the physical and conceptual periphery and center
> Mapping paradox of a "cosmopolitan" metropolis and a disaffected immigrant community
> Exploring inter-culturalism as a site for a fluid, shifting, dynamic and complex metropolis.
> Representing these premises through gentle intervention, irony, humour, surprise, beautiful imagery, private moments in public spaces, extraordinary in the ordinary. (Pather, 2012b, 92)

The execution of these concepts onto the sites and embodying them in dancers' bodies required Pather to return to Copenhagen three times between 2008 and 2009. He "fell in love with a long road" in the city that led to the "heart of an invisible population all the way into the heart of a cosmopolitan city," from Norebrohallen to the university. He embraced the idea of "a city walk" where ticket holders were bussed to the immigrant location "as a pilgrimage," and then they would walk back for a demanding three and a half hours; this spoke to an intense desire to learn, as they made thirty-four stops on their way from the immigrant ghettos into the city. This long walk, taking several hours, was deliberately crafted by Pather to be "slow" so that the audience could "see how the landscape shifted and different pieces began to shift" (2012b, 93).

In his characteristic process of working with his Siwela Sonke dancers along with local Danish dancers, Pather explored different themes around various sites, engaging with architecture or with the space itself. He also recognized astutely that apart from ticket holders, there would be an informal audience, many of them migrants who may not be aware of the Festival, nor understand the work; Pather recognizes that site-specific performances can be "potentially alienating... for people who are not aware of what is going on.... In the context of alienation and invisibility, I had to take on both a formal as well as a so-called informal audience. Somehow, I could not continue blind-sighted" (2012b, 93). With this insight, Pather "shifted gears," weaving "a series of abstract imagery" into a story, along with a mix of popular and other kinds of music to draw in the audience. The ultimate success of the project was proven in that it drew audiences all over—on the street, watching from balconies, stopping cars and bicycles, "watching the watchers watching the performance and so various permutations of watching and participating ensued" (94).

The vignettes included portraits of individuals from different cultures, on the streets or placed strategically on balconies. Somewhere midway along the city walk, dancers wore animal masks depicting racial prejudice in front of a bar with patrons drinking beer, "watching audiences watch them" (Pather 2012b, 94). The walk culminated at the university, with "its intellectual, cultural and aesthetic reserves," and with the foreigners who had traveled a long distance to get there. Pather's essay that delineates the intricate and resonant process of his creating *Blind Spot* ends with this comment for inclusion and acceptance of diverse people and their languages and cultures: "When the Sanskrit text floated across the pillars of the University at the start of this final section, it marked symbolically, a rewriting of text, or a need for it: an inclusive, ruptured, polyphonic, partly recognizable humane text. The notion was simple: these texts of who and how we are ultimately [remain] subjective and selective. The more this language remains homogenous and hermetically sealed, the more elusive the promise of the hybrid, dynamic metropolis" (2012b, 95). Pather elaborated on his comments here, namely that he urges recognition of different languages spoken by diverse populations, including migrants in metropolitan areas, and that it is important to include their linguistic and cultural heritages in creating an integrated city that does not relegate, indeed forget its migrant/outsider citizens living on the margins of urban areas (phone conversation, May 30, 2020).

Among the various locations in Copenhagen, Pather used a large courtyard in front of a stately columned building to showcase Black dancers, their faces covered with *umcako* (white powder used in traditional healing practices). They perform rigorous contemporary moves: lifting one another, tumbling and falling on the floor, one man sitting down nonchalantly while a woman struggles to find her feet under a pile of paper that she gathers around her body. The evocative song "Mallaika le" by Angélique Kidjo accompanies a duet.

On the street, a man with large, clanging bells on his ankles, his body covered with a long white garland that trails behind him, leads the audience to the next site. People standing on balconies like royalty, one even wearing a fake crown, in a playful and parodic way, greet the public gathered below like commoners separated from the higher-ups, the power holders who are above them even physically. A woman on an upstairs balcony dances a few steps of kathak to North Indian classical music. From a different balcony, a long piece of red and white fabric, the colors of the Danish flag, and similar to the dancer's dress, hangs at an intersection, draped limply downward instead of flying high, before being pulled up by the hands of a person on the balcony. The Danish flag limp, hanging down comments on the failure of the nation-state to its migrant and immigrant populations. Pather identified this site as "the nexus of where the white city started and the immigration section ended" (Pather 2018a).

On the streets of Copenhagen, two Black men dragging loads walk down a long pedestrian walkway flanked on one side by a yellow wall, as a lone White woman appears and engages in a tentative duet while another Danish dancer watches. She is carried by a Black dancer at the end, and as they move into the park, the female dancer is confronted by the male dancer. Around a carefully laid out installation of cups from traditional Danish crockery they perform at first a tender duet of siblings, which sees them intimately bound, though the woman appears uncomfortable with the man's rather aggressive physical moves, covering her face as he holds her firmly by her shoulders. Other Black dancers, led by the dancer that the woman had previously interacted with, appear as shadows in the park carrying whisks used in traditional *sangoma*, invoking the presence of the other, but also one of healing and hoping for some measure of harmony.

At the beginning of *Blind Spot*, the audience is led into an abandoned urban lot, its walls covered in graffiti. "Two men, a father and his son, appear to struggle physically," explains Pather, "while a woman sits and watches. The son, in an explosive ending of intergenerational conflict on foreign soil," takes a briefcase and runs out of the space as the audience follows (phone conversation, May 30, 2020). On another street, Black men move with bent backs as if burdened with labor, even as bells jingle on their ankles—one of Pather's unexpected juxtapositions of an emotionally heavy sight accompanied by the jaunty sound of bells. On a different street, a woman takes shelter inside a paper tent that covers her head before she pulls the paper around her like a skirt.

On the steps leading into a large building, a White man in a suit is lying down, as if struggling against the assault of a woman wearing a blonde wig. Pather explains that "the 'thread' here is that this is the 'city planner,' facing a model of the city at the beginning of the piece who demarcates land and where people should live. The end is a satiric and absurd confrontation between Gasa and him. She is rather provocative and he is both in rapture as well as wanting to get away from her" (email to Katrak, May 30, 2020). The man moves backward, then falls into a pool of water. The "pool idea," adds Pather, "was to involve most of the dancers who were in *umcako* submerge themselves and emerge with nothing on them, a ritualistic fantasy of cleaning the slate and starting over." Such use of water connects to a ritualistic cleansing except here the symbolic submersion and emergence from the pool symbolically raises the issue of "cleaning up" disparities among citizens, some of whom live on the margins literally; and metaphorically, they are on edge in their efforts to integrate into the Danish way of life. Minorities are usually beholden to assimilate into the majority culture rather than the dominant population making constructive moves to migrants.

Blind Spot, like *Cityscapes,* demonstrates Pather's unique ability to use space and to make bodies move in space, confronting divisions among people whether in Cape Town or in Copenhagen. Pather's site-specific work, guided by his significantly open-ended aesthetic vision, invites his audiences to reflect on the contemporary lives of ordinary people and their struggles.

In conclusion, the site-specific works discussed in this chapter demonstrate Pather's choreographic and conceptual labor with spatial configurations as they are etched into Black bodies' memories of exclusion, along with Pather's creative ways of reinserting these bodies into public spaces. He democratizes both the individuals and the spaces in the new South Africa. A remarkable feature of Pather's art is that he demonstrates the same vision of access and inclusion in *Cityscapes* in Durban or Johannesburg as he does for migrants who are marginalized on the outskirts of cosmopolitan Copenhagen. Increasingly, Pather is a sought-after artist who can enter a site, explore the inhabitants living in and around it, and make work that is startling and rewarding for his audiences.[18]

Pather's goals in his site-specific works discussed above continue into his site-responsive performances—*Home, The Beautiful Ones Must Be Born, Body of Evidence,* and *Qaphela Caesar*—discussed in the next chapter. Each is set in a unique location that embodies and responds to sociopolitical realities of contemporary South Africa. He selects sites that respond to his choreography as it continually explores the human body as a repository of history and memory; at times it seems he is forensically probing into this democracy's failures to its Black citizens, as if surgically carving into the body politic to discover what ails it and seeking ways to unmask the sores, unravel through his art the years of irresponsible governing that cannot meet the most basic necessities for its Black population.

NOTES

1. This bitter issue of land ownership was brought up as recently as February 2018 by the new president, Cyril Ramaposa, who replaced Jacob Zuma. In 2013, Pather as director of GIPCA, conceptualized a symposium on land (discussed in chap. 5) to mark the 100th anniversary of the 1913 Native Land Act and its continuing legacy of dispossessing and displacing Black people of their land.

2. That novel was *Devil on the Cross*, first published in 1980 in Gikuyu, then in English, (Heinemann, 1982). Ngũgĩ also published *Detained: A Writer's Prison Diary* (Heinemann, 1981). An updated version reflecting on his experience behind bars, with resonance for ongoing contemporary struggles faced by artists under repressive regimes—namely, *Wrestling with the Devil: A Prison Memoir*—was published in 2018 (New York: New Press).

3. *Pantsula*, which was rooted in South African Black townships, was initially performed exclusively by men dressed in suits, with strong group affiliations and dance competitions among groups. Today, both men and women perform the dance style and still compete in *pantsula* groups wearing street clothes and signature Converse brand sneakers. The style, performed low to the ground, with quick steps, demonstrates influences of American hip-hop and breakdancing, which are also tied to urban street culture. See the clip "The Coolest Dance You've Never Heard of: Pantsula" at https://www.youtube.com/watch?v=gMgcLo_WGig, accessed February 5, 2016.

4. A recent volume of essays entitled *Acts of Transgression: Live Art in South Africa* is coedited by Pather and Catherine Boulle (Johannesburg: University of Witwatersrand Press, 2019).

5. Pather recounted an incident during one of the segments of *CityScapes* on the beach in Durban when dancer Rushualang was "verbally attacked" by an onlooker for doing Shembe that was carefully chosen by Pather, in consultation with Rushualang and his dancers, to feature on the beach where the rhythms of Shembe and the sound of the waves would synchronize beautifully. Rushualang, "with full ownership" of Shembe,

noted Pather, confronted the negative question of why she was doing this style in public on the beach by stating forthrightly that this was her work and this was "our company," including Pather and all the dancers in that segment on the beach.

6. Schechner's deep interest in exploring ritual and performance were critiqued for troubling appropriations by Indian theater and performance studies scholar Rustom Bharucha (1990) in his pathbreaking essay "Collision of Cultures: Peter Brooks' *Mahabharata*," among other publications (see bibliography).

7. Anne Carlson uses the phrase "a critical language" as necessary for site dancers just as visual arts and other disciplines need their own vocabularies in a useful book entitled *Site Dance: Choreographers and the Lure of Alternate Spaces*, edited by Melanie Kloetzel and Carolyn Pavlik.

8. See critical theorist Andre Lepecki's essay "Choreopolice and Choreopolitics" for a useful discussion of the role of mounted police in dispersing crowds and in the political valences of performances on street corners or inside art galleries. See also my discussion in chapter 5 on Cape Town, the beautiful tourist city that is jolted with art across its central areas in Pather's curation of the *Infecting the City* public arts festival.

9. Achille Mbembe, a Cameroonian, holds academic positions at Duke University and at the University of Witwatersrand. Mbembe's concerns with race, decoloniality, and violence against the Black body are expressed in numerous publications including *Critique of Black Reason* (2017) and his seminal work, *On the Postcolony* (2001).

10. JOMBA! Contemporary Dance Experience brochure, 2005. Acquired by Katrak during a research visit in 2015.

11. In "When the Rainbow Is Not Enough...," Clare Craighead (2010) describes Shembe as "a religious and ritual dance form/movement form associated with the teaching of Isaiah Shembe. It is a slow, rhythmic and earth-bound form. Celtic is a traditional Irish dance form, characterized by fast, rhythmic foot work. Kathak is a classical Indian dance form; like Shembe, Kathak is also a religious form. It is characterized by intricate eye and hand gestures, and also involved rhythmic stamping as part of its technique."

12. KZN is KwaZulu Natal, the province in which Durban is located.

13. Jay Pather, interview by Clare Craighead, Durban, 2005.

14. Pather, 2014 program notes read by Katrak during research visit to South Africa in 2015.

15. Vanessa Manko, "Pina Bausch's *The Rite of Spring*," *Paris Review*, October 11, 2017, https://www.theparisreview.org/blog/2017/10/11/pina-bauschs-rite-spring, accessed January 15, 2018.

16. The web publication of *Changing Metropolis II* includes discussions on Copenhagen's potential and limitations in inclusion of migrants in the city. The web publication is divided into different chapters with practitioners like Pather commenting on their processes of making work in this city. The complete issue is at https://issuu.com/cphmetropolis/docs/changing_metropolis/7, accessed January 22, 2018.

17. I base the descriptions that follow on Pather's essay "The Making of Blind Spot" and on my viewing of footage of the performances on the Metropolis website (http://www.cph.metropolis.dk, accessed April 12, 2016).

18. Over the past ten years, Pather's international profile is evident in distinctive invitations and positions. Pather serves as Expert Advisor: *Live Art*, Africa 2020, commissioned by President Macron of France. He serves as chair of the Ecole Universitat de Recherche Artec International, Paris (2019–2020). In 2019, he was invited to the International Visiting Curators Program in Sydney, Australia. He was a committee member at the Decolonization of Art Institute, Berlin from 2019–2020. Pather was a Fellow at the School of English and Drama, University of London, from 2016–2018. In South Africa, he served as adjunct curator (Performance Art) for the Zeitz MOCAA (Museum of Contemporary Art Africa) in Cape Town (2017–2019). Pather was chair of South Africa's National Arts Festival Artistic committee (2010–2014) and the Dance Representative for the National Arts Festival (2005–2014). He was chair, Performing Arts Network of South Africa, from 2005–2008. Pather has presented papers at, among others, the African Knowledges Workshop, the School for New Dance in Amsterdam, the International Leadership Forum at Aix en Provence, the UNESCO Conference on Art Education in Africa, the Territoires de la creation Conference in Lille, the Metropolis Conference in Copenhagen, the World Cultural Forum in Brazil, the African Urbanism Colloquium in Cairo, and the International Theatre Institute in London.

FOUR

SITE-RESPONSIVE WORKS OF HISTORY AND MEMORY

The use of sites other than the theatre, whether site specific or site responsive, most obviously addresses use of multi-perspective, access, audience involvement and participation.... I have worked often with sites as imperfect, incomplete memory fields, archival spaces such as Constitution Hill (*The Beautiful Ones Must Be Born*), Lister Medical Centre, downtown Johannesburg (*Body of Evidence*), Cape Town City Hall and the old Johannesburg Stock Exchange (*Qaphela Caesar*). Sites in this instance provide an extant text in seemingly unshakeable bricks and mortar to work with. The immovability is tested, the veracity of the text of these monolithic spaces is destabilized and questioned through ironic interventions, displacement and a reduction in the enforced hallowedness implied by the monumental space coming up against the human frame.[1]

Jay Pather, "Laws of Recall"

THE CONCEPTS OF "SITE-RESPONSIVE" AND "site-specific" are related, though each conveys distinct nuances. In both, the public and public arenas are engaged spatially in different ways. The previous chapter discussed Pather's spatial choices for his site-specific works that are set on public streets or inside a mall or a coffee shop. Site-responsive work is similar but functions a little differently—by tapping in to an audience's knowledge of a

Fig. 4.1. Robben Island. Photographer: Katrak.

location's history and its past and present, so they may be stunned by its subversion. Specific sites such as a national museum, a war memorial, or a memorialized prison locale, such as Nelson Mandela's cell on Robben Island off the coast of Cape Town, carry their own histories that may be challenged by a creative work interacting with official versus personal stories.

In this chapter, I analyze four of Pather's site-responsive works that create vibrant interactions between the space and the content and purpose of the creative work and often question state-sanctioned histories. *Home* (2003), unfolding in nine locations, explores and explodes human desire for security and safety in a private space for Black people in the South African context. Next, in 2005, *The Beautiful Ones Must Be Born* showcases Pather's acumen at playing with multiple meanings imbued in a historic site, namely, Johannesburg's Constitution Hill, also a tourist destination for viewing prisons of the past as well as a major symbol of justice during post-independence (housing the Constitutional Court). On Constitution Hill, some spectators, standing on the Great Steps or inside Prisoner Block 4, may recall its history of incarceration and dehumanization of political prisoners even as *The Beautiful Ones Must Be Born* symbolically raises the government's reneging on commitments ten long years after independence. Pather's tour de force work, *Body of Evidence* (2008) is set in a medical building, in which the site responds to the medico-legal purpose of the work. Finally, Pather reimagines the usual activities at a city hall, a site where government officials regulate the functioning of an urban area and the lives of its citizens, by placing 2010's *Qaphela Caesar*—a story of power and betrayal—inside its corridors of power. This adaptation of Shakespeare's *Julius Caesar* was remounted at the Johannesburg Stock Exchange, another site-responsive location of deal-making and power, with lurking shadows of corruption and greed. When performed in Durban, it was a truncated production called *Caesar Interrupted*, since the funding fell short. A final (so far!) iteration of *Qaphela Caesar* unfolded on the proscenium stage of the State Theatre in Pretoria, where it was billed as "a political thriller" and was highly successful, with sophisticated set design and lighting, beautiful costumes, and virtuosic dancing.

Pather revels in deconstructing commonplace notions of governmental power vested in institutions such as city halls or state-run prisons. He is confident of what Jurgen Habermas describes as a "paradox of tolerance" that is paid at least lip service in post-apartheid society. Pather's audacious site-responsive works defy what Christopher Balme identifies as overt or indirect forms of state control over free expression, even "internalized rules and proscriptions" (2013, 100). Even when performances move outside theater buildings, "the spatial concept of a realm of theatrical interaction primarily outside the building," elaborates Balme, "merges into a conceptual entity that becomes ultimately so palpable that it functions as an extension of the institution"

(106). Balme asks, "How can the public be reached, exploited, or nurtured? . . . [What is] the nature of the public and the public sphere? What are their spatial and quantitative limits?" (105). He attests that "the public and perhaps also the public sphere in its spatial sense, come to be regarded as something that can be acted on, appealed to, influenced, and even manipulated" (105). Balme is less optimistic than an artist like Pather, whose creative works challenge rather than function "as an extension of the institution," such as a city hall or a medical building.

HOME (2003): A PLACE OF UNEASE

Pather conceived and directed *Home* with Siwela Sonke Dance Theatre, giving a recognizable site of domesticity new and disturbing meaning. Sarahleigh Castelyn remarks in her essay "'Home Is Where the Heart Is': Black South African Identities and Siwela Sonke Dance Theatre's *Home* (2003)," "*Home* . . . explores the correlation between the construction of black South African identities and the notion of home" (2011, 30). *Home* is set inside various "home" locations such as a kitchen, a bedroom, a solitary uncluttered space, a hostel, a migrant worker's cubicle, and a lounge—indoor spaces that embody a sense of entrapment for performers and spectators. The audience moves with the performers from room to room "through an 'exploded' or 'deconstructed house' . . . *Home* revisits the paradox of the desire for security and freedom, restlessness and the aching need for rest" (van Rensburg 2004).

Home was commissioned as an installation performance by the National Arts Festival (NAF) in Grahamstown for its Main Stage program in July 2003. Subsequently, *Home* was mounted at the Durban Art Gallery in October 2003 and later as part of Spier Summer Festival's tenth anniversary celebration.

In *Home*, dancers perform unfamiliar interactions with familiar objects like a table or a bed, in recognizable locations such as a kitchen or a bedroom. Indoors, bodies interact with one another and with material things that resonate with new meanings beyond their usual uses, even transcending their common uses—for instance, the kitchen table is not used for meals or for reading but as a raised platform on which the performer stands and shouts. In this kitchen, no food is being prepared to nourish the body; rather, there are violent eruptions of emotional rage and frustration, rooted in deprivation of the bounty and comfort the table was designed to support.

Pather remarked that in *Home* he was exploring the paradox of safety and flight inside a home and then playing with our viewing of this paradox. So he confesses to "playing on site"—that is, taking the usual expectation of what occurs in a domestic kitchen and having the performance unfold in another space, namely, an art gallery (interview 3, 2017). He noted in the same interview that he had already done other segments of *Home*—namely, *Hotel* (which was also part of *Cityscapes*, 2002) and *Lounge*—before he created *Kitchen* while "improvising with Nellie [Neliswa Rushualang, veteran SSDT dancer] on a solo and [he] began to think of home inside different spaces such as inside a gallery."

It remains curious and thought-provoking to imagine *Kitchen* inside an art gallery, and I wondered about Pather's choice of location. How does this site respond to the notion of home? The spectators of *Kitchen* are entering an art gallery, a public space, as voyeurs looking into a private, domestic kitchen space. This open-to-the-public private space, a kitchen, is no different from a public gallery visited by art lovers. Pather represents the political realities of the difficult lives of Black people by taking his audience right into their private homes; he makes the political personal. Further, *Daily News* insightfully notes, "The show also serves as a metaphor (through its use of a range of visual imagery, dance and performance styles) for larger global impulses of inward looking in the threat of change" (2003).

Kitchen (eighteen minutes) won one of five renowned Brett Kebble Art Awards in 2004 in Cape Town, where the show was reconstructed in collaboration with artist Greg Streak, "relish[ing] this groundbreaking step" of linking movement and visual art (Sichel 2004, 6). Pather finds "an overlapping between dance, performance and visual art. Steven [Cohen] trailblazed the blurring of boundaries for us" (quoted in Sichel 2004). The award citation notes, "This installation performance is part of a series of works that deal with shifting identities reflected in 'home' spaces.... *Kitchen* uses traditional Zulu ritual (*umcimezo*), contemporary performance text and video to evoke layers of power relations inside a rural kitchen."[2]

Home represents a unique combination of movement and visual arts, similar to *Cityscapes*, where Pather brought together dancer-actors with visual artists who captured the performances on video from their different viewpoints, then showed them inside art galleries. In *Home*, Pather uses "startling images" by different artists: "Visual artist Jo Radcliffe provides startling images of the legendary Devonshire Hotel, while Milijana Babic's unsettling home sculptures include a wrought iron swing caught in mid-air without an occupant. Angela Buckland's photography meticulously examines the bunkers of migrant workers in their temporary homes. Video artists Storm Janse van Rensburg, Greg Streak and Jan Henri Booyens complete the impressive list of visual artists whose work is featured in the production" (*Independent on Saturday*, 2003).

Attempts to create a safe space called home, something that most people consider a basic human right, have a sad history in South Africa going back to the 1913 Native Land Act, the law that stripped Black people of their land, making them homeless in the place of their birth. As Sarahleigh Castelyn recounts this history, she quotes A. J. Christopher (1994, 12): "Some 8.9 million hectares were defined as Native Reserves" where Black people could not buy property nor occupy the land via "leasing, share-cropping or labour tenancy" (quoted in Castelyn 2011, 32). Indeed, Castelyn points out that White landowners resisted this "injunction on labour tenancy [fearing] a shortage of labour" (31). Later, during apartheid, the 1950 Group Areas Act, which forcibly removed people to racially designated spaces, "was to effect," notes Christopher, "the total urban spatial segregation" (quoted in Castelyn 2011, 32). The Native Land Act, the Group Areas Act, and the relegation of Black people (unemployed in cities) to "homelands" all "provide examples of home in South Africa as a politically charged concept and location" (Castelyn 2011, 31).

Even in post-apartheid times, Black peoples' struggles to reclaim their stolen land via redistribution projects "are reminders," comments Castelyn, that they continue to endure "the loss of choice of where the home can be located.... Destruction of people's homes no doubt frequently had commensurable destructive effects on black South African identities" (2011, 31).

Pather evokes this history through his choreography of stark, even tense movements of the couple and their frustrated interactions with one another along with the angry banging of empty kitchen cabinets with no food. As the Brett Kebble Award citation notes, "The installation builds on taut complex personal relationships handled by material and philosophical contexts that are relentlessly unforgiving. The hardness foregrounds the fragility of the relationships and the impossibilities, in this instance of doing more than waiting."

In *Kitchen*, set in what is usually the hearth and heart of a home, the actions of a Black man and woman are observed from a "godly" distance by a White actor standing on top of a kitchen cabinet, playing Jesus, with arms outstretched. His very presence raises hope that the couple's misery will be alleviated. In the harsh physical movements, however, instead of comfort there is only rage and frustration. Any notion of calm and nurturing domesticity is absent; in fact, that expected feeling of safety, even if it hovers on the edges of the kitchen, is crushed.

The couple in *Kitchen* is trapped in a trying relationship (given hunger and deprivation) that is emotionally falling apart, concretized in the physical breakdown of the furniture. As the female performer enters, she calls on her ancestors by lighting the herb *imphepho* to anoint the space with its powerful fragrance. Castelyn interprets her actions as those of a traditional Zulu warrior, who is usually a male, preparing for war; here, "she adopts the performance of a type of masculinity in the face of the violence ever present in her everyday life" (2011, 37). Next, the male performer enters carrying "a *knobkerrie*—a traditional crafted walking stick that, if need be, is a weapon" (37). His movements appear frenzied. The woman opens and shuts the empty cupboards hysterically, "with the cupboard doors being worked so hard that they begin to fall off," notes Castelyn. "The kitchen, like its occupants, is fractured, and is breaking apart" (38). The atmosphere carries a foreboding of danger, "a possible threat of violence both inside and outside of this kitchen" (38).

In a hard-hitting duet that is both poignant and heartbreaking, the woman holds the man with great strength. Despite the traditional patriarchal structure of the man as head of household, here the woman supports the man against whatever threats he faces in society outside this kitchen. Castelyn indicates that although *Kitchen* unfolds in post-apartheid South Africa, the legacy of townships where Black people live in cramped, substandard housing continues to engender anger and desperation at ongoing poverty and wretchedness. *Home* is a "fractured space," as Castelyn explains, since both the inside and the outside of the home space contain a number of fragmentary elements: indoors, the kitchen cabinets are empty of food, "the crucified man" standing on top of a cupboard suggests infringement of an outside church, and the rural is symbolized by a woman sitting in a rocking chair with her hands folded in her lap, as if she is resigned and waiting. Other spaces outside the home are portrayed via video footage of a commuter train packed with Black bodies. Castelyn notes that rural and urban spaces are juxtaposed, as are the South African traditional and Christian belief systems, both "illustrat[ing] the fractured and complex reality common to the experience of home in South Africa" (2011, 39).

Kitchen opens with sounds of home reverberating not comfortingly but eerily, as a woman with a basket on her head walks in wearing sneakers with dance bells, the kind worn by Indian dancers, though always on bare feet. The bells clang unrhythmically as she stamps her feet in both African and Indian dance movements. "Dance and ritual come together," notes the *Daily News*, "to evoke intimate, interior moments of belonging/dislocation and nurturing/fleeing" (*Daily News* 2003). The woman stretches out her arms, mirroring the gesture of the Jesus figure on top of the kitchen cabinet. As the woman mops the floor, the man climbs on top of the table, then circles the woman, who suddenly lifts and carries him, cradling him upright before making him lie in her lap. The couple's agony is represented through the poignancy of their movements, which also reflect the unease within their domestic situation.

Apartheid's legacy of broken families continues to make "the experience of home," remarks Castelyn, "a site of conflict for many black South Africans" (2011, 40). Rural women's realities include waiting for husbands who may have stopped sending remittances and/or who may have other relationships in cities. The urban woman faces multiple uncertainties in dealing with poverty and imminent threats of violence both inside and outside her home. The rural and urban women "move through a partnering where both female dancers lift and hold each other" (39). *Kitchen* ends with the rural woman lifting up a bundle of firewood and balancing it on her head, draped uncannily in translucent, shining fabric, and leaving.

Home includes *Hostel*, which poignantly explores the plight of the native Black man who is rendered an outsider, a "migrant" in his own land, part of internal migrant laborers who move not from across geographical borders but within the same nation from rural to urban sites, or from one location to another for work such as in mines. This migrant laborer has no choice but to live in a cramped, alien "hostel" space where nothing belongs to him except his body—which is also at the service of his employers. The figure of the migrant is close to Pather's heart, as in his exploration of migrant-outsiders living on the margins of Copenhagen in *Blind Spot* (discussed in chap. 3) and his empathy for Black migrants from other parts of Africa to South Africa in his curation of different works for *Infecting the City* public arts festivals (discussed in chap. 5). Pather's sympathetic outreach to outsiders may also be rooted in his personal history as a descendant of Indian migrants who braved the high seas in leaving India to look for a better life. Through the use of stark video projections, *Hostel* draws a visceral link to actual migrant laborers living in claustrophobically tight spaces.

Hostel opens with a bare-chested male performer, played by Mdu Mtshali, waking up in a panic from what appears to be "a troubled sleep" (Castelyn 2011, 32). In silence, we hear his sharp breaths as he begins to stamp his feet "with a frenetic energy," comments Castelyn, indicating that "he is under duress." The meager personal items of the laborers, the hostel's occupants, are numbered, "as if catalogued and come loaded with implications of ownership" such as "a hair comb [and] a crucifix necklace" that offer windows into the men's personal lives, in which they are deprived of living with families (30). Living in the hostel, their sole purpose is to supply labor. The male bodies are never shown resting on the beds.

Castelyn comments on "the poor living and working conditions, the absence of human rights and responsibilities, social disruption and upheaval" (2011, 33). Even after independence in 1994, these hostels, with their inadequate living conditions, are still managed under the Natives (Urban Areas) Act 21 of 1923. Today, among seven hostels just outside Durban, there are "an excess of 43,000 officially registered beds" (34). Predominantly for male laborers, hostels are emblematic of disrupted families, since women and children without fathers or husbands are forced to live elsewhere. Migrant laborers not only face high-risk jobs for low pay, they also endure long separations from family.

The hostels' alienating, concrete constructions have iron gates "to separate corridors from one another in case riots erupted ... communal facilities allowed little dignity or privacy" (Castelyn, 2011, 28). Ruth Panelli notes that the physical structures of hostels themselves demonstrate "the way space can be constructed as a physical arrangement and a discourse of control" (2004, 171). The feeling of entrapment created by hostel architecture is reminiscent of Michel Foucault's concept of the panopticon (in his *Discipline and Punish: The Birth of the Prison*, 1975; an idea that comes from Jeremy Bentham, an English philosopher of the 1700s), a prison complex in which each prisoner is visible and spied upon by central command. There is no autonomy of movement or action in this rigidly controlled space.

Pather's choreography of the male dancer's movements close to his body vividly convey the feeling of being confined in a tight space, of being "oppressed by the space" (Castelyn 2011, 34). "He strains and moves through this closed space as if the air around him is thick and difficult to move through. . . . His body appears scarred. This is evident when his back is towards the audience; slides beam onto his back, and his flesh appears cut up and divided by the slides as he curls his spine and ribs and folds over, giving in to the gravity pull of the floor" (34). Castelyn analyzes the movement, affect, and political implications of *Hostel*, also noting that the "choreography of space is designed to oppress and constrain black South African masculinity" (35).

Movements from Zulu war dances, with high kicks and fighting routines, may appear out of place in this location, where the warrior preparing for battle has no chance of winning.

However, as Castelyn is quick to point out, the effect does not convey defeat or weakness. Indeed, the workers are fighting "a generalized evil.... [Their] masculinity is shaped by the space it is performed in and the space of the hostel dweller fosters this aggressive movement quality. The hostel space is constructed to contain and oppress the hostel dweller" (2011, 36). Even when the male dancer tries "to fly this space by jumping, the [visual] slides of the catalogued beds marked his body, thus visually making the link between the body and the home as an extension of each other" (37).

Hostel portrays Angela Buckland's deeply moving photographs that demonstrate that even within the confines of having only a bed to call "home," this does not stop the laborer's spirit from imprinting itself on the bed, revealing the richness of each one. In *Hostel*, although the laborer's external identity is marked by the number 522, who he is psychically and as a full human being cannot be taken away despite the small space he occupies on his bed. The authorities may identify him by the number assigned to him, so if he no longer "inhabits" that number by leaving his job, the number would simply be transferred to another laborer who would take his place. They are all "oppressed," living in what Castelyn describes as "this hostel (hostile) space" (37).

Despite the fact that the space occupied by a bed is the only "home" the migrant worker has, which is not "home" but only a functional space to rest for a few hours before his labor begins again, he nonetheless anoints the space by flicking the contents from an enamel bowl while chanting incantations in isiZulu "as mournful cello music fills the stage. He practices the exorcising and anointing of the space, calling the *amadlozi*—the ancestors—to bless the home space" (Castelyn 2011, 36).

The toll that such conditions take on male humanity triggers macho behaviors and masculinities that can quickly bleed into violence. Castelyn quotes an excellent analysis by Robert

Morrell on how South Africa was "until recently, a man's country" in which

> power was exercised publicly and politically by men. In families, both black and white, men made decisions, earned the money and held power. The law (both customary and modern) supported the presumption of male power and authority and discriminated against women. But the country's history also produced brittle masculinities—defensive and prone to violence.... For black men, the harshness of life on the edge of poverty and the emasculation of political powerlessness gave their masculinity a dangerous edge. Honour and respect were rare, and getting it and retaining it (from white employers, fellow labourers or women) was often a violent process. (Morrell 2001, 18)

Castelyn's careful re-creation of *Hostel* notes the appearance of three Black female dancers in white skirts, swaying gently from side to side while remaining in the same spot. Their hands depict bharatanatyam mudras. The color white, according to Castelyn, in "traditional South African belief is associated with the ancestral realm" (2011, 35). Hence, Castelyn remarks that the dancers wearing white costumes "suggest proximity to the ancestors, and of course, ghosts" (36). The male laborer may be dreaming of being comforted by his female relatives or ancestors.

Hostel's portrayal of "the tragic reality for millions of South African mine-workers" living in these subhuman conditions strongly strikes Matthew Krouse, arts editor of the *Mail & Guardian*, in "*Home* as a Battleground." Krouse remarks on Sphelele Nzama, who "plays a lone mineworker in a hostel, dancing solo, imagining a woman he cannot have. Above him, Pather has chosen to use the astounding photographs of Angela Buckland that she had presented in a series of 100 hostel-dwellers' beds." Krouse comments further, "Memories emerge as cadavers from cupboards and from the wings. For Pather and company, one gets the feeling, home is a place of hurt. Pather's dance piece consists of nine 'homely' locations and furthers his preoccupation with place" (Krouse 2003). Despite the despairing representations of the different segments, Krouse notes that "the coagulating agent in all of this is Pather's choreography that plays on harmony but returns in each instance to full-blown discord."

In "Where the Heart Breaks," *Sunday Magazine*'s Niren Tolsi quotes Pather's words and his thinking behind creating *Home*:

> I began to be fascinated by how within a small space inside of a home, there is so much stuff that hangs in the air. It's kind of like the spoken and unspoken emotions, all the histories which are played out and the histories which are covered up.... Going into people's lives, the stories which fall out of the closet are vast and very powerful.... All these social ideas arose through these very, very personal human stories. I began to be aware of the home space as such a paradox—that it is incredibly powerful because it seems to provide you with safety and sanctity, and when that is robbed inside the home, it's quite a betrayal. It's a big deal. (Tolsi 2003)

Pather connects the notion of home to one's sense of identity, which he believes is not fixed but fluid. He recognizes that a home feels like "a cultural space" but is actually constituted of "bits and pieces of culture from all parts of the atmosphere, making it very powerful because we are never one thing at any one time" (Pather, quoted in Tolsi 2003). Pather is "fascinated," as he notes above, by such changes. Indeed, he believes that it is "a testament to our [humanity's] adaptability.... We are so many different things and that is a sign of our resilience—the resilience of the human spirit to survive all these conquered cultures" (Pather, quoted in Tolsi 2003).

When *Home* moved to the Durban Art Gallery in November 2003, this "moveable feast," as Tommy Ballyntyne notes, features a kathak dancer from Mumbai, Vaibhav Joshi, and a young African girl whom he takes away from the dangerous playground. He is "on a journey to explore the internal meaning of the word home" (Ballyntyne 2003, 9).

Lliane Loots (2003) comments in "Home Sweet Home" that this work takes a viewer "on a dark and wonderful journey into the head and heart of Pather himself. It is almost a retrospective of his work over the past eight years," from 1996 to 2003. As the audience is made to move into the different spaces of the Durban Art Gallery, "from playgrounds to kitchens, to hostels and lounges," remarks Loots, "we are asked to question what 'home' means in South Africa." It is worth noting that Loots uses *in South Africa* rather than *for South Africans*. This makes the nation itself accountable for the many onslaughts against the human desire to create a home for its majority population. Loots quotes Pather's program notes: "Our established sense of home and family has had to shift and change—hotels, cardboard homes and bomb shelters thrive as homes, while picket fence suburbia caves in with more and more steel gates."

Loots singles out Ntombi Gasa as "one of the finest female dancers in this country," particularly for her performance in *Hotel* (part of *Home* and of *Cityscapes*) as well as her "acting and performance work [that] makes her pull the whole of *Home* together." In *Hotel* (discussed in chap. 3), a Black woman, Ntombi Gasa, and a White man Denton Douglas try to connect—physically and emotionally—as they struggle with what Loots refers to as South Africa's dark historical realities; these include the Immorality Act that forbade intimate relationships across races and the tradition of Black domestic workers caring for White children while their own children had to be raised by extended family members.

"*Home* is, in the end," remarks Loots, "about that which is hidden in our sense of private space. Pather has declared this political by opening it up into performance. *Home* makes me realise that the real political battles of this country have been about where we, as South Africans, have placed our heads to go to sleep" (Loots 2003).

In "Where the Heart Breaks," Pather comments to Niren Tolsi that in *Home* "there is no angst for the sake of angst. It's not anarchic in the sense that it goes into where the void is just black.... Home is not just a physical space. That sanctity or security is not something contained between four walls, that it's something which is kept in one's heart and in the imagination or wherever. I think in spite of all that, you do have a sense that you're still being held, there is a certain level of nurturing, that it's not entirely bleeding. At least I hope that's what comes across" (Tolsi 2003). Pather's comment that in *Home* "there is no angst for the sake of angst" is reminiscent of his 1994 essay on African contemporary dance (discussed in my introduction), in which he distinguishes the sense of alienation haunting a Westerner—expressed in postmodern and contemporary dance—from the kind of disconnection from a painful reality that South African Black people endure while suffering hunger and dehumanization. Therefore, although the feeling of alienation may be similar in response to contemporary life in Europe or in South Africa, its root causes and expressions are different. Pather's optimism, despite showing anarchy instead of security in the space of home, lies in his inclusion of nurturing as the wife holds the distraught husband in her lap, and in the presence of an elder woman looking on and holding the wife in a loving duet. The choreography embodies the hope that is especially crucial when Pather takes spectators to the edge of despair, then pulls them back into imagining the positive.

Pather adds an autobiographical note to his creation of *Home*, saying that he is "such a work person that if I do not consciously make home truly home, it so easily becomes a space in transition to work. Then again, all spaces should ideally be 'home' so that we improve the quality of work spaces as well and thereby enhance living in general" (*Daily News* 2003). Pather imagines that ideally, what people cherish in the safety and security of their private homes (even if that may not be a reality for many South Africans) would also prevail in one's public workspaces.

THE BEAUTIFUL ONES MUST BE BORN (2005): PAINFUL PAST, DISILLUSIONED PRESENT, HOPEFUL FUTURE

Pather's profound political concerns are expressed masterfully in both the astute timing and the historic setting of *The Beautiful Ones Must Be Born*, performed ten years after independence, on Constitution Hill in Johannesburg. The title, inspired by and adapted from Ghanaian novelist Ayi Kwei Armah's *The Beautyful Ones Are Not Yet Born*, connects Ghana as a postcolonial nation, independent since 1957 (the first on the African continent), to South Africa's nascent democracy. Pather recalls reading this novel when he was twenty; its politically grim postcolonial reality stayed with him. The novel is an inspiring starting point for initial rehearsals, after which he allows his choreography to grow and change. Pather selects six locations on Constitution Hill in order to examine how personal and political freedom, with its attendant hopes and disillusionments, has shaped the lives of ordinary South Africans for the past decade.

To situate the nation's Constitutional Court on the site where political prisoners were once held, especially in the notorious Old Fort Prison known as Number Four with common criminals along with political prisoners is a telling reminder of a painful past out of which a hopeful future would be forged. The Constitutional Court was opened by President Thabo Mbeki on March 21, 2004, Human Rights Day. Constitution Hill, like the Apartheid Museum and other "heritage" sites, is a tourist attraction in Johannesburg, commemorating a dark past. I visited these dungeon-like rooms in 2014 and again with my daughter Roshni in 2019, and we saw re-creations of the prisoners' cots, latrines, solitary cells, and other indignities evident in the space itself. We also entered the Constitutional Court, observing the chairs where judges sit and a large auditorium-style space for attendees. This space, in which ordinary South Africans can fight legally for justice, is now a testament to hard-won freedom. We also visited a building on Constitution Hill that holds a permanent exhibit on Gandhi's historic time in South Africa, organizing against unfair treatment of the Indian community.

In his essay "Laws of Recall: Body, Memory and Site-Specific Performance in Contemporary South Africa," Pather discusses his choice of Constitution Hill as the site for this work:

> In being played out at Constitution Hill the work also becomes a conversation with a history replete with struggle, nobility, and sacrifice. The spaces, epic in both size and history serve at once as revered temple and places of ironic nostalgia. *The beautiful ones must be born* is not an attempt at a factual critique of a fledgling democracy any more than Armah's novel was an exhaustive critique of post-independent Ghana. My experimentation with a range of dance forms, imagery, architecture, video, sound and text that emanate from several sources are there to provide frames within which you may hang your own story. (Pather 2015b, 327)

Pather's final report to the National Arts Council on New South African choreography notes that "the core" of *The Beautiful Ones Must Be Born* "lies at the centre of three great epics: Professor Mazizi Kunene's epic, *Emperor Shaka the Great*, the Indian epic, the *Mahabharata*, and the Greek tragedy, the *Oresteia*."[3] The confluence of these three culturally different classics—two epics, one from South Africa and the other from India, along with a Greek tragic trilogy that all inspire Pather's 2005 work—demonstrates his imaginative acumen in culling their linkages from past to present, of human conflict, family dysfunction, revenge, retribution, and the reconstitution of human society. In the same document, Pather notes that the "meanings contained in the grand scale epics were developed through the combination of the expressive power of contemporary dance and physical theatre with the enduring and epic qualities of traditional and classical vocabulary such as traditional Zulu ritual, Shembe Dance, Classical Ballet, Bharatha Natyam and the movements of the San and the Khoi."

Emperor Shaka's epic memorializes the courage, dignity, and warring spirit of this Zulu leader, a model inspiring ordinary Black people to recognize their own power and potential in throwing off White supremacy. In the post-apartheid context, Pather evokes challenges that ordinary Black people face even in demanding the most basic necessities of housing, education, and employment. The dilemmas explored in the *Mahabharata* include the call to dharma (duty), colliding with individual will, and with karma (destiny). The extended discourse on these philosophical concerns are contained in the *Bhagavad Gita*, in which Lord Krishna expounds the parameters of human action within the boundaries of dharma and karma to the conflict-ridden Arjuna, and by extension to all humanity. The Greek tragedy *The Oresteia*, like the *Mahabharata*, explores the personal conundrums of seeking justice versus revenge via violence; goddess Athena intervenes at the end, introducing a democratic legal system and the rule of law to resolve human conflicts.

Pather's critical yet hopeful vision recognizes that ten years into democracy there remains much work to be done to ameliorate the lives of Black people. His critique of the democratic government is different from unmediated celebrations in 2005 and later, in "Heritage Day" events glorifying *simunye*, as if unity can prevail irrespective of different economic and social struggles (Nicholson 2013, 10).[4] Indeed, Pather believes that concepts like *simunye* are more damaging than helpful. In Sichel's article "Happy to Be Back Home," Pather remarks, "My take is on a post-independence South Africa . . . and pertinent issues here. I am always fascinated by the theme of arrested violence; the imploded rage that surprises on a day-to-day basis. We veer from the most beautiful to the most ugly. A lot of it has to do with unresolved energy as South Africans have taken on the dream of *simunye*" (Sichel 2004).

The Beautiful Ones Must Be Born was commissioned by South Africa's FNB Dance Umbrella's seventeenth season.[5] In 2005,

Pather's poignant and edgy exploration of how far the South African nation has *not* come over the past decade reminds spectators of lagging social development. Along with this critical look, Pather also looks toward a future when "the beautiful ones must be born." His director note states, "In South Africa now, in the wake of ten-year democracy parties [in 2005], this dance theatre production is a conversation on several levels, with Armah's novel, with notions of freedom, impulses of violence, deferred rage, conscience, deceit, collusion, apathy, change, and mostly and most enduring, the perpetual quest for justice" (2015b, 327). Pather's evocative site-responsive work is richly multidisciplinary and interdisciplinary, infused with his use of different movement vocabularies—classical and contemporary African dance, popular forms, urban, and folk, along with video projections and theatrical placement of performers and spectators to create a layered palimpsest of kinetic, verbal, and aural effects.

Pather critiques the act of memory when it lapses into nostalgia or when it demands closure for wounds that continue to ooze. Around the time of *The Beautiful Ones Must Be Born*, 2003 Statistics South Africa placed the unemployment rate for Black people at 25.20 percent. Apart from past injustices, Pather draws attention in his "Laws of Recall" essay to the "current economic distress and wretchedness," during which one is at a despairing loss to explain the "discrepancy between one's labour and one's absurdly dire material circumstances" (2015b, 320). He continues, "I was interested in our obsession, as South Africans, with acts of remembrance and with the relationship of theatrical representation of this backward looking, subjective, inchoate state to the present. This article then is a critique of this impulse to enliven memory embodied as memorial and archive within the context of South Africa's tumultuous past. . . . As is constantly alluded to by critical theorists Jacques Lacan, Paul Ricoeur, and Michel Foucault, the act of remembering is *a preoccupation with the present*" (2015b, 320, original emphasis).

In "Laws of Recall" Pather quotes from "Symbolic Closure through Memory, Reparation, and Revenge in Post-Conflict Societies" (Hamber and Wilson 2002), in which Brandon Hamber and Richard Wilson note that

> the South African TRC has, in the interests of national reconciliation, muted feelings of vengeance, and replaced them with what it calls a more restorative model.... The nation-building discourse of truth commissions homogenize disparate individual memories to create an official version, and in so doing, they repress other forms of psychological closure motivated by ... emotions of anger and vengeance. Claims to heal the collective unconscious of the nation therefore masks how truth commissions both lift an authoritarian regime of denial and public silence, as well as create a new regime of forgetting which represses other memories and forms of psychological closure. (quoted in Pather 2015b, 321)

Pather recognizes the tension and discrepancy between what the TRC claimed in saying they were giving voice to the voiceless (thereby acknowledging their suffering) and actually achieving reconciliation. Even though the TRC was based on the human desire for closure, repressing psychological injuries leads to continuing violence, as is evident in the aftermath of South Africa's independence. For an artist like Pather, it is important to raise questions, though he offers "no readymade solution" in his site-responsive work, "only a process of animation that may at the very least bring us to the lack of resolution, a suspension that may provoke a consciousness of the moment when past and present meet" (Pather 2015b, 322).

In the same essay, Pather is critical of state-funded "static archival projects," such as the Slave Museum, the Apartheid Museum, and Constitution Hill, that serve as "islands for tourists, at best as ironical constructs, at worst in defiance of the continued presence outside their walls of what these archives enshrine and honour [as having happened in some remote past]. The static archive seems to mock the materiality of continued abnegation and poverty on a large scale" (2015b, 322). The dilemma remains: how to deal critically with "a hellish past"? Not by evoking a version of "heritage" that simply covers up the sordid past. As Daniel Herwitz remarks, it would be better for "the controversial politics of heritage" in South Africa to evoke "a stalemate around heritage" rather than "create closed fortresses of cauterized myth disguised as truth" (Herwitz, quoted in Pather 2015b, 323). Pather would rather "break down the notion of heritage and destabilize the archive in the reach for a more fluid, self-reflexive and speculative matrix" (321). To accomplish this goal, Pather uses "multiple texts—verbal, visual, kinetic—mixed media, interrupted narratives (via irony, satire, comedy juxtaposition, displacement, collage, montage, fragments, and the non sequiturs) all interacting with sites other than theatre, whether site-specific or site responsive" (326). The performative modes that Pather uses in *Beautiful Ones*—movement with multimedia and inventive props—suggest, overtly and covertly, the disillusionment with President Thabo Mbeki's controversial "Growth, Employment and Redistribution" (GEAR) policies.

The site of Constitution Hill interacts with the moving human frame set against fixed monuments, destabilizing them, even "testing [their] immovability." In outdoor site performances, there is "a contract between performance and audience. The audience can see or choose to see," Pather remarks. "Viewing is optional or partial, continuous or sporadic, depending on where one might be" (2015b, 326). *The Beautiful Ones Must Be Born* draws on what Pather regards as "imperfect, incomplete memory fields, archival spaces such as Constitution Hill" (326).[6]

Beautiful Ones showcased thirty-one dancers—eight principal dancers, fifteen ballet dancers from South African Ballet Theatre, and eight from Johannesburg's Moving into Dance Mophatong company. The work opens on the Great African Steps with sixteen Shembe dancers, plastic bottles that contain lights strapped to their backs. I discuss this work based on Pather's essay "Laws of Recall" and on a video that he made available to me. He noted that the plastic bottles are used mainly by Black Shembe followers to collect seawater from the Durban beach to take to rural areas for spiritual practices of healing connected to Zulu ritual; "holy water" used in Christian religious practices is also evoked (interview 1, 2018). Twelve classical ballet dancers in taut tutus, their arms covered in blood-red *ubovu* (red clay), join them. As the dancers begin walking down the steps, sharp and shrill sounds are heard, high-pitched human wailing as if echoed from a previous era of incarceration in this location. The sounds also evoke the harsh clang of waking up prisoners. In this conglomeration of dancers, a woman in a red skirt and top carries two plastic bottles, and another carries a tin can on her head. White umbrellas are opened and closed as they move in semicircles. Their faces are covered in *umcako* (white powder). Plastic bottles are strapped on their backs, reminiscent of carrying children. The kathak dancer Pravika Nandakishore plays a major role in this work, leading the audience from one site to another; she is a figure of continuity, reminiscent of a *sutradhara*—that is, one who connects the thread(s) of a story, common in ancient Indian drama; perhaps here, Pather is tapping into his ancestral Indian collective unconscious.

Several soloists interrupt the flow with varying stories of some imminent action. One speaks in anger, and another is lying down; Pravika Nandakishore makes the dancer get up with the sound of her ankle bells. Nandakishore dances kathak, making circles in front of the tutu-clad ballerinas and seven Black men in suits, one on top of the stairs, another next to Ntombi Gasa, who sits down with two plastic bottles in each hand. Pather's choreographic perspective makes the viewer look up to the top of the stairs and then see Neliswa Rushualang at the bottom with the ballerinas, who have sashes on their chests over their tutus. One man is dancing and speaking frantically, but no one seems to listen to him.

When Siyanda Duma, is brought forward by a priest to bear witness, he resists, as if the confession is stuck in his throat, and it stays suspended. The action then follows the dancers going up the Great Stairs on Constitutional Hill. The ballet dancers sitting on the stairs present a stark red and white image: they wear white satin gloves over their red clay-covered arms. The image of red hands hidden under white satin gloves raises the specter of blood on the hands being covered up and hidden, which symbolizes the erasure of the history of torture and other brutalities that took place on Constitutional Hill and elsewhere in South Africa.

The audience is led to the next site. As I watched the video, I became conscious of the time that it takes to walk from one location to another. Pather noted to me that he aims to get this walking rhythm right; it should not take too long and break up the continuity of the show. The audience for this show was large, nearly 150 to 200 people, so they had to be divided, and the dancers performed twice to accommodate spectators' walking time without compromising Pather's desired flow of the piece.

Act 2, "I Didn't Do It," begins at the Awaiting Trial Block with veteran SSDT dancer Neliswa Rushualang's face covered in *umcako*, wearing black, covered by a blanket, and carrying a sack of rice balanced on her head. She walks forward with a knife in her hand as she "slowly and deliberately pierces the taut, bulging sack, spilling the rice on the floor, which makes the sound of light rain" (Pather 2015b, 328). Rushualang removes her head cover, and white powder flies out. In a striking duet between her and Gasa, the two principal dancers of Siwela are on the floor, then back to back as Rushualang carries Gasa on her back. Movements of pushing and pulling, embracing and separating, convey the agony of Black peoples' lives. Gasa drags Rushualang on the floor as grand orchestral music fills the air. Next, as Gasa watches, Rushualang hugs and struggles with a Black man in a duet that expresses passion and frustration. As if mirroring this duet, Gasa dances with another Black male dancer, hugging him as he crumples down to the floor. He puts his palm out as if for support; next, he is in her lap. Two Black men dance together; one speaks and the other closes his mouth. The choreography among the dancers unfolds at times in sync and at others in deliberate disruption and tension. The men have wigs behind their heads, hanging on their backs. Pather explained that this was meant to ultimately connect with Siyanda Duma's story, which after all the large framing, hones in on the personal—around abuse, interpersonal violence and deception—and that the wigs hanging off the back of the dancers' hoodies was a symbolic reference to scalped women hanging on the shoulders of the men. Duma's story continues, interrupted by Pravika Nandakishore's kathak bells and percussion sounds. Duma's movement and verbal text reference an incident of violent rape, as the words "I didn't do it" are projected via video. The denial or the truth of the incident hangs in the air. Nandakishore recites the kathak syllables "*dhit gin na*," keeping rhythm with cymbals, then leads the audience to the next location.

Act 3, "Blow Dried," takes place at the Tower Courtyard, where five dancers wearing gray trousers and trendy Stoned-Cherrie T-shirts with Steve Biko's face as it had appeared on the front cover of the November 1977 *Drum Magazine* (Tulloch, 161). They have their hair washed in the deep sinks used by prisoners. The scene begins then with a brief ironic take on the commodifying of the struggle and within the Courtyard itself, and provides a dark comment on how quickly amnesia sets in. The work then slowly gives way and soon memories of the horror of what this place meant for prisoners, its high walls and unending degradations, are captured in the action. "The dancers perform ironically the disintegration of the dance language itself," remarks Pather, as they "collapse and slide in a final babble of sound and movement" (2015b, 329). Only deeply absorbing human sounds are audible. The painful past is visible, then recedes into the harrowing folds of the live dancer/actors' skin and bones. Biko's face is visible on the dancers' T-shirts, along with the letters DRUM for *Drum Magazine*, which was significant during the anti-apartheid struggle. Biko, architect of the Black Consciousness Movement and a hero for Pather, as for many in his generation, inspired a united front of Coloreds and Indians with Black people. Biko was at the then University of Natal studying medicine when he created the South African Student Organization (SASO), influenced by Liberation Theology.[7] While in detention Biko was killed by South African authorities on September 12, 1977, though they never admitted this crime.

In "Blow Dried," a white ballerina in goggles blows bubbles in a corner, her white tutu covered with blue net-like, gauzy fabric. She is almost invisible, a fate usually reserved for Black people. Six dancers with white hair, three men and three women, move in contemporary dance style, physically pushing bodies as if fighting. Plastic bottles are thrown out from the basins.

The audience walks to Act 4, "Motion Sickness," which unfolds at the Nelson Mandela Courtyard, where only select political prisoners were allowed to exercise. This segment is an extended metaphor for the powerful in the government, represented by a male dancer in a Black pinstriped suit walking on a treadmill whose speed is controlled by Nandakishore, while enjoying a Diet Coke. Two ballet dancers sit at the foot of the treadmill using small hand forks to tend a small patch of imported turf covering and masking a small part of the cold stone ground. Initially, the treadmill requires slow walking; gradually the speed increases, requiring the person to move faster, almost running on the spot. A video showing a township plays in the background; as the speed of the treadmill increases, the images slow down to show the details of shanty homes with paper-covered walls and a child playing in the dirt near barbed wire. The suited man is sweating profusely. It is as if he is fleeing his own background and the specter of poverty, an impossibility given that he is on a static automated running machine.

Act 5, "Nocturnal Commission," begins with three dancers sitting in a triangle on Parade Ground. Three screens, one behind each dancer, show figures of a businessman, a trade unionist, and a historical figure from the 1950s. In the center is the president in silk pajamas, ostensibly on the internet. The projections close to the president show ordinary people waiting in lines and marching at protests. He is oblivious to Black peoples' degraded lives, which are absent from his field of vision and distanced on video. Even when he is forced to look at the video, the harsh reality of poverty—its texture, smell, and deprivations—remain at a physical and emotional distance from him. The layered performance portrays the president, Thabo Mbeki, in pajamas—as he used to spend all night on the internet, presiding over a White-run liberal economy in "free" South Africa. The video tries to jog his conscience, reminding him of past struggles such as the Defiance Campaign and the current reality of the stark and wide divisions between rich and poor.

Act 6, "The Beautiful Ones Must Be Born," set on Constitution Square, is enacted alongside the Constitutional Court. "Audiences are ushered to the top of the ramparts," recounts Pather in "Laws of Recall," "to view the final act from above" as though removed from political events that have serious impact on their daily lives (2015b, 330). He continues: "Lines of classical Zulu, ballet and Indian dancers remind us for a hilarious moment of the ridiculous rainbow and then give way to a series of solos and duets. The choreography has been developed out of a series of improvisation workshops based on the incomplete gesture, hesitation and flux. Video and visual markers fill the insides of the awaiting trial block . . . with archival maps of the country as well as individuals and small groups of people waiting on roadsides" (330). The voice-over, comprising numerous emails from a production manager giving news of an ex-Siwela Sonke dancer, convicted of murder, remarks that "a complex case is being talked about" and that the audience will be kept informed. Rushualang, in a Black dress and with a Black umbrella, is in the middle.

Pather describes the deliberately fragmented rhythm of *The Beautiful Ones Must Be Born* as a whole. The show starts with ballet, then African and Indian dance in the middle, along with "sporadic, idiosyncratic movements of incomplete gesture" until by the end, the movement vocabularies fall apart; even Nandakishore's kathak is not continuous but comes across as deconstructed. Movements are "disparate, fragmented, alienated, incomplete, as if searching, thus leaving the ending open-ended" (phone conversation, June 4, 2020).

Robyn Sassen, a freelance arts writer, places Pather's *Beautiful Ones* in the legacy of artists such as Steven Cohen and others who pushed the boundaries of dance to include unusual props and in-your-face avant-garde performances that ranged from inventive to offensive and raised questions such as, "But is it art?" (Sassen 2005). It is useful to quote Sassen's views at length:

> The expression "But is it art?" has been framing challenges to visual culture since early modernism. In South Africa, the dance fraternity is finally catching on.
>
> Since 1998, artist Steven Cohen and his partner Elu have courted the discipline of dance by pushing its boundaries. Elu is a trained choreographer, Cohen self-educated in the visual arts and a maverick in dance. Their work has traditionally horrified most mainstream local critics and dancers because of its unequivocal challenges to society's values.
>
> "Elu and I brought art legitimacy into a dance environment," says Cohen in an interview. "We were the absolute first to ... accompany movement with douche-drinking, fire-up-the-arse, pornographic videos ... and call it art." ...
>
> Other practitioners may not be using the same devices as Cohen, but the visual tone of performances, judging by the pickings of this year's Dance Umbrella, was palpable.

Among the choreographers who submitted work were PJ Sabbagha, Jay Pather and Gerard Bester, all of whom used social issues to challenge the language of dance. (2005)

Pather, as a profoundly thinking artist, pushes the boundaries of his representations in a space where history is in the air. He asks two poignant questions in "Laws of Recall": "How to pit the critique offered by Armah against the pressure to remember offered by the space? How do we simultaneously acknowledge Bob Gosani's searing image of naked prisoners performing the *tausa* [a derogatory movement where prisoners were stripped naked and asked to jump and expose their rectum to convince warders that they were not hiding anything] as well as the imperative to create continuities and interruptions without current reach for redress and justice?" (2015b, 332). Pather aims to let his spectators interpret the performance as he leaves the affects—kinetic, visual, and aural—open-ended.

The Beautiful Ones Must Be Born accomplishes several of Pather's goals in his site-responsive work; Constitution Hill allows contemporary audiences to view the actual, historic locations where prisoners were held, where they ate and washed, bringing together subtly any lessons from the past that contemporary audiences wish to garner as they live in independent South Africa. The vignettes in this work are located across noteworthy sites on this hill, making the audience walk from one site to the next as they absorb what they just saw, felt, and heard before encountering the next layer of experience. Pather's choreographed embodiment of Black people's lives still mired in poverty is conveyed via this artist's characteristic layering effects, as in the segment with then President Mbeki in a pin-striped suit, with a crisp white shirt on his treadmill walking on the same spot, not acknowledging the video that frames his fleeing body. Such motion in place, not moving forward, raises the glaring specter of South Africa as a nation stuck in one spot, not transforming the dark realities of the past that continue to haunt the present.

BODY OF EVIDENCE (2008): MEMORIES OF VIOLENCE HELD IN THE BODY

Pather's landmark dance and multimedia work *Body of Evidence* connects to his 1992 work *Unclenching the Fist*, which dealt with domestic violence. The earlier work was motivated by forensic scientist Dr. Leonard Lehrer's discoveries—namely that the "bodies that were appearing before him echoed several disturbing conclusions in Fanon's (1961) invocation of a culture of violence that turns in on itself" (Pather 2015b, 333). Dr. Lehrer's staggering statistics—namely that "for every one killing motivated by political violence in the early nineties in the Eastern Cape, there were seven deaths of women who were killed by someone they knew"—inspired *Unclenching the Fist*. In 2008, sixteen years after that pre-independence show, Pather continues his forensic probing into how the human body stores memories of trauma in his inter- and multidisciplinary work *Body of Evidence*. Indeed as Niren Tolsi comments, "Jay Pather in *Body of Evidence* appears to question the unfinished business of the Truth and Reconciliation Commission. . . . He seeks to understand how brutalised psyches, ignored in the post-1994 drive towards rainbow nationalism, carry the scars of violence" (2008).

Pather aims to probe not only social memories of violence that can be talked about (as happened in the TRC hearings) but also memories stored in the interstices of the human body's tissue that are difficult to access. In order to accomplish this, Pather creates a new genre, an innovative multidisciplinary form in which art undertakes—both overtly as in the objects and tactile props used in the production (cardboard miniature replicas of township homes, bread, blue flippers, naked light bulbs) and covertly—the rage and violence rooted in deferred dreams.

Pather wanted to set his choreography inside a surgical theater (a medical space that is described as a "theater" where surgery is "performed") in order to portray, organically and symbolically, a dissected body that houses trauma in its very cells. He noted that given the "forensic theme" he wanted "to use a surgical ward, or a mortuary to get into the fiber of the body" holding memories of violence (interview 1, 2018). A scientifically surgical procedure would determine if memories of wounds, physical and psychological, from years of violence and from emotional trauma, survive in the human body's bones, ligaments, and joints. Surgical dissection would enable a diagnosis of the causes and effects of traumas such as devastating poverty and a life without dignity.

He did check out an operating theater in a now defunct hospital in the Hillbrow area of Johannesburg, but it was not usable mainly because the entire site was dilapidated and unsafe for performance. And since he could not get permission to perform *Body of Evidence* in a real surgical theater, he compromised by locating it at another unusual site: the nineteenth floor of the old Lister medical building in Johannesburg. This site-responsive setting of a medical building where bodies are healed, along with the legal word *evidence* in the title, embodies *Body of Evidence*'s overall medical-legal purpose. The title connects *body* to *evidence*—legal, medical, political, eyewitness—used in courts of law that oppressed Black people during apartheid.

Body of Evidence demonstrates a provocative tour de force in Pather's use of larger-than-life video projections based on "the drawings of Henry Vandyke Carter who illustrated the anatomical guide for students of Henry Gray in his book *Gray's Anatomy* [this iconic 1918 text has its fortieth edition in 2008]" (Pather 2015b, 333). These drawings were hardly accurate as teaching tools for medical students; rather, they "communicate a deceptive order," remarks Pather, "and symmetry." Pather shared his process of using this material: "In collaboration with visual artist Storm Janse van Rensburg, I created large-scale projections of select sections of the anatomy to form a kind of architecture within which the choreography would take place" (333–34).

In these drawings, human body parts are deconstructed and literally separated, such as a skull, foot, and spine projected as a backdrop, or on the floor for dancer-actors to trample on and symbolically brutalize. The skillful use of selected images from the 1,247 in *Gray's Anatomy* creates the artistic impression of dismembering the body. Live dancers and actors weave in and out of the tapestry of muscle and bone of their own live bodies, at times silhouetted or positioned as a small human frame dwarfed by a backdrop of a huge, inanimate human skull or foot. In a forthcoming essay for *ArtSearch*, Pather discusses the value of "literary" theater-making where research along with other layers of movement and visual art in *Body of Evidence* that uses *Gray's Anatomy* is part of his process, along with "collaborative choreography" where individual dancers have "a strong hand in the development of the final work.... A code of ethics was established at the oputset from intense discussions, individual volition and agency to step in and out of processes to the awarding of choreographic credit to all participants involved in the process. The collaborative choreographic model allowed for the research to be embodied before starting to actually rehearse the work" (Pather, forthcoming). The key in dance is to embody abstract ideas and concepts that come across to spectators via the performers' bodies. Pather accomplishes this along with his characteristic layering of movement with visual art and spatial placements on the performance arena.

Pather's use of such visual art along with dance elicits an interview question from Peter Machen—namely, do these two artistic forms function "on a continuum" or as "discretely separate disciplines?" (2009). Pather responds to Machen, "Keeping the integrity of the original forms while bringing together different disciplines to create something new and layered is always a challenge. It's a fine line to walk, but I ultimately see them on a continuum, one complementing the other, while retaining their integrity as individual forms." *Body of Evidence*'s multidisciplinary

Fig. 4.2. *Body of Evidence.* Projection of foot. Neliswa Rushualang center, Ntombi Gasa in the back, seated. Photographer: Val Adamson.

form itself, in which live bodies move and dialogue with inanimate visual art, relates dialectically to the content of this work evoking South African bodies as repositories of brutal acts.

In "Laws of Recall," Pather discusses the persistence of violence and wounding that performance can deconstruct in order to unravel or even begin a healing process. The latter would be different from the TRC's goal, which was to heal by forced closure. Instead, Pather's goal is to let healing take the time needed and to deal critically with the continuing violence in South Africa rooted in apartheid's daily onslaughts on the human body, mind, and spirit. Such memories cannot be wiped out *only* by dismantling a brutal social system. In "Laws of Recall," Pather notes "an abiding question" to himself: "What are the mechanisms inherent in performance that could possibly fill these spaces and silences in memory with their confounding schizophrenic lack of spatial and temporal demarcations, their chaos and messiness, without the neat project of reconciliation or the imperatives of healing? How can performance, as interactive, social, collaborative and experiential mechanisms, make material [that is] submerged process, and initiate fault lines, making manifest that which for many South Africans remains a deeply lodged, un-nameable, unarticulated and un-witnessed ache?" (2015b, 336–37).

Body of Evidence, via multiple layers of movement, visuality, human groans, and other symbols and objects used in the performance, succeeds powerfully in confronting the nation's bloody history and its continuing specter in South African society by probing the body's flesh—not just the mind and consciousness—as the receptacle of trauma. The bones and cells speak, even wail and shout, expressing the very haunting that pursues individuals and communities long after the actual brutality has ended. The soundtrack by James Webb creatively includes Webb's incredible recordings of sounds from within his own body—he undertook this sound experiment after discussing the conceptual goals of *Body of Evidence* with Pather. Another starkly disturbing loud rant emerges from the mouth of an enraged Black man, crouched in a cage, shouting out the same isiZulu words over and over again. Pather's program notes for *Body of Evidence* (published in his essay "Laws of Recall") uniquely focus on the intelligent body that is attuned, at times more than the weary mind, to painful knowledge: "The body remembers more than through the head. Nerve and vessel, artery and synapse, all carry information from point to point, suffusing muscle, bone and cell with a plethora of images and sound, a flicker of light, a scream or a touch. Sometimes we wish that a delete button might annihilate some of the information. But the body instead stores relentlessly, file upon file, bottomless cabinet of memory, individual and collective.... What does the body do with this ebb and flow of knowledge? What does a collective nation's memory do with history?" (2015b, 334). Pather's choreography imaginatively re-creates a body "which appears in sections from head to toe," conveying the travails of bodily oppression. He deploys the body as political, especially as bodies of Black people were criminalized simply for their racial designation during apartheid.[8]

In "Laws of Recall," Pather delineates the different segments of *Body of Evidence* opening in "Phase 1: Making Memory," with six male Black bodies in white shorts standing inside white "baby baths filled with red *ubovu*." They stand folded over like objects, "their bodies as emptied out cavities that will soon be filled," as Ntombi Gasa enters and physically straightens them up. Throughout the work, she performs the nurturing role of mother or caretaker to the men. She is dressed uncannily in a maid's uniform with a fur coat and red high-heeled shoes. Pather remarks, "The tap tap of her shoes as she runs, adjusts, waits and then goes to someone else forms a counterpoint to the haunting, extremely loud soundscape of James Webb's opening track" (2015b, 337). Reviewer Peter Frost comments that "the dance is a mix of Cunningham/Graham-inspired catch-and-release and South African street fusion" (2015).

Pather's ever-fertile imagination for extraordinary juxtapositions presents a White male (John Cartwright) in his seventies, wearing a suit, tie, hat, and goggles as he enters holding colored flowers; he is talking about geraniums, their origin, their migration across continents, and hybrids of different colors, as though obsessed with *racial* colors. He walks in with a Black man as though talking to him, but a small confrontation follows, setting up what Pather describes in his essay as "a frisson that evokes the brain" accompanied by a skull projected in the background (2015b, 338). The image of the brain evokes symbolically the deeply entrenched racial stereotypes that can emerge suddenly and without warning.

Next, two dancers in red blankets perform a duet "against shifting images of the skull and the eye socket" (2015b, 338). Their bodies are reflected inside the projected image of the skull. Their shadows are larger than their physical bodies, as if to indicate that their human potential is so much greater than what their appearances or skin colors have determined in limiting their opportunities. Pather describes the movement in "Laws of Recall": "Referencing ruptures in these body parts, the choreography is furtive, unpredictable, and the physicality is risky. The dance takes place within the confines of the outline of the skull, which shifts to the eye socket and then the eye itself. This is punctuated by the shadow of John Cartwright looming behind the projection. Walking slowly behind the gauze, he remains firmly imprinted inside the skull" (2015b, 338). The presence of a White face raises a sense of surveillance, as if watching even from the background creates a sense of unease, and fear of drastic systemic violence against Black people that never leaves them; like a continual sense of haunting.[9]

Next, in what Pather calls "Phase 2: Past Present," a human spine with distinct vertebrae is projected horizontally across the screen as a backdrop, as well as on the floor. The elongated shadow of a Black man in the ritual costume of a Zulu warrior is silhouetted in front of the spinal image; then the human figure, smaller in reality than the silhouette, emerges. Two dancers move in front of a projected image of the spine. In Sichel's words, this is "an expertly curated display of conceptual forensics which rips into conscience and consciousness."[10]

Neliswa Rushualang enters, her face covered in *umcako* although, as Pather explains, "it was never the intention to depict a white woman as much as a Black woman painted white who together with a deconstructed blond wig depicts whiteness. Her arms, feet, and neck are all deliberately kept in the original skin color—a deliberate show of artifice" (phone conversation, June 4, 2020). Rushualang's sarcastic portrayal, in Pather's words, is "through a critique and comment of a Black woman." She looks spectacular in a long ballroom gown of bluish-brown gauzy material, a huge, elongated white turban on her head with a whisk at the end. She is holding a bare electric bulb emitting a harsh

Fig. 4.3. *Body of Evidence.* Neliswa Rushualang, Ntombi Gasa, and splits in the air leap by Siyanda Duma. Photographer: Val Adamson.

Fig. 4.4. *Body of Evidence.* Rushualang holds Gasa in backbend, Siyanda Duma on the table. Photographer: Val Adamson.

light in her left hand, and her neck, covered in bandages, is held stiffly, imitating a common response of arrogant White people when they encounter Black people. Rushualang, playing a White woman, reverses the tradition of Blackface, when White actors used to appear in dark face makeup. Siyanda Duma, also with umcako on his face, wearing a white suit, accompanies her, holding an upturned open silver umbrella. "Rushualang is brought in," describes Pather, "and held in place by bandages tied around her neck that keep her movements stilted. Five men manipulate these bandages with their faces in plastic orange sacks. The projection shifts from the spine to the taut muscles of a straining neck with the skin removed" as she circles in the middle of the stage (2015b, 339). Without the skin, the neck's muscles and blood vessels reveal the inner ugliness of the White woman's pride in holding her neck rigidly, looking down on others. The truths that lie under the skin, such as racial prejudice, are exposed in the stark light.

A darkly humorous segment follows, with six men in women's bras and with buckets on their heads performing *isicathamiya* and gumboot dance to entertain both themselves and the "White" couple (Pather explains *isicathamiya*).[11] The bras symbolize the women the male miners cannot have with them. Reviewer Frost remarks: "The gumboot dance morphs into a comment on masculinity and sexuality with the guys—the bros—donning bras and camping it up. Simple but very effective." The image of a rib cage is visible in the background. Suddenly, the Black men collapse as the same nurturing Black woman played by Ntombi Gasa reenters to touch them and lift them up. They lean on her as she places healing hands on their bodies. The sounds of violin and trombone reverberate poignantly.

Suddenly the projection changes to that of a Black man's face—this is not a skeletal image, as the other projected body parts have been. On stage, another man is lying in dirt on the floor and holding a naked light bulb. One of the Black men sits on a stool. He wears a white coat like a medical doctor; his face is covered with bandages on which he props up his goggles and a straw hat. He then puts on a jacket left on the floor. Another Black man is writhing with jerking movements, as if receiving electric shocks or suffering spasms of pain.

There is a direct physical confrontation over two plastic bags as two men fight over what is "essentially a loaf of bread" (Pather 2015b, 340), falling backward with the soundscape of human groans; Pather describes this encounter as part of "Phase 3: Present Future." With the projection of throat and tongue, organs that enable speech or silence "as well as taste," adds Pather, "the blunting of taste in the reach towards survival" is expressed when hungry people will not care for taste but will eat anything that fills their bellies (340).

Cartwright reenters and whistles like a White policeman giving orders. He circles as if surveilling the two Black men. In Pather's masterful layering technique, there are other scenarios simultaneously unfolding in the background. A Black female body, Ntombi Gasa, lies on a small table as if on a surgical table, though her head and feet hang off the table. The White woman, played by Neliswa Rushualang, presides over this table as Gasa rolls off—still wearing a faux fur coat and red high-heeled shoes. There is a close-up of the rib cage image as the white-faced Rushualang holds the Black woman, Gasa, in a viper-like grasp. Pather remarks that it is as if the white-faced Duma and Rushualang "ostensibly in their home [are] stuck inside the rib cage" (2015b, 341) resembling the high-rise security gates that many of the wealthy live behind in South Africa. The incongruous costumes and the white-faced Rushualang's controlling movements over the Black woman, Gasa, are threatening.

Pather shares the genesis of Rushualang's character embodying an arrogant White woman whom she had encountered on a park bench. In a workshop, as Pather explains, Rushualang "honed in on her sense of annihilation in this encounter with someone who did not do much more than subtly turn away and tauten her neck and avert her eyes, making it impossible for Rushualang to simply sit restfully on a park bench. This tautening of the neck was to become her main metaphor and point of departures. She moved quickly from this experience of disdain to embodying it. In doing so, Rushualang felt more in control of what was, for her, a devastating moment. Her physical realization of this state of disdain included using bandages to tie her neck in a set position and with bandages coming up to her head holding at the centre a blonde wig propped up by a long stick" (Pather, forthcoming).

The vignettes of Black life inside and outside townships continue, as Black men slither onto the stage on their bare stomachs, with model houses on their backs to declare one of the major needs of the Black population—standard housing with basic amenities. They slowly traverse, from left to right, the front of the stage; they are close enough to the audience that the audience can view the nice, neat houses, before they exit. One model home with a bright red roof (as if from a storybook) is left on one side of the stage, as the sounds of beatings emerge from a straw-covered enclosure.

In another scene, one of the more mature Black dancers Siyabonga Mhlongo performs a solo using *pantsula* as the dance language in a solitary circle of light against a backdrop of large-scale projections of joints. He is interrupted by a remote-controlled toy-car that attempts to "run him over" several times. He stops, retreats, retrieves his miniature home and moves away. Two Black men wearing protective kneepads and face masks (like mine workers) enter, using hip-hop dance language against another layer of projections of the knee joint. After their movement mirroring each other on opposite points of the stage, they pick up jackhammers, approach the circle of light where the car stalls with its tinny pop song playing, and destroy the car. This is "the first and only act of pure violence on the stage," remarks Pather 2015b, 341). The nurturing Gasa enters as if to make peace. The soundscape is layered with cello music and traditional chanting, and suddenly the *adhjan*, the Muslim call to prayer (sung by the mature *pantsula* dancer Mhlongo) can be heard almost imperceptibly. Such an uncanny juxtaposition of sights and sounds is characteristic of Pather's choreography.

The feeling of being stuck in one's life in terms of employment, education, or housing is evoked as a Black man in white shorts (usually infantilizing grown men as "boys" in service of Whites) enters with his legs inside two beer crates; it seems he is stuck in them, though one leg moves in and out of the can. The men with houses on their backs return. The video projects the pelvis, then "the glands in the upper body as the sound of chants, remixed by Webb, envelopes the space" remarks Pather (2015b, 341). Glands such as the lymph nodes, the thymus and thyroid in the throat, and the pineal gland in the brain all secrete hormones to regulate the body's immune, digestive, and cardiovascular health. Pather has Cartwright "wheeled on stage in a swivel chair. He is covered in LED lights placed strategically in the areas of his own glands. He performs a ruptured monologue combining the original piece about geraniums interspersed now with actual testimonies given at the TRC" (338). His feet are inside a water basin, a more comfortable position than being stuck inside a tin can. As he takes off his trousers and is left in only his briefs, he says, "Cut off his private parts," as if playing an interrogator or torturer of a prisoner on whom he passes inhumane judgment.

"Phase 4: Perpetual Future" has three structures on stage: dancer Mxolisi Nkomonde sits inside a chicken wire coop as if in prison and speaks loudly and angrily in isiZulu, repeating a phrase as if telling a story that still makes him furious. Gasa observes this, sitting inside "a hollowed-out shell made of clear Perspex [plastic]." Rushualang enters with long white strips on her gown, dragging loaves of bread to feed the poor and hungry in the townships. She circles the stage and stands on the side. On stage right, there is a straw hut from which sounds of beatings and calls for help emerge. Suddenly two bright blue flippers used by deep-sea divers are thrown out of the hut, and a group of dancers put them on, though it is difficult to walk with them on solid ground. The video projects the image of a foot, a symbol of mobility that can be either free or restricted by rules of where Black people can walk at any given time. The mother figure helps to remove the flippers so that the men can move easily. Cartwright enters to wash the feet of one of the Black men collapsed in a chair, a deliberate biblical reference. Pather remarks, "Cartwright, in a nod to the feet washing antics of Adriaan Vlok, former minister of Law and Order under apartheid, that actually took place in an act of remorse, uses a cleaning spray and cloth to wash the feet" (2015b, 343). In fact, in *Body of Evidence*, this actual incident is rendered ironically since the Black men's feet covered in flippers are not available for washing, as the politician wishes to do, in order to ask for forgiveness. Cartwright's physical use of a cleanser indicates how inadequate this gesture is in terms of expunging government corruption. The multilayering continues as Gasa carries Nkomonde like Christ on the cross.

The hybrid form of *Body of Evidence* captures the suffering and possible healing of traumatized bodies, both during apartheid and after. Speech, action, storytelling, music, and movement drawn from classical Indian dance, classical Zulu dance, and contemporary Western dance interact with human sounds of pain and despair, visual art, and multimedia. In particular, movement interacts with visual iconography.

Pather's aim for "an elegant choreography on a cross-section of bones" (2015b, 334) beautifully expressed faced a very different outcome here—namely, not the kind of "choreography at a distance, as [he] originally imagined" (334). The wished-for "elegance" devolves, still grippingly, into reflecting the harsh realities of body, and pain for the majority. The choreography was "a result of a harrowing research process which involved acquiring bottomless stores of memory from parents and neighbors, as eliciting childhood stories from the cast" (334). Pather became very aware of what he describes as "a literal and metaphoric contradiction [between] containment and evocation of memory—especially those related to violence. How I worked with this essential paradox as well as how far the participants wished to go between containment and evocation was going to determine the very nature of the work" (334). He comments that improvisations revealed clearly that "acts of torture were and are not tied up in a hermetically sealed time or space, but only serve as points of stimulus for current, continued, systematic abnegation and invisibilities" (334). Pather remains open to unexpected inputs and painful personal stories from his dancers, musicians, and collaborators of visual art during the workshop process.

In the initial workshops, Pather observes that the dancers "found solace in objects" as anchors during the process of creating this painful work. Initially, they could not trust or translate their stories/memories into kinetic form, into movement and dance (2015b, 335). Pather shares a wide-ranging list of objects that were taken up by dancers during the workshops and that symbolized the deep-seated realities of their environments: "Anything in the immediate vicinity: mats, sheets, half bricks, wire, bandages, wigs, half eaten bread, cut grass, condoms, water, tomatoes, plastic bottles cut up as masks, buckets and dust bins became ritualistically imbued with meaning, variously literal and mysterious, dark, unavailable" (335). As director of the multimedia work, he structures the vignettes with moving or wailing bodies, visual art, and objects, creating a final canvas that is a layered palimpsest of movement, speech, visual images, and human sounds.

The eleven performers ranged in age from twenty-two to seventy-two. "I tried to find a process," remarks Pather, "that looked at the body as a filing cabinet of sound, the text referencing Elaine Scarry's writings on the inexpressibility of pain" (2015b, 335). Scarry describes "the invisible geography" of someone's pain that is pulsating in the "deep subterranean" crevices of the body and that "has no reality" for an onlooker or a listener "because it has not yet manifested itself on the visible surface of the earth" (Scarry 1985, 3). Painful memories of violence, held in the interstices of the body, mind, and spirit, remain invisible.

Several unforgettable images remain marked indelibly in spectators' minds, such as the loaves of bread dragging from the wealthy woman's gown for the poor, as much to assuage her guilt as to alleviate their hunger; also memorable are the model houses with neat red roofs carried on Black dancers' backs, or the men stuck inside pails or trying to move with blue diving flippers on, and a Black man inside a chicken wire coop-like cage.

Reviewer Caroline Smart was captivated by these sights and sounds at the 2009 National Arts Festival performance in Grahamstown, South Africa, and writes of *Body of Evidence*: "We are bewitched by light and sound... [as we] observe a moving scene where a body rises from the grave and relate to strong comment on the government's lack of attention to suitable housing. We get to see a gumboot dance performed by dancers with buckets on their heads and watch the dancers stride around in flippers, the kind that divers use. I predict that it won't be long before flippers will appear as a new form of percussive dance! The dark side uncovers horrors revealed at the Truth and Reconciliation Commission. Lest we forget" (2009, 2).

Pather demonstrates in *Body of Evidence* that "the visceral body (the flesh)," as Lliane Loots remarks in "The Body as History and Memory," "is often encoded by cultural practices, social and racial constructions and gendered conditions of use and reception—which form layer upon layer of texts that convey certain meanings and power operations" (Loots 2010, 110). Among these ideological layers, the most profound are formed by the physical realities of race and gender. Hence, there is "the need," notes Loots in the same essay, "to decode and deconstruct the dancing body, and the texts which it articulates and which it inscribes, in order to examine how discourse and ideology permeate the use and reading of this body" (110). Even as discourses of sexuality control bodies, such discussions do not have absolute power; there is room to resist and counter hegemonic modes of thought about the body. In the South African context, race, gender, and gender identity take on a heightened relevance, given the history of apartheid. One powerful tool to resist the political controls over the body during and post-apartheid is memory itself. The idea of dance-making as an "embodied response" to political realities, and the demonstration that dance texts "are never neutral" but take a stance in history and memory, is portrayed in *Body of Evidence*. Loots comments:

> Pather's harrowing dance theatre work in which the audience is taken almost physically through both the architecture of the human body, and the architecture of memory and our nation's not so resolved history. Video artists and collaborator on *Body of Evidence*, Storm van Rensburg, produced images of the internal building blocks of the human body, the spine, the skull, the rib-cage, which are set against Pather's iconic dreamlike images of bandaged, semi-naked and blinded male dancing bodies who writhe, leap, and locate the audience in a landscape of pain and hurt—both physical and emotional. Interestingly enough, these are images of the damaged male who inhabit a very male (paternal) landscape of South Africa's legacy of apartheid suffering. These bandaged men are endlessly supported and pushed up physically by female veteran dancer Ntombi Gasa, whose matriarchal presence on stage offers an image of women endlessly caught up in the roles of support and nurture.
> (Loots 2010, 117)

Loots recognizes Pather's sensitivity to damaged males, helped again and again by the maternal energy of the Black woman, embodied in this work by Ntombi Gasa.

For Loots, *Body of Evidence* evokes notions of "forgiveness and forgetting ... and how forgetting which Pather is perhaps arguing is a decision not to remember—has become a political game around allegiances to power. History ... has become a contested space for choices around what is remembered and what is forgotten" (2010, 118). Pather also reminds us that we are dealing with "the perpetual containment of memories of violence in our bones. Why do memories reappear in so many violent forms?" (director note, quoted in Pather 2015b, 334). Perhaps the work itself, as Loots remarks, embodies Pather's supposition that this work "is a witnessed reminder for the audience that art and dance, if given space to speak, is part of our nation's visceral remembering." Loots tunes in to the political resonances of *Body of Evidence* that performatively evoke what she terms as "our nation's visceral remembering" (2010, 123).

Pather probes the role of art itself in recreating the past, even as he recognizes that "memory is a necessity and a scam, a seduction and a disappointment" (2015b, 336). Can art simply present, as *Body of Evidence* does, a series of non sequiturs, bare rage conveyed loudly, the juxtaposition of unexpected images—even "absurd, impossibly apocalyptic images, repetitive and disturbing" in depicting corroding memories from which there may be no release? Rather, "there is merely affirmation of a troubled present and an uncertain future. And yet the compulsion to remember remains. But can art do otherwise?" (336). Initially, perhaps all that art can do, expresses Pather wisely, is "to enable us to test reality ... illusions and false certainties to be whittled away bringing us face to face with the truth of our desire for certainties. And perhaps that is all art can do: Make us aware of this desire" (336).

Body of Evidence demonstrates Pather's progressive politics imbued in avant-garde choreography, which includes different media, and age groups of the dancers; it is also constructed of layered stories that unfold in deliberately disjointed ways in order to capture the fragmented reality of ordinary life for the majority. Form and content are related dialectically, as this bold performance represents troubling sociopolitical issues in subtle and overt ways to raise the specters of hunger, poverty, and inequality in South African society.

QAPHELA CAESAR (2010): A SOUTH AFRICAN POLITICAL THRILLER

Qaphela Caesar won the University of Cape Town's Creative Works Award (Saunders 2016, 1). The title translates as *Beware Caesar*, conveying a dual meaning: it warns the populace to beware of Caesar's power and cautions Caesar to guard against impending danger. When asked "why Shakespeare?" Pather remarked, "I felt that the epic quality of Caesar fitted with the politics of our time. But the production destabilizes even this idea, and is really a multidisciplinary massacre of Shakespeare's masterpiece, that melds media to probe the intricacies and nuances of a post-colonial society" (Pather 2010).

Pather sets *Qaphela Caesar* in different site-responsive locations. As Sichel remarks in "Bleeding from the Walls and Ceiling," "Qaphela Caesar harnessed public space to create publicly conscious art" (2010). Initially, in 2010, Pather used the old Cape Town City Hall building; next, in 2011, the prior Johannesburg Stock Exchange; in 2012, a version called *Caesar Interrupted* in Durban; and in 2015, a proscenium stage version at the State Theatre in Pretoria, also regarded as site-responsive "because of the activism during apartheid by artists like Jay who boycotted these state funded institutions," notes Sichel. In the State Theatre venue, Pather accomplishes his "mission to prove that black male and female bodies belong on any stage," comments Sichel, "and are equally capable of arabesques and pirouettes in the almost neo-classical, highly seditious choreography and the pastiche of music and projections."[12]

South African political events from 2010 to 2015, during Pather's three site-responsive productions of *Qaphela Caesar*, were volatile and rife with corruption charges against government officials.

Fig. 4.5. *Qaphela Caesar*. Dancers in flight. Photographer: Val Adamson. Courtesy Jay Pather.

President Jacob Zuma was elected in 2009 and reelected in 2014, and he held the position until his "resignation"—read "ousted"—over corruption charges in 2018.¹³ Under Zuma's administration, charges of blatant, large-scale corruption and iniquity disillusioned the majority. As in Chinua Achebe's novel *A Man of the People*, Zuma had taken enough for the people to notice; his greed and stealing were as ostentatious as his mansions, mistresses, and amassing of personal wealth. Similar to the legislators of ancient Rome's claim that Caesar was unseated "for the good of the nation," Zuma was surrounded by corrupt senators who supposedly had national interests at heart.¹⁴

Beyond the political resonances, Pather also recognizes "the betrayal of the human" on a personal level in 2010 South Africa. He remarks, "When we think of Julius Caesar, we think about a certain political expediency, but because of the depth, quality and contemporary relevance of the writing, we get to understand the betrayal of the human. We face the fragile hold on morals and ethics and the betrayal of friendship and we are never sure when the house of cards stops falling. It puts into question so much and is particularly interesting for South Africa" (Saunders 2016, 2). *Qaphela Caesar*, as Pather's other works, reveals the political as personal, excavating deeply personal, even intimate fallouts of political chicanery that has an impact on ordinary people.

At an invited keynote that Pather entitled "Shakespeare in South Africa: Contested Terrains and Unexpected Pleasures," he presented a nuanced discussion of the paradox of doing Shakespeare in South Africa, then acknowledged the significance of historical context whenever and wherever Shakespeare is performed in Africa or, indeed, in any other part of the world. In this presentation at the Global Shakespeare Symposium (University of California, Irvine, 2018), Pather contends that we "limit the scope of Shakespeare's genius" if we simply receive him in unquestioning ways, as the colonizers intended with their "wicked ways."[15] Pather's *Qaphela Caesar* works with "concepts of transposition and adaptation in relation to coming to terms with Shakespeare" in previously colonized South Africa. For Pather, it is a "glaring anomaly" to ask "what is Shakespeare still doing in Africa?" Rather, Pather finds it artistically exciting to discover the "possibility for a range of different contexts in which Shakespeare in his breadth" can speak to diverse people across time and space. The challenge remains as to how a contemporary artist can be "faithful to his/her context, and not only to regard Shakespeare in his historical and archival position."

Pather invites the awkwardness of Shakespeare in the current atmosphere of what is increasingly called "the decolonial project" (inspired worldwide by Ngũgĩ's influential text *Decolonizing the Mind*), which undertakes "a more direct and robust response to colonialism, along with the recognition that there is nothing postcolonial within liberal economies and immense global inequities" of wealth and poverty (Pather 2018a). Pather continues:

"Colonialism is deeply imbricated in contemporary society, even after independence from colonial powers"; further, South Africa's democracy was attained on "the negotiated settlement with the colonial settlers who have remained" in power, with drastic inequality in a society based on race. Wealth remains in the hands of the White minority. Hence, within "a decolonial project" and in a country like South Africa, "given its current complexities," Pather asks what Shakespeare means.

Shakespeare was on the radar, notes Pather, even prior to colonization, as Pather cites Wole Soyinka's essay "In the Name of Shakespeare." Soyinka notes that *Hamlet* was staged on September 5, 1607, aboard the English merchant ship *Red Dragon*, off modern-day Freetown in Sierra Leone, with four Africans, one Portuguese interpreter, and one hundred fifty English sailors. In the nineteenth century, Shakespeare returned to the colonies when, as Pather remarks, "English literary texts are a mask for colonialism and camouflage in Indian education, in South Africa and Africa" (Soyinka, 2016).

In our present time, Pather notes that Shakespeare thrives in South Africa, with various productions and adaptations. In 1985, nearly twenty years before his adaptation of *Julius Caesar*—at the height of apartheid and the State of Emergency, when Pather returned from NYC—he directed his reworked *Tempest* in which Sycorax and Caliban are the heroes. Sycorax stage-manages the play, and her son, Caliban, is not a monster but a tall, charming, beautiful man who calls out Prospero for occupying the island. Ariel is not always "an obedient sprite." Pather points out instructively that there are clues in Shakespeare's text itself for transposition, such as when Sebastian describes the island as "deserted and uninhabitable," mirroring a typical failure, Pather reminds us, of Whites to see Black people or regard them as human. Yet at the wedding scene, the stage directions in Shakespeare read, "The villagers come out to dance." Pather asks, "Where did they come from? Where are they during the course of the play?" (2018a).

In Pather's version, the stage is full of Black performers walking around, though Sebastian and his companions do not see them. Pather notes that he "was poking fun at the idea of invisibility and visibility." At the end, "with minor script changes," Pather remarks in his presentation, "Caliban and Ariel stage a coup and take over the island. This was after all during the Emergency, I was 25, and it was in 1985 and we needed all the inspiration we could get to live in the middle of all that."[16]

Pather narrates a fascinating historical incident that connects Shakespeare to Nelson Mandela during Mandela's imprisonment on Robben Island; Mandela read Shakespeare in a volume made available by another prisoner, Venkataraghavan, who smuggled in Shakespeare's *Collected Works* as his "Indian Bible." The warders left it alone, making it possible to pass the volume to thirty-three prisoners between 1975 and 1978. Each one selected a favorite passage and signed his name in the book. Mandela selected a passage from *Julius Caesar* about sacrifices made for political issues and signed his name.

Pather comments on the "initial impulse" for his 2010 *Qaphela Caesar*—namely, that it was "during a time of great political upheaval in South Africa after Mandela. . . . South African politics sat at a momentous and powerful junction topped by the unprecedented burning of ANC membership cards reminiscent of the historic burning of passes. The themes of patriotism, personal ambition, betrayal, corruption, conspiracy and trust all became powerful features of our current political themes" (2018a). Mainly, Pather notes in the same talk that his "interest lay in the tension between the Caesar persona and that of Brutus representing the good fight . . . the struggle between the past and the expediency of the present."

The choice to use the old Cape Town City Hall as a venue for the 2010 *Qaphela Caesar* "had resonance and significance," notes Pather, adding that he "made [the production] for City Hall to begin with" (2018a). The front of City Hall in Cape Town remains an icon "representing the good fight," since it holds the balcony from which Mandela addressed South Africa and the world when he was first released. "He walked straight from prison to the balcony," Pather recalls, "and spoke." During this time, Pather notes, there were "extreme events (that) played out and lent their energy to the production—the end of apartheid in 1994, ushering in a new era, then in 1995, the TRC as a vehicle and container of trauma was introduced given as a gift for the people of South Africa but we think more and more for the rest of the world." Pather's criticism of the TRC expressed in his previous dance-theater productions (discussed in chap. 2) is restated here as relevant for the "excesses" that Pather finds in Shakespeare's text:

> The vision [of the TRC] was tempting in its neatness, its clean arc trying to narrativize trauma in a linear, cause and effect configuration. Yet, what the TRC was attempting to address, [i.e.,] apartheid, was covered in unending, immersive, pervasive, multimodal [impacts]; not what singular dictators did but what ordinary people did to other ordinary people. In the wake of such sophisticated, strategic, systemic execution of colonial and apartheid trauma, the TRC posited the straightforward confessional exposition, dramatic builds, climactic admissions, quick turnarounds and a grand gesture of compassion and neat endings. It felt like a performance for the North and remaking of a Chekhov or Ibsen, rather than what I think of as seepage, spillage, and overflows in order to understand the kinds of excesses that I found in *Julius Caesar*. The sense of things not being contained, not telling a neat story [in which] even the iambic pentameter was impossible to sustain because it is imposed to hold passions and energies that were so visceral.... *Qaphela Caesar* [evokes concepts such as] seepages in the realm of truth, chaotic overflow, challenges to neat endings, body excesses, overflow that goes beyond the restrained narrative of truth and reconciliation. (2018a)

Qaphela Caesar at City Hall begins after Caesar is already killed. In one room, we see a pile of suits that the politicians left behind when they fled the scene. Initially, Pather's idea of using City Hall was to include a walk (iconic in several of his works to spark ordinary folks' curiosity and to gather audiences), starting from Parliament, coming down Parliament Street, passing Church Square, using some of the balconies for performance, then passing the Iziko Slave Lodge and finally arriving at City Hall. Pather wanted to draw a connection between Parliament and City Hall, but not having adequate funds, he had to set the entire work inside City Hall's fourteen rooms.

Qaphela Caesar was performed for five days, traversing the rooms, each given an evocative title by Pather, such as "a large room for nostalgia, debris and deal making, a room for a press conference [in the space and on the furniture used by the World Cup media], a room for courage and conscience, a room of power, sex and prophesy, a room for farewells, the women know" (Pather forthcoming). Pather discusses the ambience in each room, his choreographic choices, costumes, and the soundscape—for instance, "a smoking room full of politicians in suits with their pants around their ankles, shuffling around aimlessly. Hanging limply from their mouths are white balloons used as speech bubbles that inflate and deflate in the earnestness to please and say the politically expedient thing. Caesar, in the centre of it all, makes ridiculous gestures to an opera singer's rendition of Brindisi (The Drinking Song) from La Traviata" (Pather forthcoming). Another reviewer comments that "the opening scene in the City Hall was prescient. The announcement of Caesar's death at a press conference in a room still festooned with paraphernalia from the FIFA 2010 World Cup is an unwitting reminder of further international corruption and intrigue" (*Daily News* 2016).

In the middle of the show, "among other disruptions" Pather remarks that he "staged an interjection with actor Mwenya Kabwe handing out original scripts to the audience, imploring them to get us back 'on track' and insulting their lack of proper Queen's English in their reading" (Pather forthcoming). Kabwe "goes into a frenzy about the text, literally stops the action," as some audience members have to read loudly, "potentially humiliating, nonetheless funny if not disturbing" (Pather 2018a). The audience was jolted suddenly when asked to read a line of dialogue, after which they were promptly criticized for "intonation" and "flat vowels" and for not respecting the rules of "iambic pentameter." Such interventions have "a personal investment" for Pather, who believes that in "gently criticizing the Queen's English, [he] brings witness to a society forming and reforming itself, looking backward and forward to enrich and grapple with the present" (Pather 2018a). For Pather, as for others from former British colonies, the Queen's English was used as a tool of control and access. In Pather's case, as narrated earlier in his biography (see the introduction), he had to attend a language laboratory in order to remove the "deviant sounds" of his native South African Indian accent. Pather recalls that such experiences raised a range of emotions in him, to repeat words over and over in order to attain "the correct sounds" of the Queen's English.

Qaphela Caesar at City Hall explores the giddiness of attaining, holding on to, and abusing power via contemporary dance, tango, punk rock, film, and opera, described on the Gordon Institute for Performing and Creative Arts (GIPCA) site as "a rich and multi-layered work. . . . Shakespeare's classic text about honour, patriotism and friendship has been reworked by Pather to examine corruption and political power from a modern African perspective. *Qaphela Caesar* explores betrayal, prophesy, the power of political structures and the position of the individual within it. The deconstructed performance will take the audience on a journey through 14 rooms within the historical City Hall, alternating between installation and performing art and incorporating dance, spoken text, multimedia and opera" (Pather 2010).

The integral link between art and politics evident in all of Pather's creative works functions in specific ways in *Qaphela Caesar*—at times openly, at other times subtly, as "for a moment, art moved into the background," to use Benjamin Wihstutz's words, "and the theatre as a political space came to the fore" (Wihstutz 2013b, 183). Wihstutz relies on Foucault's potent concept of heterotopic space, namely "an exceptional space, which is subject to other rules and conditions and separated from everyday social life.... Michel Foucault believed heterotopias to represent specific, institutionally grounded places, which differ from other places in our societies due to their space-time relationship" (185). Pather uses City Hall as a heterotopic site that is connected both to present anxieties surrounding political strife in South Africa and, through his adaptation of Caesar, to the historical past and Cape Town residents' memories. Pather's adaptation is so profoundly contextual to his society, along with the site-responsive environment of City Hall, that he coalesces past and present, Caesar's history and South Africa's.

On the occasion of Pather winning the Creative Work Award at UCT for *Qaphela Caesar*, Saunders comments that Pather "believes that the relationship between art and politics is ingrained and that even making art which is not politics is taking a political stand" (Saunders 2016, 3). Pather himself explains the connection between art and politics, applicable not only to *Qaphela Caesar* but to all his work: "Art gives us a way towards finding those metaphors, those symbols, the kind of tangential experience to understand the nuances of the past, a troubled present and suspended future. It is becoming more and more necessary for art to bear witness to all that is going on as we enter an era of feeling abandoned and lonely, unseen and invisible" (Saunders 2016, 3).

Along with the performance, Pather, as director of GIPCA, held the *pre-past-per-form* conference on interdisciplinary and performance art that "provided an academic underpinning and legitimacy... to South African contemporary art" (Sichel 2010). Sichel's review of *Qaphela Caesar* at Cape Town City Hall, entitled "Bleeding from the Walls and Ceilings," marks 2010 as the year in which "South African dance's site-specific installation-style performance comes of age" (Sichel 2010).

By 2010, Sichel notes that "Pather is an old hand at deconstructing cultural, religious, socio-political issues twinned with his obsession with architecture and landscape as harbingers of identity and history." He is adept at researching and interrogating a subject, "then extracting essences of song, dance, dramatic, ritualistic and art-making tradition. The resulting often anarchic, iconography is born not out of random choices and superficially imposed experiments, but out of an intensive shared process and a deep knowledge of whom and what forms the director and choreographer is working with" (Sichel 2010). In each carefully considered movement or use of media in this work, Sichel notes that Pather succeeds in making his performers "engage as the exotic, the erotic [as] post-colonial, post-apartheid, post-democratic (con)texts come into simultaneous play. Location, location, location."

After its Cape Town performances, *Qaphela Caesar* was commissioned by FNB Dance Umbrella, Johannesburg, where its site-responsive location was the old Stock Exchange building, in which the movement of finance and capital is as powerful and rife for economic and political corruption today as it was in Caesar's time—just with different kinds of currency.[17] Even today's fast-paced, internet-driven transactions replicate issues of power brokers, friendships, and lobbyists jockeying for influence, similar to the circumstances of Caesar's time. In both locations, City Hall and the Stock Exchange, "the themes were heavily influenced," comments Pather, "by these spaces of political and economic power."[18] Pather notes that these site-specific productions "were also a comment on the architecture that hosted the works" (Pather forthcoming).

A third version of *Qaphela Caesar*, called *Caesar Interrupted*, was performed in 2012 in Durban—a version that gets its title from the fact that Pather did not get enough funding to mount the

Fig. 4.6. *Caesar Interrupted*. Ntombi Gasa crouched under a wooden plank and Nhlakanipho Cele in red high-heeled sandals carrying a fan on his back and a poster. Photographer: Val Adamson.

entire show. The festival organizers who had already announced this work on the program wanted Pather to do a twenty-minute version, which was "ridiculous" to him. Hence, he did *Caesar Interrupted* using footage from his earlier adaptations, to convey "a sense of loss" (Pather 2018a). This experience conveys for Pather "a betrayal of Caesar that parallels a betrayal of our artists because [the organizers] could not come up with a small amount of funding for this Company to perform their full work" (2018a). This scenario parallels misspent funds and cuts to arts funding, due implicitly to government corruption.[19]

The 2015 iteration of *Qaphela Caesar* on a proscenium stage at Pretoria's State Theatre was "extremely popular" notes Pather, though getting back to the story line was "a capitulation" for him, even as he acknowledges monetary commitments of fulfilling a commission and paying his dancer-actors (2018a) On the proscenium stage he was able to use projections and creative lighting, at times filling the stage with uncanny shadows. Shakespeare's text is heard via video inserts of actors reading different character parts. For Pather, "a crucial scene in the whole show" evokes the ongoing (since 2008) xenophobic attacks in South Africa on "foreigners," typically Africans from other parts of the continent. In a chilling scene, a man is questioned, "What is your name? What are you doing here?" (2018a).

In his director's note for the 2015 production at the State Theatre in Pretoria, Pather comments that "the original story is riddled with political intrigue, personal betrayals, staggering deception, superstitions, prophecies, and high drama. At the centre of it all is the tension between the good fight of the past and the political expediency of the present, as well as the lust for power, the mysterious roots of this power and the collapse of conscience."[20] The overlapping issues of Shakespeare's historical drama and contemporary South Africa ring true, such as the dangers of power grabbing, betrayals by close friends, and the general disaffection of a wider public.

At the State Theatre Pather weaves his choreographic and directorial magic, holding the audience captive for an hour and fifty minutes as he inundates them with virtuosic movement and multimedia images that re-create the Shakespearean tragedy for South Africa's contemporary realities, in which self-serving leadership and amassing of personal wealth prevail in the halls of power. The human body is the repository of political power and betrayal conveyed via Pather's choreography, a hybrid of contemporary dance, traditional *sangoma* ritual movements, and video projections.

The musical score includes opera, classical music, and other human sounds, at times overlapping or even interrupting one another. "Above all," remarks Pather in his director's note, "the dance production is a political thriller performed to the highly charged 'Death and the Maiden' by Schubert and other works by contemporary composers to evoke a fast-paced kinetic re-imagining of Shakespeare's work while providing commentary on the politics of our time, of memory, history and future." Within the layered soundscape of opera and classical music, suddenly a pop song intervenes—Barbra Streisand's "The Way We Were" rendered by a drag queen—while in the background "black-and-white struggle footage offered irony and nostalgia" (Saunders 2016, 4). Pather, skilled at layering both his choreography and musical choices, comments that he likes "the disparate forms to be able to hold the space. I wasn't interested in making a dry, political statement. I wanted to create a theatrical spectacle and bring together the skills of choreography, directing and cabaret and bring them to bear on a political story" (Saunders 2016, 4). It is fascinating to marvel at Pather's use of multiple disciplines on a hybrid canvas—dance that showcases the human body in striking movement, along with video images, animation, backdrop projections of buildings, a human face or a pig mask, and underwater projections that make water seem to move on stage with striking lighting effects, all of which "hold the space" for the audience. It is worth noting that Pather, "cognizant of moving the work from rich architectural contexts to a proscenium stage, worked with the designer to create a constantly shifting architectural surrounds from the Parliament buildings to cityscapes, opening of parliament regalia, etc." (phone conversation, June 4, 2020).

In "Tonight/What-s-on/Gauteng," Pinto Ferreira (2015) writes lyrically about the "utter beauty" of the set "juxtaposed with sinister discomposure. The tranquility of the clinical white, pale-lit set is starkly contrasted with three austere pig-masked actors sitting in the auditorium, staring into the distance. Their diabolical and ominous presence evokes an unsettling awareness of impending evil." Ferreira compliments Pather's effective combining of voice-over with "miraculously choreographed sequences" and images of "satirical projections of the Union Buildings, placing the political unrest of ancient Rome in a contemporary context."

Fig. 4.7. *Qaphela Caesar*. Dancers with string and balloons. Photographer: Val Adamson. Courtesy Jay Pather.

The reviewer, Ferreira praises Wilhelm Disbergen's set and lighting design, which he believes steal the show. "His [Disbergen's] impeccable multi-media constructions are not only aesthetically invigorating, they serve as an integral part of the development of the work, contributing to the social commentary and the enthralling subtext." Fereira asserts that there is definitely "a place for this kind of avant-garde theatre, invitingly thought-provoking and superb performances, in South Africa."

As in Shakespeare, Pather's Caesar (Nkanyiso Kunene) is not a particularly prominent or vocal character but rather the catalyst for the action—in particular, Brutus' (Sandile Mkhize) psychological conflict when his loyalty to Caesar is at odds with political expediency couched in false patriotism that haunts him until his own suicide. Cassius (Monde Marafana) leads the conspirators to murder Caesar to prevent the latter's rise to power. And although Caesar is warned by a soothsayer "to beware the ides of March" (a date forever associated with Caesar's killing), he ignores the warning, as well as his wife Calpurnia's (Lorin Sookol) premonitions of his impending murder.

The 2015 video recording of the performance opens with three pig-masked men stepping onto the stage from their seats among the audience, implying that such human-pigs are among the populace. Pigs, associated generally with negative, even repulsive connotations of greed and gluttony, appear to be indicative of these pig-masked men, who turn out to be deceitful and untrustworthy; they are, in fact, part of the nation's power structure. The symbolism of the pig head is analyzed astutely by the Tracey Saunders: "The blame for the current state of the nation is not laid exclusively at the door of politicians. One of the more insidious characters in *Qaphela Caesar* is the well-heeled and slick human attired in a designer business suit and adorned with a large pig's head. The constant and relentless presence of the new-liberal economy is not merely big and gross but a sensual, sophisticated and sensuous persona" (Saunders 2016, 3).

The three pig-masked men, also embodying pigheadedness, mount the stage as two men and two women enter from either side. They come together as the backdrop image of a large pig invades the audience's vision. My analysis and the characters' dialogue are based on watching a video of the production. The voice-over intones, "Can you see your face, noble Brutus?" implying that the men wearing the pig masks are the traitors who will deceive Brutus into betraying his friend Caesar. Other voice-overs follow: "I do fear Caesar chosen by the people for king" and "honor is the subject of my story."

Caesar's wife, Calpurnia, in red blouse and long gold skirt, enters and falls harshly on the floor, reminiscent of the Physical Theater style. A group movement piece follows, with vigorous jumps, tumbles, and general frenzy, as we notice the backdrop portraying a sprawling, ornate building in contemporary South Africa. A diagonal shaft of light reveals a person carrying a shawl

Fig. 4.8. Dancer with pig face mask. Photographer: Val Adamson. Courtesy Jay Pather.

for Caesar, as if giving him the mantle of power. The bearer of the gift lays the shawl down on a lighted circle. The many facets and prongs of accepting leadership are in the air: Will Caesar be successful? Will he be deposed by murder?

One person opens the shawl and drapes it around Caesar's body as the voice-over remarks, "Such men are dangerous." As one sits in the chair, the word *ambition* floats in the air. Others without pants rally around the one in the chair to represent sycophantic power grabbers, moving as if simulating a sexual act leading to orgasm. The group carries white balloons that are popped, symbolizing that ambition will amount to nothing. The backdrop images display word bubbles, such as those used in illustrated works like graphic novels and comic books, to indicate who is speaking or thinking.

The words reaching the audience are "the abuse of greatness when it disjoins remorse from power." Ever since Cassius gathered conspirators to his side, the landscape is like a "hideous dream," "a phantasm . . . [that needs] wary walking." The light coming from a diagonal panel in the middle and two other straight strips reflects the fragmentation of thoughts invading the conspirators as though they are troubled by conflicts. As two vertical panels of light turn red and red light spills on the floor, a violin sounds lyrically. Then an opera singer's words chime in as the lights turn to a soft blue, while a man and woman dance a beautiful pas de deux. Pather's choreography is deeply affective in pas de deux dances, as in *A South African Siddhartha*, in *Hotel*, and here in *Qaphela Caesar*. A further layer is added as a dancer in the background appears with stripes on his face as though he is duplicitous, someone not to be trusted. As Brutus's wife Portia (Leagan Peffer) keeps asking her husband what troubles him—since, as his wife, she has the right to share his agony—two pig-masked male dancers reenter as if embodying Brutus's dark thoughts.

Pather's layering of images, movements, and sounds creates a multidimensional landscape of people in the midst of chaotic psychological and political strife. The backdrop moves to underwater images of fish and animals. Pather's choreography is augmented by his choices of creative lighting, which focus on the ballet pointe shoes before the dancers are lit and their bodies are seen; as Brutus' wife Portia (in her death throes) goes into a frenzied repetition of *entrechat* jumps, two pig-masked men enter and carry her away.

A soprano sings an impossibly high note, screeching almost painfully as a dancer sits uncomfortably in a red chair. Then, as if being tortured by electric shots, he twitches. A *sangoma* figure with a white-painted face and a flower on his head is visible, along with two other figures in white masks and with white scarves, as in *sangoma* ritual ceremonies. Others enter with white balloons, as in a previous scene, as if carrying flimsy promises that burst into thin air in no time. They sit as if around a board table awaiting the man in the red chair, who then climbs unceremoniously on top of the table; the lights are low and bluish-gray as the jockeying for power is implied and chairs fall. Some dancers remain fixed in the chairs like prisoners. Lights on the stage floor move like ocean waves, evoking shifting allegiances of power. Water, represented by the lighting, appears to take over the surface of the stage, where one dancer sits in the chair and nonchalantly observes others (even as they are drowning) screaming and fighting. The flood appears to invade the space as the struggle continues. A warning cry comes to Brutus—"Fly my lord, fly, farewell"—but Brutus kills himself.

The backdrop shows crowds of people, and, startlingly, a Black woman wearing a white wig and very high platform shoes appears, carrying a candelabra with three lit candles, singing Barbra Streisand's popular song "The Way We Were." "If we had the chance to do it all again" she sings, "tell me, would we, could we?" This is followed by a line that would sound like a platitude if it were not so tragically true of South Africa's political realities: "What's too painful to remember, we should simply forget." Painful memories, lack of accountability, and a need to forget all invade the audience's consciousness.

Lights suddenly get very bright, and we hear the tragic line about Brutus: "This was the noblest Roman of them all. This was a man." An ornate, embroidered shawl, a symbol of the one who is in power, reappears as if ready for the next new leader. It is placed on the floor. The pig-masked men return, but the woman stops them from taking the shawl. The leaders in front pretend to be sharing but look voraciously at the shawl, and the pig-headed dancer simply dances around in joy knowing that whoever gets the shawl will in any event be in his pocket.

Qaphela Caesar on the proscenium stage was received with critical acclaim, regarded as "an interdisciplinary contemporary adaptation" of Shakespeare's classic, examining "corruption and political power from a modern African perspective" (Artslink 2015). Sibusiso Mkhwanazi in "Danger, Gevaar, Ingozi" recognizes Pather's skill in combining "the disciplines of dance, music, photography and video to tell the story of politics and the resultant constant power struggles.... One of the most critical issues discussed by the piece is patriotism and is a topical subject in our society. The age-old question of who qualifies as an African is a constant undercurrent on stage as dancers from all races—with assistance from some nifty lighting—delve deep into the argument" (Mkhwanazi 2015). Mkhwanazi also appreciates "how much of a deconstruction" this adaptation is in Pather's hands in that it includes "sangomas complete with a Zulu soundtrack of praise songs." Sichel recognizes Pather's skillful hybridity in bringing together "the spoken, visual and performed texts, astutely synergized with Shakespeare's play and Pather's mixed media installation style, and conceptual wizardry [that] vividly spoke to South African realities of the time. The director-choreographer and his company caused a sensation with their courage, inventiveness, creativity and artistry" (Sichel 2016, 14).

In 2015, when this work was staged at the State Theatre the student movement around #FeesMustFall was at its height. Pather's re-creation of Shakespeare's classic spoke to the political corruption rife within South Africa. This tumultuous time (2015–16) of student protests and unrest on several campuses, when major urban universities had to shut down, reflects what Pather "refers to [as] the current state in South Africa as being one of a low-grade depression that is worsened by the very personal nature of the betrayal that people experience and the fear that there is no hope of recovery" (Saunders 2016, 3).

The political situation in South Africa in 2015 makes this tale of power and honor even more relevant than it was in 2010. As Pather remarks: "Opened *Qaphela Caesar* last night amidst a massive attack of the State on students and it all has been feeling far too relevant for my liking. Here's an extract from a text fragment at the end of the first Act." [21]

> CAESAR:
> Let me have men about me that are fat;
> Sleek-headed men and such as sleep o' nights:
> Yond Cassius has a lean and hungry look;
> He thinks too much; such men are dangerous.
> He reads too much; would he were fatter!

Pather is "self-reflexively" critical that using a Shakespeare play was based on his conviction that art and politics are integrally connected. As a consummate artist who has his finger on the pulse of his nation's political fortunes, Pather believes that "Art gives us a way towards finding those metaphors, those symbols, the kind of tangential experience to understand the nuances of the past, a troubled present and suspended futures. It is becoming more and more necessary for art to bear witness to all that is going on as we enter an era of feeling abandoned and lonely, unseen and invisible" (Saunders 2016, 1).

Pather's conclusion to his keynote for the Global Shakespeare Symposium at UCI posits "an abiding question" to himself—namely,

> the mechanisms inherent in performance that can possibly fill spaces and silences, interactive, collaborative, experiential... initiate fault lines making manifest for South Africans' deeply lodged unarticulated, unnamable, unwitnessed ache... for people to negotiate order and predictability in their lives. My dialogic approach is not existential but political, to get closer to the interiority of the many layers and fabric and touch spaces of vulnerabilities.... The alchemy at the meeting ground of artist, politics and the nation bring tentative answers, open-ended means. Shakespeare is a means to an end, rather than an end. (2018a)

With *Qaphela Caesar*, Pather was inspired by Shakespeare's text to transform it into an extravaganza of movement, video projections with political meanings, and creative lighting and sound, all of which reflect the political miasma of South Africa under Zuma's corrupt regime.

In conclusion, the site-responsive works discussed in this chapter challenge the enormous inequities among the races in South Africa, and the spaces—physical, mental, psychological—that they can occupy legitimately in this democracy. In *Home*, Pather sensitively tunes into the urgent needs of the majority for a safe home and the parameters of what a "home" means for a rural or urban Black family, for a worker living in a hostel, or for an interracial couple struggling anxiously in *Hotel*. The failures of the state are evoked in sharp contrast to struggling families in line for bread while the president is on his treadmill, oblivious to video images of wretched lives in townships in *The Beautiful Ones Must Be Born*. Similar to the form of this latter work, the vignettes in *Body of Evidence* excavate the individual's and the nation's history and memories held inside the body's bone marrow and cells, raising provocative, even painful questions of accountability, responsibility, and the continued waiting by the majority for opportunities to earn a livable wage. Despite greedy politicians struggling to hold on to power represented in 2015 in *Qaphela Caesar*, the masses prevail, as they do also in Zuma's eventual ouster in 2018.

Pather's choreographic and musical choices, along with the conceptual layering of his site-responsive works, give audiences epiphanic, theatrical moments to learn from and to see with their hearts, and may inspire them to participate in struggles for social justice. In the next chapter, I discuss Pather's continuing spatial explorations, expressed adventurously in his curations of the public arts festivals *Infecting the City* and *Live Art* in Cape Town.

NOTES

1. My thanks to Pather for sharing a copy of this essay with me in July 2015. Since then, the essay has been published in Greg Homann and Marc Maufort, eds., *New Territories: Theater, Drama and Performance in Post-apartheid South Africa* (Bruxelles: P.I.E. Peter Lang, 2015), 317–44.

2. *Umcimezo*, a traditional Zulu ritual where a bride to be goes to various neighbors' homes accepting gifts, is used ironically in *Kitchen* since the couple is already married.

I am grateful to Adrienne Sichel for a copy of the Brett Kebble Award citation, 2004.

3. My thanks to Pather for sharing his copy of this unpublished final report with me.

4. In 2013, *The Mercury*'s Greg Nicholson, in "Where a Nation Meets/Meats," quotes Mamphela Ramphele's unifying words: "From our collective struggle was born a nation based on a constitution that protects the pillars of democracy with respect for the rule of law" (September 26 2013, 10). Ramphela warns against "tribalism and a return of racial politics [that] risks the destruction of all that we have built together." The same article quotes Deputy President Kgalema Motlanthe's expected state line: "Heritage Day . . . defines us as a people with a shared future. It symbolizes the totality of our humanity, our history, our socio-political evolution and the

need to overcome our fragmented past to use such victory as a bridgehead to build a future defined by unity, democracy, non-racialism, non-sexism, justice and prosperity for all our people."

5. As Heather Mackie (2003) remarks, "Philip Stein, one of Johannesburg's great arts gurus, and the man who really started up the Dance Umbrella, never failed to evince a childlike enthusiasm about this event, and the surprises, energy and diversity it displays. Now in its 17th season, the annual FNB Dance Umbrella has become an established event on Johannesburg's arts calendar."

6. Pather recounted that during the process of researching and visiting the site for this work, he was reminded disturbingly that this location is not only for tourists but is also used as an event site, for commercial use. He overheard a conversation about renting the space for a birthday party and the "problem" of lighting the space. The solution was to use "pink lights that would glow through the space and would still give a sense of the prison." Although he did not include this type of event to critique in *Beautiful Ones*, he did use the idea of young folks washing hair as if in a spa (phone conversation, June 4, 2020).

7. In a phone conversation (June 4, 2020), Pather explained that although the University of Natal during apartheid was for Whites only, a few Black people were allowed in "with Ministerial permission" if there were no universities for Black people that taught a particular subject. This was the case for Biko, who wanted to study medicine and there was no university for Black students that offered medicine.

8. This is reminiscent of the 1978 play *Sizwe Bansi Is Dead*, cowritten by Athol Fugard, Winston Ntshona, and John Kani, which unfolds during apartheid. Sizwe remarks poignantly that "our [Black] skin is trouble." It is sad and ironic that such racial designations still haunt the new nation as represented in Pather's works.

9. As I write these words about systemic racism in South Africa, I am unnerved by the events in Minneapolis, US, on May 25, 2020, where yet another Black man, George Floyd, was killed by a White policeman whose White hand is bloodied forever as he pressed down with his knee on Floyd's neck for eight minutes and forty-six seconds and murdered him. "Black Lives Matter" and "I can't breathe" (Floyd's words before he died) were rallying cries of protests and demonstrations, peaceful and violent, expressing rage and frustration. Protests went on for ten days after his killing, across 140 cities and towns in all fifty states, with curfews in several major cities and the National Guard called into 21 cities. Injustice against

Black people and their oppression goes back nearly four hundred years in the history of slavery.

10. Sichel's comments on *Body of Evidence*, for the National Arts Festival, 2009, http://mg.co.za/multimedia/2012-10-04-memories-0-violence-1.

11. Pather notes in "Laws of Recall" that *isicathamiya*, an originally rural form of a cappella singing and dancing, was "devised largely by migrant workers in the KwaZulu Natal region. The word translates as 'walking softly' referring in part to the cramped living conditions that made it imperative that the practice of this form used little space and was soft, a far cry from its roots in the wide-open fields of the rural parts."

12. Email to Katrak, October 22, 2015.

13. The political upheaval had been ongoing since Mandela stepped down as president and Thabo Mbeki became president in 1999, with his deputy Jacob Zuma. Mbeki and Zuma's power struggles finally forced Mbeki to leave office in 2008. From the inception of Zuma's presidency in 2009 until 2017, he faced charges of rape and corruption. He survived several impeachment votes and calls for his resignation. Finally, when faced with a no-confidence vote on February 22, 2018, he resigned before the no-confidence vote on February 14, 2018. Cyril Ramaposa is now the president.

14. The many calls for President Zuma to step down are similar to the situation of Robert Mugabe, the Zimbabwean president who refused to abdicate power after thirty-seven years as president. Finally, recent political events in Zimbabwe, with a short military takeover, forced Mugabe to resign on November 21, 2017. There were jubilations in the streets of Harare and across Zimbabwe. Mugabe, ninety-three, died on September 6, 2019 in Singapore.

15. All quotations by Pather here are from his keynote presentation, transcribed from a video recording, for the Global Shakespeare Symposium, University of California, Irvine(UCI), January 2018.

16. See the introduction, where I discuss Pather's adaptation of *The Tempest* in 1985.

17. In selecting such sites, Pather (2018a) comments that apart from the challenges of dealing with the authorities and building managers, the biggest hurdle is the quality of the floor in terms of safety for dancers, especially for contemporary dance movements that require high jumps, at times changing positions in the air and then landing on the ground.

18. Director's note, *Qaphela Caesar*, 2015.

19. One highly controversial recent South African government policy to fund arts development in nonurban areas, although not problematic in itself, makes funding increasingly and seriously insecure for well-established companies such as Pather's Siwela Sonke Dance Theatre (twenty-two years old in 2018) and Loots's Flatfoot Dance Company (twenty years old in 2018), among other established companies that have produced a significant body of work over the past twenty years along with their commitment to training the next generation of dancers. Hence, cuts to funding training programs is a severe blow to the very lifeblood of these companies. In a timely article entitled "Funding Shock for Dance Companies" (Loots 2016), Lliane Loots argues usefully that the government would do well to rethink this policy of putting money into rural programs that are barely off the ground at the expense of companies with twenty- to thirty-year records of training the majority of dancers in South Africa. Although Loots admits that it is encouraging to support "the new kids on the block," such a move "lacks the wisdom of ensuring a sustained dance industry by continuing to fund tried and tested companies that hold the local dance industry afloat." Loots strategically suggests "a middle-ground" whereby the National Arts Council (NAC) continues to fund the more established companies with the proviso that they mentor new companies and pass along legacies of "good governance and artistic integrity that supports the old and the new."

20. My thanks to Adrienne Sichel for sending me a copy of this program via regular mail from Johannesburg.

21. Email to Katrak, October 22, 2015.

PART III

CURATORIAL CHOREOGRAPHIES
Challenges of Curating Public Art Festivals (2007-Present)

FIVE

A NEW KIND OF PERFORMANCE— CURATION OF LIVE ARTISTS

> Public art has always been part of who we are on this continent and in this country given our history of public ritual, public protest and celebration. The interconnectedness of the African "us" meets challenge after challenge in a public, social way, brought to vibrant life in artistic expression. There is too that part of our history that impeded this public interconnectedness, throwing people apart and far away from each other, a physical and psychic separation still waiting to be healed. Infecting the City is a small attempt at igniting the interconnectedness.... We are confident that, whether through shared rapture or mutual puzzlement, the Festival offered possibilities for public engagement across a range of divides.... The provocation and extraordinary achievements of our artists provided assertive directions and inspiration for public engagement.
>
> Jay Pather, "Curator's Note, 2012"

PATHER'S SUCCESS IN INTERDISCIPLINARY PERFORMANCES inside theater spaces, and in site work outdoors, is rooted in linking his creative work to critical discourse, theory to praxis, and the whole to politically progressive goals. Pather's scope as curator and his activities of curation are similar to—and, at times, on a larger public scale than—his site-selective and site-responsive choreography. Pather's site and curatorial work share similar resonances in providing access to high-quality art for ordinary citizens, startling them with unexpected sights and sounds that may provide a release from daily struggles, and he often leaves the works open-ended. In the site-specific *Cityscapes*, Pather as choreographer and director primarily selected particular works and locations for the pieces; such choices involve curatorial skills, though on a smaller scale than Pather's curation of large-scale public arts festivals such as *Infecting the City* (ITC), which he co-curated with Brett Baily in 2008, and then as sole curator from 2012 on, and *Live Art*, which he has curated since 2012, both of which I analyze in this chapter. I also trace Pather's journey as curator from 2007 on. Curating such public arts festivals fulfills Pather's goals of democratizing space, of creating opportunities for different publics to share the same space, and to start conversations across racial and class divides that remain daunting even during post-apartheid.

Pather's distinctive qualities as curator include selecting innovative, often risky work by established and new artists; collaborating with them to select appropriate, even provocative locations for their work; identifying city routes for his audiences to traverse freely as they respond or walk away; and exerting his overall acumen in having works speak to one another (as in a theater season). Pather's concept-infused curator notes, and his theorizing on curation in essays, contend that the task of curation (the word derives from the Latin, "to take care of") functions differently in visual art comprising objects than in live art, which can be unpredictable and bold. Curating a festival of public art that showcases live artists and spectators is distinct from curating inanimate objects inside a museum.

The main deviation from curation of an exhibition inside a museum resides in "taking care of" live performers and artists with their own human circumstances and their creative works, which can be risky or edgy and can challenge audiences to step out of their comfort zones. Such impact also requires a curator such as Pather to plan for the preemption of disgruntled spectators at best and for hostile ones at worst. At times, certain shows in the center of Cape Town have elicited direct violence from motorists, who can threaten live artists and then drive away.

Pather regards curating live art to be the most challenging, even "impossible" as his essay "The Impossibility of Curating Live Art" states, since this performance genre requires that curators remain open and "keep pace with this ever-shifting art form" (2019b, 90). His own curatorial experience guides his analysis "to consider the limits of the terms curation and curator, the conceptual shifts necessary to meet the artist's intentions and the contexts or constrains of a given work, and to probe possibilities for a new vocabulary" (93) for live art. I discuss below Pather's articulation of this "new vocabulary" and how it functions in his curation of live art festivals.

David Bunn's discussion of the challenges faced by South African artists in the city of Johannesburg are applicable to other South African metropolitan centers: "The city is associated with a failure of mediation between levels, with a kind of metaphoric skin that no longer communicates properly with an interior body. The failure of this traffic between levels is variously figured: as a hardening and sloughing of the surface; sedimentation, rather than mining of deep penetration" (Nuttall and Mbembe 2008, 146). Bunn further adopts a "disease" analogy between the plague and the role of art; he comments on "the diseased skin and its relative autonomy. In the time of the plague, it seems, it requires a very special aesthetic effort to find joy in the space between disease and love, between the present time of desire and the ineluctable progress of illness" (146–47). Such concepts of infection and inserting art into the body's struggle are close to Pather's articulations of infection and the body in his curating *Infecting the City* public art festivals.

Pather's curatorial activities in and around Cape Town span several ventures—he served as co-curator of Spier Contemporary in 2007, creating with curator Clive van den Bergh a two-month long art exhibition of one hundred artists on the Spier

Estate. From 2010 to 2015, as director of University of Cape Town's Gordon Center for Performing and Creative Arts (GIPCA), he curated multifaceted activities—*ITC* public arts festivals since 2008 and *Live Art* since 2012, along with organizing exhibitions, symposia, and interdisciplinary workshops with performers and choreographers, scholars, and scientists as well as literary, media, and visual artists.

Since 2016, after GIPCA's five-year funding ended, Pather was successful in getting a three-year grant of just over nine million rand from the Andrew W. Mellon Foundation (2016–19 and extended to 2023) to revive GIPCA under the new name Institute for Creative Arts (ICA). The ICA is

> based in the University of Cape Town's Humanities Faculty, formerly known as the Gordon Institute for Performing and Creative Arts (GIPCA). Since 2008, the Institute has fostered innovative practice and research in the creative and performing arts that works across the disciplines of music, dance, fine art, drama, literature and film, with a particular focus on black practitioners and issues that affect black South Africans.... A key premise of the ICA's work is that interdisciplinary practice in South Africa, and live art in particular, help us to understand the complexity of our contemporary society—one that is chronologically "post" apartheid, but that continues to grapple with material redress, land redistribution and systemic racism.[1]

Pather as "performance-curator" embodies a role played increasingly by artists across the globe, as Tom Sellar discusses in his significant essay "The Curatorial Turn" in a special issue of *Theater*: "Performance curators are ideally invested, simultaneously, in critical discourse of cultural politics, social engagement, the history of art, dramaturgy, and performance studies. They have been embraced as an essential link between theory and praxis, able to join separately developed disciplinary strands; they have been hailed as a possible negotiator of institutional and genre categories at a time when institutions are rethinking their limitations [such as involving a vast public that may not go to museums or theaters], artists are blurring forms with unprecedented fluidity, and discourses ... are resolutely, and freely, interdisciplinary" (Sellar 2014, 22). As "performance curator," Pather is a skilled thinker and interlocutor in collaboration with the artists he showcases. He also functions as "a possible negotiator of institutional and genre categories," to use Sellar's words, by fostering interdisciplinary, multidisciplinary, and live art performances across Cape Town.

Further, curatorship, a "mode of self-presentation," as Paul O'Neill posits in *The Culture of Curating and the Curating of Culture(s)*, is "employed by artists and curators alike as both a communicative medium and a genre of artistic production" (cited in Sellars 2014, 23). Pather is a prominent example of an "artist-curator" who invites and facilitates discussions by artists, philosophers and researchers about and beyond performance, and who also commissions creative works from his wide network. He aims, in his curation, to fulfill one of the foremost roles of performance curators—namely, "to make and rethink the connection between art and public." This link is critically important in contemporary times, as is evidenced by shrinking audiences (especially among youth) for traditional, classical works inside theaters. Pather uses outdoor sites and digital media to draw in spectators of different generations, creating new connections and dialogues among artists and their publics, combating the many historical odds of a segregated social structure.

CO-CURATING SPIER CONTEMPORARY: FOSTERING NEW SOUTH AFRICAN ARTS

The Spier Estate, Pather explained, was in solidarity with social justice work and fostering artists (phone conversation, June 7, 2020). In 2002–3, there was a strong sense that many Black artists felt ostracized and ignored by the art world. Spier Contemporary, a visual art exhibition with some performance, aimed to change that. Another trajectory was the Spier Summer Festival that in 2006–7 did not have a large audience. Hence, the Spier Estate invited Pather and others to discuss alternatives. Spier Summer Festival became the first 2008 *Infecting the City* festival that moved to Cape Town.

The *Spier Contemporary 2007* catalog, edited by Pather, includes an opening statement by the Africa Centre (also the publisher), founded in 2005, namely, "to provide a new arts and cultural voice in Africa, for Africans" to address the disturbing reality that excellent African art is currently found not on the continent but outside of it (Pather 2007, 268). This reality is rooted in colonialist plunder of art objects that often takes years of negotiations between governments and museums to rectify (by returning the artifacts to their rightful cultural homes). The Africa Centre's goal is to challenge this dishonest piracy, which leads to a dearth of variety of artworks by local artists, by teaming up with Spier "to represent a new South African contemporary art voice" (Pather 2007, 1–3). Spier aims to bring together "a hundred South African artists working with an amazingly diverse set of media within extraordinarily different cultural contexts. The opportunity to use visual art as a medium to reflect the 'state of the nation' offered both daunting and exciting possibilities" (Pather 2007, 2).[2] Spier's efforts fostered cross-disciplinary work and performance in exhibiting art.

Pather, co-curator with Clive van den Berg of Spier Contemporary in 2007, was on the selection team for creative work solicited from urban and rural South Africa. The Africa Center records that the inaugural exhibition included ninety-two artists on the Spier Estate in December 2007, running until February 20, 2008, and then moving to Johannesburg for March 16 through May 31, and finally to Durban for August 1 through October 31. Spier Contemporary's aim was to encourage innovation and foster new artists by providing a platform to showcase their work. There were eleven physical locations where artists could submit their work, including digital submissions, which were uncommon for rural artists. This curatorial activity of selecting and mentoring artists laid the foundation for Pather's own aesthetic innovations and cultivated his keen eye for a multidisciplinary array of creative expressions in his curation of *Infecting the City*, and *Live Art* since 2012.

Curator Clive Van den Berg's intention, stated in the catalog's opening chapter, was to be inclusive and provide space for artists to express themselves and to have a platform for their work. In Van den Berg's travels across South Africa, he discovered that for artists, "the dominant subject was 'the mutant body: Bodies altered by fear, resentment, disease, abuse, neglect, or one sensed an uncertainty about how to fit in'" (Pather 2007, 5)— this plethora of emotions was trapped within bodies under apartheid for years. Berg adds that for artists "using performance, the body seems to enact its own doubt or denial" (5). Performers also "disrupt the sanctity of spaces, of comfort zones and of written or unwritten taboos." Berg's ideas on both the physical body and disrupting space resonate in Pather's work. Fascinatingly, rather than resignation at apartheid injustices, Berg notes that alternatives to "what might have been" were explored, including "moments in our history when trajectories other than separation and alienation were possible" (Pather, ed., 2007, 6). A common aspect of the exhibition was "a relocation of ritual to space, emblematic of a larger fluidity of actions and their symbolic representation" (7). The location of the exhibition was "in a temporary building [with] walls made by piling shipping containers as if in a giant Lego fantasy.... The roof [was] a series of tensile wings ... [with] views out to the landscape" (7). The energy flowing between the sounds of nature and the ambience surrounding the artwork brought the outside and inside together. Playing with site in this way was key to Pather's *Cityscapes*, in which he situated dancer-actors outdoors on the steps of well-known buildings, or in front of concrete columns. Alternately, he brought spectators indoors, into a small room where they were crammed together while viewing *Hotel* (discussed in chap. 3), or inside a domestic kitchen set in an art gallery (*Kitchen*, discussed in chap. 4). Spier Contemporary's uses of space reflect the themes and concerns of artistic works similar to Pather's goals in his site works, and later in his curating of public arts festivals.

The Spier Contemporary 2007 project, as noted by one of the selectors, Thembinkosi Goniwe, in "Reflections from Uneven Ground," appropriately used "a flexible selection procedure," since artists worked with such vastly different economic opportunities in different parts of South Africa: "cosmopolitan and urban, to remote and rural areas" (Pather 2007, 9). Additionally, the disparities of gender, race, class, and "even access to education, information and facilities that enable art of quality . . . racially marked social locales" and played a role in the artworks produced (10). Hence, Goniwe observes, large-scale installation works mostly came from urban areas, whereas rural artists had mainly "non-technological artworks" that did not use "computerized innovations"; these need to be evaluated in relation to the rural conditions that inform them and be judged through a reframing of the dominant criteria upon which contemporary art is judged. At the same time, it is important not to ghettoize submissions, because artwork from rural areas is as much a part of the new South Africa as art from cities, which do not have a sole claim on transformative art. With such ideals, it was nonetheless a daunting task to review some two thousand submissions—the sheer volume emphasized the fact that art production was thriving (Goniwe, in Pather 2007, 12).

Among the diverse artworks in the catalog, Steven Cohen's *Cleaning Time (Vienna): 3 Interventions on DVD* demonstrated his admirable insights in a bold outdoor performance, taking "the theatrical out into reality," as he notes, "and deconstruct[ing] social functioning through [his] uninvited, unexpected, and sometimes unwelcome, public interventions." Above all, Cohen asserts, "I chose to make art, not entertainment" (Pather 2007, 76). In *Cleaning Time*, Cohen replicates a story he had heard in childhood from his grandparents that "Jews in Vienna during the time of the holocaust had been forced to clean the streets with toothbrushes. This is well verified by witnesses in literature and on the internet" (76). Cohen provocatively decides "to clean the streets of the Heldenplatz with a giant toothbrush and a diamond up [his] arsehole," as he remarks in the Spier Catalog, when he is invited to Vienna for the First International Festival of Jewish Theatre. The two striking images in the Spier Catalog include Cohen wearing a close-fitting, off-the-shoulder top, a gas mask on his genitalia, and very high-heeled red shoes.[3] His bare thighs and legs assume a balletic posture in one pose, and in another he shows his buttocks when he is on all fours, leaning forward to clean the floor with a huge toothbrush.

Cohen's comment about the painful past of the Jewish genocide echoes the many discriminations suffered by Black people in South Africa. Cohen writes passionately about the acts of remembering and not forgetting the past via "new methods.... Shocking and radical is an appropriate language for dealing with unspeakable horror" (Pather 2007, 76). Cohen asks "if it is possible to look with self-critical irony at the atrocity of genocide.... Stone monuments are too easy to ignore" (76). His further comment that "the danger is not in the way we remember as much as in the way we forget" (76) echoes Pather's goal of having spectators face uncomfortable realities of ongoing poverty and inequities through his own creative work and his critical curatorial practice.

DIRECTOR OF GIPCA 2010–2015: INFECTING A CITY WITH PERFORMANCE

Rarely has a festival set out "to infect" a city. This is the uncanny and original aim set out in Brett Bailey and Jay Pather's co-curators' note for *Infecting the City* in 2008—specifically, that the festival has "a singular aggressive aim—to infect the city with performance that captures the complexities of our daily lives.... The underlying intention is to feature works that bravely take on new ways of expression, of collaboration... and of integrating the classical and the contemporary."[4] In 2009, 2010, and 2011, Bailey continued as curator, and Pather was sole curator from 2012 on. From its inception, the festival attracted artists and spectators to "invade roads and pavements, shop windows and fountains, tops of buildings and underground parking areas. Balconies and street corners all became performance spaces and spaces where the ordinary was reimagined."

In 2008, *Infecting the City* invaded Cape Town's central areas with art for a diverse public. This city is situated in what Achille Mbembe calls a "postcolony, marked by a timespace with the multiple, contradictory moments of everyday life in Africa read against the persistent accretions of slavery, colonialism, apartheid and neo-liberal forms of democracy" (Mbembe 2001, 24). However, as Pather and Mark Fleishman argue, "while Cape Town is undeniably and unavoidably a part of this postcolony, it often seems as if it has been dragged into it kicking and screaming, seemingly reluctant to completely shed its tag as the colonial 'mother city'" (Fleishman and Pather 2014, 102).

In their essay entitled "Performing Cape Town: An Epidemiological Study in Three Acts," Fleishman and Pather tune in to this city's rhythms as framed by medical discourse, with the word *epidemiological* mirroring the original impulse to infect the city with "something from the outside [that] has entered the body of the city, a kind of pathogenic micro-organism that has the capacity to cause tissue injury or overt disease" (2014, 101). The festival's aim was "to worry, disturb, render uneasy" the onlooker-inhabitants of the city (2014, 101). Fleishman and Pather cite Susan Sontag's essays, "Illness as Metaphor" and

Fig. 5.1. Cape Town Harbor. Photographer: Katrak.

"AIDS and Its Metaphors," which warns against using illness "as a figure or metaphor" and thereby distorting its meaning.[5] That said, Fleishman and Pather emphasize that most performances in *ITC* are "politically productive, in the ways in which they go about worrying at and elucidating what is occurring at a level less immediately visible to those who pass through the city on any given day. Ironically, then, as infections, they contain the radical potential to expose contamination and point the way towards health" (102).[6]

Just as visitors may pass through the city, so do "the infectious but ephemeral festival events themselves." Hence, it is "'not a place for being or belonging,' but more interested perhaps in trading on its looks," comments *Performing Cities*' editor, Nicholas Whybrow, "which include the natural beauty of its location effectively in between two major oceans of the world and the looming presence of Table Mountain" (Whybrow 2014, 11).

Along with Cape Town's natural beauty, it also boasts "an exceptionally high degree of biodiversity, with over 9000 species of plants occurring in the area," remark Fleishman and Pather, "around 6200 of which do not grow anywhere else in the world; or its extensive winelands, as picturesque as its wines are sought after—wild and cultivated beauty side by side" (103). Amid such beauty, it may seem counterintuitive to speak of infection and disease. However, in terms of placing performances in Cape Town, Fleishman and Pather adopt

> a more radical conception of beauty. This is one that is less concerned with form, proportion, harmony and boundedness, intending as such to produce a calming and pleasurable response, than with the *limits* of form: with disproportion, disharmony and boundlessness, intending to produce a response that is altogether more agitational, exciting and disruptive, and from which any pleasure that is derived is, as Zizek says, "procured by displeasure itself" (1989, 202). Such a conception of beauty ... operates as a foreign body.... As such it is potentially transformative, offering alternative perspectives and possibilities for the majority of the city's inhabitants who are often excluded from both art and the city. (Zizek, quoted in Fleishman and Pather 2014, 104)

Fleishman and Pather contend that the emphasis lies not on disrupting Cape Town's natural beauty but rather on its built environment enshrined in colonialism and slavery—"the ugly part of South African history" (Fleishman and Pather 2014, 104). The intention is "to show how a dialogue—or what may be more accurately called a spat—between this kind of clawing colonialist beauty," remarks Pather, "and the infectious beauty of these public performances, begins to emerge" (104). Pather's use of the colloquial word *spat* accurately evokes the emotions of discerning citizens, who recognize that the city's "clawing colonialist beauty" hides its ugly history as well as its continued inclusion of Black people only for labor inside the city, and the exclusion of their homes in townships relegated to areas outside the city.

Cape Town's tourist attraction lies not in its culture or history but rather in its "prized beauty," whitewashed, as it were, by excluding Black citizens from the city center. Indeed, Cape Town was "the ideal apartheid city" the site where segregation policies were formulated and where they continue to operate in the huge distances between the city center, White suburbs, and Black townships.

In his essay "The Periphery as Threshold," Pather looks back to what "infecting a city" such as Cape Town means even today, since "spatially, the remnants of apartheid continue to be heavily reflected and present. The majority of the city's Black population resides in far-flung townships in an area known as the Cape Flats. These were holding grounds for migrant workers brought in from rural areas to work in the city during apartheid" (2018b, 66).[7] The city center contains the business district and stretches out to predominantly White suburbs. Pather reminds us of the sobering realities during post-apartheid, since there were no

> major shifts in economic power or land distribution [which] only reinforced a landscape where the spatial [and racial] demarcations of the city remain largely intact and unaltered. Within this context the idea for "infecting" a city is very much about letting the outside in, however temporary. The word infection is loaded with negativity, anxiety and alarm. The body as a sacrosanct yet contested space, sealed shut with skin yet vulnerable and porous is an apt metaphor for land and country, constitution and status quo. Within the context of a public art festival in South Africa then, the active willful infection of a city is as much a playful intervention on etymology as it is a conscious, virulent act of unmaking and reconstituting place. (2018b, 66)

Pather recognizes problems of "access and mobility that make it difficult to be truly social across class and race in our public spaces," given the history of keeping urban spaces out of reach for the majority. Hence, Black people who rely on public transport that ends at specific times, have to forego evening performance.

Even if they stay in the city after work and witness a performance, they have to catch the last available public transport. Sadly, performers have to face an "empty" city center after dark, which is, ironically, as Pather bemoans, "also the time when the magic of performance thrives" (2018b, 66).

Another tourist destination for the politically minded is Robben Island, off the coast of Cape Town, where its most famous prisoner, Nelson Mandela, was held for eighteen (of twenty-seven) years. However, Robben Island has a longer history than Mandela's incarceration. Ato Quayson points out that the Island was "an instrument of colonial public-health policy from 1846–1931" (Quayson 2007, 175). This island "throughout its colonial history... has been a visible site of banishment and exclusion," comment Fleishman and Pather, where "lepers and lunatics could be secluded away from the rest of 'decent' society." They draw a connection between disease being "banished" to Robben Island and "Cape Town [which] has always feared infection" remaining un-diseased (Quayson quoted in Fleishman and Pather 2014, 103).

Bodies moving in cities, in and around buildings, or near sites of stunning natural beauty such as Table Mountain in Cape Town enable the spatial realm, to borrow Stephen Pile's words, "to determine their [peoples'] behaviors in a whole range of ways" (quoted in Whybrow 2014, 17). Pile also recognizes that the space of the city itself, with its "unconscious logics constructs [inhabitants'] experience." For artists, such engagements with cities evoke historical information (such as the discovery of bodies buried under a building) or memories of events such as Nelson Mandela's first address to the people after his release from twenty-seven years in prison, from the balcony of Cape Town City Hall.[8] Whybrow analyzes "a spatial engagement itself... with the welcome result that various forms of 'creative criticality' or hybrid text, often inflected by first-hand experience or memoir," examine how a city is brought to life through performance (2014, 3). Pather curates performances in sites that cover up painful histories—such as at Preswich

Fig. 5.2. Nelson Mandela's cell on Robben Island. Photographer: Katrak.

Memorial in Cape Town, where buried slave bones were discovered. Pather locates a site performance there with modern-day Black people who are conducting ordinary human activities, such as barbecuing, and hair braiding that may not be visible inside the "tourist" city.

Fig. 5.3. "Leper Colony Graveyard" on Robben Island. Photographer: Katrak.

INFECTING THE CITY (*ITC*) IN PUBLIC ARTS FESTIVALS: 2008–2011

"Infection" constitutes the potent driving force of Bailey and Pather's co-curation in 2008. Under the theme of "time," they commissioned new works such as *Dreamtime* and collaborative projects such as *22 mins 37 sec* and *Waking Time*. *Dreamtime* is described in the program notes as evoking "mystifying images of sleep, memories that haunt us, the languor of reverie, the visitations of ancestors, demons or angels" (program notes).[9] These abstract concepts are conveyed via "visual, audio and performing artists working in the fields of opera, choral and African song, video, African and Indian dance and theatre." The dancers performed different styles—classical Indian kathak by Pravika Nandkishore, *bharatanatyam* by Savitri Naidoo, and Siwela Sonke-trained Neliswa Rushualang in traditional African and contemporary dance.

22 minutes 37 seconds is the exact span of time in which this work was performed. It celebrated the urban space with humor evoked via provocative juxtapositions such as "unlikely cartoon characters, clay-covered dancers, bizarre roller skaters, and vibrant musicians collid[ing]" This playful piece disturbs the order of Thibault Square, a concrete and brick area surrounded by tall, bland architecture "where the corporate world marches to a clockwork regimen and stories lie buried in cement." This work echoes Pather's own masterful juxtapositions in several works such as a nonspecific figure blowing in with the wind into a room, then stepping out of a closet holding a CD as the interracial couple's anxieties and secrets pervade the ambience in *Hotel*.

The 2009 theme of "Home Affairs" (the name of the government agency that deals with immigration) reflected the political backlash against migrants from the African continent. It was intended to inspire audiences to think about difficult issues facing refugees. In addition, a six-week collaborative course included twelve artists from South Africa and beyond who created *Exile and Limbo* in relation to this theme. Resonant images included depictions of a man holding many suitcases, refugees evoking displacement, and "pyramids" depicting slaves all aiming to astonish Cape Town viewers. Troubling issues of immigration and the mistreatment of fellow Africans in South Africa reemerge in Pather's curated works for *ITC* 2012 (discussed below).

The name *Infecting the City* was expanded in 2010 to *Infecting the City Public Arts Festival* to indicate the vast canvas of work; this included visual art, performance, dance, and installation art placed on major streets and at Cape Town's urban landmarks, to encourage thought and dialogue among artists and spectators. Ordinary people could enjoy artworks in city squares and historic buildings, making such curatorial work "inseparable from its context," to use Sellar's phrase, "requiring a curator to originate or complete its framework" (2014, 23). He remarks that since the 1990s the art world has seen a rise of "global art biennials . . . [that have] nourished a new class of nomadic, internationally orientated curators" who, according to Sellar, are "enlarging perspectives to include contemporary non-Western art . . . [and to] incorporate curatorial strategies into their own creative work" (23).

The 2010 theme of "Human Rite" had artists thinking about the role of "rites and rituals as tools for transformation and healing." Artists were urged "to ask: What cries out for transformation or healing? Who needs to be included in the social fabric of the City? And how do we amplify and liberate the energy of the CBD [Central Business District] of Cape Town?" Artists sought to uncover stories rendered invisible, to assert their human rights as citizens of the city, and looked for "what needs to be righted, and 'rited.'"[10]

The theme of ritual was a way of celebrating community along with the somber history of slavery in South Africa. The Slave

Lodge, adjacent to St. George's Cathedral and Company Gardens, that could not be visited by Black people during apartheid, is a memorial and reminder of the past. The Khoisan Action Group's performance memorializes this past, using elements of healing with a garden of indigenous herbs, marking the massacre site of the Khoi and other groups. Usha Seejarim created a mandala, taking sand from places across Cape Town that marked sites of human rights violations. The mandala took a week to create, and after a week the sand was returned to the ocean, capturing both the significance of creating this work from a natural though ephemeral element like sand, which evokes time (as in the phrase, "time/sand slips through one's fingers") and actualizes the impermanence of an artwork that returns the borrowed sand back to its original home on the seashore. No such returns of stolen lands to their rightful owners have occurred to this day in South Africa's ongoing struggle over land dispossession. Ritual uses of herbs or sand memorialize human violations during a painful past.

In 2011, the theme of "Treasure" inspired artists to create works that highlight Cape Town's prized possessions, those both known and forgotten by its inhabitants, including a focus on waste and garbage transformed by performers to make audiences aware of recycling in *Slices of Life*. Bailey's curator's note, worth quoting at length, asserts that the unrecognized "treasures" of Cape Town include its Black people and their music and art, along with the workers who make the city function:

> We want to turn the public spaces of Cape Town into stimulating, creative places where you can be intrigued, touched and informed by the arts, where you can see your world through different lenses.
> In 2011, we celebrated the rich variety of wonderful "Treasures" that are found in the Cape. We placed a long-overdue spotlight on the people, music and performance styles from the many cultures that have made Cape Town their home. We commemorated our monuments, buildings and communal spaces, and our precious natural resources. We drew attention to the workers who keep our City running, and the valuable recyclable materials we throw out

as rubbish.... The Festival-goers witnessed people from different traditions and communities who performed actions and sounds that they have rehearsed and perfected. Each performance has a deep meaning for the performers.

But was each of these performances really an art form? And can one say exactly why any of them should not be called art?

We live in a country where certain cultural viewpoints have always told us "this is more valuable; that is less valuable. This is a real Treasure. That is just junk."... If South Africa belongs to all who live in it and is to truly be home to so many communities with so many diverse treasures, we need to broaden our minds and embrace everybody's cultural expressions as our National Treasures.[11]

Bailey reminded audiences to appreciate the artistic products of a vast spectrum of Cape Town citizens and to recognize cultural work from different sectors without stereotypical judgments of art as high and low, worthy or not, but to instead embrace diverse precious products created by the inhabitants of this city.

In 2011, as director of GIPCA, Pather's collaborative curation explored the changing role of artistic directors, including himself, in new democracies in "Directors and Directing." Pather conceptualized these initiatives and wrote analytic notes about them. In October 2011, scientists and artists shared statistics and aesthetics for "Hot Water: Art and Climate Change." Performances on saving the earth from the human footprint included contemporary South African dancer and ardent environmentalist Tossie Van Tonder's work, entitled *The End*. In 2012, GIPCA held symposia on "The Beautiful Project" exploring notions of beauty and ugliness; "The Exuberance Project" devised by Rael Salley challenged stereotypes of "the dark continent" and investigated "what is abundant, enthusiastic, unrestrained and joyful in contemporary creative and performing arts of Africa" (Pather 2011). Also in 2011, GIPCA hosted a staggering twelve events under the title "Great Texts/Big Questions" that included scholars and artists.

Among them, prominent scholar of the Indian Ocean World Isabel Hofmeyr discussed Gandhi's book *Hind Swaraj* (*Indian Self-rule*), "written in 1909 on the SS Kildonan Castle as he returned from London to South Africa. [It] is the only book that we have in which he expounds his ideas of non-violence and satyagraha ('passive resistance'). Although it is widely regarded as his rebuke to anti-colonial Indian activists who argued that the violence of imperialism could only be ended with counter-violence, Gandhi's analysis suggests that such a strategy merely absorbs the logic of imperialism and makes one resemble one's enemy" (Pather, 2011).

INFECTING THE CITY (ITC) 2012: DISTURBING CAPE TOWN'S PRISTINE URBANITY

Pather's first solo curation of the *ITC* 2012 festival intervenes deliberately via provocative artworks, subverting Cape Town's "good looks" and shaking up this city's "stasis," its complacency in its "neo-liberal economics," and its resistance to change (Fleishman and Pather 2014, 103). Pather's spatial imagination unfolds as he works with artists who "use the city as a backdrop," as he notes in "The Periphery as Threshold," and with others who "are more investigative of the spaces they create their work for" (2018b, 66). In the same essay, Pather expresses particular frustration with "realities lived (the continued lack of change and the persistence of overwhelming poverty and unemployment)" that he wishes to bring into sharp focus for his audience by curating "continuities and flows between experiences of realities lived ... with those that are performed. This insertion of performativities inside of a highly charged city, are both overt and covert, and aim to be part of existing dialogue, simply and modestly affording other frames and lenses with which to view, experience and re-imagine the contested city." Here, Pather underlines the usefulness of different kinds of performative "insertions" that can ignite discussions among citizens about their city, even as they discover new ways of perceiving it.

As curator, Pather enlivens the 2012 theme of "Making Public Space Public" by "curating the Festival on *a set of routes* [where] works were positioned next to each other along different routes, effectively *mapping the city with art*" [emphasis added]. He connects artistic work to the spaces in which they unfolded. His concept of "remaking place" informs his "curatorial choices with regards to sites, works, routes, and programming from restaged work given new breath in *surprising spaces* to performances devised especially for the spaces they are performed in" (2018b, 66). For Pather, there is "a clear and strong political commentary as well as inter cultural experiences that audiences seem to stumble into" as they walk along "routes" in Cape Town with its "continued separations, the poverty, the lack of transformation and the continued imposition of colonial symbology" (66). Productions moving along a "route" gather audiences along the way and take them "to parts of the city which they may not normally visit or pass by in their normal every day.

In his keen attention to the city and its citizens, Pather draws attention to current violence against Black people from across the continent who are treated as "foreigners" and who therefore try to remain hidden in Cape Town. Such invisibility for self-protection, versus visibility that can lead to conflicts, relates to Pather's "curatorial practice [that] very often touches on the notions of visibility and invisibility. . . . Periphery and center make apparent that which remains submerged" (2018b, 66).

Pather's curator's note in 2012 asserts his goal of "public engagement: Infecting the City is about . . . unlocking communal spaces and giving ordinary citizens access to extraordinary art." This is showcased effectively in a live performance of a work by a South African composer on a grand piano wheeled into the Cape Town Train Station and used mostly by Black commuters. A railway station, a liminal space marking an in-between place of departure and arrival (different from the touristy in betweenness that functions for pleasure), is animated unexpectedly by music played off a classical piano that enlivens the listeners' consciousness, infusing energy into their monotonous train rides to and from work. Pather pushes the boundaries of transforming a train station into a sort of symphony hall with a grand piano "rest[ing] on the gleaming white tiles of the Station concourse" and having pianist Justin Krawitz perform compositions of two Cape Town composers including "the world premiere of celebrated composer Hendrik Hofmeyer" (Pather 2012a).

Pather was deeply gratified by this experiment of presenting classical music at a railway station "frequented by people who would not ordinarily find themselves appreciating the arts." Further, these spectators' deep humanity was evident in their desire "to donate money to the artist," explains Pather, "and these are not middle-class citizens who can afford to pay for the arts. Their levels of appreciation are absolutely unheard of." Pather deliberately includes classical arts performances rather than the usually expected contemporary work when presenting art outdoors.

SETTINGS OF WATER AND BONES: *ITC* 2012

Along the route of the 2012 *ITC* festival, Mandisi Sindo's *The Sacrifice* is set in a space that adds a layer of subversion—namely, "inside a manicured water feature comprising a long trough of water as well as the adjoining fountains on St. George's Mall," a central area in Cape Town, carefully paved for the crowds of tourists (Fleishman and Pather 2014, 105). Pather posits a striking image for this performance that "resembled the eruption of a festering blister performed as it was inside a water feature meant to bring calm to the inner-city shopper and tourist. The clear water in the fountain was soon filled with muddy red clay." *The Sacrifice* deploys "a wide range of elements: traditional Xhosa ritual, contemporary dance, opera, live percussion and striking visual imagery." This overtly violent work narrates the portrayal of baiting and sacrificing a bull, "used as a metaphor," comments Pather, "for the willful shedding of blood, and subsequently redemption and reconciliation" (Fleishman and Pather 2014, 105). However, there is no winner in this struggle, as "the dying bull unsuccessfully attempts to console the distraught killer. The work, in foregrounding the restlessness of the killer, ultimately speaks to the impossibility of reconciliation." Mandisi Sindo includes "a choir of pallbearers dressed in black suits, knee deep in the fountains, who sang traditional Xhosa burial songs" as excerpts of the opera *REwind* (based on TRC hearings, discussed in chap. 2) by Philip Miller were heard. This artist's layering of performative elements—Xhosa ritual sounds, opera, drums—to portray a theme of sacrifice and violence inside the unique space of Cape Town's water feature creates a deeply troubling performative effect.

Among the thirty-two performances that were part of the *ITC* festival in 2012, "this work drew audiences," remarks Pather, "who surrounded the work sometimes almost four rows deep, providing little visibility to those in the fourth row, but who nevertheless remained to the end" (Fleishman and Pather 2014, 107). Even acknowledging the visceral power of this performance, Pather is realistic about how far such transgressive agendas can go. After the performance ends, the effects linger for some time until they evaporate. And the *Infecting the City* technicians and artists are compelled to clean up the space and leave it as it was according to agreement with the city. "Where, one may well ask," questions Pather thoughtfully, "is the residue or outcome of this performance—notions one associates with the enactment of ritual—to remind us of the intensities just experienced?" (106). The city has to recompose its "normal" beautiful look and keep its tourists contented. Cape Town "pretends" to be "an international [rather than an African] city," notes Pather. Such wishful thinking is rooted in its "racial dimension. [It] is the only city in the country controlled by the White-led Democratic Alliance rather than the ruling African National Congress and as a consequence is intent on proving it can do things better" (107).

Different from *The Sacrifice*, which is set at a manicured water feature, is *teka munyika* ("to take and give" in Tsonga), which presents a unique recollection of a gruesome past (*ITC* 2012). This collaboration between choreographer Sello Pesa and visual artist Vaughn Sadie unfolds at "a public space of great contestation," comments Pather, "the Prestwich Place Memorial." This space is "currently comprised of an ossuary that contains the bones of more than 3000 slaves and other individuals from the seventeenth century" (Fleishman and Pather 2014, 108). The performance style for *teka munyika* includes "a triad of vignettes"—one displays a professional hair stylist braiding hair (on the street in front of the memorial), usually a lengthy process, which the audience watches while waiting for something to happen. Another performer is sipping wine and enjoying a picnic on the green lawn, onto which he invites "unwitting accomplices ... alongside evacuated graves" (109). The third segment takes place in the adjoining parking lot, where a performer plays loud music, his car doors and trunk open, as he barbecues sheep head and sheep skin, "a staple meat dish for those from the townships unable to afford the choice cuts," as Pather explains. Nothing much happens except that these activities are enough to disrupt the pristine memorial space with intrusions from human activities common in townships such as hair braiding, cooking a sheep's head with an unsettling, burning smell, and a picnic next to slaves' bones. Pather describes these everyday occurrences as "understated acts of nuanced irony" and notes that they "demand a different kind of attention" (110).

Pather further argues that these acts present "a conundrum of performance style. . . . Here was a performance mode that one could call hyper-real, a slice of naturalism mirroring in great detail the anaesthetized apathy of the current populace, and the slumbering remains of past inhabitations buried deep in the ossuary" (Fleishman and Pather 2014, 110). The specters of the past enter present consciousness, disturb viewers, and force them to face "the worst excesses of the past and the numerous social crises of the present" rather than remaining indifferent and distant, true to Cape Town's laid-back reputation that glories in mystifying its seamy history.

THE "OTHER" AFRICANS: ABJECT, DISABLED, "FOREIGN": ITC 2012

Pather comments on three performers—Mbikayi, Kayumba-wa-Yafolo from Kinshasa (who performed for Spier Contemporary 2010) and Akindiya from Lagos—as "alien interventions" that purposefully use body coverings such as newspapers, tapes, and bandages along with other "markings as central tropes in the work." Such "ritualized hiding or altering of the outer surfaces of the skin," argues Pather, "amounts to a meditation on the notion of the outsider and on (in)visibility, (in)authenticity and, ultimately, belonging and inclusion—or the lack thereof" (Fleishman and Pather 2014, 113).

Nigerian artist Olaniyi Rasheed Akindiya, in a "durational installation" entitled *Abawon (Stains)* explores "how the city responds to its neglected and abjected others" (Fleishman and Pather 2014, 114). In this work, the artist impersonates a mentally challenged pregnant woman, carrying a baby on "her" back, walking the streets of Cape Town, and pushing a wheelbarrow. Invading public spaces, supermarkets, malls, and parks, the artist is prominent in his installation, which uses wood and thread. "Through a series of provocative interventions, *Abawon (Stains)* invites us to explore how we react to waste, gender equality, the mentally impaired, people living with HIV/AIDS, and disability." Akindiya embodied an aberrant, visible presence by "wrap[ping] himself conspicuously in traffic hazard tape and strap[ping] himself to a pole outside Cape Town Station," inviting scrutiny from "a possibly hostile xenophobic public" against outsiders/"foreigners" from the continent, which demonstrates a new kind of troubling segregation among Black people in South Africa. Pather describes Akindiya's performance as an integral part of "acts of insertion even though co-opted in moments by the city. . . . The gesture is ultimately performative: temporary, enacted, possibly transformative but ultimately time bound and framed tightly within how the city seeks to perform itself to its visitors, its tourists" (116). Hence, despite a distinct insertion by portraying an abject, mentally disturbed individual in Cape Town's pristine space, the city ignores such art, not taking it into its bosom but rather focusing on recomposing itself in its beauty. The ugly insertion was regarded as temporary and aberrant, not the norm.

In another performance, Philippe Kayumba-wa-Yafolo (Kinshasa-born and working at the time in Cape Town) with three performers covered entirely, except for faces and hands with newspapers, experiences direct hostility. They occupy a traffic island in Adderley Street, located in Cape Town's CBD, where they engage calmly in domestic chores until they become agitated and occupy more space. "A malicious pedestrian" sets fire to the newspaper covering one of the performers, bringing "into sharp focus the levels of tension," notes Pather. "In this performance, the tension literally ignited" (Fleishman and Pather 2014, 114). Such an attack on a performer who looks like an outsider is vicious; it sends a dark message that the artist would be better off remaining "invisible."

Another artist, Maurice Mbikayi, based in Kinshasa and also a "foreign" national, is "quietly disruptive" with his unique, attention-grabbing performance that "stopped traffic and forced people to stare" (Fleishman and Pather 2014, 113). Mbikayi "covered his entire body in white bandages [as if to avoid "infection"], and then rode a horse through the busy thoroughfare of the Grand

Parade opposite the Cape Town City Hall led by a woman wearing a gas mask. In referencing the protection of skin and lungs from infection, he ironically drew attention to the fragility of skin" (113).

As these kind of performances and interventions on this level and scale proliferate, it is no surprise that *ITC* festivals continue to grow remarkably—from around ten artworks in 2008 to nearly sixty in 2013. "There has been a 300% increase in submissions to participate between 2012 and 2013," notes Pather, "and the audience has diversified and grown, all testimony to an assured public interest in a Festival of this nature."[12]

THE SIXTH *ITC* FESTIVAL, 2013: CAPE TOWN "IGNITED, MYSTIFIED, AND INTRIGUED"

The 2013 festival showcased Cape Town as "the backdrop, stage, and audience to a mesmerizing showcase of live culture across all artistic disciplines," comments Pather, "that will ignite, mystify and intrigue the Mother City. . . . In collaboration with several national and international partners GIPCA presents a diverse range of works that embrace interdisciplinarity whilst engaging with public spaces in compelling ways. These emerge from the University of Cape Town's Creative and Performing Arts departments, the culminating presentations of 2012–2013 Donald Gordon Creative Arts Fellows and Award Winners, as well as workshops and commissioned international pieces. GIPCA also partners with the Public Culture CityLab (African Centre for Cities, UCT) on *Thinking the City*, a series of talks and discussions seeking to strengthen thinking and practice at the intersection of culture and public space" (Pather 2013a).

Pather's curatorial vision and practice continue to select adventurous artists who use a variety of media that disrupt Cape Town's beautiful landscape and orderliness. To invade the city through artworks served "to encourage audiences to discover, define and experience" spaces that used to be out of bounds for many, with works such *Uvuko! Resurrection*, *The Diagnosis*, and *Ilulwane*, among others (Pather 2013a).

Uvuko! Resurrection, directed by local Cape Town artist Mandla Mbothwe, with eight members of the Steve Biko Center, uses the sounds of spirituals with historical narration of the city; as such, it is an experimental "multi-media, interdisciplinary multiple site-specific artwork" (Pather 2013a). As the group walks along many city streets, they sing and speak about historical events and leaders, along with the performers' own personal stories and their village names. Such sights and sounds "conjure up the deep-seated local stories that lie dormant, pulling us inexorably to a sacred space." This performance invokes the past to remind onlookers of their relation to the city. In one segment, the performers "ritually bathe in containers of water, encircled by a ring of fire as a drummer and praise-singer appear" (Pather 2013a). The image of a "ring of fire" evokes the horrible violence on the heels of independence of "necklacing," the act of throwing burning tires around victims' necks.

Capeofon is by Norwegian musician and composer Ole Hamre, who is renowned for his work "with the transformation of speech into music [that] captures the sights of Cape Town and the vocalisations of Capetonians" from different backgrounds. "Each note on Hamre's custom-built keyboard is linked to an intoning local person as Hamre 'plays' the choir on the huge screen, accompanied by live musicians and Umcolo choral participants from Kenmere Primary School. *Capeofon* offers a new gift by the citizens of the Mother City" (2013a).

The Diagnosis documents sights and sounds in the city at night, in a nocturnal performance by artists who intervene in different locations around the city, playing with the conscious and the subconscious by interrogating "the nonsensical automatons of ordinary life. *The Diagnosis* is an experimental sleepwalk." It is created by artists Leila Anderson and Stan Wannet, the latter of whom is "a multimedia sculptor from the Netherlands with training in visual art and electrical engineering." Pather interprets *The Diagnosis* as employing "the ordinary in the extraordinary and the simple towards spectacular ends.... Both artists took turns to lie asleep in the window attracting curious passers-by to their shop. Inside the shop was a myriad of artefacts concerned with archive and archival practice" (Pather 2013a). One amazing aspect, which used television monitors and projectors, demonstrated what the two artists "had been up to the night before ... when they would create performances with no one watching, document these and play them inside the store during the day while they slept. The play on dream-states and waking was both a spectacular remaking of a meditative space in the middle of the busy-ness of the city." In conjoining and reversing the usual waking and sleeping times, *The Diagnosis* deconstructs both the daytime rat race to make a living and the night hours of creative dreams and of performing without onlookers.

A highly provocative work, *Ilulwane* ("bat" in isiXhosa, or "one who floats at night"), by Cape Town video and performance artist Athi-Patra Ruga, portrays South African traditional ritual along with contemporary dance and media in the unusual setting of the Long Street Baths at night, bathed in red light. The program notes state that "*Ilulwane* is a derogatory term for a Xhosa man circumcised in a hospital rather than in the traditionally sanctioned initiation ceremony. The figure of the *Ilulwane*, recognized as neither boy nor man, creat[ed] a space in which masculinity, masquerade, identity and sexuality can be interrogated and the tension between tradition and modernity explored" (Pather 2013a). *Ilulwane* "reclaimed a public swimming pool," remarks Pather. "Replete with high heels and a bevy of synchronized swimmers below him, Ruga was hoisted high after being dunked in the pool, reclaiming tradition, sexuality, public space as a personal odyssey in one spectacular performance performed with an audience of 600 people" (Pather 2013a). *Ilulwane* is a bold performance in which the intimate ritual of circumcision is taken out of its traditional context

Fig. 5.4. *Ilulwane*. Athi-Patra Ruga. *Infecting the City* 2012. Photographer: Sydelle Willow Smith. Courtesy Jay Pather.

and is then recuperated in a public bath. The ritual is no longer private but in full view of no fewer than six hundred onlookers.

An unusual presentation called *Cooking Information in the Streets of Ikapa*, performed by wire sculptor and painter Gloria Mbhele and located in Cape Town's CBD, presents Mbhele laboring over "a wire and *papier-mache* construction, using flour, a domestic kitchen staple to bind the City's digested and discarded news into a sculptural form" as she selects the significant from the unimportant, leaving it to the audience to form their own opinions on the news. The artist, interested in gender, sculpts women "in various poses—carrying babies, looking through binoculars—dotted around the city centre." Linking a food item like flour "to bind" the city news, without selecting the significant from the minor, sheds light on both the quality of political news that surrounds people and the increasing difficulty of filtering true from false, weighty from trivial, and discerning what might evaporate by day's end.

The 2013 festival featured Vincent Mantsoe, an internationally renowned South African dancer-choreographer who returned home to perform from his base in France. Mantsoe, born in Soweto, acknowledges waking up "every day to the sound of the drum his mother played to greet the Ancestors. A descendant of a long line of *sangomas* (traditional healers), Mantsoe participated in traditional rituals involving the use of song and dance" (Pather 2013a). Mantsoe's *NTU* explores the abstract idea of nothingness from which "something takes form." It was acclaimed by the *New York Times* as a performance "so extraordinarily contained that the end effect is like seeing the shape, the figure, push its way free of encompassing clay."

Another internationally renowned South African dancer-choreographer, Dada Masilo, performed *Death and the Maidens*, in which she probes the different motivations of tragic heroines from a female perspective. "Masilo riffs Chilean writer Ariel Dorfman's celebrated play" of the same title in stunning movement to explore female anguish, even retaliation (Pather 2013a). The program notes state that "Masilo's 'maidens' are not victims, and death is not necessarily masculine." In this work, Masilo "continues an engagement with the heroines of literature and drama that began with her acclaimed solo work, *The Bitter End of Rosemary*."[13] This artist, renowned for her hybrid adaptations of classical ballets such as *Swan Lake*, effectively marginalizes ballet, though she is a virtuosic dancer in her performance of both ballet and her South African dance traditions.

The range of multidisciplinary works featured in the 2013 festival, apart from the ones discussed above, included some "must-sees" such as "gospel singers on bicycles and a mob of over 300 skateboarders cruising through the city. . . . As part of the Africa Centre's youth program, 'Arts Aweh!' Infecting the City will transport 400 high school scholars from across greater Cape Town to the City Center to engage and interact with the Festival and its artists."

In 2013, Pather was director of GIPCA conceptualized symposia such as "Thinking the City" and "Ways to do Public Art: People in Space make Place." Pather remarks:

> *Thinking the City* partnered with the Public Culture CityLab (Africa Centre for Cities, UCT), March 12–15, 2013. This series of talks and discussions is presented as part of the African Centre's annual Infecting the City Public Art Festival, and seeks to strengthen thinking and practice at the intersection of culture and public space, particularly in Cape Town.
>
> Cape Town has a long history of public art and culture, and has more recently embraced the notion of a "creative city." This is an exciting prospect for creative practitioners, yet the question of "creative city for whom" keeps bubbling to the surface of public debate, as different interest groups lay claim to the creative expression, and of, public space. *Thinking the City* will contribute to the Infecting the City programme by unpacking a series of examples and contested territories related to cultural practice in the city, in order to foster a more critical dialogue about creative practice in public space. (Pather 2013a)

Also in 2013, Pather organized LAND, marking the centenary of the brutal Native Land Act of 1913, which dispossessed Black people of their land during colonial times; land repatriation to rightful owners continues to be a serious problem today. Pather describes LAND as

> an event comprising performances, visual art installations, public lectures and panels about land, territory, ownership and art.... South Africa is characterized by a series of disjunctive experiences in a land of extraordinary contrast; its natural splendor belies the brutal experiences of slavery, forced removals and continued poverty. In deference to the centennial of the infamous Native Land Act of 1913, there has been a national focus on land as a vessel of trade, trauma, and restitution. The material inscription of colonisation, with the Land Act as its formalisation, remains performative—still determining where people live and intersect, and how people move through space. It results in diverse and opposing ideas, values, dreams that constantly disrupt the country's present. (Pather 2013a)

The year 2013 was marked by "a national focus on land as a vessel of trade, trauma, and restitution. The material inscription of colonization, with the Land Act as its formalization, remains performative—still determining where people live and intersect, and how people move through space.... Twenty years into our democracy ... LAND focuses on contemporary practices, the traumas and the hauntedness that manifest as a result of this condition." Thus LAND unfolds at various contested sites in Cape Town such as "the controversial Prestwich Memorial" and its grounds, where human remains, including the unmarked graves of Black people and freed slaves, were uncovered from the eras of colonialism and slavery.[14] Other sites include the Grand Parade and the Castle of Good Hope, Cape Town City Hall, Rondebosch Common, and District Six [with its history of displacing Colored South Africans], and there are walking tours in central city and other areas to foster discussion of colonial and slave legacies.

Pather's curation of the *ITC* festival in 2014 (with fifty-four local and international artists and 102 performances over six days) deepens through his pubic engagement, with new works created for the festival, restaged productions from participating arts organizations, and collaborative pieces conceived under his curatorship. The captivating narrative recorded in his essay "Motion Sickness" about one of his curated dance works at *ITC* 2014 and its reception at Cape Town's railway station is worth quoting at length:

> A middle-aged black woman burdened with bags hurries across the Cape Town Station concourse. Clenching a season ticket together with a plethora of bags, she is aiming for the station platforms hoping to get into a train that will take her back to the Cape Flats. This movement in and out of the city by black working-class people replicating patterns of migrant labour has become deeply inscribed topography, unaltered in the postcolonial city. These patterns of movement continue as a result of pervasive economic asymmetries that are deeply etched in the landscape of South Africa,

even though macro political movements twenty years into our democracy hopelessly attempt to signify the opposite in its empty discourse of social cohesion and economic development.

The woman stops though, arrested by a happening in the middle of the concourse. Twelve dancers from Jazzart Dance Theatre reenact ancient Nam rhythms in a contemporary dance work. The dancers are dressed in ordinary clothing and perform extraordinary movement. Kinetically vigorous as well as lyrical, the bodies of the dancers embody both the pain and tensions of a working-class community while the freedom in the movement signals the body's capacity to break free to release itself from the entrapment, to move without restrain. The sight itself is very rich. But even richer is the interaction with an audience comprised of people who have been taken by surprise by a full-length dance work that resonates with their own experiences in the middle of a train station of a regular weekday afternoon. I watched the woman stopping in her tracks, furtively looking around her to see if she is in the way of a film shoot of something, and then letting go of the bags, settling down and watching till the end of the hour-long production. (Pather 2015c)

Pather delights in observing this Black, middle-aged woman initially avoiding the performance assuming it was for someone else, then "settling down" to enjoy it for an hour. Such response fulfills his goal of bringing technically stunning dance performance to the commuters, who are predominantly Black people, inside a public transport center.

Pather aims to be in tune with spectators (as the incident above demonstrates) as he is in recognizing performance that can inspire dancer-actors. He describes how a performer "can transform a functional space into a place 'of dreams' where dialogues of possibility are rife." He continues: "When a performer goes into performance mode, the altered psychological and physiological state that demarcates them from the passer by hurrying along with shopping bags, the impact is extreme and loaded. A level of insanity, disruption, playfulness, irresponsibility combined with the control and discipline of performance meets bemused onlookers torn between having their journey interrupted and watching" (Pather, quoted in Davidoff 2006, 144).

Pather's curator's note for the 2014 festival, held a few months after Mandela passed away in December 2013, connects South Africa's "chequered history . . . bristl(ing) with contradiction" that was epitomized in the mourning period that showed both "deep sorrow and joyous celebration played out equally" (Pather 2014d). Mandela's passing marked the end of an era under South Africa's first Black president, a period filled with "dizzying heights and terrible lows." By 2014, twenty years after democracy, there was widespread disillusionment, partly evident in the very difficulties of curating itself, which involved more than "simply gathering works," remarks Pather, "that converse with each other and the City."

For Pather, the far more challenging aspect of curating "resembles something of an abyss in a developing city: from sourcing spaces to securing viewing areas for large groups of people, to incorporating logical movement from work to work and public footfall. Ultimately, a public art festival is about art and the public. And as long as that public is not just a small group of in-the-know followers of art, but a complex nation of inequality, varying access, varying levels of free time; as long as it is about publics then the Festival programmes more than just the art works" (Pather 2014d). Increasingly, Pather recognizes that his curation needs to factor in "a giddy range of unknowns" along with being provocative.

Pather's (2014d) curatorial goals always honor the fact that "a public art festival is about art and the public," one that creates access across a range of publics of different races and classes, with "varying levels of free time"—some of whom can enjoy artworks as well as interact "with the strangers next to [them]—of our gloriously complex publics with all its inequities and difficulties, deeply yearning for that glue amongst us to stick and last a little longer than our twenty years." Since "the public" is not a homogenous entity, curators need to deal with publics and get them on board to support decolonizing projects, some of which may have to be reconceptualized, with new spaces for their performance.

Pather relies on challenges of moving diverse audiences through the city by creating "routes," a format that he used for his site work *Blind Spot* (discussed in chap. 3), where the audience walked for over three hours from the immigrant location on the outskirts of Copenhagen into the main city. With *ITC*, one program would begin at "the top of Company's Gardens and the next work would be further along a particular route finally making its way to point Z which may be across the city" (Pather 2015c). Along the route, works that were easily accessible and other more challenging ones were juxtaposed "to cut through," as Pather argues in the same essay, "a particular homogeneity that pervades artistic enterprise." Spectators could respond to different sights, sounds, smells, and "texts evoking the histories of the spaces that were being passed, evoking the city as a sensorium."

Performances ranged from Nigerian artists Emeka Ogboh's *Verbal Mapping II*, based on what the artist describes as "calls made by Lagos bus conductors, melodically shouting out their bus routes to potential passengers or notifying passengers of the next stop. The noisy bus conductor is an icon of the Lagos sonic map, a lyrical wordsmith dishing out Lagos bus routes like freestyle rap." Pather notes that these calls were installed on Adderley Street, where South African taxi drivers have their own calls to passengers. Another work transforms "cold walls into ones which may hug you as you walk by animated as they are with real people, embedded and sewn into the existing walls," demonstrating how a helpful hugging human touch can nurture a passer-by.

As in a collaboration in 2013 with Africa Center's youth program Arts Aweh, which transported high school students from across Cape Town to the festival, in 2014, Youthscapes brought in groups of young people from various parts of the Cape both as spectators and as active participants who could take workshops on space, architecture, movement, and composition. For Pather, "Youthscapes, led by several creative leaders... will hopefully go some way toward re-inscribing the City as a shared space—one that is inspiring, evocative, and safe for all." Here, as an artist-mentor, Pather demonstrates his commitment to making creative skills available to young people, hoping that they would find the city captivating and "safe for all."

In 2015 (March 8–14), Pather's curatorial work on the *ITC* festival was accompanied by a symposium presented by GIPCA entitled "Remaking Place," demonstrating his continued exploration of place and space not only in performance but also in theoretical undertakings with scholars that still retain a focus on the changing parameters of public art. Pather remarks that this symposium

> runs parallel with the *Infecting The City* Festival and features luminaries in public art discourse such as Gabi Ngcobo, co-founder of the Center for Historical Reenactments, Lewis Biggs of the International Award for Public Art; Wang Dawei, Dean of Fine Art, Shanghai University and Marilyn Douahala Bell, from the highly respected Douala' Art in the Cameroon.... The Symposium's sessions fall in and amongst the *Infecting The City* programme, making it possible to attend both events.
>
> Public Art is fast becoming a crucial nexus for South African art—it not only encourages innovation and excellence in art, but proffers crucial issues around the relationship of art to community, audience involvement and engagement, access, and bringing key questions around heritage, personal identities and governance into the public realm.
>
> The increase in visiblity and commissioning of Public Art nationally brings an awareness to the potential for the animation of a site that is accessible and available to a diverse audience, rendered equal in their pleasure, surprise, shock or discomfort by a common, unprecedented occurrence. At its height, public art allows for diverse meanings as well as coherence in the middle of complex, barely intersecting subjectivities. But the question resurfaces: Has it? (Pather, 2015d)

One of the most successful GIPCA-hosted projects over several years, the "Great Texts/Big Questions" public lecture series that illuminates current intellectual and creative thinking in South Africa culminated in a published volume, *Relocations: Reading Culture in South Africa* edited by Imraan Coovadia, Alexandra Dodd, and Cóilín Parsons (2015). The authors range from novelists to poets, to artists, and social activists.

Pather's considerable achievements as curator of *ITC* public arts festivals over the years lie in what he calls, "a provocation" that aims to challenge Cape Town's inertia in dealing with its painful past and its ongoing segregation policies. Pather is in line with what Erika Fischer-Lichte, in "Policies of Spatial Appropriation," describes as "the double dialectic" of festivals, namely "liminality and periodicity, on the one hand, regulation and transgression, on the other" (Fisher-Lichte and Wihstutz 2013, 235). Fischer-Lichte posits that "festivals enable a temporal transcendence, for they forge their own temporality, which breaks with normal daily life. . . . Although subject to regulation, the quintessence of a festival action consists in the transgression of certain rules, namely those that impose constraints on daily life" (235). Pather knows this paradox too well—ITC festival upheavals are temporary in Cape Town. Life returns to normal within the city as it performs itself "in a range of ways with a certainty and a history that has endured and that is inscribed in a manner that is as brash and unselfconsciously opportunistic as it is highly sophisticated, deeply entrenched and subtle" (Fleishman and Pather 2014, 117).

In this climate, what resonances of performances, however disturbing during the time that they occupy certain spaces, remain for spectators? Pather posits that after six years of curating this festival, "some shifts are occurring" (Fleishman and Pather 2014, 117). As an adventurous curator, he is open to a variety of ways in which temporary disruptions in a highly managed tourist city can touch and transform participants and onlookers. To explain what he calls "shifts" in perception inspired by *ITC* performances, Pather returns to his favorite analogies of infection, the body, invading viruses, and how the human immune system responds. He quotes Catherine Belling, who notes that the battle between the human body and invading microbes "occurs not at the level of 'the human self', but at 'the cellular level of the immune system' that is not entirely human at all. What is occurring at the cellular level is invisible to the naked eye, impossible to see without technological assistance" (Whybrow 2014, 117). Pather has availed himself of such bodily metaphors of dis-ease and battle in his *Body of Evidence* (discussed in chap. 4), where memories of violence are held inside the human muscles, bones, and cells. In *ITC* performances as well, Pather achieves political resonances through metaphor, which he regards as "the only way of figuring what is, in fact, occurring. In such metaphors 'each cell of [the] human immune system' becomes 'a miniature human self within a society at war' and is 'engaged in direct combat with microbes'" (quoting Belling 2003, 95, in Fleishman and Pather 2014, 117). Pather equates the idea of change occurring at the cellular level and healing from dis-ease to the impact of art that occurs not always visibly or immediately, but that can take place at a later time, at a subterraneous level, and out of sight. Such inspiration for transformation can equip bodies to battle the diseases of poverty and unemployment and build strength to work toward social justice.

Pather's curation of *ITC* public art festivals as GIPCA's director (2010–15) continues under its new identity, Institute for Creative Arts (ICA). An Andrew W. Mellon grant provided funding for the group from 2016 to 2019 and has been renewed through 2023. ICA's goals follow in GIPCA's legacy by fostering interdisciplinary creative and performing arts, collaborative research projects, and live art, communicating with various publics, and addressing concerns related to community and urban spaces. ICA was inaugurated on April 5, 2016, in Hiddingh Hall at UCT with Pather as director, who remarked:

It is becoming clear that the work lies in questioning the boundaries between modalities—this is to say that it is not just music, drama, dance, or fine art, where the audiences are not quintessentially one public, but a range of publics where space is not one space, but several, stable and mobile, gazed at and immersive, characters are not singular and homogenous, but complex, heterogeneous and blur between "self" and the playing.

The decolonizing project asks us for our conservatoires and modalities to be questioned, the simple question of access to a gallery space or a theatre is not answerable with a series of development programmes of bussing children into these spaces. The publics are not the problem, the problem may lie in the conception itself, the spaces, the modalities, the inherited claims of purity, the sets of codes available to a few. (Pather 2016a)

ICA's opening program showcased Pather's continuing fascination with spaces and their significance, hidden histories, and contemporary trajectories. Two creative works, Khanyisile Mbongwa's *Umnikelo Oshisiwe* (*A Burnt Offering*) and Owen Manamela-Mogane and Themba Mbuli's *#Untitled*, question the physical location of this launch—namely, Hiddingh Hall, built in 1911 during South Africa's colonial period. *Commute 2* by iQhiya, with a mini bus taxi common in many South African cities and used mainly by Black people to travel from their township homes to city centers for work, metaphorically traverses the distance between townships outside Cape Town and city center.

In 2016 (May 13–14), one of the first noteworthy ICA events curated by Pather was the interdisciplinary 3rd Space Symposium: Decolonisation and the Creative Arts. Pather describes the parameters and goals of this event as aiming to examine the "imperative to decolonise the university, the role of the creative arts in provoking change, and the dialectic between the settled nature of academic curricula and the spontaneity of transformation" (Pather, 2016b). He explains further that in the context of South Africa, such decolonization is critical since at the core of the #rhodesmustfall and #feesmustfall movements lie ideas of representation, identity, heritage, symbolism and art works. The creative and performing arts do not exist in a vacuum. It is within these contexts that the ideas around the 3rd Space Symposium evolved. As part of its ongoing project to facilitate interdisciplinary research and dialogue in the creative and performing arts that disrupts boundaries, the ICA brings together addresses, panel discussions, public debate, performances, film screenings and art exhibitions to explore the subject.

Ideas pertaining to history and heritage, language, hybridity, the creative economy and curriculum will be explored by academics, performers, curators, musicians, choreographers and playwrights. The Symposium will also provide a platform for probing the potential of the university curriculum to respond to the fluidity of transformation, and to generate forms for carrying transformation forward. (Pather 2016b)

Pather reflects on his curatorial journey since 2004, when he headed an initiative called *Republic* for JOMBA! in Durban, which later re-emerged as *Paradise* and involved workshops and performances in different disciplines "from curation to choreography to lighting and sound workshops, lectures on live art practice, architecture, and city planning." He notes that in 2007, as chair of the selection committee for the National Arts Festival with visual and performing artists, choreographers and theater makers, "the curatorial intention was to expand the scope of performance." Spier 2007 and 2010 aimed to inspire new work. At a GIPCA 2010 conference titled, *pre-post-per-form* convened by Pather, "the idea of a festival dedicated entirely to live art arose." He sensed an energy among artists and theorists to be part of such a festival.

LIVE ART FESTIVALS SINCE 2012: CHALLENGES AND THE INCREASING "IMPOSSIBILITY" OF CURATION

Pather's curation of *Live Art* festivals involved extensive conceptualizing and research that he shares in analytic notes on a variety of works that took place in 2012, 2014, 2017, and 2018 (2020 postponed until 2021 due to Covid-19). His curatorial process involves selecting established and emerging artists and working with them to identify locations for their work. This intellectual and on-the-ground performance activity has resulted in a landmark publication entitled *Acts of Transgression: Live Art in South Africa*, edited by Pather and Catherine Boulle. This is the first text in South Africa to explore live art from its many parameters, undertaking "a rigorous conceptual engagement with rather than a chronological overview of, live art in South Africa," as the editors note in their introduction. Pather and Boulle are concerned "specifically [with] understanding live art against shifting notions of crisis" and how "artistic agency" is expressed during times of "political urgency" (Pather and Boulle 2019, 11). This volume of twenty-five chapters is a seminal contribution to scholarship on live art, with key insights into how to curate "performative practices of disruption and ambivalence," in Sarah Nuttal's words, or in Boulle's analysis of "the anarchism of live art [through] the lens of pioneering performance artists Steven Cohen, whose dissonant works offer profoundly political interpretations in this time of turbulence" (quoted in Pather and Boulle 2019, 11). Pather and Boulle (2019, 2) recognize that "in South Africa, live art is born of extremity. Its syncretic form has evolved in response to rapidly changing social climates, colonial imposition, cultural fragmentation and political upheaval; its affective tenor of excess and irrationality embodies the unpredictability of crisis. It proffers a new language that resists the narratives of certainty and linearity through which a neocolonial agenda has been perpetuated (even if sometimes inadvertently) in this country, reflecting—without seeking to resolve—the inscrutability and urgency of states of socio-political flux."[15]

Pather, as director of GIPCA since 2010 (ICA since 2016), has curated *Live Art* festivals that involve, as he theorizes, curatorial skills different from those needed for *ITC* public arts festival performances. Gabrielle Pinto, in "Unpacking the ICA Live Art Festival with Director Jay Pather," remarks on "the critical place" that ICA occupies "in the South African creative landscape because it nurtures challenging and constructive dialogues, which in the past have remained swept under the thick dust-collecting carpet of high-brow academia" (Pinto 2017). Another of Pather's goals throughout his creative journey, namely to make high-quality art accessible to diverse publics, is fulfilled through ICA's (as GIPCA's before it) many activities, as Pinto also endorses: "Through fellowships, open lectures, symposiums and learner-ships, the ICA has made thought-leaders and artists accessible to the public. It has facilitated important conversations that previously were held in tight liberal academic circles and seldom reached beyond the confines of the theatre or the white walls of the 'sacrosanct gallery'" (Pinto 2017). Among the many creative ventures, Pather, as the institute's director, "has spearheaded audacious projects," continues Pinto, "with passionate rigour such as the three-week Live Art Festival which brings performances to Cape Town once-off. . . . This ambitious undertaking [showcases] the astonishing power art has to expedite the practice of democracy" (Pinto 2017).

Pather's commitment throughout his career to socially conscious art and to synergistic connections between art and politics, art and activism, and space and race continues with new elements of surprise and new structures in curating live art. To Pinto's question, "To what extent is Live Art a form of activism?" he responds, "It is often difficult to separate one from the other, and it is activism that may be aligned with several issues of social justice whether it is around class, race, gender, sexual identity and so forth. But at its core in attempting to undo the way we think, in surprising us with new forms, new ideas, new structures, the activism also cuts deeper than sloganeering or simple agitation. Combining this with dismantling familiar and comfortable aesthetic choices is a multi-pronged approach to vibrant and visceral, even perhaps 'entertaining' activism" (Pather, quoted in Pinto 2017).

Although Pather's essay "The Impossibility of Curating Live Art" makes a bold assertion—namely, that curating "in the context of live art has run its course," he explores new provocations for himself and other curators by the need to take on "the writing of new grammars." The latter is necessary in curating "unresolved performance art that resists definition and framing, against a backdrop of global and national turbulence. The curation of anarchy or crisis is a contradiction in terms." Pather desires to create a space where embodying such "new grammars" would come from artists and their creations, rather than having ideologies imposed upon them by art experts or curators. Indeed, curators need to recognize the artistic ferment of "new grammars" that might well be disjointed, even chaotic, reflecting a contemporary world that is harsh, imbalanced, and teeming with inequities. Pather recognizes the potency of live art and its creators who remind audiences, crucially, especially in the present "resurgence of right-wing thought globally... to dig deep into the core of civic responsibility which is not to establish dogma or one way of doing things but by testing the limits of what we can comprehend and allow a range of forms to exist. To undo dogma and allow individuals freedom of movement and self-identity. In simply starting with the premise of undoing established forms, live art troubles established ways of thinking and allows us to practice fluidity, openness and mature, personally felt and executed democracy" (Pather, quoted in Pinto 2017).

Curators of live art face new provocations in a digital age, with increasing use of technologies and the internet. At times it is more accurate, comments Pather, "to understand Live Art as art that lives. There could be a live performer present or not" (interview 1, 2018). The audience is also challenged, since intuitively it expects a live performer, and it feels counterintuitive to view a performer via the intervention of technology. Pather is willing to go along with such absence of the artist's live bodily presence; indeed, he argues creatively in the same interview that "increased technology shrinks space." Pather succinctly describes the difference between performance art and live art as "performance art is now live art" (interview 1, 2018). In his interview with Gabriella Pinto, he expands on this idea:

> Performance art referred to the departures visual artists in particular made from creating object centred art such as painting or sculpture, and when art making became embodied and performative. Live Art as a term emerges later and with rising interests in technology and electronic media, incorporates performance but includes as well living works where the artist may not be present and "performing." These include live installations (existing for a particular duration) that incorporate technology and electronic media.... Live art is not public art in the traditional sense of the word. So, we are looking at an interaction that is more daring, challenging and dynamic. More risk can be difficult to sit through at times, but when it strikes, the rewards are overwhelming. (Pather, in Pinto 2017)

Curating live art involves working with production teams, pedestrian issues, security, venue management, traffic officers—all much more complex than a single curator's task for a visual art exhibition inside a gallery. Live art outdoors needs to contend with the spaces used along with being mindful of the time it takes spectators to reach the next performance. Curating space and time are crucial in ensuring the flow of the performances. Live art uses a variety of spaces; in fact, in Pather's lyrical description, "Live art works bend space, whether disowning the white cube, confounding the proscenium arch or spilling out onto a street or cyberspace. The curation of space involves extending the question of whether the space serves as a malleable canvas for the question that the artist poses and provides immense possibilities also for encounters with a range of publics" (2019, 99). The process of realizing an artist's vision from idea to execution to reaching an audience is complex, and curators would do well not to exert too much control, especially in outdoor venues. In the interview with Pinto, Pather comments further that "space is all important for most artists working in this form.... Space is material, a piece of language that artists use.... We work very hard to match work to space, but in the programming of multiple works where we are also factoring easy access for audiences, it can be challenging" (Pinto 2017).

Live art curation necessitates a rethinking of some central notions of curation, such as setting up specific themes for a festival. At the same time, by giving up "overt framing," live art may come across as "rudderless," even bordering on anarchy that also—perhaps paradoxically—needs to be showcased, even if that involves some containment. Allowing such freedom enables the creative work to breathe instead of forcing it into predetermined frames. Curators like Pather are bold enough to accept that "the central premise of live art is to break away from a convention that promotes predictability, repetition and easy, reductive association amongst works." Uncertainty, playfulness, even anarchic resonances are welcome in live art. Since live art "emerges from the fringes of such disciplines as the visual and performing arts, social sciences and electronic media and inhabits a suspended territory ... [following] its own laws, topography, dynamics and logics," it is much trickier to work with "themes," although the latter certainly provide anchors to viewers.

The inaugural *Live Art* festival in 2012 featured thirty artists under the title *Make-up Your Mind* and aimed "to be a space for interrogation and exploration of contemporary art forms." The festival would "embody themes of presence, identity and gender ... featuring artists who emerge from a wide range of fields, often collapsing disciplinary boundaries" (Pather 2012c). Festival events took place in a variety of venues, including the Cape Town City Hall, UCT's Hiddingh Campus, roadsides, and a farm. Interdisciplinary and daring, the festival challenged spectators with "conflicting ideas about how we perceive and not just what we perceive" taking on "the mantra of our times: 'But is it art?' both an earnest question and a cliche that inspires irritation and impatience" (Pather 2012c). Live art comes into being with the disillusionment of "the collapse of established systems based on prejudice, and postcolonial subjectivities [that] have all contributed to a healthy and robust bewilderment around contemporary art, particularly that emerging from South Africa" (Pather 2012c). Further, the kind of risky innovations by live artists who break boundaries rely on open-minded spectators who encounter and respond to "fresh work that sits on the edge" (Pather 2012c). The festival featured established South African artists such as Nelisiwe Xaba in *Uncles and Angels* and new path-makers forging unusual directions, such as Tebogo Munyai's *Right Inside*, Gabriella Pinto and Iman Isaacs, Richard September, and Thema Mbuli. The *Sunday Independent* named *Live Art* 2012 one of its five best art events in South Africa.

In curating *Live Art* 2014, Pather featured thirty-nine "works of innovation by artists that demonstrate an edge in performance art practice" (Pather 2014c). In his introduction to the program, Pather remarks that the works "emerge from diverse disciplines: visual arts, dance, theatre, music, architecture and literature, works will be maverick, mongrel, collaborative, interdisciplinary, vexing. Some may be a breeze, others may need a strong stomach or a thick skin or some programme notes.... [We want to] honour the artists named in these pages who have persisted in pushing the boundaries of their work inviting discomfort, debate and critique in unique and singular experiences" (Pather 2014c). In 2014, Pather could still group and juxtapose works around subjects such as "Framed (and Framing)," "The Body and Its Mortality," "Republic (or Nation, Authority, Nationalisms)," "Abject Object," "The Periphery as Threshold," and "Femininities."

In his essay "The Impossibility of Curating Live Art," Pather recognizes that it is necessary to create new platforms for live art and to strive toward an "expan[sion] of our languages and our visions. In lieu of, but hopefully moving towards, such a vision, [he] offer[s] five elements which [he] understand[s] as starting points in the creation of new grammars for curation" (Pather 2019b, 97). These begin significantly with "Spatialities," then move to "Rhythm," "Opacity," "Terminologies," and "Audience." Pather concludes his essay with this subheading: "Death of the Curator" (102).

Under one of the principal elements, "Spatialities," for *Live Art 2014* Pather worked "with space as a curatorial tool and with the notion of the outsider as part of South Africa's developing democracy" (2019b, 98). As chair of a panel entitled "The Periphery as Threshold," Pather described how Cameroon-based performance artist Christian Etongo's work *Quartier sud*, "sliced raw fish, used copious amounts of bread flour, a range of foods, water and alcohol, body painting, and a series of body actions that included deftly maneuvering under, across, and through a maze of tightly tied up string" (2018b, 66). Etongo explored illegal immigration involving conflicts between those on the periphery and those in the center, though these two spatial points "may not be far off from one another," comments Pather, "replacing each other in turbulent exchanges" (2018b, 66).

Live artists in the 2014 festival broadly shared the notion of the "periphery as threshold" in theme and form, along with working "with extremities, spillage, overflow and a 'bubbling over' or excess" (2018b, 66). Pather argues in his essay "The Periphery as Threshold" that the periphery, relegated to the outer ends of cities, "contained and subjugated, starts to breed excesses and overflow" (66). He aims to explore "how the periphery becomes a kind of threshold, a space or a lens through which the centre out of which they have been expelled, may be viewed" (66). There is much to learn about the center and its policies in keeping certain populations excluded from city centers as "the continued presence of black shack settlements in South Africa in spite of a supposed democracy," comments Pather. When excluded "peripheral" people come to the center, their very presence disrupts the center's order and its "public relations image.... It is ultimately how the periphery responds, acquiescent and compliant or fierce and oppositional, that the centre reveals its truths. In turn and if communities that are on the peripheries of society use force in an effort to be more visible and move to the center of a society, how the society responds will be significant" (66–67). The center can respond "with greater force" and once again exclude the undesirables with no hope for "future inclusion."

Gavin Krastin's piece *Rough Musick* (*Live Art* 2014) presented the "periphery" in the very body of this "queer artist of European descent" covered in ash, "as the 'other'" (Pather 2018b, 66). Pather describes *Rough Musick* as "a work with asphyxiation and the performance of other extremities by leading audiences lying on a cart drawn by a donkey on the outskirts of the city. The audience members were given old iron and aluminum plates and utensils and were asked to beat these repeatedly. They created a bizarre soundtrack, the 'rough music' in the title, as they followed Krastin's abject near naked body in freezing temperatures. *Rough Musick* referenced a practice that originated in the small villages of medieval England as a means for the public to disgrace and humiliate petty criminals, sexual deviants and 'others'" (66).

The *Live Art* 2014 festival featured dancer-choreographer Mamela Nyamza's evocative work *19 Born 76 Rebels*, which used live dogs interrupting the performance in a public space. The title evokes the 1976 Soweto uprising against Bantu education, when apartheid police used dogs to attack protestors. "The work begins to inhabit a space of disruption," notes Pather. In this striking work, two tall, elegantly attired woman, one dressed in the colors of apartheid South Africa, the other in the ANC colors, raise (as it were) the ghost of Marie Antoinette's disdainful remark at the hungry masses: "Let them eat cake." Such gestures evoke parallels with current South African society, with staggering levels of poverty and hunger.

A work by Boyzie Cekwana called *In Case of Fire, Run for the Elevator* is described by the artist as a "story of food and its intricate, uneven and invisible poetics . . . the disquiet of an angry stomach grumbling at the deafening din of culinary correctness. . . . [It] honors imbecility and pokes fun at heroism, authority and the republic. It flirts with ambitions of legitimacy as it scours the uncertain terrain of artistic acceptability" (Pather 2019b, 97). Pather notes that Cekwana's work "was another tipping point in the shifting landscape of live art—his use of stasis and reduction as indicative of a plateau of despondency and impotence on which movements such as #Rhodesmustfall was born. This then fires another wave of energy that has imbued the works of artists appearing in subsequent festivals in 2017 with all the volatile iridescence that dominated the Fallist protests" [#feesmustfall protestors were called the Fallists] (97).

In Pather's 2014 curation around the theme of "The Body and Mortality," he recounts an unpredictable experience around Chuma Sopotela's work *Inkukhu Ibeke Iqanda* ("The chicken has laid its eggs") inside a room of the old Cape Town City Hall, when "the unplanned and overwhelming smell of the fresh cow dung on which Sopotela performed" was too much for certain spectators who had to leave for air (Pather, 2019b, 90). Such unpredictable challenges posed by smell leads Pather "to point to the need to search for other grammars" for curating live art, different from curation of objects (2019b, 90).

In "Curating Liveness (From Temperature to Smell)" (a subheading in the essay "The Impossibility of Curating Live Art"), Pather (2019b, 87) discusses the activity of curating "presence [that] is inherently unpredictable," hence it requires that curators are prepared when the unanticipated stares them in the face. Pather provides examples from his own curation at the 2017 *Live Art* Festival when Jelili Atiku performed *Come Let Me*

Clutch Thee, which dealt with the devastating impact of oil spills in the Niger Delta that destroy the environment and threaten biodiversity and food supply. In this work, Pather notes that "the bride's train was affixed to a trail of approximately 50 plastic cans of raw petroleum" that began to melt in the heat and spilled on the Iziko South African National Gallery's "pristine floors" (87). The unpredictability "at its most elemental," he comments, "especially when the territory is untrammelled, is to invite a walk through fire, illuminating and scalding at the same time. And it is this walk that asks for different sets of philosophical, political and social ideas around the curation of performance" (87).

By 2017, "the nature of crisis and overt disruption becomes more and more a language unto itself," reflects Pather, so that it was impossible to curate around a theme or even a set of themes since the submissions were vastly different. Further, Pather notes that "the question of form existed in an entirely new and much more contested space than had been the case three years prior" (2019b, 99). Pather's aesthetic-political vision is finely tuned to the changing sociopolitical landscape of deepening crisis in South Africa in terms of leadership, corruption, and the widening gap between rich and poor.

Pather links "levels of unpredictability, mobility and transformation [to] societies in crisis" like South Africa, where dreams of *simunye* and a rainbow nation have failed and have created an atmosphere ripe with "tension . . . turbulence that makes particular demands on artists. In such a climate of crisis, conventional theater and dance is struggling to remain relevant, whereas live artists' wide-ranging responses encapsulate instability" (2017, 142). Pather cites social struggles around #Feesmustfall and #Rhodesmustfall that disrupted conventional protest modes.[16] For Pather, such disruption itself "emerges as a particular performative form," one that needs receptive curators to showcase different forms of live art.

Along with such radical changes, curators need to question "the grand narrative perpetuated by colonial forms [that] is premised on the idea that there is only one rhythm, or flow.... Colonial rule imposed this fallacy. Rhythm is as crucial to curation as it is to performance—listening to the 'heartbeat' within and between works" (2019b, 99). How, asks Pather, can the decolonial project shake off this rhythm of a colonial heritage, and "how much of this asks us to be far more speculative, patient and courageous in how we consider new rhythms in curation as the decolonial project unfolds and unravels hundreds of years of colonial practice?" (99). Pather's creative notion of "new rhythms" in curation of *Live Art*, aligned to decolonial goals, parallels his concept of "new grammars," vocabularies, and methods.

In curating *Live Art* 2017, Pather sensed the energy of "overflow" that was "unpredictable." Further, he felt that live artists "wanted to be left alone" and not be taken care of in conventional curatorial methods of organizing themes and frames for their work. Pather characterizes the 2017 festival as marked by "idiosyncrasy. An effervescence, a sense of something new happening, a direct, immediate encounter" (2019b, 102). Prominent artists such as Steve Cohen, and iQhiya presented work at this festival. iOhiva is a performance art collective of twelve underrepresented Black women who wanted to hold a discussion rather than "perform." Mamela Nyamza's *De-Apart-Hate* conveys the historical and continuing reality of "hate" and "apart"-ness rooted in apartheid via idiosyncratic juxtapositions of a seesawing, unsteady bench that serves as a coffin, a pulpit, and a plank to sit against as this bold performer opens her legs and places the Bible at her crotch; then, as she sticks her tongue out and licks a finger, she keeps turning the pages, intoning, "It never ends" and "Ah men" (Van Straaten, Nicola. 2016).

Live art such as Nyamza's *De-Apart-Hate* is a form of activism not only because it challenges the status quo concerning social justice issues of race, class, gender, and religious dogma exerted especially on women, but in how "it is undoing the way we think, in surprising us with new forms, new ideas, new structures," notes Pather. He adds, "Combining this with dismantling familiar and comfortable aesthetic choices is a multi-pronged approach to vibrant and visceral, even perhaps 'entertaining' activism" (2019b, 97). Live art such as Nyamza's dismantles recognizable forms, troubling spectators to think beyond traditionally accepted gender roles or religious doctrines even as she inspires openness and freedom of thought in South Africa's democracy.

In the search for new vocabularies to curate live art, Pather cites the work of Albert Khoza at the 2017 *Live Art* festival, whose work *Take in Take out (to live is to be sick to die is to live)* is "a traditional holistic practice of healing the body that makes use of indigenous plants. Not a performance so much as an offering of himself and the traditions of his ancestors, Khoza shares this healing practice in an exploration of death, disease, and sickness.... Khoza believes that theatre, dance, and art in general are weapons of change" (Pather 2017c). Pather regards Khoza's work as a "reminder that what we are calling live art was in existence on the African continent for centuries. Unidentified as such, sporadic snatches of this appear and disappear in contemporary performance" (Pather 2017c). Pather is inspired by Khoza's work as demonstrating that live art is not a new category of performance but that it has existed for centuries in Africa. Hence, it behooves curators to transform "the terminology of contemporary Western practice," notes Pather, taking his cue from Khoza's 2017 work that "signaled an urgent need for the interrogation of terminology appropriated to fit unwilling contexts" (Pather 2017c).

Pather concludes his essay "The Impossibility of Curating Live Art" with strong advocacy for the curator to become "increasingly invisible ... to cease to live (and interfere) in the creation of presence, to disappear completely [which] may be the most productive strategy: a curatorial approach that refines and redefines the edges of involvement and disengagement, seeking out the delicate balance between these two positions in order to give life to new works that are probing and provocative while remaining speculative and unknowable" (2019b, 103). Pather advocates boldly that curators take a back seat and let artists take the lead in presenting live art. In his innovative and analytic attention to space and race in the context of his society, Pather's curatorial activities, in the selection of performances and in his essays on site and live art, offer powerful tools for artists elsewhere in Africa and beyond. It is important not simply to move shows out of theaters and galleries into public spaces and to make them accessible but to focus on "the visibility of the artwork *as* an artwork" (2019b, 103).

Live Art 2018 took place over two weeks and presented forty creative works, with artists like Donna Kukama, Albert Khoza, Nelisiwe Xaba, and Gavin Krastin. Their performances ranged from gut-wrenching excavations of Black history in a performance installation, to a nude body evoking beauty and vulnerability, to the slave-holding Cape Coast Castle, and performances inside the Company Gardens and the Iziko Slave Museum. I spent a mind-blowing week in Cape Town experiencing these "boundary-defying artists [who] expressed present traumas, recalled ghosts and memories from past histories, and engaged in performance formats ranging from installations, dance, and narrative, to African-based ritual and sound. Several live performances evoked ancestry and the archive by showing the body as either a site of subversion and sexuality or of disease and healing.... The festival offered its audiences the opportunity to bear witness to lost lives in images such as the work shirts, a paper dress hung on a chain, a nude body in a spectacle of beauty and pain, and through our participation in the flower trade [learning about South Africa's incredible biodiversity]" (Katrak 2019, 172, 180).[17]

In conclusion, this chapter has traversed over a decade of Pather's curatorial activities, from 2007 to 2019, discussing his key work as a performance curator who selects and locates venues and, with his keen sensibility and perspicacity, discovers and mentors new artists in public arts festivals in Cape Town, alongside his theoretical essays such as "The Periphery as Threshold," his concept-driven curator notes, and his coediting the volume *Acts of Transgression: Live Art in South Africa* (2019). Additionally, in curating live art festivals, this artist with his finger keenly on pulse of the deepening social crisis in South Africa and artists' responses to it posits the "impossibility" of curatorial activities in the traditional sense of selection and placement; rather, with characteristic boldness, Pather advocates that curators remain open and prepared for the unexpected and unimaginable. Further, with characteristic humility, he proposes that curators not be intrusive in an artist's creation and performance of live art but that they instead get out of the way of artists' unpredictable moves and allow maximum space—physical, emotional, and psychological—to the creative artists themselves.

NOTES

1. "About the ICA," http://www.ica.uct.ac.za/ica/about, accessed March 2, 2018.
2. In business since 1692, Spier Wine Farms, located in Stellenbosch, around forty miles from Cape Town, is one of South Africa's oldest wine farms. Spier's noteworthy legacy includes fostering art, along with creating fine wines and cultivating food that sustains the environment.
3. Red high-heeled shoes show up in different Pather works—in *Body of Evidence*, Ntombi Gasa wears them along with an incongruous fur coat; in *Qaphela Caesar*, the transvestite wears red stiletto heels; in *rite*, Black men in shorts wear white wigs and red high-heeled shoes.
4. Pather and Bailey's co-curatorial note for *ITC* 2008 can be found at https://en.wikipedia.org/wiki/Infecting_the_City#cite_ref-4), accessed March 25, 2019.
5. Susan Sontag's two essays "Illness as Metaphor" and "AIDS and Its Metaphors" (New York: Picador, 1990) are foundational in studies of illness. However, recent research in medicine posits that healing and the arts are congruent in the care of patients with diseases like Parkinson's

and dementia. In March 2003, the Society for the Arts in Healthcare and the National Endowment for the Arts held a symposium in Washington, DC that brought together experts in the arts, social services, medicine, media, and the government "to develop a strategic plan for advancing the arts in healthcare." At this gathering, Dr. Michael Samuels, in "Art as a Healing Force: Alternative Therapies in Health and Medicine," stated that the healer and the artist both stimulate the rational and intuitive parts of the brain and have positive impacts on the body's immune system among other benefits. https://www.arts.gov/sites/default/files/NEA_SAHConceptPaper.pdf, accessed July 25, 2018.

At my own institution, the University of California, Irvine, a recent initiative called Medical Humanities, a collaboration among the Schools of Humanities, Arts, and Medicine, is engaged in the synergy of healing and empathy with medical knowledge. Invited speakers have included poet-physicians, disability scholars, physician-authors on palliative and end of life care.

6. This is reminiscent of when, in more recent times, President Mbeki was receiving much criticism for his Minister of Health, and Mbeki himself was refusing to accept AIDS's dire consequences in South Africa.

7. Pather's essay "The Periphery as Threshold" was part of a symposium held in conjunction with *Live Art* festival 2014. I am grateful to Pather for sharing a copy with me. It is now published in *Klaxon* 5, 2018.

8. Nelson Mandela's first speech on being released was reported in the *New York Times* on February 12, 1990, in an article entitled "South Africa's New Era; Transcript of Mandela's Speech at Cape Town City Hall: 'Africa It is Ours.'" Here is an excerpt:

> *Amandla! Amandla! i-Afrika, mayibuye!* [Power! Power! Africa it is ours!] My friends, comrades and fellow South Africans, I greet you all in the name of peace, democracy and freedom for all. I stand here before you not as a prophet but as a humble servant of you, the people. Your tireless and heroic sacrifices have made it possible for me to be here today. I therefore place the remaining years of my life in your hands. . . . I extend special greetings to the people of Cape Town, the city to which, which has been my home for three decades. Your mass marches and other forms of struggle have served as a constant source of strength to all political prisoners.

9. I am very grateful to Sarah Davies Cordova for sharing these program notes from *Infecting the City* 2008 with me from her time in Cape Town.

10. Brett Bailey, curator's note, Institute for Public Art, 2011, https://www.instituteforpublicart.org/case-studies/infecting-the-city-public-arts-festival/, accessed July 31, 2016.

11. Ibid.

12. *Infecting the City*, 2013, http://www.infectingthecity.com/2013/.

13. Masilo, a renowned choreographer and winner of the prestigious 2008 Standard Bank Young Artist for Dance Award, has created ten original works including her own versions of *Romeo and Juliet, Carmen,* and *Swan Lake*, which were performed across Europe. She has also collaborated with internationally acclaimed South African artist William Kentridge on *Dancing with Dada*, performed at the Market Theatre in Johannesburg. See the introduction for a discussion of Pather as an inspiring conceptual artist for the generation younger than him, such as Masilo, Mamela Nyamza, and Nelisiwe Xaba.

14. "Preswich Place in Green Point in Cape Town has long been a subject of class and racial conflict in the Western Cape.... In the 1820s the area was sub-divided and sold, it then became part of the developed urban core of the Cape. In the 1960s, Blacks and Coloreds were forcibly removed from the area to the Cape Flats. In 2003, construction activities in the area uncovered human bones and as required by the South African Heritage Resources Agency (SAHRA) Act, construction was halted and Archeologists from the University of Cape Town (UCT) were contracted to investigate. Exhumations of the human remains began." http://www.archivalplatform.org/blog/entry/prestwich_place, accessed February 28, 2017.

15. Pather shared his unpublished essay "The Impossibility of Curating Live Art" with me in 2018. It is now published in Jay Pather and Catherine Boulle, eds., *Acts of Transgression: Live Art in South Africa* (Johannesburg: University of Witwatersrand, 2019), 82–104. See also the editors' introduction (1–16) in the same volume. *Acts of Transgression: Live Art in South Africa* has been shortlisted for the 2020 Humanities & Social Sciences (HSS) award for Best Non-Fiction, Edited Volume as noted on the ICA site, http://www.ica.uct.ac.za/ica/news/2020HSSAwards.

16. See my discussion of these protest movements in chapter 3.

17. Please see Katrak's detailed write-up on *Live Art* 2018 in the Institute for Creative Arts' Newsletter at http://www.ica.uct.ac.za/ica/news/LAFreport2018. Additionally, see Katrak on *Live Art* 2018, "Legacies of Loss and Trauma, Healing and Redemption: Cape Town *Live Art* Festival," *TDR: The Drama Review* 63, no. 4 (winter 2019): 172–80.

CONCLUSION
Choreographic Reinventions and New Directions

JAY PATHER, PERFORMANCE, AND SPATIAL POLITICS IN SOUTH *Africa*, a first monograph on this world-class artist, recognizes his stature in provocative site works, his contributions as a theorist of space, and his unique, prolific, and multifaceted creations over four decades that have significant impact in South Africa, on the African continent, and globally. I have argued that this innovative choreographer and curator utilizes spaces—geographical, bodily, mental, and psychological—in conjunction with race in order to challenge apartheid and post-apartheid divisions, and to intervene via art in social justice. Pather's evolving spatial politics are in line with his nation's political landscape during and after apartheid, within a "democracy" that has yet to fulfill its promises to the majority.

As choreographer, Pather draws from an eclectic palette of dance styles—classical Zulu and Xhosa dance, Indian classical, ballet, modern, and contemporary dance, along with South African popular movement styles such as *pantsula*, *kwasa kwasa* (originally from the Congo), *isicathamiya* (Zulu a cappella singing with gentle rhythmic movements), gumboot dance, Zulu ritual practices of *sangoma*—that is, traditional healing—as well as the language of gesture and multimedia that can reach audiences with many languages. Startling juxtapositions, hybrid movement alongside visual art, and other media are characteristic of Pather's signature style.

Pather's choreography and curation of large-scale public arts festivals are intercultural and interdisciplinary. They blur artistic boundaries between and among disciplines—not only dance and theater but movement with visual art, video, and other digital media for audiences in South Africa, parts of Europe, Asia, and the United States. Pather's imagination is guided by decolonial agendas, by alternative uses of space, and by technological creativity, all of which open up new gateways and clear away exclusionary barriers that are the perimeters that Pather continues to upend and remove.

Along with such multimodal creative tools, Pather focuses on the body's ability to convey emotion and meaning, as well as on the body as a literal and symbolic site on which he inscribes individual, social, and national histories. Pather contends that the body, even more than the mind, is the repository of memory, particularly mental residues of violence that continue to breathe inside the muscles, bones, and cells of the human body.

Pather's engagement as a thinker and choreographer/director with issues of the past and memory brings particular illuminations to the troubled history of South Africa, and by extension to violent scenarios in other parts of the world such as Rwanda and Myanmar. As he remarks in his essay "Legacies of Violence: South Africa, 20 Years after Democracy" (presented at the "O.P.E.N. Talk" part of Singapore's International Arts Conference in 2014), "the fear in the evocation of the apartheid past is indeed one of the elements at the core of the contestation around memory, its representation, access, evocation and effect" (Pather 2014). The temporal dimension in dealing with the past relates integrally to space, especially to apartheid's mapmaking, which forced Black people out of cities or into "homelands" in arid parts of the county. Although migrations of vast numbers of people from native to diasporic locations, by necessity or by choice, is a mark of the twentieth and twenty-first centuries, internal migrations, and migrations from rural to urban areas, mark the flows of ordinary people seeking new homes and livelihoods. Black people, however, in South Africa were forbidden during apartheid to move geographically from so-called rural, native "homelands" to cities unless they had employment in the city.

Dealing with the past is a contentious issue in South Africa. Pather quotes Mandela's often repeated reminder of "a past that threatens to live with us like a festering sore." However, the TRC that set out to "heal" these "festering sores" was an inadequate response for Pather, as he argues, to "centuries old sustained, institutionalized violence, and an underestimation of the sophistication of apartheid" (Pather 2014a). Pather finds comments by Mandela's fellow prisoner, intellectual Neville Alexander, useful although problematic: "The strategic-political and ultimately moral-historical question is how to move towards understanding without ever forgetting, but to remember without constantly rekindling the divisive passions of the past" (Alexander 2003, 117). How people remember past injuries is part of a journey of healing in which a mandate such as recalling the past "without constantly rekindling the divisions passions of the past" is hardly possible. The past, colonialism, and apartheid are processes that are not fixed in time and space as conceptualized by postcolonial and decolonial thought. Hence, past wounds do arise without warning and often violently in as deeply scarred a society as South Africa.

Even deeper than racial divisiveness, Pather insists on "continued economic distress and dire material circumstances [that] ensure that the remembrances of such acts of violence and depravation have clear reference to the immediate present" (Pather 2014a). Journeying into the past is less about seeking closure and more about the present realities in which long hours of labor do not result in a living wage. Pather rationalizes "the obligation to remember . . . because much of apartheid's brutality lay in a psychic abnegation of all kinds, of rendering the clearly visible, invisible" (2014a). Here he cites the continuing harsh realities of exploitation that are simply denied. "For the victim, this pretense is all the more violent in its assertion that they the victim(s) [are] not present, that they lack the human qualities of presence, that what they are experiencing is not real, that they do not feel" (2014a).

Pather's theory-praxis engagements with memory and history, the body and ritual, his spatial explorations in site-specific and site-responsive choreography, and his curation of public arts festivals—*Infecting the City* and *Live Art*—are remarkable. Pather demonstrates creative foresight in selecting established artists even as he mentors emerging ones, working with them in identifying appropriate, often unexpected, even provocative locations for their works. In touristy Cape Town, the very use of previously forbidden sites—the city center, the public library, the slave museum, or city hall—is political. Even with apartheid's "demise," a long way remains to restore democratic uses of public spaces, making "public space truly public" in Pather's words. He argues that apartheid was effective in "evacuating cities as places for living" (Fleishman and Pather 2014, 111). This system, which forced Black people into townships away from city centers, gave White bodies claims to the suburbs, and "cities became empty shells, places into which bodies would stream for the day but leave for the night" (111). Local transport used mostly by Black people stop at a certain time at night, when performances take place. Pather is aware that such infrastructure matters need to be addressed to include diverse audiences.

MIXING GENRES AND BODIES: CHOREOGRAPHING TO IGOR STRAVINSKY'S *THE FIREBIRD*

Although I regard Pather's choreography for *The Firebird* (2016) as a fascinating next step in the continuing progression of his oeuvre, particularly in his explorations of space and movement in space with aesthetic-political goals, Pather himself in revisiting this 2016 choreographic experience in 2020 was more speculative, believing that his choreography for *The Firebird* remains "unfinished" (phone conversation, June 7, 2020). He recognizes incredible moments of working together with Janni Younge as director. He had created "a choreographic frame" as he does for all his works, but in *The Firebird* he commented that "the frame remained as a structure; it was not realized in a full-fledged, layered, and performed work." The audience did not perceive anything missing (I saw the show in Los Angeles) and received the show with standing ovations wherever it was performed. However, recognizing that this was a new form of working with dancers and inanimate puppets, he decided to leave his choreography "unfinished." Pather is thoughtful and candid about feeling "unfulfilled perhaps because what was new was within grasp but not achieved through lack of time and resources. The clash between the economy's insistence on a schedule and delivery, the large puppets that had so much traction, and a punishing travel schedule created some compromises in choreography that I felt uncomfortable about. This may be part of the fallout or collateral damage of creating something new and [a] new form, that 'the unfinishedness of the choreography' was probably part of this" (phone conversation, June 7, 2020).

Similarly, *The Firebird* was a new direction for Pather in 2016; he reinvents himself in his first foray of working with human dancers holding inanimate puppets. The dancers learn to manipulate giant puppets made of paper and sticks; the latter add to the human forms as bodily extensions supporting and directing their movements in a large-scale show. In this work, form and content are connected integrally as they relate to South Africa's political climate.

Pather's choreographic juxtaposition of "the *toyi-toyi*, a dance of protests and a derivative of Southern African dance ... with a classical *pas de deux* between a puppet and a dancer" represents "the complexities of contemporary South Africa [that] are achingly present" (Pather 2016c).[1] Pather's "Choreographer Note" recognizes the racial and political markers operating in the very reality of "these bodies flung together," a human and a puppet, that have to "make sense of each other and with each other bring up challenge, resistance, resilience, fear, and hope. The intensities of the context under which the work is created asks us as artists to go beyond just being clever, to succumb to telling a story, our story, the stories" (2016c). The danced story moves away from Stravinsky's Russian folktale and is rooted in South Africa as well as pushed beyond the Ballet Russes innovations to include mixed genres and bodies.

As choreographer, Pather undertook a different process of creating movement than in his previous works since he had "to figure out a way in which different kinds of puppetry in dance could work [and] how to combine the specificity of puppetry with the intuitive meaning of dance. Dance can be so suggestive whereas the puppets are so specific" (2016c). For some of Pather's dancers, moving with the huge puppets was a new challenge.

Along with an innovative form that brought animate and inanimate presences on stage, *The Firebird* project was a "creative collaboration spanning two years" with award-winning director Janni Younge, award-winning choreographer Pather, and Cape Town's Handspring Puppet Company which fabricates larger-than-life puppets. Handspring Puppet Company is famous for their work *War Horse*, which traveled internationally in 2007.[2] Both Younge and Pather have always "welcomed diverse voices, movement styles and nuanced puppetry detail" originating and developed in Cape Town. Pather's choreographic tour de force was first presented at Cape Town's Artscape Theatre; next, it traveled to the National Arts Festival in Grahamstown before embarking on a US tour. In a highly positive review, "The Firebird Stuns Audiences at Artscape," Thola Antamu (2016) writes that

Stravinsky's "original score seamlessly combined with dance and giant puppets is a thrilling multisensory experience" (Antamu 2016). Further, Antamu recognizes the show as "a visual storytelling of South African history, pain, hope, enthusiasm, defeat and success. Choreographer Jay Pather has completely reimagined the ballet, so that African dance jumps, dreamlike, into ballet, which bounces into *pantsula*, shuffles into tap and leaps elegantly into contemporary dance styles."

In the US, *The Firebird* was performed in Philadelphia, Washington, DC, Chicago, and Los Angeles, with live music played by the cities' resident orchestras. The musicians who played Stravinsky's *Firebird* score sat behind the dancers with their huge puppets. I was in the audience on August 4, 2016, at Los Angeles's Hollywood Bowl, a huge outdoor amphitheater (with a capacity to hold 17,500 spectators) and a popular venue for summer performances, with pleasant, balmy nights true to its desert location. It felt heartwarming to recognize that in some ways I had come full circle with my project, beginning my journey with this monograph in my California location, traveling multiple times to Pather's home in South Africa, also meeting him in his ancestral home of Chennai, India, and now witnessing his choreographed *Firebird* in my Los Angeles abode.

The female protagonist-dancer called The Seeker (Jackie Manyaapelo) displays a range of emotions reflected by dancers maneuvering the puppets, which function "as visual metaphors for the emotional content"; passion and inspiration are embodied in the firebird, doubt and aggression are conveyed by puppet animals, and "innocence and playfulness [are evoked in] the form of children"; the puppet children's innocence "is captured in the translucent vellum, a soft and flexible material which when dry, forms a beautiful but brittle skin" (Pather 2016c). Pather noted to me that in the original "Fokine ballet, there is an evocation of innocence. In our version, post-1994, it is independence" (interview 6, 2016). Michel Fokine's initial, original choreography for *Firebird*, based

Fig. C.1. *The Firebird* at the Hollywood Bowl, Los Angeles. Photographer: Luke Younge. Courtesy Janni Younge and Suzy Bell.

on a Russian folktale, emphasized tropes of innocence, blessings, and curses; Younge's concept and Pather's choreography focused on challenges faced by The Seeker (reminiscent of Pather's 1999 work *A South African Siddhartha*, discussed in chap. 1) after South Africa's hard-won independence. Like Fokine's successful collaboration with Sergei Diaghilev's Ballets Russes, so was Pather's with Janni Yonge and the Handspring Puppet Company.

This *Firebird* rewrites the original narrative behind Stravinsky's music and Russian folklore by transporting it into the sociopolitical South African landscape, with The Seeker in the body of a young woman in this new democracy. Her "political innocence," as Pather described it was a familiar emotion even for progressives after independence in 1994, brimming with hope for a new postapartheid world (interview 5, 2016). Beside The Seeker is a figure described as The Alchemist of Honesty (Ntombi Gasa) embodying the wisdom of the ancestors, a female guide helping The Seeker to balance creative and destructive thoughts, "bringing them together to birth a fully formed idea and support it with power and vision" (Pather 2016c). The Seeker gains self-confidence as she "celebrates integration and intercultural acceptance," realizing also that underlying a sense of inclusion remains ongoing inequality. "She calls on her critical insight (the snake-like creatures)," comments Pather "to tear down the illusions she has built and [that] pull her ideas apart" (Pather 2016c). Even with the hope of a new nation, Pather contends, "the unfinished business of material equity" persists. However, "the doubt and rising rage is always accompanied by the firebird metaphor, a source of creativity, the ability to make and chart new ground. When both forces work in opposition to each other there is potential for great destruction and drawing the disparate ideas of rage and creation together suggests a regeneration that is not superficial" (Pather 2016c).

Pather comments that for this work "a diverse layering of styles of dance became very important. Classical African dances and ballet in the earlier parts of the work help us probe the naivete of the original rainbow nation" (Pather 2016c). Pather's hybrid choreography weaves together contemporary South African dance as influenced by classical African dance and by ballet. Suzy Bell, a South African arts commentator who saw the Los Angeles show, shared with me her blog notes, which refer to Pather using multiple styles "in an attempt to create something new," breaking recognizable form to create a new direction/structure for the work:

> Pather's classical Zulu and Tswana African dance with Ukrainian tradition Russian dance in *The Firebird* creates a lush richness of diversity. He describes this as a somewhat forced marriage to break form in an attempt to create something new. I love that he included classical Indian dance hand movements to heighten the creative form.... The war shuffling *toyi-toyi* dance is particularly apt for its curated inclusion in Pather's choreography.... The cross-cultural pollination of these dance forms on one stage is admittedly challenging ... but that is the creative point in breaking form to create new.[3]

Director Janni Younge notes in an interview with Suzy Bell, as recorded on Bell's blog, that "when torn apart, something new comes from that." Younge (2016) excavates "the imaginative potential of the firebird-as-phoenix, a new and more encompassing force of life, rising from the ashes." Younge adds in her director note that she "needed a way to express both the cyclic nature of progress and the potential for new life to spring from the ashes." Like Pather, she recognizes both what she calls "the miracle of democracy" along with the realities of post-independence, when "cracks" in the post-apartheid era are "beginning to show." In particular, Younge points out that "racial tensions we once imagined were gone forever have re-asserted themselves" (Younge 2016).

Such divisiveness is tearing South African society apart and connects to what Bell notes in her blog as "Younge's and SA's acclaimed choreographer Jay Pather's creative umbilical cord connection to their current political context." Bell continues, "We as South Africans know it's messy, it's real, not re-imagined. . . . [Younge and Pather] courageously attempt to share a new visual form to express a fresh contemporary voice. . . . Dancers perform while engaging with and carrying giant puppets weighing up to 200 kilos (440 pounds). This is what acclaimed SA playwright Neil Coppen refers to as the *Abnormal Load* of South African society (#AbnormalLoad for Europe, US, Syria et al)." Bell appreciates Younge's artistic courage in mounting this "mammoth creative technical production . . . married with dance and live animation along with an orchestra of 110 performing live on stage, seated behind the total of fifteen performers, some holding multiple puppets."

Ultimately a sense of wonder returns to the post-1994 world in *The Firebird* when The Seeker is able to balance the forces of creativity and destruction in the deeply moving puppets of children, golden-colored, held gently by human hands of the dancer-puppeteers evoking hope for the future. In his artistic world, so profoundly grounded in the material inequities facing the

Fig. C.2. Backstage at the Hollywood Bowl, August 4, 2016, after performance of *The Firebird* with Ntombi Gasa of SSDT in middle, Katrak to her left, and Katrak's daughter Roshni to Gasa's right. Photograph taken by a cast member.

majority in his nation, Pather's vision remains hopeful, holding on to the dual anchors of "passion and creativity" that ultimately rise inside The Seeker and by implication in the spirits of ordinary South Africans for social justice (Pather 2016c).

Throughout Pather's own artistic journey he has sought, almost as a seeker himself, the power in art, through various modes of expression, to evoke new avenues of possibilities for joy and connectedness for diverse South African citizens. His work engages the conjuncture of space and race whether in his 1999 dance-theater work *A South African Siddhartha* (chap. 1), where the male seeker wanders the Karoo until attaining enlightenment as the Buddha, or in *The Firebird*, where the female seeker in post-independence South Africa dances a gamut of emotions—exhilaration, doubt, disillusionment, and finally hope in this nascent democracy of twenty-two years in 2016.

At the time of concluding this book during the 2020 Covid-19 global pandemic, in terms of new forms Pather is training dancers and facilitating online choreographic projects. Such online platforms continue to move art into another sphere opened up under the constraints of social distancing and fears of infection and can inspire artists to create new initiatives that participate online in social justice causes.

In 2020, both the Covid-19 global pandemic and the centuries old disease of racism were brought to the fore in the police killing of George Floyd on May 25 in Minneapolis, US. Floyd's repeated cry of "I can't breathe" is a rallying point of the Black Lives Matter uprising. "I can't breathe" is also the experience of asphyxiation of the lungs caused by Covid-19 that has killed over 150,000 people in the US; among them, more Black citizens (in proportion to their population) have died, many with underlying health conditions rooted in their lack of access to health care, often surviving in what are called "food deserts." In the fight against racism, will this latest killing of an unarmed Black citizen "be a moment or a movement?" And what is the role of artists hit in unprecedented ways by the virus, leading some to be fatalistic and others to create online art? The pandemic has uncovered, remarks Pather, "the truth of what exists, uncovering excesses and profound absences, just as our understanding of Black people who suffer disproportionately to their numbers [both in South Africa as in the US], given systemic and unspoken racism" (phone conversation, June 7, 2020). Noting that performances, for example, have been relegated to the very end of a lockdown, for Pather, it is important for artists to talk through at this time how art possibly can go back to being "an essential service, for healing, for public health and social responsibility. To be part of the healing process in a society, as it was (and in some instances continues to be) on the African continent" (phone conversation, June 9, 2020).

As director of the Institute for Creative Arts (ICA), Pather notes in the April 2020 ICA newsletter:

COVID-19 has been an encounter with a concrete wall, not always the lucid film of opportunity some would have us image it. Transitioning to online meetings, teaching, performance and art exhibitions does present a way to deal with this reality—valiant and occasionally rewarding, it is also frustrating, lonely, imperfect and reductive. A talking head on a screen is hardly a model for the complexities and nuances of human endeavour and communication. The urgency of seeing through crisis to some kind of other side has touched all of us, but acknowledging its reality is a sobering place to start.[4]

Although this crisis has challenged "the coming together of diverse publics," ICA has announced innovative online programs scheduled April through November 2020, such as "the first series of a new ICA Podcast featuring interviews with South African artists and curators about live art" inspired by the published volume *Acts of Transgression: Contemporary Live Art in South Africa*. Another planned event is a public art symposium featuring presentations by contributors to ICA's forthcoming book *Restless Infections* (2021), a collection of scholarly essays on *Infecting the City* recognized as "the largest and longest running public arts festival in the country."[5] *Restless Infections* on ITC promises to be as path-breaking as *Acts of Transgression* has been on live art.

Since my discovery of Pather's work, and for the past few years, I have devoted myself excavating his artistic oeuvre, which I trust will be illuminating for dancers and scholars, for performers and festival organizers, and for all who partake in Pather's creative endeavors to deploy art as a vehicle for social change for the people of South Africa, for Africans on the continent, and for artists and ordinary people globally. As an original theorist of space, Pather connects places and bodies to the historical and political environments of his nation with resonances beyond South Africa. He makes inanimate spaces alive with bodies in his transformational choreography and curatorial practice. His site-specific and site-responsive creations make key interventions with his underlying purpose throughout his own passionate creative journey: the performing arts can inspire change. They are, as this book ascertains, processes of shared learning and methods for seeking social justice in a variety of spaces—private, domestic, intimate, public—for a diverse population in South Africa and across the world.

NOTES

1. I am grateful to Siwela Sonke's Ntombi Gasa for a copy of this program from the Cape Town production, which she kindly gave to me when I saw her in Los Angeles. She plays the role of the Alchemist of Honesty in *The Firebird* with much passion and a stage presence that came across to me even in the vast expanse of the Hollywood Bowl. Pather's "Choreographer Note" is also reprinted in the Hollywood Bowl Summer Program, p. 14.

2. In "Puppet Masters' Big Leap" in the *Los Angeles Times*, Karen Wada reviews how "War Horse's' Lifelike Creatures Put Heart and Soul into Play." Basil Jones and Adrian Kohler of Cape Town's Handspring Puppet Company are the creators of these larger-than-life animal puppets. In *War Horse*, they "tried to create believable horses that could carry the emotional weight of the show." This meant being sensitive to re-creating a horse's grunt or shake of the head, "transforming detail into something much more like soul or spirit." As noted by Nicholas Hayter, director of the National Theater in London, where *War Horse* was presented first in 2007, Jones and Kohler "can become obsessive about a particular muscle they want to represent in a particular way. This feeds into a genuinely spiritual sense of what happens when you ask a puppet to interpret the life of a living creature. Something really mysterious happens." Karen Wada, "Puppet Masters' Big Leap," *Los Angeles Times*, July 1, 2012. In the audience at the Hollywood Bowl, my daughter and I felt a similar "spiritual sense" when watching the human dancers interacting with the animal puppets, and with two golden child puppets in *The Firebird*.

3. Suzy Bell's blog can be accessed at http://www.ireallyloveafrica.tumblr.com.

4. Jay Pather, ICA newsletter, April 2020.

5. Pather, ICA Newsletter.

APPENDIX
INDIANS IN SOUTH AFRICA
A Chronological Time Line

A USEFUL TEXT, *A Documentary History of Indian South Africans*, edited by Surendra Bhana and Bridglal Pachai, includes materials from early migrants (1860–1914) and relies on archives and libraries with materials "largely political in orientation," as in "official documentation: letters of complaint, petitions, last wills and testaments, memorials and so on," since personal and family letters were rare (Bhana and Pachai 1984, xi). I borrow from and add to Bhana and Pachai's time frame in order to trace a chronological history of Indians in South Africa under four periods: (1) 1860–1944, (2) 1945–60, (3) 1961–82, and (4) post-1982.

(1) During **the early period 1860–1944**, indentured laborers had a much harder time adjusting to life than free Indians, who, according to Bhana and Pachai, could move freely around the country. "The documents recapture instances of the misery," they remark, "that accompanied indenture. There are complaints of low wages, long hours, low rations, inadequate attention to social and medical needs, and also of beatings" (Bhana and Pachai 1984, 2). Bhana and Pachai usefully include a "diversity of documents, often written by hired scribes suggest[ing] the complex process of an immigrant people's assimilation into a newly forming, wider society" (3). Documents include as "The Coolies

petition the Durban Corporation for better wages" (3); "Muslims of Durban complain about the vexatious curfew law" (6); "Pillay and others petition the Viceroy of India" (10); "Suicides among indentured Indians" (17); and "Narayanan searches for his wife and child," a poignant case in which Narayanan was not informed that his wife and child were considered "invalid" and "had been sent back" to India (22). Even the entrenched racism underlying White supremacy is evident in a document entitled "Muslim traders petition against Free state law of 1884"—a case of "thirteen Gujarati Muslims [known at the time as 'Arabs'] ... [who] wished to be classified as citizens, not as 'coloureds' [which at that time meant Black] (31). Several documents testify to how Indians resisted unfair laws such as "The Dealers' Licenses Act," judged accurately by the petitioners as "an attempt to weed out small traders." This petition by Mohammed Cassim Camroodeen and others to the Secretary of State, Joseph Chamberlain, dated December 31, 1898, provides evidence that "argued convincingly that the Act gave local boards the power to behave despotically" (36).

Indians entered the Transvaal in 1881 with Sheth Abubakar, who opened a shop in Pretoria and purchased land on one of its principal streets. Other traders followed in his wake. Their great success roused the jealousy of European traders, who commenced "an anti-Indian campaign in the newspapers, and submitted petitions to the Volksraad or Parliament, praying that Indians should be expelled and their trade stopped" (Gandhi 1928, 1954, 33). Prejudicial statements such as "Indians have no sense of human decency, [that] they suffer from loathsome diseases, [that] they consider every woman their prey" became rampant. Indians did not read the newspapers and were shocked at the turn of events. Their appeals to President Kruger fell on deaf ears.[1]

Indians were deprived of the right to purchase land in many areas and were often given undesirable areas in which to live and trade. Gandhi compares the Transvaal-mandated racism against

Indians to the caste system in India, which carried notions of pollution and defilement—prejudices that Gandhi himself would campaign to abolish later in his life. The situation for Indians in the Free State was similar to that in the Transvaal, though in the Cape Colony, because of the presence of Malays and the fact that some Indian Muslims married Malay Muslims, the scenario was not as overtly racist and restrictive as it was in the other colonies. However, even in the Cape, two laws "copied from Natal were passed, namely, the Immigration Restriction Act and the Dealers' Licenses Act" (37).

As discussed usefully in Surendra Bhana's book *Gandhi's Legacy: The Natal Indian Congress 1884–1994*, Gandhi, much like other Indians educated in Britain, believed in Britain's guarantee of "Imperial equality" to all its subjects. "What we wanted in South Africa," remarked Gandhi in 1901, "was not a White man's country; not a White brotherhood, but an Imperial brotherhood" (quoted in Bhana 1997a, 11). Gandhi was "outraged" when he witnessed Indians as "victims of a dilemma," remarks Huttenback, "rooted in a historical change in the evolution of the British Empire" (Huttenback 1971, vi). This "change" was rooted in the movement of Indians to other parts of the empire where they faced prejudicial treatment. "It became increasingly difficult," continues Huttenback, "for the British Government to justify what was in practice a double imperial standard—one for White men and the colonies of settlement and another for non-Europeans and the dependent empire" (vii). In particular, Indians were "guaranteed" by Queen Victoria to receive the same treatment as "all other subjects of whatever race or creed"; despite this guarantee, immigrant Indians faced harsh realities in South Africa. Gandhi himself realized later, during the long road to liberate India from the colonial yoke, that this was hardly a promise of political rights and equality. As noted by historian Chattopadhyaya in *Indians in Africa: A Socio-Economic Study*, "British imperialism in Africa, as elsewhere in the British Empire, was tempered by as much humanitarianism as was justified by its political and economic interests" (Chattopadhyaya 1970, 1).

Just as it did with anti-trade laws, racism by Whites pervaded immigration laws that sought to force indentured laborers to return to India after their five-year term or to pay a hefty and prohibitive tax of three pounds sterling each year to remain in South Africa. This was resisted in the document "An unjust and uncalled-for Immigration Bill, 1894," filed by "Abdoolla Hajee Adam, Parsee Rustomjee, Doroosamy Pillay and others to the Natal Governor on 8 August 1894" (Bhana and Pachai 1984, 53). Indians were charged with "invading" several colonies. "The Natal Formula was soon to be adopted by the rest of South Africa" (53). "Further Immigration Restrictions, 1903" attempted "to tighten control over the entry of free Indians into Natal" (61).

Bhana recounts that when the Natal Indian Congress (NIC) was established in 1894, at a time when there were forty-two thousand Indians in Natal, its goal was to protect the "rights the Indians believed they enjoyed as subjects of the British crown" (Bhana 1997b, 1). However, Natal's Whites, in their efforts to assert White supremacy, tried to disenfranchise Indians. Although Gandhi had decided to return to India, he was convinced by major Indian merchants to organize and resist such legislation. The Whites in power, who "were in the process," comments Bhana, "of consolidating their subjugation of the African people," did not want to deal with the "complication" of dealing with Asians as well (3). They wanted their labor but were not prepared when large numbers of them decided to stay on in South Africa even as petty traders. A remark by General Smuts to Gandhi is instructive: "This country is the Kaffirs'. We Whites are a handful. We do not want Asia to come in" (11).

Bhana records that "in 1893, there were 16,051 indentured Indians compared to 24,459 'free' Indians" (Bhana 1997b, 3). As with any dominant group, the Whites were not interested in the diversity of the Indian community, which consisted of different religions, languages, and cultural practices. Those from Southern India spoke Tamil and Telugu; those from the north and east of India spoke Punjabi, Bhojpuri, Gujarati, and Bengali. There were Hindus, Muslims, and some Parsis and Christians. "The NIC [Natal Indian Congress] was a secular body that sought to rise above these cultural, religious, and linguistic differences," even though joining any political organization did not mean that people left their ethnic affiliations behind; rather, they added them, remarks Bhana, "to their primary list of affiliations" (Bhana 1997b, 5). "It would be a mistake," adds Bhana, "to imagine that an altered political identity wiped away ethnicity" (6).

Prejudice against Indians was rooted in what Chattopadhyaya describes as "trade-jealousy" of the European traders, especially in the Transvaal. Even the Indian community's limited economic success, which was rooted in their practice of frugality, was used to launch racist stereotypes about their unsanitary ways of life, a condition caused by not having sufficient living areas for decent housing. There was also the fear of miscegenation, of Indians marrying Europeans. Another complaint was that the Indians sent remittances home instead of investing in the land where they lived—understandable historically, since their situation was precarious, and they remained unwelcome. They were made to feel as the "other" in race, religion, language, and social customs by the Europeans, especially the Dutch settlers in the Transvaal, who demonstrated "innate antipathy 'to anything approaching equality between the White and the Colored races'" (Chattopadhyaya 1970, 121).

Dada Abdulla, the very person, who had brought Gandhi to South Africa, made his residence available to Gandhi and others who initiated the NIC on August 22, 1894. One of the underlying problems of the NIC was that from its inception it was dominated by wealthy merchants who wanted economic benefit from their resistance to Whites. Bhana records that in 1921 (and until 1961) the NIC moved away from relying on the "Imperial equality" doctrine evoked for Indians as subjects of the British Crown.

In its initial days, the NIC wanted to educate White people about Indians. Therefore, it maintained a membership of businesspeople and excluded working-class Indians through the simple expedient of keeping membership fees prohibitively expensive for their meager wages. Hence, even as the NIC became known in India and England, it did not have support of the majority of South African Indians. Bhana notes that in 1913 the organization faced "a crisis" because the *satyagraha* campaign needed to include the vast majority of the population, and the business community could not identify with these goals. Bhana usefully points out that "Gandhi's role was influential but it was not central in the sense that the movement for the entire period was not controlled by him. There has been a tendency in early works on Gandhi to see the movement in monolithic terms, and his role as pivotal. I am largely in agreement with Maureen Swan whose seminal work has shown the existence of an intricate network of political, semi-political, religious, and ethnic organisations whose perspectives Gandhi could not ignore" (Bhana 1997a,17).[2] Indeed, Gandhi's ability to grasp the diversity among Indians and to work with various groups divided by religion and culture is "a reflection of his greatness," notes Bhana.[3]

There were groups and leaders who disagreed with Gandhi, such as P. S. Aiyar, who ran *Colonial Indian News* (1901–03) before establishing the *African Chronicle* in 1907, in which he expressed views that differed from Gandhi's and the NIC's. Nevertheless, Gandhi's charismatic personality drew thousands to him. Increasingly, he emphasized that his strength was rooted in his spirituality as he reflected on religious matters in *Indian Opinion* between 1904 and 1910.

Documents on "the dramatic way in which the *satyagraha* campaign unfolded from 1906–1914," comment Bhana and Pachai, demonstrate why satyagraha appealed to the Indians. "It marshalled their inner-most resources, and thereby gave them the dignity which their legal disabilities sought to deny" (Bhana and Pachai 1984, 112). Gandhi himself describes satyagraha as "soul force pure and simple.... It was not a weapon of the weak" (Gandhi, 1928, 1954).

One key issue that Bhana points out is that ultimately, Gandhi had not been born in South Africa, so his positions were "typical of sojourner politics, an aspect of which was that the Indians did not think of South Africa as their home.... This must, in part explain why they could not identify with 'children of the soil' in South Africa" (Bhana 1997a, 22). Further, Gandhi, "as a moral crusader" who used truth and nonviolence as weapons to resist injustice, was not embraced by all Indians. While the satyagraha campaign began in September 1907 in the Transvaal, Gandhi's wish to see it embraced in Natal was not welcomed. Between 1907 and 1909, his main supporters were former indentured laborers who were willing to resist nonviolently and go to jail. The separation of Gandhi's initial business supporters and his satyagraha philosophy was based on what Bhana describes as "ideological differences" between the merchants, who were looking out for their own self-interest, and Gandhi, who by 1913 was interested in "an enlarged vision of the welfare of all Indians in South Africa" (29).

Bhana characterizes Gandhi's "enduring legacy" as his ability to create "Indianness" for those in South Africa by uniting several disparate elements within the community. Although he considered Indians to be distinct from the "kaffirs," and hence more "acceptable" to Whites, history judges Gandhi's shortsightedness negatively in such racialized evaluations. Whites used such separations to their own advantage with classic divide-and-conquer policies that caused further divisions between Black people and Indians, as they regarded the latter "as a separate racial category. This racialization became embedded in South African politics" (Bhana 1997a, 31).

The overall situation for Indians worsened with the constitution in 1910 of the Union of South Africa, bringing together the different colonies of Natal, Cape, Transvaal, and the Orange

Free State. Bhana and Pachai consider 1914 to be "a watershed of considerable importance," as it marks the date of an agreement between then president of South Africa, J. C. Smuts, and M. K. Gandhi that "represented an attempt, inconclusive though it might have been, at resolving the many grievances felt by the Indians in such diverse areas as social political matters, and *satyagraha*" (Bhana and Pachai 1984, xii).

Gandhi's time in South Africa ended with the Smuts-Gandhi Agreement and the Indian Relief Act, which attempted to strike a compromise between the Indians and Smuts. Gandhi realized that the future road to freedom and equality had to be worked out by South Africa's Indians themselves. The South African Indian Congress (SAIC), formed in 1923, was largely conciliatory, as they carried on Gandhi's legacy. This was not acceptable to all factions of the Indian community, some of whom were eager to join forces with Black people and conduct a joint struggle against racism. Moonsamy Naidoo was opposed to the South African Indian Congress because he felt "a few wealthy 'Mohammedans and banias' had no mandate to speak on behalf of the community," according to Bhana and Pachai (1984, 161).

(2) **The period from 1945–60** is marred significantly by apartheid, which made racism systemic, and marked by defiance. After 1945, new leadership rejected Gandhian ideals of passive resistance that they believed kept Indians in "a status of permanent inferiority" (Bhana and Pachai 1984, 184). Once apartheid was established in 1948, Indians and Colored communities were swept up in its racial laws, where they occupied an uncomfortable buffer zone between White and Black people.

Resistance from 1946 to 1948 includes Indians forging connections with other organizations, foreshadowing "the multiracial front of the 1950s," as Bhana indicates (1997b, 71). Specific resistances were mounted around issues of land. Smuts offered Indians "limited political rights in return for acceptance of segregation" via the Asiatic Land Tenure and Indian Representation

Act, which the Indians called the "Ghetto Act." February 20 and June 13 of 1946 were declared days of protest and work stoppage. Bhana narrates, "Fifteen thousand Indians gathered at the Red Square in Durban and solemnly pledged to oppose the law. From there, a procession of passive resisters, led by Monty Naicker, marched to the corner of Gale Street and Umbilo Road where five tents were erected on a vacant municipal lot. There the first eighteen passive resisters took their stand" (73). They were arrested a week later but only given a warning. The next time passive resisters like Sorabjee Rustomjee, M. D. Naidoo, Dr. K. Goonam, and R. A. Pillay were jailed. By August 1946, 300 protestors had gone to jail. From Durban, among 724 resisters, 82 were women (73). The resisters crossed the Natal-Transvaal border at Volksrust on January 25, 1948, to defy the unjust 1913 land law that forbade Indians from moving into the Transvaal.

Anti-Indian Whites in Natal voted against giving Indians any representation in politics. The press followed suit. Boycotts of Indian traders were encouraged. The hardest blow came with the Nationalist government's hard line from 1948 onward. Divisions deepened among supporters and opponents of passive resistance. Increasingly, a united front of all oppressed racial groups known as "a Black alliance" against Whites gained favor (Bhana 1997b, 80). In the 1949 Durban riots, fueled by anti-Indian sentiment, Indians were the target of attacks by Black people, which led to 123 deaths and much destruction of property. Rather than blaming individuals, the South African Indian Congress (SAIC) and the ANC "issued a joint statement on 6 February 1949, in which the disturbances were blamed on institutionalized inequality and the preaching of 'racial hatred' and 'intolerance' in 'high places.' A coordinating council was created on 15 April, the function of which was to generate greater co-operation between Africans and Indians" (81).

In 1956, the South African Institute of Race Relations sponsored a symposium with the theme of "The Indian as a South

African" (Bhana and Pachai 1984, 239). The four authors who presented papers "argued that the Indian South African, then in the fourth and fifth generation, was 'by birth and residence... thoroughly South African'" (quoted in the South African Institute of Race Relations, "The Indian as a South African," 55–71, cited in Bhana and Pachai, 1984, 239). The authors argued strongly that the one-hundred-year anniversary of Indian settlement (1860–1960) is only thirty years short of when Europeans settled in this land. However, as Dr. S. Coopan and Dr. A. D. Lazarus remark, "Political propaganda has endeavored to make the White electorate believe that the Indian is an alien, unassimilable element in South Africa, a threat to 'White' civilization. Latterly there has been an attempt to infect the African mind in the same way. It is hardly believable that it could seriously be held that less than 410,000 Indians could endanger the security of 2 and ½ million Europeans and 8 million Africans!" (Bhana and Pachai 1984, 239).

A key problem for the Indian community was in its very naming. The Natal Indian Congress, established during Gandhi's time in South Africa, had outlived that designation. There was a move to change the name to the South African People's Congress in order to do away with Indian exclusivity. But nothing came of this as the community wanted to retain its ties to Gandhi and to India rather than to South Africa. Of course, there were members among the Indian community, such as Pather and others, who related their struggle for equality with that of the Black population.

As Bhana and Pachai comment, "By 1960 Indians had become truly integral and permanent members of South African society, but they enjoyed none of the civil rights accorded to its white citizens" (1984, 185). A major blow was struck to the Indian struggle when the ANC was banned in 1960, and again when a state of emergency was declared after the Sharpeville massacre, in which innocent Black people protesting unfair laws were shot, sometimes in the back, by police.

(3) **The period from 1960–82** saw an increased move by Indians to work with disadvantaged Black people and to find common ground in the struggle for equality. Giving Indians representation in the government was a contentious issue. "By 1961," remark Bhana and Pachai, "the South African Government gave official recognition to the de facto situation and decided that Indians were henceforth to be regarded as a permanent part of the population. The hope of repatriating Indians, faint though it once might have been, was at last laid to rest" (1984, 249). The South African Indian Council of 1968 was regarded by some Indians as a tool of the racist government intended to foster "ethnically-based" groups rather than insisting "that South Africa's future be determined non-racially by all her people in democratically representative institutions" (249). Other conciliatory members, such as Amichand Rajbansi, executive chairman of the South African Indian Council, wanted to negotiate with the government. "Separate can't be equal," the opponents argued (250). There were racist elements within the Indian community that looked down on Black people and did not espouse the one-person one-vote philosophy. Rather, they wanted to carve out favors from the Whites in power.

In a powerful address as part of the President's Council in September 1980, P. T. Poovalingam agreed to serve on the council with the understanding that if there was no meaningful participation by Africans in the body's deliberations within twelve months, he would resign. He resigned after a year. In his inaugural address of February 6, 1981, he declares, "I am a South African. I am not an Indian." He continues to poignantly present his family history: "My father was an Indian who came to this country as an ordinary indentured Indian immigrant. The fact that his older brother was a magistrate in Madurai in India and the fact that my father was well educated through the Tamil medium, a language that shares with Mandarin Chinese the distinction of having been in constant usage for over 5000 years, the fact that my father was educated in his native Tamil language gives credence to his own claim that he was a victim of a glib-talking British 'coolie-catcher'" (quoted in Bhana and Pachai 1984, 270). He asserts that what is important is that he is "as much South African as any one of the honorable members here" (270).

Among other prominent Indians who were part of the liberation struggle, Ahmed Mohamed Kathrada (1929–2017) was arrested in 1963 and convicted, with Mandela, in the Rivonia trial. Kathrada, imprisoned for twenty-five years (Mandela was held for twenty-seven), was not released until 1989. "New leaders such as J.N. Singh and I.C. Meer were active from their student days," remarks Bhana, "active in trade union work, influenced by the ferment of the Second World War" (Bhana 1997b, 69). Others such as Billy Nair joined the armed wing of the ANC, Umkhonto we Sizwe (Bhana 1997b, 68). ANC Secretary-General Walter Sisulu addressed an NIC meeting in Durban along with A. J. Luthuli, president-general of the ANC (69).

(4) **Post-1982.** After the Soweto uprising of 1976, and with growing anti-apartheid sentiment worldwide, investors began withdrawing from South Africa, leading to a loss of 25.2 billion rand between 1984 and 1987 (Bhana 1997b, 132). Sanctions were put in place after local protests in many parts of the United Kingdom and the United States.[4] By 1988 there was a serious loss of confidence in the Botha regime, which increased military repression rather than seeking political solutions. The White supremacists lost much of their support in the 1989 election, and by 1990, F. W. de Klerk took several steps toward opening up a road to political negotiation, such as unbanning the ANC and releasing Mandela and others from prison.

NOTES

1. Similar campaigns fueled the xenophobic violence perpetuated against migrants from the African continent—for instance Ethiopians in 2008 and others in ensuing years.

2. See also Maureen Swan, *Gandhi: The South African Experience* (Johannesburg: Ravan, 1955).

3. The Ahmed Kathrada Foundation's Lives of Courage Project, in partnership with South African History Online, documents "the lives of less well-known, rank and file political activists" such as Reggie Vandeyar, an ordinary, working-class person whose political activities as a member of the Transvaal Indian Congress, the South African Communist Party, and the ANC and its armed wing, Umkhonto we Sizwe, led to his arrest and conviction in 1964. He served a ten-year sentence on Robben Island with his co-accused, Shirish Nanachai and Indres Naidoo. He was released in 1973 and kept under house arrest for ten years. Ismail Vadi notes in his book *Reggie Vandeyer: Portrait of a Revolutionary* that Vandeyer exemplifies "the role of an activist as an intermediary between the leaders and the masses." The book was published on Vandeyer's eightieth birthday in 2011 (Vadi 2011, 2).

4. Student protests across US universities pressured administrations to divest from companies doing business in South Africa since such investments, in effect, supported the apartheid regime. The protests were geared also to educate people in the United States about the unfair realities of daily life under apartheid, a blot on humanity, for the majority of South Africans.

BIBLIOGRAPHY

A NOTE ABOUT ONLINE SOURCES
FOR DANCE SCHOLARSHIP

Increasingly, space for the performance arts in print media—local and national newspaper and magazine reviews and so on—is scarce in South Africa, and reviewers and arts commentators rely on websites to post their interviews and critiques of dance works. Yet these very sites that belong to businesses, whose online presence changes and is often short-lived, by their very nature add to the ephemerality of the performance, especially since they rarely inform the critics, performers, companies and festivals who depend on the platform for visibility. This leads to the troubling reality of sites that were active when I began this research in 2014 (and included materials from 1996 onwards) no longer functioning in 2020. I include them here because I have quoted from these sources (that I luckily have in print form), in order to provide documentation of the material "disappeared" from online venues.

Alexander, Neville. 2003. *An Ordinary Country: Issues in Transition from Apartheid to Democracy.* New York: Berghahn.
Anderson, Patrick, and Jisha Menon, eds. 2009. *Violence Performed: Local Roots and Global Routes.* Basingstoke: Palgrave Macmillan.
Antamu, Thola. 2016. "The Firebird Stuns Audiences at The Artscape." Artslink.co.za, June 25.

Arkin, A. J., K. P. Magyar, and G. J. Pillay, eds. 1989. *The Indian South Africans*. Pinetown, South Africa: Owen Burgess.

Artslink. 2015. "Qaphela Caesar at The State Theatre." October 9. https://www.artlink.co.za/news_article.htm?contentID=38885.

Ashton, Len. 2001. "Insights into a Tenacious People." *Argus Tonight*, February 7.

Auslander, Philip, and Carrie Sandahl, eds. 2004. *Bodies in Commotion: Disability and Performance*. Ann Arbor: University of Michigan Press.

Bakhtin, Mikhail M. 1981. *The Dialogic Imagination*. Translated by Caryl Emerson and Michael Holquist. Austin: University of Texas Press.

Ballyntyne, Tommy. 2003. "On *Home*." *Sunday Magazine*, November 2.

Balme, Christopher. 2013. "Thresholds of Tolerance: Censorship, Artistic Freedom, and the Theatrical Public Sphere." In *Performance and the Politics of Space: Theatre and Topology*, edited by Fischer-Lichte and Wihstutz, 100–13. New York: Routledge.

Bates, Crispin, ed. 2001. *Community, Empire and Migration: South Asians in Diaspora*. Basingstoke: Palgrave Macmillan.

Bell, Suzy. 1998. "Taking a Stand." *Mail & Guardian*, August 14–20.

———. 2000a. "The Great SA Dance." *The Independent on Saturday*, March 18.

———. 2000b. "A Dance of National Importance." *The Independent on Saturday*, April 22.

———. 2000c. "At Last, a Dialogue on Indian Dance." *The Independent on Saturday*, April 22.

———. 2000d. "Siddhartha: An Uncontested Triumph." *The Independent on Saturday*.

Belling, Catherine. 2003. "Microbiography and Resistance in the Human Culture Medium." *Literature and Medicine* 22: 84–101.

Berning, Gillian, ed. 1994. *Gandhi Letters: From Upper House to Lower House, 1906–1914*. Durban: Local History Museum Education Series No. 4.

Bevernage, Berber. 2012. *History, Memory, and State-Sponsored Violence: Time and Justice*. New York: Routledge.

Bhabha, Homi. 1994. *The Location of Culture*. London: Routledge.

Bhana, Surendra. 1997a. *Gandhi's Legacy: The Natal Indian Congress, 1894–1994*. Pietermaritzburg: University of Natal Press.

———. 1997b. *The Natal Indian Congress 1894–1994*. Pietersmaritzburg: University of Natal Press.

Bhana, Surendar, and Bridglal Pachai, eds. 1984. *A Documentary History of Indian South Africans*. Cape Town: David Philip.

Bharucha, Rustom. 1984. "A Reply to Richard Schechner." *Asian Theatre Journal* 1, no. 2 (autumn): 254–60.

———. 1990. "Collision of Cultures: Some Western Interpretations and Uses of Indian Theater." In *Theater and the World: Performance and the Politics of Culture*, 13–41. London: Routledge.

———. 2000. "Interculturalism and Its Discriminations: Shifting the Agendas of the National, the Multicultural, and the Global." In *The Politics of Cultural Practice: Thinking through Theater in an Age of Globalization*, 20–44. London: Athlone.

———. 2014. "The Search for Justice in Truth and Reconciliation." In *Terror and Performance*, 104–47. London: Routledge.

Blair, Rhonda, and Amy Cook, eds. 2016. *Theatre, Performance and Cognition: Languages, Bodies and Ecologies*. London: Bloomsbury.

Brandstetter, Gabriele. 2015. *Poetics of Dance: Body, Image, and Space in the Historical Avant-Gardes*. Oxford: Oxford University Press.

Brannigan, Erin. 2015. "Dance and the Gallery: Curation as Revision." *Dance Research Journal* 47 (1): 5–25.

Burt, Ramsay. 1995. *The Male Dancer: Bodies, Spectacle, Sexualities*. London: Routledge.

Burton, Antoinette. 2016. *Africa in the Indian Imagination: Race and Politics of Postcolonial Citation*. Foreword by Isabel Hofmeyr. Durham, NC: Duke University Press.

Byam, Dale L. 1999. *Community in Motion: Theatre for Development in Africa*. Westport, CT: Bergin & Garvey.

Carlson, Marvin. 1989. *Places of Performance: The Semiotics of Theatre Architecture*. Ithaca, NY: Cornell University Press.

Casey, Edward S. 1993. *Getting Back into Place: Toward a Renewed Understanding of the Place-World*. Bloomington: Indiana University Press.

———. 2007. *The World at a Glance*. Bloomington: Indiana University Press.

Casper, Monica, and Eric Wertheimer, eds. 2016. *Critical Trauma Studies: Understanding Violence, Conflict and Memory in Everyday Life*. New York: New York University Press. See especially Martin Beck Matuštík with Gabriele Schwab, "Future's Past: A Conversation about the Holocaust," 122–34.

Castelyn, Saraleigh. 2011. "'Home Is Where the Heart Is': Black South African Identities and Siwela Sonke Dance Theatre's *Home* (2003)." *African Performance Review* 5 (2): 30–42.

Chattopadhyay, Anindita. 2010. "The Funny Man." *The Hindu*, January 10, 2010.

Chattopadhyaya, Haraprasad. 1970. *Indians in Africa: A Socio-Economic Study*. Calcutta: Bookland.
Christopher, A. J. 1994. *The Atlas of Apartheid*. London: Routledge, Johannesburg: Witwatersrand University Press.
Cole, Catherine, M. 2010. *Performing South Africa's Truth Commission: Stages of Transition*. Bloomington: Indiana University Press.
———. 2020. *Performance and the Afterlives of Injustice*. Ann Arbor: University of Michigan Press.
Coleman, David. 1997. "More Trauma Than Drama." *The Mercury*, August 27.
Coovadia, Imran, Alexandra Dodd, and Cóilín Parsons, eds. 2015. *Relocations: Reading Culture in South Africa*. Cape Town: Gordon Institute for Performing and Creative Arts (GIPCA) and University of Cape Town Press.
Cordova, Sarah Davies. 2016. "African Refugees Asunder in South Africa: Performing the Fallout of Violence in *Every Year, Every Day, I Am Walking*." In *Choreographies of Twenty-first Century Wars*, edited by Gay Morris and Jens Giersdorf, 85–109. Oxford: Oxford University Press.
Cordova, Sarah Davies, and Antoinette Sol. 2015. *Hippolyte Carnot, Gunima: Nouvelle africaine du dix-huitième siècle*. Paris: L'Harmattan.
———. 2016. "Glasser, Sylvia (b. 1940 –, Polokwane, South Africa)." In *Routledge Encyclopedia of Modernism*. New York: Taylor and Francis. doi:10.4324/9781135000356-REM1663-1.
Craighead, Clare. 2010. "When the Rainbow Is Not Enough: Site-Specificity, the Body as a Site, Multiculturalism and Intercultural Practice in Jay Pather's *CityScapes* (Durban, 2002)." *South African Theater Journal* 24 (1): 259–78.
Daily News. 2003. "No Place Like Home." October 23.
———. 2016. "Qaphela Caesar." June 14.
Dangor, S. E. 2004. "Negotiating Identities: The Case of Indian Muslims in South Africa." In *South Asians in the Diaspora: Histories and Religious Traditions*, edited by Knut A. Jacobsen and P. Pratap Kumar, 243–68. Leiden: Brill.
Davidoff, Terri. 2006. "Deconstructing Jay Pather's Location Specific Theatre: Creating Space for Transformative Dialogues." *South African Theatre Journal* 20 (1): 128–49.
de Certeau, Michel. 1984. *The Practice of Everyday Life*. Translated by Steven Rendell. Berkeley: University of California Press.
De, Esha, and Sonita Sarkar, eds. 2002. *Trans-Status Subjects: Gender in the Globalization of South and Southeast Asia*. Durham, NC: Duke University Press.

Derrida, Jacques. 1994. *Specters of Marx: The State of the Debt, the World of Mourning, and the New International*. New York: Routledge.

Desai, Ashwin. 1966. *Arise Ye Coolies: Apartheid and the Indian, 1960–1995*. Johannesburg: Impact Africa.

Desai, Ashwin, and Goolam Vahed. 2007. *Inside Indenture: A South African Story, 1860–1914*. Durban: Madiba.

Dhupelia-Mesthrie, Uma. 2000. *From Canefields to Freedom: A Chronicle of Indian South African Life*. Cape Town: Kwela.

Douglas, Gilbert, et al. 2006. "Under Fire: Defining a Contemporary African Dance Aesthetic—Can It Be Done?" *Critical Arts: South-North Cultural and Media Studies* 20 (2): 102–15.

Ellapen, Jordache. 2018. "Queering the Archive: Brown Bodies in Ecstasy." *Scholar and Feminist Online*. http://sfonline.barnard.edu/feminist-and-queer-afro-asian-formations/queering-the-archive-brown-bodies-in-ecstasy-visual-assemblages-and-the-pleasures-of-transgressive-erotics/.

Epprecht, Marc. 2013. *Sexuality and Social Justice in Africa: Rethinking Homophobia and Forging Resistance*. London: Zed Books.

Eze, Michael Onyebuchi. 2010. *Intellectual History in Contemporary South Africa*. Basingstoke: Palgrave Macmillan.

Fanon, Frantz. (1963) 2004. *The Wretched of the Earth*. Translated by Richard Philcox. New York: Grove. First published by Presence Africaine.

Farber, Yael. 2008a. *Theatre as Witness: Three Testimonial Plays from South Africa; in Collaboration with and Based on the Lives of the Casts*. London: Oberon.

———. 2008b. *Molora*. London: Oberon.

Farred, Grant. 2000. *Midfielder's Moment: Coloured Literature and Culture in Contemporary South Africa*. Boulder, CO: Westview.

Ferreira, Pinto. 2015. "Tonight/What-s-on/Gauteng." Review of *Qaphela Caesar*. IOL, http//www.iol.co.za/tonight/what-s-on/guatend/theatre-review-qaphela-caesar-1936470.

Finkelpearl, Tom. 2000. *Dialogues in Public Art*. Boston: MIT Press.

Fischer-Lichte, Erika. 2013. "Politics of Spatial Appropriation." In *Performance and the Politics of Space: Theatre and Topology*, edited by Erika Fischer-Lichte and Benjamin Wihstutz, 219–38. New York: Routledge.

Fischer-Lichte, Erika, and Benjamin Wihstutz, eds. 2013. *Performance and the Politics of Space: Theatre and Topology*. New York: Routledge.

Fitt, Sally, and Anne Riordan, eds. 1980. *Dance Focus: IX: Dance for the Handicapped*. Reston, VA: National Dance Association.

Fleishman, Mark, and Jay Pather. 2014. "Performing Cape Town: An Epidemiological Study in Three Acts." In *Performing Cities*, edited by Nicolas Whybrow, 99–119. Basingstoke: Palgrave Macmillan.

Foster, Susan Leigh, ed. 1995. *Choreographing History*. Bloomington: Indiana University Press.

Foucault, Michel. 1972. "Questions on Geography." In *Power/Knowledge: Selected Interviews and Other Writings, 1972–1977*, edited by Colin Gordon, 63–77. New York: Pantheon.

———. 1975. *Discipline and Punish: The Birth of the Prison*. Translated by Alan Sheridan. New York: Random House.

———. 1984. "Des Espace Autres." *Architecture/Movement/Continuite*, October, 1–9. http://web.mit.edu/allanmc/www/foucault1.pdf. Based on a lecture from March 1967.

———. 1998. "Different Spaces." In *The Essential Works of Foucault* vol. 2: *Aesthetics, Method, and Epistemology*, edited by James D. Faubion, 175–85. New York: New Press.

Franko, Mark. 2015. *Dance as Text: Ideologies of the Baroque Body*. Oxford: Oxford University Press.

Friedman, Sharon, ed. 2012. *Post-Apartheid Dance: Many Bodies Many Voices Many Stories*. Cambridge: Cambridge Scholars.

Frost, Peter. 2015. "On *Body of Evidence*." *Cue Media*, July 12.

Gandhi, Ela. 1994. *Mohandas Gandhi: The South Africa Years*. Cape Town: Maskew Miller Longman.

Gandhi, M. K. (1928) 1954. *Satyagraha in South Africa*. Translated from Gujarati by Valji Govindji Desai. Ahmedabad: Navjivan.

Garland-Thomson, Rosemarie. 2009. *Staring: How We Look*. Oxford: Oxford University Press.

Ghosh, Amitav. 2010. "Foreword." In *Eyes Across the Water: Navigating the Indian Ocean*, edited by Pamila Gupta, Isabel Hofmeyr, and Michael Pearson, ix. Pretoria: Unisa.

Gibbs, James, Ketu H. Katrak, and Henry Louis Gates Jr., eds. 1986. *Wole Soyinka: A Bibliography of Primary and Secondary Sources*. Westport, CT: Greenwood.

Glasser, Sylvia. 1991. "Is Dance Political Movement?" *Journal for the Study of Human Movement* 6 (3): 112–22. First published 1990, *The Dance Journal* 1 (1): 7–11.

Goodlife Reporter. "Rajesh's Important Durban 'Breyani.'" *The Mercury*, April 6.

Gopie, Rajesh. 2008. *Out of Bounds: A Play.* Mowbray, South Africa: Junkets.
Gordon Institute for Performing and Creative Arts (GIPCA). 2013. "Land: Performances, Installations, Film Screenings." Brochure from the GIPCA office, University of Cape Town.
Govender, Ronnie. 2008. *The Lahnee's Pleasure.* Auckland Park: Jacana Media.
Govinden, Devarakshanam. 2008a. *"Sister Outsiders": The Representation of Identity and Difference in Selected Writings by South African Indian Women.* Pretoria: University of South Africa Press.
———. 2008b. *A Time of Memory: Reflections on Recent South African Writings.* Durban: Solo Collective.
Gupta, Pamila, Isabel Hofmeyr, and Michael Pearson, eds. 2010. *Eyes across the Water: Navigating the Indian Ocean.* Pretoria: University of South Africa Press.
Hadley, Bree. 2014. *Disability, Public Space Performance and Spectatorship: Unconscious Performers.* Basingstoke: Palgrave Macmillan.
Hamber, Brandon, and Richard Wilson. 2000. "Plays, Politics and Cultural Identity among Indians in Durban." *Journal of Southern African Studies* 26 (2): 255–69.
———. 2002. "Symbolic Closure through Memory, Reparation and Revenge in Post-Conflict Societies." *Journal of Human Rights* 1 (1): 35–53.
———. 2010. "The Unwieldy Fetish: Desire and Disavowal of Indianness in South Africa." In *Eyes across the Water: Navigating the Indian Ocean*, edited by Pamila Gupta, Isabel Hofmeyr, and Michael Pearson, 109–21. Pretoria: Unisa.
Hansen, Thomas Blom. 2012. *Melancholia of Freedom: Social Life in an Indian Township in South Africa.* Princeton, NJ: Princeton University Press.
Hofmeyr, Isabel. 2010. "Africa as a Fault Line in the Indian Ocean." In *Eyes across the Water: Navigating the Indian Ocean*, edited by Pamila Gupta, Isabel Hofmeyr, and Michael Pearson, 99–108. Pretoria: Unisa.
Hopkins, D. J., Shelley Orr, and Kim Solga. 2009, 2011. *Performance and the City.* Basingstoke: Palgrave Macmillan.
Horowitz, Donald, L. 1991. *A Democratic South Africa? Constitutional Engineering in a Divided Society.* Berkeley: University of California Press.
Houston, Andrew, ed. 2007. *Environmental and Site-Specific Theatre.* Toronto: Playwrights Canada.

Hunter, Victoria. 2015. *Moving Sites: Investigating Site-Specific Dance Performance*. London: Routledge.
Hutcheon, Linda. 1989. *The Politics of Postmodernism*. London: Routledge.
Huttenback, Robert, A. 1971. *Gandhi in South Africa: British Imperialism and the Indian Question, 1860–1914*. Ithaca, NY: Cornell University Press.
The Independent on Saturday. 2003. "Bright New Season of Dance," October 25.
Itzkin, Eric. 2001. *Gandhi's Johannesburg: Birthplace of Satyagraha*. Johannesburg: Witwatersrand University Press in association with Museum Africa.
Jacobsen, Knut A. and Pratap P. Kumar, eds. 2004. *South Asians in the Diaspora: Histories and Religious Traditions*. Leiden: Brill.
Jameson, Fredric. 1981. *The Political Unconscious: Narrative as a Socially Symbolic Act*. Ithaca, NY: Cornell University Press.
Jeffery, Celina. 2015. *The Artist as Curator*. Bristol: Intellect.
Jeyifo, Biodun, ed. 2002. *Modern African Drama: A Norton Critical Edition*. New York: Norton.
Katrak, Ketu H. 1986. *Wole Soyinka and Modern Tragedy: A Study of Dramatic Theory and Practice*. Westport, CT: Greenwood.
———. 2002. "Changing Traditions: South Asian Americans and Cultural/Communal Politics." *Massachusetts Review* XLIII (1): 75–88.
———. 2006. *Politics of the Female Body: Postcolonial Women Writers of the Third World*. New Brunswick, NJ: Rutgers University Press.
———. 2008. "Literary Matters: Research Methods in Reading Ethnic Literatures." In *Ethnic Studies Research: Approaches and Perspectives*, edited by Timothy Fong, 257–79. Lanham, NY: Alta Mira.
———. 2009. "The Arts of Resistance: Arundhati Roy, Denise Uyehara and the Ethno-Global Imagination." In *Violence Performed: Local Roots and Global Routes*, edited by Patrick Anderson and Jisha Menon, 244–63. Basingstoke: Palgrave Macmillan.
———. 2011. *Contemporary Indian Dance: New Creative Choreography in India and the Diaspora*. Basingstoke: Palgrave Macmillan.
———. 2018. "Defying Boundaries, Excavating Histories, Revising Trauma." ICA. Last modified October 8, 2018. http://www.ica.uct.ac.za/ica/news/LAFreport2018.
———. 2019. "Legacies of Loss and Trauma, Healing and Redemption." *Drama Review* 63, no. 4 (winter 2019): 172–80.
Kloetzel, Melanie, and Carolyn Pavlik, eds. 2009. *Site Dance: Choreographers and the Lure of Alternate Spaces*. Gainesville: University Press of Florida.

Knowles, Ric. 2007. "Environmental Theatre." In *Environmental and Site-Specific Theatre*, edited by Andrew Houston, 68–99. Toronto: Playwrights Canada Press.
Krouse, Matthew. 2003. "*Home* as a Battleground." *Cue Magazine*, June 28.
———. 2003. "Home Is Where the Hurt Is." *Mail & Guardian*, July 4–10.
Kumar, P. Pratap. 2004. "Taxonomy of the Indian Diaspora in South Africa: Problems and Issues in Defining Their Identity." In *South Asians in the Diaspora: Histories and Religious Traditions*, edited by Knut A. Jacobsen and P. Pratap Kumar, 376–92. Leiden: Brill.
Kuppers, Petra. 2014. *Studying Disability Arts and Culture: An Introduction*. Basingstoke: Palgrave Macmillan.
Kwon, Miwon. 2003. *One Place After Another*. Boston: MIT Press.
Lazarus, Neil. 1990. *Resistance in Postcolonial African Fiction*. New Haven: Yale University Press.
Lefebvre, Henri. (1974) 1994. *The Production of Space*. Translated by Donald Nicholson-Smith. Oxford, UK; Cambridge, MA: Blackwell Publishers.
———. 2004. *Rhythmanalysis: Space, Time and Everyday Life*. Translated by Sturat Elden and Gerald Moore. London: Bloomsbury.
Lepkoff, Daniel. 1999. "What Is Release Technique?" *Movement Research Performance Journal* 19 (Fall/Winter).
Leseth, Anne. 2010. "Michezo: Dance, Sports and Politics in Tanzania." *Anthropological Notebook* 16 (3): 61–75.
Lippard, Lucy. 1984. *Get the Message? A Decade of Art for Social Change*. New York: E. Dutton.
Loots, Lliane. 1999. "On Jay Pather's *Forked Tongues*." *The Mercury*, November 5.
———. 2001. "Resituating Culture in the Body-Politic." *Agenda: Culture Transgressing Boundaries* 49: 9–14.
———. 2002. "Reinvention of Dance." *The Mercury*, February 8.
———. 2003. "Home Sweet Home" On Jay Pather's *Home*. Local newspaper, Durban.
———. 2009. "Navigating African Identities, Otherness and the 'Wild, Untamed Body' in Dance Training and Pedagogy in South Africa: A Case Study of Flatfoot Dance Company's Dance 'Development Programmes,'" *Congress of Research on Dance (CORD) Proceedings* 41, supplement 1, 293–99.
———. 2010. "The Body as History and Memory: A Gendered Reflection on the Choreographic 'Embodiment' of Creating on the Socially

Constructed Text of the South African Body." *South African Theater Journal* 24, no. 1 (January): 105–24.

———. 2011. "Revisiting Gender Ecology and Eco-Feminism: A Profile of Five Contemporary Women Water Activists." *AGENDA* 25 (2): 6–16

———. 2012. "Voicing the Unspoken: Culturally Connecting Race, Gender and Nation in Women's Choreographic and Dance Practices in Post-Apartheid South Africa." In *Post-Apartheid Dance: Many Bodies, Many Voices, Many Stories*, edited by S. Freidman, 51–71. Newcastle upon Tyne: Cambridge Scholars.

———. 2013. "'Body Politics' and Negotiating Gender Violence and Child Sexuality through Flatfoot Dance Company's Youth Arts Interventions Programmes in KwaZulu-Natal: A Case Study (2003–2013)." *AGENDA*, 27 (3): 28–38.

———. 2015. "'You Don't Look Like a Dancer!' Gender and Disability Politics in the Arena of Dance as Performance and as a Tool for Learning in South Africa." *AGENDA* 29 (2): 122–32.

———. 2016. "Funding Shock for Dance Companies." *The Mercury*, July 20.

———. 2020. "Choreographies of Identity, Self and the 'African' Dancing Body in Negotiating Contemporary Dancing Histories and Practices in KwaZulu-Natal Post 1994: A Case Study of Flatfoot Dance Company." Doctoral dissertation, University of KwaZulu-Natal. https://researchspace.ukzn.ac.za/handle/10413/18212. Accessed May 15, 2020.

Machen, Peter. 2009. "'Dance Me to the Edge of Art': Peter Machen Talks to Jay Pather." *Mail & Guardian*, October 17–19.

Mackie, Heather. 2003. "South Africa: Dance Umbrella: The Beautiful Ones Must Be Born." *Business Day*, February 11.

Maharaj, Brij, Ashwin Desai, and Patrick Bond, eds. 2011. *Zuma's Own Gold: Losing South Africa's "War on Poverty."* Trenton, NJ: Africa World.

Maqoma, Greg. 2016. "Beyond the Euphoria of Movement." TEDx Talks, October 18. https://www.youtube.com/watch?v=XubYaoshp6s.

Martin, Randy. 1998. *Critical Moves: Dance Studies in Theory and Politics.* Durham, NC: Duke University Press.

Mathur, D. B. 1986. *Gandhi, Congress and Apartheid.* Jaipur: Aalekh.

Mbembe, Achille. 2001. *On the Postcolony.* Berkeley: University of California Press.

———. 2017. *Critique of Black Reason.* Durham, NC: Duke University Press.

McCann, Jamie Alexandra. 2008. "Embracing Differences: Integrating the Topic of Disability into the University Dance Curriculum." Master of fine arts thesis, University of California, Irvine.

Middeke, Martin, Peter Paul Schnierer, and Greg Homann, eds. 2015. *The Methuen Drama Guide to Contemporary South African Theatre*. London: Bloomsbury.

Mkhwanazi, Sibusiso. 2015. "Danger, Gevaar, Ingozi." *Culture Review Magazine*. http://www.culture-review.co.za/culture-qaphela.

Molefe, Doreen. 2015. "Dance Brings Caesar to Life!" *Daily Sun*, October 21.

Moopen, Jeyasperi. 2015. "Negotiating Movement between Two Cultures: Socially and Politically." Conference Presentation at Confluences 8: Negotiating Contemporary Dance in Africa. University of Cape Town, School of Dance, July 16–18, 2015.

Morrell, Robert. 2001. "The Times of Change: Men and Masculinity in South Africa." In *Changing Men in Southern Africa*, edited by Robert Morrell, 3–37. Pietermaritzburg: University of Natal Press.

Mukherji, Anahita. 2011. "Durban Largest 'Indian' City outside India." *Times of India*, June 23. https://timesofindia.indiatimes.com/city/mumbai/Durban-largest-Indian-city-outside-India/articleshow/9328227.cms?referral=PM.

Munro, Brenna M. 2012. *South Africa and the Dream of Love to Come: Queer Sexuality and the Struggle for Freedom*. Minneapolis: University of Minnesota Press.

Naicker, Lee-Ann. 2014. "Aspects of South African Indian and Colored Identity as Reflected in Four Selected Post-Apartheid Plays." Thesis #9811098, Tshwane University of Technology. Accessed at University of California, Irvine, August 2015.

Natal Witness. 2000. "Modern Parable of One Man's Search for Enlightenment." March 17.

Ndebele, Njabulo. S. 1994. *South African Literature and Culture: Rediscovery of the Ordinary*. Manchester: Manchester University Press.

Ngũgĩ, wa Thiong'o. 1981. *Detained: A Writer's Prison Diary*. London: Heinemann. Republished in an updated version entitled *Wrestling with the Devil: A Prison Memoir*. New York: New Press, 2018.

———. (1998) 2002. "Enactments of Power." In *Penpoints, Gunpoints, and Dreams: Towards a Critical Theory of the Arts and the State in Africa*, 37–69. Clarendon: Oxford University Press. Reprinted in Biodun Jeyifo, ed. *Modern African Drama: A Norton Critical Edition*. New York: Norton, 2002.

Nicholson, Greg. 2015. "South Africa: Where 12 Million Live in Extreme Poverty." *Daily Maverick*, February 3.

———. 2013. "Where a Nation Meets/Meats." *The Mercury*, September 26, 10.

Nuttall, Sarah, and Achille Mbembe, eds. 2008. *Johannesburg: An Elusive Metropolis*. Durham, NC: Duke University Press.

Panelli, Ruth. 2008. "Social Geographies: Encounters with Indigenous and More-Than-White Anglo Geographies." *Progress in Human Geography* 32 (6): 801–11.

Pather, Jay. 2006. "A Response: African Contemporary Dance? Questioning Issues of a Performance Aesthetic for a Developing Continent." *Critical Arts: South-North Cultural and Media Studies* 20 (2): 9–15.

———, ed. 2007. *Spier Contemporary Catalogue: Exhibition and Awards*. Cape Town: Africa Centre.

———. 2010. "Performances: *Qaphela Caesar*." GIPCA/ICA. Accessed April 12, 2011. http://www.ica.uct.ac.za/GIPCA/projects/2010/QaphelaCaesar.

———. 2011. Program Notes. GIPCA/ICA. Accessed May 15, 2015. http://www.ica.uct.ac.za/gipca/projects/2011.

———. 2012a. *Infecting the City* 2012, curator notes. Accessed March 26, 2014. http://www.infectingthecity.com/2012/curators-note/. Now found at https://www.instituteforpublicart.org/case-studies/infecting-the-city-public-arts-festival/. Accessed May 21, 2020.

———. 2012b. "The Making of *Blind Spot*: From Lab to Biennale." In *Changing Metropolis II*, edited by M. V. Polli, 89–95. Copenhagen: Kobenhavns Internationale Teater. https://issuu.com/cphmetropolis/docs/changing_metropolis.

———. 2012c. *Live Art* Inaugural Festival 2012, curator notes. http://www.ica.uct.ac.za/ica/projects/LiveArtFestival2012.

———. 2013a. *Infecting the City* 2013, program notes. http://www.ica.uct.ac.za/GIPCA/projects/2013/InfectingTheCity, http://www.ica.uct.ac.za/GIPCA/projects/2013/ThinkingTheCity, and http://www.ica.uct.ac.za/gipca/projects/2013Land.

———. 2013b. "Shifting Spaces, Tilting Time: Public Art and the African City." In *Rogue Urbanisms: Emergent African Cities*, edited by Edgar Pieterse and AbdouMaliq Simone, 433–44. Johannesburg: Jacana Media.

———. 2014a. "Legacies of Violence: South Africa, 20 Years after Democracy." Unpublished essay. Presented at the Open Participate Enrich Negotiate (O.P.E.N) Conference, Singapore, June 27.

———. 2014b. *Live Art* Festival 2014, curator notes. http://www.ica.uct.ac.za/ica/projects/LiveArtFestival2014.

———. 2014c. *Live Art* Festival 2014, introduction. http://www.ica.uct.ac.za/sites/default/files/image_tool/images/389/Album1/2014%20Programme.pdf.

———. 2014d. *Infecting the City* 2014, curator/program notes. Accessed January 15, 2015. http://www.infectingthecity.com/2014/cape-town/curators-note and http://www.infectingthecity.com/ITC-2014-Artist-Prog.pdf.

———. 2015a. "A Love Affair with Spaces." TedxUCT, Build.image(I) NATION series, University of Cape Town. Accessed October 26, 2015. https://www.youtube.com/watch?v=1kgNZ3G8lMY.

———. 2015b. "Laws of Recall: Body, Memory, and Site-Specific Performance in Contemporary South Africa." In *New Territories: Theatre, Drama, and Performance in Post-Apartheid South Africa*, edited by Greg Homann and Marc Maufort, 317–44. Bruxelles: P.I.E. Lang.

———. 2015c. "Motion Sickness." In *Movement Cape Town*, edited by Zahira Asmal. Cape Town: The City.

———. 2015d. "Remaking Place." GIPCA Symposium. http://www.ica.uct.ac.za/ica/projects/Symposiums/RemakingPlace.

———. 2016a. "Launch of the Institute of Creative Arts (ICA)." ICA. http://www.ica.uct.ac.za/GIPCA/projects/2016/ICALaunch.

———. 2016b. "3rd Space Symposium: Decolonisation and the Creative Arts." ICA. http://www.ica.uct.ac.za/GIPCA/projects/2016/3rdSpaceSymposium.

———. 2016c. Choreographer note, *The Firebird* program. Cape Town and Los Angeles, Hollywood Bowl.

———. 2017a. "Negotiating the Postcolonial Black Body as a Site of Paradox." *Theater* 47 (1): 139–61.

———. 2017b. "Right to Reply: UCT Is Not a Closed and Controlled Gallery." *Daily Maverick*, August 11, 2017.

———. 2017c. ICA *Live Art* Festival program. February 10–26. http://www.ica.uct.ac.za/sites/default/files/image_tool/images/389/Album1/ICA%20Live%20Art%20Festival%20Programme%20-%20final.pdf.

———. 2018a. "Shakespeare in South Africa: Contested Terrain with Unexpected Pleasures." Keynote, Global Shakespeare Symposium, University of California, Irvine, January 19.

———. 2018b. "The Periphery as Threshold." *Klaxon* 5, 66–78.

———. 2019b. "The Impossibility of Curating Live Art." In Pather and Catherine Boulle, *Acts of Transgresssion: Contemporary Live Art in South Africa*, 82–104.

———. Forthcoming. "Caught up in multiply-layered skirts or what's a stripper doing in Julius Caesar?" *ArtSearch*.

Pather, Jay, and Catherine Boulle, eds. 2019. *Acts of Transgresssion: Contemporary Live Art in South Africa*. Johannesburg: University of Witwatersrand Press.

Pather, Jay, and Bailey, Brett. 2008. Co-curators notes for *Infecting the City*. In Pather and Fleishman, "Performing Cape Town."

Pearson, Michael. 2010a. "The Idea of the Ocean." In *Eyes Across the Water: Navigating the Indian Ocean*, edited by Pamila Gupta, Isabel Hofmeyr, and Michael Pearson. Pretoria: Unisa.

———. 2010b. *Site-Specific Performance*. Basingstoke: Palgrave Macmillan.

Pillay, Kribben. 1995. *Looking for Muruga: A Play in Two Acts*. Durban: Asoka Theatre Publications.

Pinto, Gabriella. 2017. "Unpacking the Live Art Festival with Director Jay Pather." *Between 10and5*. February 24. https://10and5.com/2017/02/24/154001/.

Praeg, Juanita. 2020. "The Political Promise of Choreography in Performance and/as Research: First Physical Theatre Company's Manifesto and Repertory, 1993–2015." Dissertation, Rhodes University.

Purpura, Lia. 2006. *On Looking: Essays*. Louisville, KY: Sarabande.

Quayson, Ato. 2007. *Aesthetic Nervousness: Disability and the Crisis of Representation*. New York: Columbia University Press.

Radhakrishnan, Smitha. 2003. "'African Dream': The Imaginary of Nation, Race, and Gender in South African Intercultural Dance." *Feminist Studies* 29, no. 3 (fall): 529–37.

———. 2005. "'Time to Show Our True Colors': The Gendered Politics of 'Indianness' in Post-Apartheid South Africa." *Gender & Society* 19, no. 2 (April): 262–81.

Ranciere, Jacques. 2009. *Aesthetics and Its Discontents*. Translated by Steven Corcoran. Cambridge: Polity.

Ranger, Terence. 1975. *Dance and Society in Eastern Africa, 1890–1970*. London: Heinemann.

Rebentisch, Juliane. 2013. "Rousseau's Heterotopology of the Theatre." Translated by Gerrit Jackson. In *Performance and the Politics of Space: Theatre and Topology*, edited by Erika Fischer-Lichte and Benjamin Wihstutz, 142–65. New York: Routledge.

Reddy, Vasu. 2006. "The Poetics and the Politics of African Contemporary Dance: Contesting the Visceral." *Critical Arts: South-North Cultural and Media Studies* 20 (2): 116–20.

Reeder, Melanie. 1999. *Disagreement: Politics and Philosophy*. Minneapolis: University of Minnesota Press.

———. 2012. *A Sangoma's Story: The Calling of Elliot Ndlovu*. Johannesburg: Penguin.

Rendell, Jane. 2006. *Art and Architecture: A Place Between*. London: I.B. Tauris.

Robertson, Heather. 2002. "Space Explorer." *Sunday Times*, April 14.

Roche, Jennifer. 2015. *Multiplicity, Embodiment and the Contemporary Dancer: Moving Identities*. Basingstoke: Palgrave Macmillan.

Rosenberg, Leonard, and Goolam Vahed. 2014. *Dirty Linen: "Other" Durban, 1870s–1980s*. Durban: Durban University of Technology.

Said, Edward. 1983. *The World, the Text, and the Critic*. Cambridge, MA: Harvard University Press.

Samuel, Gerard M. 2007. "Undressing the (W)rapper: Disability Dance." *Ponto de Vista* 9: 131–43.

———. 2009. "Eclipsed on Centre Stage: The (Dis)Abled Body." *CORD Proceedings*, 1–5.

———. 2010. "Shampoo Dancing and *Scars*: Disembodiment in Afro-Contemporary Choreography in South Africa." Proceedings of ASTR/CORD Joint Conference, Seattle, Washington.

———. 2012. "Left Feet First: Dancing Disability." In *Post-Apartheid Dance*, edited by Sharon Friedman, 127–46. Newcastle upon Tyne: Cambridge Scholars.

Sandahl, Carrie, and Philip Auslander, eds. 2005. *Bodies in Commotion: Disability and Performance*. Ann Arbor: University of Michigan Press.

Sassen, Robyn. 2005. "But Is It Art?" *Art Throb*. Last modified June 1, 2005. http://artsouthafrica.com/archives/archived-featured-articles/212-main-archive/archived-featured-articles/1234-but-is-it-dance.html.

———. 2015. "Just Who Does Contemporary Dance Think I Am?" *My View: The Arts at Large* (blog), March.

Saunders, Tracey. 2016. "Jay Pather's Qaphela Caesar wins UCT Creative Works Award." *Daily News*, June 14, 1–5. https://www.news.uct.ac.za/article/-2016-06-14-jay-pathers-qaphela-caesar-wins-uct-creative-works-award Accessed September 12, 2016.

Scarry, Elaine. 1985. *The Body in Pain: The Making and Unmaking of the World*. New York: Oxford University Press.

Schechner, Richard.1984. "A Reply to Rustom Bharucha." *Asian Theatre Journal* 1, no. (2) (Autumn): 245–53.

———. (1988) 2003. *Performance Theory*. New York: Routledge.

———. 1994. *Environmental Theater: An Expanded New Edition Including "Six Axioms for Environmental Theater."* New York: Applause.

Schwab, Gabriele. 1996. *The Mirror and the Killer-Queen: Otherness in Literary Language*. Bloomington: Indiana University Press.

———. 2010. *Haunting Legacies: Violent Histories and Transgenerational Trauma*. New York: Columbia University Press.

Sellar, Tom. 2014. "The Curatorial Turn." *Theater* 44 (2): 21–29.

Sellar, Tom, and Bertie Ferdman, eds. 2014. "Performance Curators." Special issue, *Theater* 44 (2).

Sethia, Tara. 2012. *Gandhi: Pioneer of Nonviolent Social Change*. Boston: Pearson.

Shapiro, Johanna. 2011. "Dancing Wheelchairs: An Innovative Way to Teach Medical Studentsabout Disability." *American Journal of Medicine*, 886–87. doi:10.1016/j.amjmed.2011.03.008.

Sichel, Adrienne. 1995. First Encounters of Contemporary African Choreography held in Luanda, Angola, November 17–20. Sichel's personal copy held at the Ar(t)chive, University of Witwatersrand, Johannesburg.

———. 1996. "Transposing History and Dance to Inform—The Siwela Sonke Dance Company Ensures That KwaZulu Natal Pupils Come to Terms with Their Socio-political Backgrounds." *The Star*, October 30, 1996.

———. 1999. "Pather's Show, *Miracle*." *The Mercury on Friday*, March 26.

———. 2002. "Cityscape 'Happenings' Catch Durban Off Guard." *The Sunday Independent*, April 14.

———. 2003. "Radical Dance Set to Shake Up Johannesburg." Reprinted as "When Jay Pather Shook Johannesburg in 2003," *Dance Gazette*, 2015. https://issuu.com/goethejoburg/docs/gazette_final1lowres.

———. 2004. "Happy to Be Back at Home." *The Sunday Independent*, October 12.

———. 2009. Commentary on *Body of Evidence*. The Ar(t)chive, School of the Arts, University of Witwatersrand.

———. 2010. "Bleeding from the Walls and Ceiling." October 5. The Ar(t)chive, School of the Arts, University of Witwatersrand.

———. 2010a. "Bringing Pages of History Alive." September 7. The Ar(t)chive, School of the Arts, University of Witwatersrand.

———. 2010b. "Grappling with South African Physical Theatre." *South African Theatre Journal*, 41–50.

———. 2010c. "Lifedance." *The Sunday Independent*, November 28, 2010.

———. 2014a. "Legacies of Violence/Art Resolution: Mamela Nyamza and Fellow Trailblazers." Unpublished essay. Presented at the Open Participate Enrich Negotiate (O.P.E.N) conference, Singapore, June 27.

———. 2014b. "Riotously Creative Rite Debuts on Home Ground." The Ar(t)chive. Published in *JOMBA! Khuluma Digital blog*. https://drive.google.com/file/d/0B4S7HewuDpAXZWJVQnA4WVhZdDg/view?ts=5f05a4b9

———. 2015. "Confessions of, and Observations by, a Reluctant Dance Critic." *South African Dance Journal* 3, no. 1 (winter): 109–19.

———. 2016. "Enigmatic Bodyscapes: Sampling South African Dance." In *Critical Stages/Scenes Critiques* 13 (June/July): 1–21. http://www.critical-stages.org/13/the-landscape-of-south-african-contemporary-dance/.

———. 2018. *Body Politics: Fingerprinting South African Contemporary Dance*. Johannesburg: Porcupine.

Smart, Caroline. 2009. "Body of Evidence," *ARTSMART KZN Arts News*, October 17, 1–3. http://news.artsmart.co.za/2009/10/body-of-evidence_17.html.

Smith-Autard, Jacqueline M. 2002. *The Art of Dance in Education*. London: A & C Black.

Soja, Edward. W. 1989. *Postmodern Geographies: The Reassertion of Space in Critical Social Theory*. London: Verso.

———. (1996) 2000. *Thirdspace: Journeys to Los Angeles and Other Real-and-Imagined Places*. Oxford: Blackwell.

Sontag, Susan. 1990. *Illness as Metaphor and AIDS and Its Metaphors*. New York: Picador.

Soyinka, Wole. (1962, 1988, 1993) 2002. "Theater in African Traditional Cultures: Survival Patterns." Reprinted in Soyinka, Wole. 1988. *Art, Dialogue and Outrage: Essays on Literature and Culture*. Ibadan: New Horn Press. Also reprinted in Jeyifo, Biodun, ed. *Modern African Drama: A Norton Critical Edition*. New York: Norton.

———. (1976) 2006. *Myth, Literature and the African World*. London: Cambridge University Press.

———. 1999. *The Burden of Memory, the Muse of Forgiveness*. New York: Oxford University Press.

———. 2016. "In the Name of Shakespeare." In *Living Shakespeare: A Collection of Essays*, edited by Virginia Crompton. London: British Council. https://literature.britishcouncil.org/assets/Uploads/05.-shakespeare-lives-nigeria-wole-soyinka-digital-download.pdf.

Spivak, Gayatri Chakravorty. 2003. *Death of a Discipline*. New York: Columbia University Press.

———. 2012. *In Other Worlds: Essays in Cultural Politics*. London: Routledge.

Stevens, Maurice. 2009. "From the Past Imperfect: Towards a Critical Trauma Theory." *Letters: Newsletter of the Robert Penn Warren Center for the Humanities* 17, no. 2 (spring): 1–5. https://www.vanderbilt.edu/rpw_center/Letters/letterss09.pdf.

Stories. 2015. "The Coolest Dance You've Never Heard of: Pantsula." Video, 2:13. https://www.youtube.com/watch?v=gMgcLo_WGig.

Swan, Maureen. 1955. *Gandhi: The South African Experience*. Johannesburg: Ravan Press.

Taussig, Michael. 1993. *Mimesis and Alterity: A Particular History of the Senses*. London: Psychology Press.

Thiara, Ravi K. 2001. "Imagining? Ethnic Identity and Indians in South Africa." In *Community, Empire and Migration: South Asians in Diaspora*, edited by Crispin Bates, 123–52. Basingstoke: Palgrave Macmillan.

Thompson, James. 2009. *Performance Affects. Applied Theatre and the End of Effect*. Basingstoke: Palgrave Macmillan.

Tichman, Paul. 1998. *Gandhi Sites in Durban*. Durban: The Local History Museums.

Tiérou, Alphonse. (1989) 1992. *Dooplé: The Eternal Law of African Dance*. Translated by Deirdre McMohan. Chur, Switzerland: Harwood Academic.

Tolsi, Niren. 2003. "Where the Heart Breaks" *Sunday Magazine*, October 16, 2003.

———. 2008. "Grappling with Violence." *Mail & Guardian*, February 21. https://mg.co.za/article/2008-02-21-grappling-with-violence/.

Tulloch, Carol. 2016. *The Birth of Cool: Style Narratives of the African Diaspora*. London: Bloomsbury.

Vadi, Ismail. 2011. *Reggie Vandeyer: Portrait of a Revolutionary*. Lenasia, South Africa: Ahmed Kathrada Foundation.

Vahed, Goolam, and Bhana Surendra. 2015. *Crossing Space and Time in the Indian Ocean: Early Indian Traders in Natal, a Biographical Study*. Pretoria: Unisa.

Van Niekerk, Natasha. 2000. "Talking to Director and Choreographer of A South African Siddhartha, Jay Pather." *Berea Mail*. March 10.

Van Rensburg, Storm Janse. 2004. "Jay Pather." *Artthrob* 88, November. https://artthrob.co.za/04dec/artbio.html, accessed July 25, 2015.

Van Straaten, Nicola. 2016. "Mamela Nyamza's Constant Reinvention." *Between 10and5*. September 16. http://10and5.com/2016/09/16/mamela-nyamzas-constant-reinvention.

Viswanathan, Gauri. 1989. *Masks of Conquest: Literary Study and British Rule in India*. New York: Columbia University Press.

Whybrow, Nicholas. 2014. *Performing Cities*. Basingstoke: Palgrave Macmillan.

Wihstutz, Benjamin. 2013a. "Introduction." In *Performance and the Politics of Space: Theatre and Topology*, edited by Erika Fischer-Lichte and Benjamin Wihstutz. New York: Routledge.

———. 2013b. "Other Spaces or Space of Others? Reflections on Contemporary Political Theatre." In *Performance and the Politics of Space: Theatre and Topology*, edited by Erika Fischer-Lichte and Benjamin Wihstutz, 182–97. New York: Routledge.

Woods, Bryan. 2010. "MoLoRa: The Independent Interview with Yael Farber." *Independent Weekly*, March 17, 2010.

Woodward, Keith, and John Paul Jones III. 2005. "On the Border with Deleuze and Guattari." In *B/ordering Space*, edited by H. Van Houtum, Olivier Kramsch, and Wolfgang Zierhofer, 235–48. New York: Ashgate.

Xaba, Nelisiwe. 2006. Program Notes for *They Look at Me and That Is All They Think*. 9th JOMBA! Contemporary Dance Experience.

Younge, Janni. 2016. Director note in *The Firebird* program. Cape Town and Los Angeles' Hollywood Bowl.

Zizek, S. 1989. *The Sublime Object of Ideology*. London: Verso.

Zuern, Elke. 2011. *The Politics of Necessity: Community Organizing and Democracy in South Africa*. Madison: University of Wisconsin Press

INDEX

access, 3, 6, 11, 16, 30, 46, 48, 56n8, 109, 113, 128, 134n9, 142, 147, 148, 155–157, 163, 166, 168, 173, 175, 186, 208, 237, 261, 282, 288, 293, 302, 316, 317, 318, 321, 324, 327, 335, 350
Acts of Transgression, 205n4, 323, 336, 338n15, 351
Adamson, Val, x, xxix
adaptations, 4, 102, 134n2, 210, 256, 257, 262, 264, 272; deconstruct, 272, 312
aesthetic-political, 1, 2, 18, 24, 25, 26, 28, 53, 55, 79, 106, 110, 126, 149, 332, 343, 340
Africa Center, 286, 312, 317
African Literature Association, xvii
African National Congress, 29, 85, 97, 99n12, 258, 305, 361, 362, 364
Afro-fusion, 37, 40, 51, 86. *See also* Sylvia Glasser
Afrovibes Festival, 23, 34, 42, 44, 54, 60n32, 62n37
Ahimsa-Ubuntu, 37, 67, 72, 76–80, 83–89; sound design, 90, 95, 183
Albany Hotel, 174, 175, 181, 183
Andrew W. Mellon Foundation, 284
apartheid, xiii, xv, xvi, xvii, xxii; ban names, 105; challenge, 1, 2, 3, 5–6, 7–8; ended, 32, 45, 72, 79, 80, 84, 96, 99n12, 101, 102, 103, 104, 107, 113–114; "Re-moving Apartheid," 114–116, 128, 135n17, 142, 150, 151, 164, 170, 180, 216, 224, 238, 240, 293, 299, 330, 333, 340, 341–342, 360, 364, 365n4; separating races, 9, 27; trauma, xxiv; xxv; wounds, 12, 13, 20, 30, 31
Armah, Ayi Kwei, 224, 227
Ar(t)chive, The, xviii, xxviii. *See also* Adrienne Sichel
anti-Indian, 354; anti-trade, 356, 361
art, xxiii, 5, 6, 25, 253; activism, 333, 334; bear witness, 273; and community, 318; healing, 336n5; impact, 320, 321; and metaphors, 262, 273; and politics, 261, 262, 273, 324; and public, 285, 288, 316; and space, 302
audience, 148, 190, 236, 270, 300, 308, 318; formal and informal, 200–201, 315; challenge, 282; shrinking, 285; diverse, 324
avant-garde, 163, 191, 235, 253

Baartman, Sarah, 58n23
Bailey, Brett, 23–24, 282, 284, 289, 337n10

388 INDEX

Bakhtin, Mikhail, 41
ballet, 16, 17, 25, 26, 30, 42, 47, 57n11, 84, 85, 86, 91, 93, 95, 124, 130, 131, 157, 159, 179, 183, 225, 229, 230, 231, 233, 234, 235, 271, 289, 312, 339, 344, 345, 346, 347
Balme, Christopher, 210–211
Bausch, Pina, 189
Beautiful Ones Must Be Born, The, 7, 8, 11, 157, 165, 170, 209, 224–236, 274, 276n6. *See also* Constitution Hill
Bell, Suzy, xxix, 17, 38–40, 90, 91, 92, 95, 124–125, 347–348, 352n3
Belling, Catherine, 320
Bester, Gerard, 236
Bhabha, Homi, 28, 41–42, 146, 168
Bhagavad Gita, 226
Bhana, Surendra, 355, 356, 357, 359, 360, 361, 364
Bhana, Surendra, and Pachai, Bridglal, 88, 353, 358–359, 360, 362, 363, 364
Biko, Steve, 28, 29, 56n7, 232, 233, 276n7, 309
Blind Spot, 10, 20, 151, 156, 197–204; "city walk," 200–201, 317
Black consciousness, xvi, 27, 28, 29, 56n7, 78, 81, 233
Black Lives Matter, 276n9, 350
Blough, Leslie, xxx
body, xiv, xix, 2, 21, 25, 106, 108, 109, 140, 149, 159, 166, 169, 180, 204, 238, 250, 237–238, 241, 287, 293, 320, 335; body, as political, 242; body remembers, 240–241; and dance, 18, 340; burdens on, 53; and history, 73; infection, 283; as site, 3, 9, 11, 12, 13, 105
Body of Evidence, xiii–xv, xix, 11, 12, 13, 100n16, 106, 111, 123, 126, 147, 195, 208, 210, 274, 277n10, 320, 336n3; embodiment, 200, 237–254; location, 238. *See also Unclenching the Fist*
Boulle, Catherine, 205n4, 323, 338n15

Brett Kebble Art Award, 10, 14, 213, 214
British imperialism, 355, 356
Brutus, Dennis, xvii, 105, 134n3
Buckland, Angela, 213, 219, 220
Bunn, David, 28
Busby, Daniel Gary, xxviii

Cape Town, xvi, xxv, xxix, 2, 4, 8, 9, 10; along "routes," 302, 304, 306, 307, 309, 312, 313, 317, 319, 321, 337n8, 342; Arena Theatre, 103; Baxter Theatre, 34, 132; biodiversity, 292–293; CAPAB (now Artscape), 122; Cape Flats, 314, 338n14, 344; central areas, 290, 311; *Cityscapes*, 171, 187, 209, 262; Confluences 8 Dance Conference, 62n40; Dance for All, 57n11; Gugulethu township, 136; Handspring Puppet Company, 55, 344, 352n2; inertia, 319, 324, 327, 331, 335, 336; *Infecting the City* festival, 54; Jazzart Dance Theatre, 88, 107; launching ICA, 284; *Live Art* festival, 35; Long Street, 27, 24, 32, 33; Magnet Theatre, 19, 44; natural beauty, 292; Preswich Memorial, 314; prime apartheid city, 148, 162; public hostility, 283; railway station, 3, 148, 302–303, 307, 314; Rhodes statue, 167; Robben Island, 294, 299, 300, 301; tourists, 293
Cape Town City Hall, 11, 206, 254, 258, 294, 308, 314, 327, 331, 337n8, 342
Carlson, Anne, 163, 206n7
Carlson, Marvin, 160
Carter, Henry Vandyke, 238
Casey, Edward, 140, 142, 151, 155–156
caste system, 355
Castelyn, Saraleigh, 211, 213–220
Cekwana, Boyzie, 22, 23, 44, 331
censorship, 45, 52, 104, 105, 145
Chennai, xvi, xxvii, xxx, 29, 55, 76, 345

INDEX

choreography, xiii; aesthetic-political, 26; affective, 270; ancestry, 27; avant-garde, 36, 253; award-winning, 14, 55, 90, 128; *Blind Spot, Hostel*, 151, 218; *Body of Evidence*, 241, 243, 248, 249; body, 214; city centers, 8, 19, 197, 298, 301, 302, 309, 310, 311, 316, 317, 318; city, xvi, xix, 6; *Cityscapes*, 157, 170, 178; collaboration, 22–23, 42, 153, 239; conceptual, 24, 147, 150; confront exclusions, 96; contemporary, innovative, 46, 49, 51, 83, 147; curation, 340; dance and visual art, 20, 238; danced activism, 180; dance-theatre, 76; democratic, hybrid, 41, 42, 43, 47; disruption, 232; diverse styles, 16–17, 18, 21, 38–40, 88; epics, 225; *Firebird*, 342–347; *From Before*, 183; ground-breaking, xxv, 1, 2, 7; on history and memory, xxiv, xv, xvi, xxiv, 76; *Home*, 221; hope, 223; improvisation, 234; Indian and African, 67, 95, 265; interdisciplinary, 25; kathak and gumboot, 84, 91, 92; *Kitchen*, 214; lighting, 271; limits of, 21; migrant history, 79, 82; "onus," 108; Pina Bausch, 189; politically progressive, 133; *Qaphela Caesar*, 254, 266; *Republic*, 322; *Rite*, 103, 188, 193, 195; site, 34, 134, 163; spatial vision, 110; theory into practice, 19, 342; *toyi-toyi*, 52, 343, 347; *Unclenching the Fist*, 123; violence, 106

City Hall, 55, 259–262

Cityscapes, 8, 9, 10, 88, 128–129, 133, 147, 149, 155, 157, 170–179, 204, 205n5, 213, 282, 287; *Cityscapes Re-Routed*, 171. *See also* site-specific

classical African dance, 346, 347

classical Indian dance, 16, 37, 38, 39, 40, 80, 249, 347; Bharatanatyam, 17, 91, 220, 225; kathak, 17, 39, 43, 49, 84, 85, 87, 91, 129, 130, 206n11, 221, 235; Odissi, 17, 92, 94

classical music, North Indian, 202; at a railway station, 3, 303; Western, 148, 178, 265, 266, 303

Cohen, Steven, 213, 235, 288–289, 323, 333

Cole, Catherine M., 112–113

colonial legacy, 18, 32, 41, 45, 70, 72, 82, 126, 141, 257, 286, 290, 292, 294, 313, 321, 333, 341, 355; "colonial symbology," 167, 302

"Coloured," xv–xvi, 12, 55n2, 233, 354, 357, 360

Constitution Hill, 157, 165, 166, 209–210, 224, 231, 236; constitutional court, 224, 234. *See also Beautiful Ones Must Be Born*

contemporary African dance, xviii, 16, 44, 46–49, 63n43, 92, 186, 188, 227

Contemporary Indian Dance, xv, xvi, xvii, 57n14

contemporary South African Dance, 44, 46, 47, 49

Copenhagen, xxv, 20, 151, 197, 198, 200, 202, 207n16

Coppen, Neil, 348

Cordova, Sarah Davies, xxviii, 337n9

covid-19, 350, 351

Craighead, Clare, xxix, 172–177, 183, 206nn11&13

crossing over, vi, 143, 146, 147, 170, 172

cultural boycott, 36, 97n6

curator/curation, v, xxiv, xxiii, xxiv, xxv, 1, 2, 3, 19, 23, 24, 25, 33, 34, 42, 43, 44, 54, 72, 185, 275, 281, 282; performance-curator, 284, 285, 286, 287, 289, 290, 299, 302, 308, 316, 317, 318, 319, 322, 323, 325, 326, 327, 329, 331, 332, 333, 334, 335, 336, 339, 351

Dada Abdulla, 97n4, 357

Dance for All, 56–57n11

dance and history, 72, 87; and visual art, multimedia, 20, 22
dance-drama, 16, 21, 29, 53, 82, 108; to performance, 109
Davis, Desire, 22
De, Esha and Sarkar, Sonita, 4
Deboo, Astad, xxx
decolonial project, 257, 317, 321, 333, 340
Defiance Campaign, 72, 85, 86, 234
democracy, xxv, 1, 2, 3, 5, 6, 8, 29, 38, 46, 80, 81, 107, 114, 116, 117, 130, 145, 147, 150, 153, 158, 161, 166, 170, 180, 191, 204, 224, 225, 226, 227, 257, 275n4, 290, 314, 315, 316, 324, 325, 329, 330, 334, 337n8, 340, 346, 348, 349
Denton, Douglas, 179–181, 222
Denyschen, Jessica, xviii, xxviii
Derrida, Jacques, 116–117
Diaghilev, Sergei, 346
Disbergen, Wilhelm, 267
domestic violence, 14, 53, 118, 121, 122, 123–126, 136n22, 237n44
Duma, Siyanda, 231, 232, 244, 245
Durban, xix, xx, xxv, 6–7, 8, 9, 10, 27, 30, 33, 82, 102, 118, 122, 123, 128, 129, 130, 134, 142, 149, 157, 162, 166, 171, 174, 177, 178, 204, 254, 263, 286, 322, 354, 361, 364
Durban City Hall, 6–7
Durban Art Gallery, 174, 211, 221, 222
Dutch East India Company, 74; Khoikhoi-Dutch wars, 74; small-pox epidemic, 74

Egungun, 117, 136n20
Emperor Shaka the Great, 225, 226
Essa, Saira, 37, 78, 102, 103
Eze, Michael Onyebuchi, 80–81

Fanon, Frantz, 110, 123, 135n11, 237
#FeesMustFall, 167, 273, 322, 331, 332
FIFA 2010 World Cup, 26
Firebird, The, 4, 54–55, 134n7, 136n24, 342–349; US tour, 352nn1&2

First Physical Theater Company, 50, 63n47; Juanita Praeg, 63n48. *See also* Gary Gordon
Fisher-Lichte, Erika, 319
Fleishman, Mark, 19, 44, 290, 292
FNB Dance Umbrella, 14, 50, 57n18, 90, 179, 187, 192, 226, 263
FNB Vita Award, 14, 90, 119
Fokine, Michel, 345
foreigners, xxiv, 20, 107, 201, 265, 302, 307. *See also* outsiders
forensic science, 12, 20, 122, 237, 238
Forked Tongues, 7, 96, 113, 118, 126–129
Foster, Susan Leigh, 72–73
Foucault, Michel, 140, 141, 164, 199, 218, 227, 262
From Before, 8, 10, 17, 156, 171, 183, 184, 187
"free" Indians, 353, 356
Fugard, Athol, xxiv, 31, 104, 276n8
fusion, 39, 40, 41, 75, 85, 99n13, 118, 128, 129, 167, 172. *See also* Afro-fusion, hybrid

Gandhi, Mohandas, 38, 67, 70, 71, 73, 77, 78–83, 86, 95, 97n4, 98–99n10, 102, 110, 135n11, 225, 301, 354, 355, 356, 357, 358, 359, 360, 362
Gasa, Ntombi, xix, xx, xxi–xxii, xxviii–xxix, 10, 15, 44, 79, 92, 119, 124, 131, 153, 179, 181, 183, 188, 192, 193, 203, 222, 230, 242, 244, 245, 246, 247, 248, 249, 252, 264, 274, 336n3, 346, 349, 352n1
gay, xxiv, 26, 30, 31, 53, 103, 105, 158
geography, 3, 4, 27, 54, 84, 96, 137, 140, 141, 154, 161, 163, 164, 250
Ghosh, Amitav, 68, 73
Glasser, Sylvia, 36, 40, 44, 51–52, 53. *See also* Afro-fusion
Global Shakespeare Symposium, xxiii, xxviii, 34, 134n1, 183, 256, 274
Gopie, Rajesh, 80; *The Coolie Odyssey*, 98n8
Gordon, Gary, 50–51, 63nn47–48
Gordon Institute for Performing and

Creative Arts (GIPCA), 33, 34, 54, 261, 262; collaborative curation, 300–301; Director Pather, 205n1, 289–322, 323; renamed Institute for Creative Arts (ICA), 284, 308
Gosani, Bob, 236
Govender, Suria, xxix, 40, 62n36
Govender, Ronnie, xxii, xxix, 37, 100n14
government of India, 70, 81
Gray, Henry, 238–239
Group Areas Act, 60–61n34, 84, 87, 99n14, 100nn14–15, 214. *See also* land dispossession
gumboot dance, 16, 18, 39, 57n13, 84, 85, 86, 87, 124, 177, 245, 251, 339
Gupta, Pamila, 68

Hall, Stuart, 41, 146, 167
Handspring Puppet Company, 55, 134n7, 344, 346, 352n2
Hayes, Peter, 103, 105–107, 134n4
Hector Peterson, 102, 135n13
Hesse, Hermann, 90, 91
Hinkel, Alfred, 24, 33, 36, 37, 104, 127
history of slavery, 277n9, 298
Hofmeyr, Isabel, 70, 72, 78, 301
Home, 5, 10, 151, 204, 209, 211–223, 274
homelands, 5, 140, 151, 214, 340, 341
homosexuality, 25, 30; homophobia, 26
Hostel, 75, 151, 211, 213, 216–220, 222
Hotel, 5, 9, 10, 140, 174, 175, 179–183, 212, 222, 270, 274, 288, 297
Houston, Andrew, 161, 162
Huttenback, Robert, 355
hybrid, 18, 25, 37, 40–43, 45, 47, 49, 57n14, 92, 149, 201, 242, 249, 265, 266, 272, 312, 322, 339, 347

immigrants, 200, 202, 298, 317, 353, 355, 356, 363; refugees, 298
Immorality Laws, 180, 222
in-between, 28, 54, 83, 137, 143, 145, 147, 148, 302–303

indentured, 38, 41, 61n34, 67, 70, 74, 80, 81, 82, 86, 97nn4–5, 98n8, 172, 353, 354, 356, 359, 363
independence, xiii, xvii, xxiii, 7, 14, 33, 38, 53, 72, 79, 96n1, 107, 113, 115, 118, 119, 135n11, 144, 146, 147, 210, 217, 224, 226, 228, 237, 257, 309, 345, 346, 349
Indian migration, 68, 72, 74, 76, 79
Indian Ocean, 38, 67, 68, 175, 301
Indian Opinion, 71, 99n10, 358
Indians in South Africa, 76, 81, 99n11, 353–365
Indian Ocean World, 68, 69, 301
indigenous, xv, xvi, 16, 17, 42, 48, 51, 55n2, 74, 75, 76, 82, 83, 104, 141
Infecting the City, xix, 4, 24, 25, 27, 33, 34, 54, 62n39, 163, 171, 185, 206, 217, 275, 281, 282, 283, 286, 287, 290, 297, 298, 301, 302, 304, 308, 311, 312, 313, 318, 337n9, 338n12, 342, 351
Institute for Creative Arts (ICA), 34, 284, 320, 338n17, 350
infection/ disease, 283, 291, 290, 292, 293, 294, 297, 307, 308, 320, 350, 351
installation, xix, 3, 20, 35, 174, 175, 186, 202, 211, 213, 214, 261, 263, 272, 284, 288, 298, 306, 313, 326, 335
intercultural, 8, 15, 17, 37, 39, 49, 88, 126, 149, 172, 173, 340, 346
interdisciplinary, xiii, 1, 22, 24, 25, 26, 28, 35, 41, 43, 46, 54, 128, 227, 262, 272, 281, 284, 285, 309, 320, 321, 322, 327, 328, 340
interethnic dialogue, 40
international, 31, 32, 34, 38, 54, 55, 89, 103, 114, 187, 197, 198, 200, 207n18, 233, 250, 251, 262, 274, 289, 298, 304, 307, 312, 314, 318, 320, 331, 334, 338n13, 340, 344
invisibility, 7, 26, 39, 72, 96, 105, 168, 196, 198, 199, 200, 258, 302, 306, 307, 342
isicathamiya, 18, 86, 130, 245, 277n11, 339
Island, The, 31

Jazzart Dance Theater, xxix, 24, 27, 32, 33, 88, 103, 104, 107, 122, 123, 315
Jina, Keiron, xxix, 25–26, 59nn24–28, 63n22
Job, Jacki, xxix
Johannesburg, xxix, 9, 10, 11, 14, 37, 46, 56n6, 59n24, 61n34, 62n34, 62n36, 80, 103, 104, 105, 129, 146, 149, 162, 168, 171, 179, 180, 183, 186, 187, 188, 189, 196, 204, 208, 209, 210, 224, 229, 238, 254, 263, 276n5, 283, 286, 338n13
JOMBA!, xviii, xxix, 7, 14, 47, 119, 126, 186, 187, 188, 193, 322

Kani, John, xxiv, 56n6, 104, 276n8
Kathrada, Ahmed Mohamed, 364, 365n3
Katrak, Ketu H., *Contemporary Indian Dance*, xv; *Politics of the Female Body*, 4; *Wole Soyinka and Modern Tragedy*, 136n18
Kentride, William, 59n23, 338n13
Kitchen, The, 10–11, 152–153, 192, 211, 212–216; inside art gallery, 212, 222, 275n2, 288
Khoi and San, xv, 55n2, 74, 299
Khoza, Albert, 334, 335
kinetic, 13, 21, 112, 227, 229, 236, 250, 265, 315
Knowles, Ric, 162
Krawitz, Justin, 303
Kumar, Pratap, P., 81, 82
Kunene, Mazizi, 225
Kunene, Nkanyiso, 267

Laban, 49–50
Lalloo, Dr., xxix
land, 4, 5, 10, 38, 51, 67, 68, 74, 75, 76, 82, 83, 85, 87, 96, 100n15, 104, 115, 139, 170, 185, 187, 199, 203, 213, 214, 216; land dispossession, 74, 82, 84, 85, 87, 141; 1913 Native Land Law, 361; reclamation, 142, 151, 193, 205n1, 214, 299; redistribution, 284, 293, 354, 357, 360, 361, 362; symposium, 313–314, 354, 360
language lab, 261
Laws of Recall, 12, 14, 96, 117, 119–122
Lefebvre, Henri, 140, 149, 150, 152, 163, 185
Lehrer, Leonard, 122, 237
Lenasia, 60–61n34
lesbians, 25, 58n21, 105, 158
liminality, 143, 162, 302, 319
Live Art festival, xix, 15, 24, 33, 34, 35, 54, 60n33, 62n39, 107, 163, 205n4, 275, 282, 283, 284, 285, 320, 322–335; activism, 324; technology, 325–326, 342
locations, xiv, xxiii, 3, 4, 9, 10, 11, 23, 24, 27, 28, 31, 37, 43, 47, 49, 88, 104, 115, 139, 140, 146, 147, 148, 179, 190, 196, 197, 198, 200, 202, 204, 209, 210, 211, 212, 214, 217, 218, 220, 230, 232, 236, 254, 263, 282, 287, 309, 317, 321, 323, 340, 342, 345; gallery, 152, 168, 169, 174–175; indoor/outdoor, 152, 153, 155, 161, 162, 164, 165, 170; relocation/dislocation, 87, 107, 172, 199, 216
Loots, Lliane, xxix, 44, 47, 49, 61n34, 63n44, 171–172, 173, 174, 178, 222, 251–253, 278n19
Lupton, Julia, xxviii

Mahabharata, 206n6, 225, 226
Maharaj, Manesh, xxix, 61n34
Maharaj, Smeetha, xxix, 38–39, 61–62n34, 79–80, 97nn5–6; and Singh, Vasugi, 39
Marafana, Monde, 267
Mbeki, Thabo, 224, 229, 234, 236, 277
Mandela, Nelson, xvii, 39, 56n7, 62n36, 67, 73, 80, 105, 107, 115, 134n3; *Julius Caesar*, 258; Winnie Mandela, 135n15, 144, 167, 209, 233, 11, 258, 259, 277n13, 294, 316, 337n8, 364

INDEX

Mantsoe, Vincent, 44, 51, 53, 312
Maqoma, Gregory, 44, 48, 51, 53, 60n30, 75–77
Marikana massacre, 170
masculinity, 25, 26, 59n27, 103, 218, 219, 220, 245, 310, 312
Masilo, Dada, 24, 25, 44, 58n19, 312, 338n13
Mbeki, Thabo, 224, 229, 234, 277n13, 337n6
Mbembe, Achille, 140, 149, 169, 206n9, 283, 290
Meer, Fatima, 67, 77, 79, 99n12
Mellon, Andrew W., 34, 284, 320
memory, xiv, xv, 2, 5, 11, 12, 13, 18, 108, 111, 119, 122, 125, 172, 208, 227, 238, 240, 249–250, 253, 272, 274, 289, 320; and history, 204, 340, 342; past, present, and future, 273. *See also* violence, trauma, body
migrants, xv, 15, 20, 37, 68, 76, 82, 107, 151; in *Blind Spot*, 198–199, 200, 201, 204, 207n16, 213, 217, 297, 314, 340–341, 353, 364n1
mine workers, 220, 247
Miracle, 89
Mkhize, Sandile, 267
Moopen, Jeyasperi, xxix; Afro-fusion, 40, 62n36; *From Canefields to Freedom* (docudrama), 80, 98n7; Tribhangi Dance Theater, xx, xxix, 114, 179
Mugo, Micere Githae, 31, 104
Mumbai, xvi, xxv, 14, 17, 55, 61, 221, 237
Moving into Dance Mophatong, 36, 44, 51, 60n30, 179, 229
Mugabe, Robert, 277n14
multicultural, 36, 95, 168, 173, 174
multidisciplinary, xiii, 1, 14–15, 20, 21, 22, 26, 28, 36, 40, 54, 96, 106, 109, 227, 237, 239, 254, 261, 285, 287, 312
multimedia, 1, 3, 15, 20, 21, 26, 28, 49, 50, 80, 147, 149, 229, 249, 250, 261, 265, 272, 309, 339

museum, 23, 25, 70, 104, 164, 171, 188, 207, 209; Apartheid Museum, 224, 228, 282, 285, 286; Iziko Slave Museum, 228, 260, 335
Mzizi, Thulebona, 90

Nandakishore, Pravika, xxix, 43, 99n13, 124, 127, 129, 131
nation, 3, 93, 95, 115; history, 149, 157, 165, 191, 202, 209, 228, 241, 252, 253, 255, 268, 273, 274, 276n8, 286, 297, 307, 340; land, 313–314, 316, 318, 328, 339, 340, 346, 349, 351; rainbow nation, 96, 111, 112, 127, 129, 130, 132, 133, 144, 157, 167, 179, 202, 217, 222, 224, 230, 232, 233, 235, 236, 237, 332, 347; slogans, 118
National Arts Festival, xix, 14, 32, 89, 103, 105, 122, 207n18, 211, 251, 277n10, 322, 344
Natal Indian Congress, 85, 355, 356, 357, 362
Native Land Act, 205n1, 213, 214, 313
New York City, xviii, 8, 10, 14, 17, 30, 31, 102, 103, 133, 156, 162, 171, 183, 184
Ngũgĩ wa Thiong'o, xviii; 2, 11, 12, 31, 102, 104, 136n23, 142–143, 150; *Wrestling with the Devil: A Prison Memoir*, 205n2; *Decolonizing the Mind*, 256
Nkomonde, Mxolisi, 196, 248, 249
Ntshona, Winston, xxiv, 104, 276n8
Nuttall, Sarah, 140, 149, 283
Nyamza, Mamela, xix, 24, 25, 44, 58nn20–21, 60, 136n22, 330, 333, 334, 337–338n13

Olympic games, 129
Oresteia, 135n12, 225, 226
Orlin, Robyn, 24–25, 33, 57n18, 59n23
Outsider, xx, xxii, 9, 20, 83, 76, 83, 91, 107, 201, 216, 217, 306, 307, 329. *See also* foreigner

Pakeezah, 198
pantsula, 10, 18, 57n13, 99n13, 123, 124, 129, 149, 156, 157, 174, 177, 178, 179, 205n3, 247, 248, 339, 345
Paradise, 43, 322
Pass Books, 135n13
Pather, Gita, xxix, 125
Pather, Jay, v, xiii, xxvii, xiii-xvi, xxv, xxvii, xxxi, 1; aesthetic-political, 1, 2, 24, 25, 26, 28, 55, 79, 106, 110, 126, 149, 332, 346; African Contemporary dance, 48–49; audience, 13–14; autobiographical note on *Home*, 223; avant-garde, 10–11; awards, leadership, 14–15, 32–33, 128; bio, 27–35; body as site, 11–14; co-editor, *Acts of Transgression: Live Art in South Africa*, 205n4; collaboration, 6, 253; constituency, 44–45; critical of Gandhi, 78–79; curator, 23–27; democratize, deconstruct space, 6–9, 210; early memories, 172; evolving spatial politics, 53–55; Fulbright, 30; goals of site work, 148–150, 315; hybrid, 41–42; international work, 14, 34, 54, 207n18; mentor, 43, 52; passion for dancing, 29–30; as "performance-curator," 284; as pedestrian, 19, 160; progressive politics, xv, 2, 14, 149, 253, 281; Siwela Sonke, 15–18; South African Indians, 35–40; space as political and historical, 3–6; Tamil origin, 72; theorist, 18–22, 150; visionary, 32. *See also* site-specific and site-responsive

Pather, Jay, published essays: "Caught up in Multi-Layered Skirts or What's a Stripper Doing in Julius Caesar?," 193, 195–196; "The Impossibility of Curating Live Art," 283, 325, 328–329, 334; Keynote (talk), Global Shakespeare Symposium, UC Irvine, xxiii, 256–258; "Laws of Recall: Body, Memory and Site-Specific Performance in Contemporary South Africa," 19, 208, 225, 227, 228, 234, 236, 240–241, 242, 243; "Legacies of Violence: South Africa 20 Years After Democracy" (talk), 5, 340; "A Love Affair with Space" (TedX talk), 19, 185; "The Making of Blindspot: From Lab to Biennale in Copenhagen," 197–204, 207n17; "Motion Sickness," 42, 314–315; "Negotiating the Post-Colonial Black Body," 32–37, 119, 166–170; "Performing Cape Town" (with Mark Fleishman), 20, 290, 294, 303, 305–306, 307, 319, 342; "The Periphery as Threshold," 24, 25, 34, 35, 50, 293, 301, 329, 337n7; "Purush: The Global Dancing Male" (symposium talk), 29–30; "A Response: African Contemporary Dance," 48–49; "Shifting Spaces, Tilting Time," 11, 12, 19, 114, 118, 128–132, 139, 180

Pather, Jay, program/director/curator notes: *Beautiful Ones*, 227–228; *Body of Evidence*, 240–241, 253; *Cityscapes*, 175–177; *Firebird*, 344, 346–347; *Home*, 312–313; *Infecting the City 2008*, 289–290, 336n4; *Infecting the City 2012*, 23–24, 185, 281, 302; *Infecting the City, 2013*, 308–309; *Infecting the City 2014*, 316; *Live Art 2014*, 328; *Qaphela Caesar*, 255–256, 265, 277n18, 336n3; *rite* 188
Pearson, Mike, 164–165
performance, xxiv, xxv, xix, 1; from dance-theater to performance, 96, 109, 112, 113, 117, 123, 126, 129, 165, 298; genres, 3; live, xviii, 13, 31, 33, 34, 35, 44, 48, 49, 50, 51, 54, 57n17, 75, 86, 87, 88, 92, 102, 106, 109; site, 4, 5; spaces, 2. *See also* access, body, memory, intercultural, multidisciplinary
Pillay, Kribben, xxix, 37

political is personal, 6, 8, 9, 96, 101, 152
postmodern, 20–21, 39, 154, 162
Praeg, Juanita, 63n48
Preswich Memorial, 4, 295, 305, 314, 338n14
public art, xix; belonging, 148, 178, 186, 206n8, 318; curator note, 281; festivals, 4, 23, 24, 27, 33, 34, 36, 54, 60n2, 217, 282–338, 298, 313, 316, 320, 323, 336, 340, 342; gallery, 10–11; versus live art, 326; symposium, 351
public space, 6, 7, 8–9, 13, 19, 21, 55, 140, 148, 155, 158, 159, 161, 173, 175, 177, 200, 204, 212, 254, 293, 299, 302, 305, 306, 308, 310, 313, 330, 335, 342
puppets, 55, 134n7, 343; and humans, 344, 345, 346, 348, 352n2

Qaphela Caesar, xxxiv, 11, 26, 117, 134n1, 195, 196, 204, 208, 210, 254–275; *Caesar Interrupted*, 210, 254, 263–264; Creative Works Award, 254
Quayson, Ato, 294

race, system, xv, 1, 2, 6, 29, 70, 173, 190; discriminations, 168; divisiveness, 341; and space, 3, 5, 6, 8, 11, 101, 132, 293, 324, 335; stereotypes, 242, 245, 357; systemic racism, 276n9, 360; tensions, 348
Radcliffe, Jo, 213
Ramaposa, Cyril, 277n13
Ratnam, Anita, xvi, xxvii
Republic, 186–187, 322
resistance, 3, 52, 74, 81, 82, 83, 86, 87, 98, 99, 191, 301, 357, 360, 361
RE-WIND, 113, 304
Rhodes statue, 167, 168, 169
#Rhodesmustfall, 322, 331, 332
rite, 10, 55–63, 187–196, 207n15, 336n3
Rite of Spring, 4, 103, 187; Nijinsky, 1
ritual, 27, 37, 91, 92, 117, 123, 140, 153, 159, 160, 162, 179, 188, 189, 193, 203, 206n11, 216, 263, 281, 287, 298, 299, 304, 306, 309, 310, 311, 312, 335, 342
release technique, 18, 57n15
Robben Island, 134n3, 209, 258, 294, 365n3
Robertson, Heather, 39, 43, 172, 175
Rushualang, Neliswa, x, xix, xxviii, 15, 44, 79, 92, 124, 127, 153, 188, 193, 205n5, 212, 230, 231, 235, 240, 243–248, 249

Sabbagha, P. J., 27, 60n30, 63nn47–48, 236
Said, Edward, 28
Samuel, Gerard, xvi, xxix, 44, 57n8
Samuel, Harold, xxii, xxix
Samuel, Michael, xxix
Sangoma, 90, 92, 93, 117, 203, 265, 271, 272, 312, 339
Sassen, Robyn, 190–191, 235–236
satyagraha, 38, 78, 79, 80, 83, 86, 98, 301, 358, 359, 360
Scarry, Elaine, 250–251
Schechner, Richard, 31, 161–162, 164, 206n6
Schwab, Gabriele, xxviii, 7–8, 12–13, 28, 109, 113, 120, 136n25, 144–145. *See also* trauma
Sellar, Tom, 284–285, 298
settlers, 51, 72, 74, 75, 76, 82, 83, 84, 97n5, 257, 357
sexuality, xxiv, 31, 59n25, 103, 105, 106, 118, 120, 245, 252, 310, 335
Shakespeare, 4, 11, 134n1–2; adaptation, 210, 259, 261, 265, 266, 267, 272, 273, 274; *Julius Caesar*, 254, 255, 256, 257; and Mandela, 258; *Tempest*, 257–258
Sharpeville Massacre, 56n7
Shembe, 175, 179, 183, 205n5, 206n11, 225, 229–230
Shifting Spaces, Tilting Time, 99n13, 118, 128–133
Sichel, Adrienne, xviii, xxvii–xxviii, 22–23, 46; on *Ahimsa-Ubuntu*, 77, 86–88, 89, 98n7, 156; on *Body of Evidence*,

Sichel, Adrienne (*cont.*)
  243, 277n10; on *Cityscapes*, 156, 171, 174, 175, 178–179; on Glasser, 36–37; *Hotel*, 181, 187; *Kitchen*, 203, 213, 226; on Laban, 49–51, 52, 56n6, 57–58nn18&21, 60n29–30, 63; on *Qaphela Caesar*, 254, 262–263, 272, 273, 275n2, 278n20; on *rite*, 187–188, 189, 191–192, 213, 226, 260, 272–273; "Legacies of Violence" (unpublished essay), 61n17. *See also* Ar(t)chive
Simon, Barney, xxiv
simunye, 36, 53, 96, 100n18, 118, 127, 128, 130, 173, 179, 226, 332
Singh, Ashwin, xxii, xxix
Singh, Vasugi, 38–39
site-responsive, xiv, 3, 4, 10, 11, 54, 134, 152, 160, 165, 170, 204, 208, 209, 201, 227; *Beautiful Ones*, 224–236; *Body of Evidence*, 237–254; *Home*, 211–223; *Qaphela Caesar*, 210, 254–274, 281, 342, 351
site-specific, 3, 4, 9–10, 13, 14, 15, 19, 54, 88, 104, 128, 134, 139, 140, 148, 150, 155, 156, 157, 158, 159, 160, 161–162, 165; anchors, 157–163; balconies, 201; *Blind Spot*, 197–204, 229, 263, 282; *Cityscapes*, 170–186; deconstruct space, 3, 10; glance, 156; goals, 8, 158; malls, 10; *republic*, 186–187; *rite*, 187–196; site-selection, 6, 9; site-specific to proscenium, 196; street, 160, 197, 201, 202
Siwela Sonke Dance Theater (SSDT) Company, v, xiii, xix, xx, xxiii, xxviii, 10, 14, 15–17, 24, 33, 36, 43, 46, 52, 56nn8&10, 79, 83, 88, 89, 90, 92, 118, 124, 125, 146, 147, 153, 171, 179, 186, 193, 200, 211, 278n19, 297, 352n1
Sizwe Bansi Is Dead, 276n8
slavery, 56, 277n9, 290, 292, 298, 313, 314
Sneddon, Elizabeth, 51
social change, xv, xxiii, 19, 25, 89, 123, 125, 351

social justice, xxiv, 1, 30, 31, 55, 72, 76, 134, 187, 275, 285, 320, 324, 333, 339, 349, 350, 352
Soja, Edward, 140, 141, 153, 154, 163
Sookol, Lorin, 268
Sontag, Susan, 290–291, 336n5
Sopotela, Chuma, 188, 196, 331
South African Constitution, 32, 131
South African dance styles, 3, 18, 57n13, 67, 312
South African Dance Theater, 118
South African Indians, xxii, 27, 29, 35, 38, 76, 82, 88, 99n11, 107, 358. *See also* appendix I
South African Indian Council, 362, 363
South African Siddhartha, A, 37, 38, 67, 89–96; dance forms, 91–92, 117, 270, 346, 349. *See also* Suzy Bell
Soweto, 56n7, 75, 135n13, 312, 330, 364; uprising, 102
Soyinka, Wole, xvii, xxiii, 45, 56n5, 111, 116, 136nn18&20, 150; on Shakespeare, 257
space, xiii, xxiii, xxiv, xxviii, 1; innovative, 3, 6, 10, 339, 349; Ngũgĩ, 2; space and race, 1
spatial politics, xxiii, 1, 2, 3, 5, 8, 14, 23, 55, 34, 35, 36, 67, 84, 96, 101, 126, 141, 152–153; avant-garde, 163; evolving, 2, 10, 53, 54; spatial imagination, 301; spatial journeys, 95; spatial locations, 4, 133
Stein, Philip, 276n5
Spier Contemporary 2007, 283, 287, 322
Spivak, Gayatri Chakravorty, 41
Stravinsky, Igor, 4, 54, 187, 188, 193, 195, 342, 344. *See also rite* and *Firebird*
Streisand, Barbra, 266, 271
State Theatre, 254, 265, 273

Tamil, 72, 181, 357, 363–364
Tempest in Africa, The, 104, 134n1
Testimonies, 7, 96, 117, 118–119
Tierou, Alphonse, 46–47

Tolsi, Niren, 221, 222–223, 237
torture, 18, 92, 110, 119, 231, 248, 250, 271
townships, 4, 10, 15, 57n13, 99n13, 130, 146, 149, 151, 157, 167, 169, 198, 205n3, 215, 247, 248, 274, 292, 293, 305, 321, 342
toyi-toyi, 52, 343, 347
Trial of Dedan Kimathi, The, 31, 104
trauma, xiii, xxiv, 1, 7, 11, 12, 13, 41, 60n33, 75, 87, 109, 113, 135nn12&14; apartheid, 114–117; Ronnie Govender, 100; land, 313, 314, 335; *Laws of Recall*, 120–122. See also Gabriele Schwab, domestic violence, body, land, Truth and Reconciliation Commission
transitional, 28, 54, 112, 137, 143; Soyinka, 116; Schwab, 144–145
Truth and Reconciliation Commission (TRC), xv, 7, 53, 96, 107, 110–114, 228, 237, 240, 248, 251, 259, 304, 341; "Re-moving Apartheid," 7, 114–117, 118, 119, 120, 121, 124, 134n9, 135n12
Turner, Victor, 162
Tutu, Desmond, 38, 67, 107, 110

ubuntu, 38, 67, 80–81, 96
umcimezo, 213, 225, 275n2
Unclenching the Fist, 11, 14, 96, 118, 122–126, 237. See also *Body of Evidence*
University of California, Irvine, xxiii, xxviii
University of Cape Town, xvi, xvii, 32, 33–34, 43, 166–167, 284

Van den Berg, Clive, 283, 287
Vandeyar, Reggie, 365n3
van Rensburg, Storm Janse, 238, 252
van Tonder, Tossie, 11–12, 300; interview with Sichel, 59n6
violence, xiii, 5, 13, 14, 20, 24, 25, 26, 53, 60n29, 105, 106, 109, 111; against outsiders, 302, 364n1; colonial, 87; Fanon, 110; gender-based, 195–196; institutionalized, 341; memories, 237–240, 250–253, 320, 340; post-apartheid, 112–114, 135n11, 142, 145, 147, 177, 180, 191, 192, 206n9, 215, 216, 219, 220, 226, 228, 232, 243, 247, 283, 304, 309; systemic, 243
visible/invisible, 7, 8, 12, 39, 72, 132, 133, 168, 198, 199, 200, 258, 302, 304, 306, 335, 367
visual art, xxiv, 3, 14, 20, 21, 23, 28, 31, 42, 54, 55, 59n23, 109, 111, 147, 149, 152, 162, 165, 174, 187, 191, 206n7, 213, 235, 238, 239, 240, 249, 250, 282, 284, 286, 298, 305, 310, 313, 326, 328, 340

Webb, James, 100n16, 188, 241, 242
Webber, Tammy Ballantyne, xxviii
white supremacy, 226, 354, 356
Whybrow, Nicholas, 291, 294, 320
Wihstutz, Benjamin, 160–161, 163, 164, 262, 319

Xaba, Nelisiwe, 25, 44, 58n23, 328, 335, 338n13
Xhosa dance/ritual, 17, 47, 91, 303, 304, 339

Younge, Janni, 4, 57, 136n24, 343, 344, 347, 348; and Handspring Puppet Company, 55, 134n7, 344, 346, 352n2. See also *Firebird*

Zulu dance, 16–17, 39, 40, 41, 47, 83, 91, 218, 249, 347; Zulu ritual, 153, 213, 225, 230, 243, 275n2, 339
Zuma, Jacob, 168, 205n1, 255, 274, 275, 277nn13&14
Zanzibar, 14, 17

KETU H. KATRAK is Professor in the Department of Drama at the University of California, Irvine. She is author of *Contemporary Indian Dance: New Creative Choreography in India and the Diaspora, Politics of the Female Body: Postcolonial Women Writers of the Third World,* and *Wole Soyinka and Modern Tragedy: A Study of Dramatic Theory and Practice.*